## To the Reader

In publishing ANNUAL EDITIONS we recognize the enormous role played by the magazines, newspapers, and journals of the public press in providing current, first-rate educational information in a broad spectrum of interest areas. Many of these articles are appropriate for students, researchers, and professionals seeking accurate, current material to help bridge the gap between principles and theories and the real world. These articles, however, become more useful for study when those of lasting value are carefully collected, organized, indexed, and reproduced in a low-cost format, which provides easy and permanent access when the material is needed. That is the role played by ANNUAL EDITIONS.

This tenth edition of *Annual Editions: Physical Anthropology* contains a variety of articles relating to human evolution. The writings were selected for their timeliness, relevance to issues not easily treated in the standard physical anthropology textbook, and clarity of presentation.

Whereas textbooks tend to reflect the consensus within the field, *Annual Editions: Physical Anthropology 01/02* provides a forum for the controversial. We do this in order to convey to the student the sense that the study of human development is an evolving entity in which each discovery encourages further research and each added piece of the puzzle raises new questions about the total picture.

Our final criterion for selecting articles is readability. All too often, the excitement of a new discovery or a fresh idea is deadened by the weight of a ponderous presentation. We seek to avoid that by incorporating essays written with enthusiasm and with the desire to communicate some very special ideas to the general public.

Included in this volume are a number of features designed to be useful for students, researchers, and professionals in the field of anthropology. While the articles are arranged along the lines of broadly unifying subject areas, the *topic guide* can be used to establish specific reading assignments tailored to the needs of a particular course of study. Other useful features include the *table of contents* abstracts, which summarize each article and present key concepts in bold italics, and a comprehensive *index*.

In addition, each unit is preceded by an overview that provides a background for informed reading of the articles, emphasizes critical issues, and presents *key points to consider* in the form of questions. Also included are *World Wide Web* sites that can be used to further explore the topics. These sites are cross-referenced by number in the topic guide.

In contrast to the usual textbook, which by its nature cannot be easily revised, this book will be continually updated to reflect the dynamic, changing character of its subject. Those involved in producing *Annual Editions: Physical Anthropology 01/02* wish to make the next one as useful and effective as possible. Your criticism and advice are welcomed. Please complete and return the postage-paid *article rating form* on the last page of the book and let us know your opinions. Any anthology can be improved, and this one will continue to be.

*Elvio Angeloni*

Elvio Angeloni
*Editor*
*E-mail address: evangeloni@paccd.cc.ca.us*

# Contents

**UNIT 1**

## Natural Selection

Six articles examine the link
between genetics and the
process of natural selection.

The concepts in bold italics are developed in the article. For further expansion please refer to the Topic Guide and the Index.

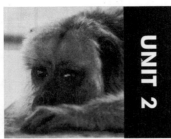

## UNIT 2

## Primates

Eight selections examine some of the social relationships in the primate world and how they mirror human society.

The concepts in bold italics are developed in the article. For further expansion please refer to the Topic Guide and the Index.

# Physical Anthropology

01/02

*Tenth Edition*

## EDITOR

### Elvio Angeloni
*Pasadena City College*

Elvio Angeloni received his B.A. from UCLA in 1963, his M.A. in anthropology from UCLA in 1965, and his M.A. in communication arts from Loyola Marymount University in 1976. He has produced several films, including *Little Warrior,* winner of the Cinemedia VI Best Bicentennial Theme, and *Broken Bottles,* shown on PBS. He also served as an academic adviser on the instructional television series, *Faces of Culture.*

McGraw-Hill/Dushkin
530 Old Whitfield Street, Guilford, Connecticut 06437

**Visit us on the Internet**
*http://www.dushkin.com*

# Credits

**1. Natural Selection**
Unit photo—Courtesy New York Library Picture Collection.
**2. Primates**
Unit photo—United Nations photo by George Love.
**3. Sex and Society**
Unit photo—© National Geographic Society, Washington, DC.
**4. The Fossil Evidence**
Unit photo—Courtesy of the American Museum of Natural History.
**5. Late Hominid Evolution**
Unit photo—Courtesy of WHO.
**6. Human Diversity**
Unit photo—United Nations photo.
**7. Living With the Past**
Unit photo—Courtesy of the American Museum of Natural History. 201—Map by Patrica Wynne. 202—Courtesy Gorney Bravin & Lee, NY.

# Copyright

Cataloging in Publication Data
Main entry under title: Annual Editions: Physical Anthropology. 2001/2002.
    1. Physical anthropology—Periodicals. I. Angeloni, Elvio, *comp.* II. Title: Physical anthropology.
ISBN 0–07–243330–2        573'.05        ISSN 1074–1844

Tenth Edition

Cover image © 2001 by PhotoDisc, Inc.

Printed in the United States of America        1234567890BAHBAH54321        Printed on Recycled Paper

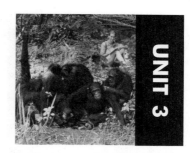

UNIT 3

# Sex and Society

Six articles discuss the relationship between the sexes and the evolution of a social structure.

## Overview    104

UNIT 4

## The Fossil Evidence

Four selections discuss some of the fossil evidence for hominid evolution.

The concepts in bold italics are developed in the article. For further expansion please refer to the Topic Guide and the Index.

UNIT 5

# Late Hominid Evolution

Seven articles examine
archaeological evidence
of human evolution.

The concepts in bold italics are developed in the article. For further expansion please refer to the Topic Guide and the Index.

The concepts in bold italics are developed in the article. For further expansion please refer to the Topic Guide and the Index.

# Topic Guide

This topic guide suggests how the selections in this book relate to the subjects covered in your course.

The Web icon ( ) under the topic articles easily identifies the relevant Web sites, which are numbered and annotated on the next two pages. By linking the articles and the Web sites by topic, this ANNUAL EDITIONS reader becomes a powerful learning and research tool.

| TOPIC AREA | TREATED IN | TOPIC AREA | TREATED IN |
|---|---|---|---|
| **Aggression** | 7. Machiavellian Monkeys<br>8. What Are Friends For?<br>11. Dim Forest, Bright Chimps<br>12. To Catch a Colobus<br>13. Coping With Crowding<br>15. These Are Real Swinging Primates<br>20. Apes of Wrath<br>26. Hard Times Among the Neanderthals<br>31. Archeologists Rediscover Cannibals<br>**15, 16, 18, 26, 28, 31, 34** | **DNA (Deoxyribo-nucleic Acid)** | 3. Curse and Blessing of the Ghetto<br>33. Black, White, Other<br>**29, 30, 31, 33, 34** |
| | | **Dominance Hierarchy** | 8. What Are Friends For?<br>15. These Are Real Swinging Primates<br>19. What's Love Got to Do With It?<br>20. Apes of Wrath<br>**15, 16, 18, 19, 20, 21** |
| | | **Evolution** | 40. Natural History of Art<br>**11, 12, 13, 14** |
| **Anatomy** | 6. Five Sexes, Revisited<br>16. War Between Men and Women<br>19. What's Love Got to Do With It?<br>21. Sunset on the Savannah<br>23. New Human Ancestor?<br>25. *Erectus* Rising<br>26. Hard Times Among the Neanderthals<br>27. Gift of Gab<br>28. Dating Game<br>29. Who Where the Neandertals?<br>30. Fate of the Neandertals<br>31. Archeologists Rediscover Cannibals<br>32. Lost Man<br>37. Profile of an Anthropologist<br>**20, 21, 22, 23, 24, 25, 26** | **Forensic Anthropology** | 37. Profile of an Anthropologist<br>**32, 33, 34** |
| | | **Genes** | 3. Curse and Blessing of the Ghetto<br>4. Saltshaker's Curse<br>33. Black, White, Other<br>41. Dr. Darwin<br>**28, 29, 30, 31** |
| | | **Genetic Drift** | 1. Growth of Evolutionary Science<br>3. Curse and Blessing of the Ghetto<br>**11, 12, 13, 14** |
| | | **Genetic Testing** | 3. Curse and Blessing of the Ghetto<br>5. Fortune Teller<br>**11, 12, 13, 14, 28, 29** |
| **Archaeology** | 25. *Erectus* Rising<br>28. Dating Game<br>31. Archeologists Rediscover Cannibals<br>32. Lost Man<br>37. Profile of an Anthropologist<br>**22, 23, 24, 25, 26** | **Homo erectus** | 25. *Erectus* Rising<br>31. Archeologists Rediscover Cannibals<br>**22, 23, 24, 25, 26, 28** |
| **Art** | 40. Natural History of Art<br>**4, 6, 8** | **Homo sapiens** | 28. Dating Game<br>29. Who Were the Neandertals?<br>30. Fate of the Neandertals<br>**25, 26, 28** |
| **Australo-pithecines** | 21. Sunset on the Savannah<br>22. Early Hominid Fossils From Africa<br>23. New Human Ancestor?<br>**22, 23, 24** | **Hunting and Gathering** | 11. Dim Forest, Bright Chimps<br>12. To Catch a Colobus<br>24. Scavenger Hunt<br>26. Hard Times Among the Neanderthals<br>29. Who Were the Neandertals?<br>30. Fate of the Neandertals<br>**16, 18, 22, 23, 24, 25, 26** |
| **Bipedalism** | 19. What's Love Got to Do With It?<br>21. Sunset on the Savannah<br>22. Early Hominid Fossils From Africa<br>23. New Human Ancestor?<br>24. Scavenger Hunt<br>**19, 20, 21, 22, 23, 24** | **Hunting Hypothesis** | 8. What Are Friends For?<br>17. Myth of the Coy Female<br>24. Scavenger Hunt<br>**17, 22, 24, 26** |
| **Blood Groups** | 33. Black, White, Other<br>34. Racial Odyssey<br>**29, 31, 32, 33, 34** | **Locomotion** | 15. These Are Real Swinging Primates<br>19. What's Love Got to Do With It?<br>21. Sunset on the Savannah<br>22. Early Hominid Fossils From Africa<br>23. New Human Ancestor?<br>**15, 16, 22, 28** |
| **Catastrophism** | 1. Growth of Evolutionary Science<br>**11, 12, 13, 14** | **Mutation** | 1. Growth of Evolutionary Science<br>**12, 14** |
| **Chain of Being** | 1. Growth of Evolutionary Science<br>**11, 12, 13, 14** | **Natural Selection** | 1. Growth of Evolutionary Science<br>2. Darwin's Influence<br>3. Curse and Blessing of the Ghetto<br>4. Saltshaker's Curse<br>16. War Between Men and Women<br>33. Black, White, Other<br>34. Racial Odyssey<br>36. Tall and the Short of It |
| **Cro-Magnons** | 28. Dating Game<br>**4, 5, 6, 7, 25, 26** | | |
| **Disease** | 3. Curse and Blessing of the Ghetto<br>4. Saltshaker's Curse<br>5. Fortune Teller<br>16. War Between Men and Women<br>34. Racial Odyssey<br>39. Viral Superhighway<br>41. Dr. Darwin<br>**6, 13, 28, 30, 32, 33, 34** | | |

# ◉ AE: Physical Anthropology

The following World Wide Web sites have been carefully researched and selected to support the articles found in this reader. If you are interested in learning more about specific topics found in this book, these Web sites are a good place to start. The sites are cross-referenced by number and appear in the topic guide on the previous two pages. Also, you can link to these Web sites through our DUSHKIN ONLINE support site at *http://www.dushkin.com/online/*.

**The following sites were available at the time of publication. Visit our Web site—we update DUSHKIN ONLINE regularly to reflect any changes.**

## General Sources

### 1. American Anthropological Association (AAA)
*http://www.ameranthassn.org/index.htm*
Maintained by the AAA, this site provides links to AAA's publications (including tables of contents of recent issues, style guides, and others) and to other anthropology sites.

### 2. Anthromorphemics
*http://www.anth.ucsb.edu/glossary/index2.html*
A glossary of anthropological terms is available at this Web site.

### 3. Anthropology in the News
*http://www.tamu.edu/anthropology/news.html*
Texas A&M provides data on news articles that relate to anthropology, including biopsychology and sociocultural anthropology news.

### 4. Anthropology on the Internet
*http://www.as.ua.edu/ant/libguide.htm*
This Web site provides addresses and tips on acquiring links to regional studies, maps, anthropology tutorials, and other data.

### 5. Anthropology 1101 Human Origins Website
*http://www.geocities.com/Athens/Acropolis/5579/TA.html*
Exploring this site, which is provided by the University of Minnesota, will lead to a wealth of information about our ancient ancestors and other topics of interest to physical anthropologists.

### 6. Anthropology Resources on the Internet
*http://www.socsciresearch.com/r7.html*
Links to Internet resources of anthropological relevance, including Web servers in different fields, are available here. *The Education Index* rated it "one of the best education-related sites on the Web."

### 7. Anthropology Resources Page
*http://www.usd.edu/anth/*
Many topics can be accessed from this University of South Dakota site. South Dakota archaeology, American Indian issues, and paleopathology resources are just a few examples.

### 8. Library of Congress
*http://www.loc.gov*
Examine this extensive Web site to learn about resource tools, library services/resources, exhibitions, and databases in many different subfields of anthropology.

### 9. The New York Times
*http://www.nytimes.com*
Browsing through the archives of the *New York Times* will provide a wide array of articles and information related to the different subfields of anthropology.

### 10. The PaleoAnthro Lists Home Page
*http://www.pitt.edu/~mattf/PalAntList.html*

Spend time at this site and the related PaleoChat site, at *http://www.pitt.edu/~mattf/PaleoChat.html*, to exchange information related to physical anthropology.

## Natural Selection

### 11. Charles Darwin on Human Origins
*http://www.literature.org/Works/Charles-Darwin/*
This Web site contains the text of Charles Darwin's classic writing, *The Origin of Species*, which presents his scientific theory of natural selection.

### 12. Enter Evolution: Theory and History
*http://www.ucmp.berkeley.edu/history/evolution.html*
Find information related to Charles Darwin and other important scientists at this Web site. It addresses preludes to evolution, natural selection, and more. Topics cover systematics, dinosaur discoveries, and vertebrate flight.

### 13. Fossil Hominids FAQ
*http://www.talkorigins.org/faqs/fossil-hominids.html*
Some links to materials related to hominid species and hominid fossils are provided on this site. The purpose of the site is to refute creationist claims that there is no evidence for human evolution.

### 14. Harvard Dept. of MCB—Biology Links
*http://mcb.harvard.edu/BioLinks.html*
This site features sources on evolution and links to anthropology departments and laboratories, taxonomy, paleontology, natural history, journals, books, museums, meetings, and many other related areas.

## Primates

### 15. African Primates at Home
*http://www.indiana.edu/~primate/primates.html*
Don't miss this unusual and compelling site describing African primates on their home turf. "See" and "Hear" features provide samples of vocalizations and beautiful photographs of various types of primates.

### 16. Chimpanzee and Great Ape Language Resources—Anthropology
*http://www.brown.edu/Departments/Anthropology/apelang.html*
This series of Web sites on primates includes the Primate home page and the Gorilla home page. It provides links to the entire text of Darwin's *Origin of Species* and more.

### 17. Electronic Zoo/NetVet-Primate Page
*http://netvet.wustl.edu/primates.htm*
This site touches on every kind of primate from A to Z and related information. The long list includes Darwinian theories and the *Descent of Man*, the Ebola virus, fossil hominids, the nonhuman Primate Genetics Lab, the Simian Retrovirus Laboratory, and zoonotic diseases, with many links in between.

### 18. Jane Goodall Research Center
*http://www.usc.edu/dept/elab/anth/goodall.html*
The Jane Goodall Research Center, a program of the University of Southern California's Anthropology Department, is a

repository for data gathered over more than 30 years at Gombe National Park, Tanzania. Search this site for information about primate research.

## Sex and Society

### 19. American Anthropologist
*http://www.aaanet.org/aa/index.htm*
Check out this site—the home page of *American Anthropologist*—for general information about anthropology as well as articles relating to such topics as biological research.

### 20. American Scientist
*http://www.amsci.org/amsci/amsci.html*
Investigating this site will help students of physical anthropology to explore issues related to sex and society.

### 21. Bonobo Sex and Society
*http://songweaver.com/info/bonobos.html*
Accessed through Carnegie Mellon University, this site includes a *Scientific American* article discussing a primate's behavior that challenges traditional assumptions about male supremacy in human evolution.

## The Fossil Evidence

### 22. The African Emergence and Early Asian Dispersals of the Genus *Homo*
*http://www.sigmaxi.org/amsci/subject/EvoBio.html*
Explore this site and click on this title to learn about what the Rift Valley in East Africa has to tell us about early hominid species. An excellent bibliography is included.

### 23. Anthropology, Archaeology, and American Indian Sites on the Internet
*http://dizzy.library.arizona.edu/users/jlcox/first.html*
This Web page points out a number of Internet sites of interest to different kinds of anthropologists, including physical and biological anthropologists. Visit this page for links to electronic journals and more.

### 24. Long Foreground: Human Prehistory
*http://www.wsu.edu:8001/vwsu/gened/ learn-modules/top_longfor/lfopen-index.html*
This Washington State University site presents a learning module covering three major topics in human evolution: Overview, Hominid Species Timeline, and Human Physical Characteristics. It also provides a helpful glossary of terms and links to other Web sites.

## Late Hominid Evolution

### 25. Archaeology Links (NC)
*http://www.arch.dcr.state.nc.us/links.htm#stuff*
North Carolina Archaeology provides this site, which has many links to physical anthropologists' sites such as the paleolithic painted cave at Vallon-Pont-d'Arc (Ardeche).

### 26. Human Prehistory
*http://users.hol.gr/~dilos/prehis.htm*
The evolution of the human species, beginning with the *Australopithecus* and continuing with *Homo habilis, Homo erectus,* and *Homo sapiens* is examined on this site. Also included are data on the people who lived in the Palaeolithic and Neolithic Age and are the immediate ancestors of modern man.

## Human Diversity

### 27. Cult Archaeology Topics
*http://www.usd.edu/anth/cultarch/culttopics.html*

This fun site provides information on interesting pseudoscientific theories that have attracted scholarly attention. The Lost Tribes and the Moundbuilder Myth, and Cryptozoology: Bigfoot and Nessie are among the many myths debunked here.

### 28. Hominid Evolution Survey
*http://www.geocities.com/SoHo/Atrium/1381/index.html*
This survey of the Hominid family categorizes known hominids by genus and species. Beginning with the oldest known species, data includes locations and environments, physical characteristics, technology, and social behaviors. Includes charts and citations.

### 29. Human Genome Project Information
*http://www.ornl.gov/TechResources/Human_Genome/ home.html*
Obtain answers about the U.S. Human Genome Project from this site, which details progress, goals, support groups, ethical, legal, and social issues, and genetics information.

### 30. OMIM Home Page-Online Mendelian Inheritance in Man
*http://www3.ncbi.nlm.nih.gov/omim/*
This database from the National Center for Biotechnology Information is a catalog of human genes and genetic disorders. It contains text, pictures, and reference information of great interest to students of physical anthropology.

### 31. Patterns of Human Variability: The Concept of Race
*http://www.as.ua.edu/ant/bindon/ant101/syllabus/ race/race1.htm*
This site provides a handy, at-a-glance reference to the prevailing concepts of race and the causes of human variability since ancient times. It can serve as a starting point for research and understanding into the concept of race.

## Living With the Past

### 32. Ancestral Passions
*http://www.canoe.ca/JamBooksReviewsA/ ancestral_morell.html*
This review of Virginia Morell's book, *Ancestral Passions,* a biography of the famously dysfunctional Leakey family, will likely spur you to the bookstore in order to learn more about the history of paleontology and the thrill and trials of the hunt for human origins. It is this evolutionary detective story that is the book's true drama. Jump over to *http://url.co.nz/african_trip/tanzania.html* to read an individual's account of a recent trip "In the Cradle of Humankind."

### 33. Forensic Science Reference Page
*http://www.lab.fws.gov*
Look over this site from the U.S. Fish and Wildlife Forensics Lab to explore topics related to forensic anthropology.

### 34. Zeno's Forensic Page
*http://forensic.to/forensic.html*
A complete list of resources on forensics is presented on this Web site. It includes general information sources, DNA/serology sources and databases, forensic medicine anthropology sites, and related areas.

**We highly recommend that you review our Web site for expandedinformation and our other product lines. We are continually updatingand adding links to our Web site in order to offer you the most usableand useful information that will support and expand the value of yourAnnual Editions. You can reach us at: http://www.dushkin. com/annualeditions/.**

# Unit 1

## Unit Selections

1. **The Growth of Evolutionary Science,** Douglas J. Futuyma
2. **Darwin's Influence on Modern Thought,** Ernst Mayr
3. **Curse and Blessing of the Ghetto,** Jared Diamond
4. **The Saltshaker's Curse,** Jared Diamond
5. **The Fortune Teller,** Kenneth S. Kosik
6. **The Five Sexes, Revisited,** Anne Fausto-Sterling

## Key Points to Consider

❖ In nature, how is it that design can occur without a designer, orderliness without purpose?

❖ What is "natural selection"? How does Gregor Mendel's work relate to Charles Darwin's theory?

❖ In what ways has Charles Darwin influenced modern thought?

❖ Why is Tay-Sachs disease so common among Eastern European Jews?

❖ What is the "saltshaker's curse," and why are some people more affected by it than others?

❖ What do genes actually do and how predictive are they of human social behavior?

❖ To what extent should a person be informed of a future genetically caused disease about which nothing can be done?

❖ How many human "sexes" are there and why?

 **Links**     **www.dushkin.com/online/**

These sites are annotated on pages 4 and 5.

As the twenty-first century begins and we reflect upon where science has taken us over the past 100 years, it should come as no surprise that the field of genetics has swept us along a path of insight into the human condition as well as heightened controversy as to how to handle this potentially dangerous knowledge of ourselves.

Certainly, Gregor Mendel, in the late nineteenth century, could not have anticipated that his study of pea plants would ultimately lead to the better understanding of over 3,000 genetically caused diseases, such as sickle-cell anemia, Huntington's chorea, and Tay-Sachs. Nor could he have foreseen the present-day controversies over such matters as surrogate motherhood, cloning, and genetic engineering.

The significance of Mendel's work, of course, was his discovery that hereditary traits are conveyed by particular units that we now call "genes," a then-revolutionary notion that has been followed by a better understanding of how and why such units change. It is knowledge of the process of "mutation," or alteration of the chemical structure of the gene, that is now providing us with the potential to control the genetic fate of individuals.

The other side of the evolutionary coin, as discussed in the unit's first two articles, "The Growth of Evolutionary Science" and "Darwin's Influence on Modern Thought," is natural selection, a concept provided by Charles Darwin and Alfred Wallace. Natural selection refers to the "weeding out" of unfavorable mutations and the perpetuation of favorable ones. The reproductive aspects of this process are also a matter of continuing investigation.

It seems that as we gain a better understanding of both of these processes, mutation and natural selection, and grasp their relevance to human beings, we draw nearer to that time when we may even control the evolutionary direction of our species. Knowledge itself, of course, is neutral—its potential for good or ill being determined by those who happen to be in a position to use it. Consider the possibility of eliminating some of the harmful hereditary traits discussed in "Curse and Blessing of the Ghetto" and "The Saltshaker's Curse," both by Jared Diamond. While it is true that many deleterious genes do get weeded out of the population by means of natural selection, there are other harmful ones, Diamond points out, that may actually have a good side to them and will therefore be perpetuated. It may be, for example, that some men are dying from a genetically caused overabundance of iron in their blood systems in a trade-off that allows some women to absorb sufficient amounts of the element to guarantee their

own survival. The question of whether we should eliminate such a gene would seem to depend on which sex we decide should reap the benefit.

The issue of just what is a beneficial application of scientific knowledge is a matter for debate. As discussed in "The Fortune Teller" and "The "Five Sexes, Revisited," who will have the final word as to how these technological breakthroughs will be employed in the future? Even with the best of intentions, how can we be certain of the long-range consequences of our actions in such a complicated field? Note, for example, the sweeping effects of ecological change upon the viruses of the world, which in turn seem to be paving the way for new waves of human epidemics. Generally speaking, there is an element of purpose and design in our machinations.

Yet, even with this clearly in mind, the whole process seems to be escalating out of human control. It seems that the whole world has become an experimental laboratory in which we know not what we do until we have already done it.

As we read the essays in this unit and contemplate the significance of genetic diseases for human evolution, we can hope that a better understanding of congenital diseases will lead to a reduction of human suffering. At the same time, we must remain aware that someone, at some time, may actually use the same knowledge to increase rather than reduce the misery that exists in the world.

**Natural Selection**

# The Growth of Evolutionary Science

## Douglas J. Futuyma

Today, the theory of evolution is an accepted fact for everyone but a fundamentalist minority, whose objections are based not on reasoning but on doctrinaire adherence to religious principles.

—James D. Watson, 1965*

In 1615, Galileo was summoned before the Inquisition in Rome. The guardians of the faith had found that his "proposition that the sun is the center [of the solar system] and does not revolve about the earth is foolish, absurd, false in theology, and heretical, because expressly contrary to Holy Scripture." In the next century, John Wesley declared that "before the sin of Adam there were no agitations within the bowels of the earth, no violent convulsions, no concussions of the earth, no earthquakes, but all was unmoved as the pillars of heaven." Until the seventeenth century, fossils were interpreted as "stones of a peculiar sort, hidden by the Author of Nature for his own pleasure." Later they were seen as remnants of the Biblical deluge. In the middle of the eighteenth century, the great French naturalist Buffon speculated on the possibility of cosmic and organic evolution and was forced by the clergy to recant: "I abandon everything in my book respecting the formation of the earth, and generally all of which may be contrary to the narrative of Moses." For had not St. Augustine written, "Nothing is to be accepted save on the authority of Scripture, since greater is that authority than all the powers of the human mind"?

When Darwin published *The Origin of Species,* it was predictably met by a chorus of theological protest. Darwin's theory, said Bishop Wilberforce, "contradicts the revealed relations of creation to its Creator." "If the Darwinian theory is true," wrote another clergyman, "Genesis is a lie, the whole framework of the book of life falls to pieces, and the revelation of God to man, as we Christians know it, is a delusion and a snare." When *The Descent of Man* appeared, Pope Pius IX was moved to write that Darwinism is "a system which is so repugnant at once to history, to the tradition of all peoples, to exact science, to observed facts, and even to Reason herself, [that it] would seem to need no refutation, did not alienation from God and the leaning toward materialism, due to depravity, eagerly seek a support in all this tissue of fables."[1] Twentieth-century creationism continues this battle of medieval theology against science.

One of the most pervasive concepts in medieval and post-medieval thought was the "great chain of being," or *scala naturae.*[2] Minerals, plants, and animals, according to his concept, formed a gradation, from the lowliest and most material to the most complex and spiritual, ending in man, who links the animal series to the world of intelligence and spirit. This "scale of nature" was the manifestation of God's infinite benevolence. In his goodness, he had conferred existence on all beings of which he could conceive, and so created a complete chain of being, in which there were no gaps. All his creatures must have been created at once, and none could ever cease to exist, for then the perfection of his divine plan would have been violated. Alexander Pope expressed the concept best:

Vast chain of being! which from God began,
Natures aethereal, human, angel, man,
Beast, bird, fish, insect, what no eye can see,
No glass can reach; from Infinite to thee,
From thee to nothing.—On superior pow'rs
Were we to press, inferior might on ours;
Or in the full creation leave a void,
Where, one step broken, the great scale's destroy'd;
From Nature's chain whatever link you strike,
Tenth, or ten thousandth, breaks the chain alike.

Coexisting with this notion that all of which God could conceive existed so as to complete his creation was the idea that all things existed for man. As the philosopher Francis Bacon put it, "Man, if we look to final causes, may be regarded as the centre of the world . . . for the whole world works together in the service of man . . . all things seem to be going about man's business and not their own."

"Final causes" was another fundamental concept of medieval and post-medieval thought. Aristotle had distinguished final causes from efficient causes, and the

*James D. Watson, a molecularbiologist, shared the Nobel Prize for his work in discovering the structure of DNA.

Western world saw no reason to doubt the reality of both. The "efficient cause" of an event is the mechanism responsible for its occurrence: the cause of a ball's movement on a pool table, for example, is the impact of the cue or another ball. The "final cause," however, is the goal, or purpose for its occurrence: the pool ball moves because I wish it to go into the corner pocket. In post-medieval thought there was a final cause—a purpose—for everything; but purpose implies intention, or foreknowledge, by an intellect. Thus the existence of the world, and of all the creatures in it, had a purpose; and that purpose was God's design. This was self-evident, since it was possible to look about the world and see the palpable evidence of God's design everywhere. The heavenly bodies moved in harmonious orbits, evincing the intelligence and harmony of the divine mind; the adaptations of animals and plants to their habitats likewise reflected the devine intelligence, which had fitted all creatures perfectly for their roles in the harmonious economy of nature.

Before the rise of science, then, the causes of events were sought not in natural mechanisms but in the purposes they were meant to serve, and order in nature was evidence of divine intelligence. Since St. Ambrose had declared that "Moses opened his mouth and poured forth what God had said to him," the Bible was seen as the literal word of God, and according to St. Thomas Aquinas, "Nothing was made by God, after the six days of creation, absolutely new." Taking Genesis literally, Archbishop Ussher was able to calculate that the earth was created in 4004 B.C. The earth and the heavens were immutable, changeless. As John Ray put it in 1701 in *The Wisdom of God Manifested in the Works of the Creation,* all living and nonliving things were "created by God at first, and by Him conserved to this Day in the same State and Condition in which they were first made."[3]

The evolutionary challenge to this view began in astronomy. Tycho Brahe found that the heavens were not immutable when a new star appeared in the constellation Cassiopeia in 1572. Copernicus displaced the earth from the center of the universe, and Galileo found that the perfect heavenly bodies weren't so perfect: the sun had spots that changed from time to time, and the moon had craters that strongly implied alterations of its surface. Galileo, and after him Buffon, Kant, and many others, concluded that change was natural to all things.

A flood of mechanistic thinking ensued. Descartes, Kant, and Buffon concluded that the causes of natural phenomena should be sought in natural laws. By 1755, Kant was arguing that the laws of matter in motion discovered by Newton and other physicists were sufficient to explain natural order. Gravitation, for example, could aggregate chaotically dispersed matter into stars and planets. These would join with one another until the only ones left were those that cycled in orbits far enough from each other to resist gravitational collapse. Thus order might arise from natural processes rather than from the direct intervention of a supernatural mind. The "argument from design"—the claim that natural order is evidence of a designer—had been directly challenged. So had the universal belief in final causes. If the arrangement of the planets could arise merely by the laws of Newtonian physics, if the planets could be born, as Buffon suggested, by a collision between a comet and the sun, then they did not exist for any purpose. They merely came into being through impersonal physical forces.

From the mutability of the heavens, it was a short step to the mutability of the earth, for which the evidence was far more direct. Earthquakes and volcanoes showed how unstable terra firma really is. Sedimentary rocks showed that materials eroded from mountains could be compacted over the ages. Fossils of marine shells on mountain-tops proved that the land must once have been under the sea. As early as 1718, the Abbé Moro and the French academician Bernard de Fontenelle had concluded that the Biblical deluge could not explain the fossilized oyster beds and tropical plants that were found in France. And what of the great, unbroken chain of being if the rocks were full of extinct species?

To explain the facts of geology, some authors—the "catastrophists"—supposed that the earth had gone through a series of great floods and other catastrophes that successively extinguished different groups of animals. Only this, they felt, could account for the discovery that higher and lower geological strata had different fossils. Buffon, however, held that to explain nature we should look to the natural causes we see operating around us: the gradual action of erosion and the slow buildup of land during volcanic eruptions. Buffon thus proposed what came to be the foundation of geology, and indeed of all science, the principle of uniformitarianism, which holds that the same causes that operate now have always operated. By 1795, the Scottish geologist James Hutton had suggested that "in examining things present we have data from which to reason with regard to what has been." His conclusion was that since "rest exists not anywhere," and the forces that change the face of the earth move with ponderous slowness, the mountains and canyons of the world must have come into existence over countless aeons.

If the entire nonliving world was in constant turmoil, could it not be that living things themselves changed? Buffon came close to saying so. He realized that the earth had seen the extinction of countless species, and supposed that those that perished had been the weaker ones. He recognized that domestication and the forces of the environment could modify the variability of many species. And he even mused, in 1766, that species might have developed from common ancestors:

> If it were admitted that the ass is of the family of the horse, and different from the horse only because it has varied from the original form, one could equally well say that the ape is of the family of man, that he is a degenerate man, that man and ape have a common origin; that, in fact, all the families among plants as well as animals have come from a single stock, and that all animals are descended from a single animal, from which have sprung in the course of time, as a result of process or of degeneration, all the other races of animals. For if it were once shown that we are justi-

fied in establishing these families; if it were granted among animals and plants there has been (I do not say several species) but even a single one, which has been produced in the course of direct descent from another species . . . then there would no longer be any limit to the power of nature, and we should not be wrong in supposing that, with sufficient time, she has been able from a single being to derive all the other organized beings.[4]

This, however, was too heretical a thought; and in any case, Buffon thought the weight of evidence was against common descent. No new species had been observed to arise within recorded history, Buffon wrote; the sterility of hybrids between species appeared an impossible barrier to such a conclusion; and if species had emerged gradually, there should have been innumerable intermediate variations between the horse and ass, or any other species. So Buffon concluded: "But this [idea of a common ancestor] is by no means a proper representation of nature. We are assured by the authority of revelation that all animals have participated equally in the grace of direct Creation and that the first pair of every species issued fully formed from the hands of the Creator."

Buffon's friend and protégé, Jean Baptiste de Monet, the Chevalier de Lamarck, was the first scientist to take the big step. It is not clear what led Lamarck to his uncompromising belief in evolution; perhaps it was his studies of fossil molluscs, which he came to believe were the ancestors of similar species living today. Whatever the explanation, from 1800 on he developed the notion that fossils were not evidence of extinct species but of ones that had gradually been transformed into living species. To be sure, he wrote, "an enormous time and wide variation in successive conditions must doubtless have been required to enable nature to bring the organization of animals to that degree of complexity and development in which we see it at its perfection"; but "time has no limits and can be drawn upon to any extent."

Lamarck believed that various lineages of animals and plants arose by a continual process of spontaneous generation from inanimate matter, and were transformed from very simple to more complex forms by an innate natural tendency toward complexity caused by "powers conferred by the supreme author of all things." Various specialized adaptations of species are consequences of the fact that animals must always change in response to the needs imposed on them by a continually changing environment. When the needs of a species change, so does its behavior. The animal then uses certain organs more frequently than before, and these organs, in turn, become more highly developed by such use, or else "by virtue of the operations of their own inner senses." The classic example of Lamarckism is the giraffe: by straining upward for foliage, it was thought, the animal had acquired a longer neck, which was then inherited by its off-spring.

In the nineteenth century it was widely believed that "acquired" characteristics—alterations brought about by use or disuse, or by the direct influence of the environment—could be inherited. Thus it was perfectly reasonable for Lamarck to base his theory of evolutionary change partly on this idea. Indeed, Darwin also allowed for this possibility, and the inheritance of acquired characteristics was not finally prove impossible until the 1890s.

Lamarck's ideas had a wide influence; but in the end did not convince many scientists of the reality of evolution. In France, Georges Cuvier, the foremost paleontologist and anatomist of his time, was an influential opponent of evolution. He rejected Lamarck's notion of the spontaneous generation of life, found it inconceivable that changes in behavior could produce the exquisite adaptations that almost every species shows, and emphasized that in both the fossil record and among living animals there were numerous "gaps" rather than intermediate forms between species. In England, the philosophy of "natural theology" held sway in science, and the best-known naturalists continued to believe firmly that the features of animals and plants were evidence of God's design. These devout Christians included the foremost geologist of the day, Charles Lyell, whose *Principles of Geology* established uniformitarianism once and for all as a guiding principle. But Lyell was such a thorough uniformitarian that he believed in a steady-state world, a world that was always in balance between forces such as erosion and mountain building, and so was forever the same. There was no room for evolution, with its concept of steady change, in Lyell's world view, though he nonetheless had an enormous impact on evolutionary thought, through his influence on Charles Darwin.

Darwin (1809–1882) himself, unquestionably one of the greatest scientists of all time, came only slowly to an evolutionary position. The son of a successful physician, he showed little interest in the life of the mind in his early years. After unsuccessfully studying medicine at Edinburgh, he was sent to Cambridge to prepare for the ministry, but he had only a half-hearted interest in his studies and spent most of his time hunting, collecting beetles, and becoming an accomplished amateur naturalist. Though he received his B.A. in 1831, his future was quite uncertain until, in December of that year, he was enlisted as a naturalist aboard *H.M.S. Beagle,* with his father's very reluctant agreement. For five years (from December 27, 1831, to October 2, 1836) the *Beagle* carried him about the world, chiefly along the coast of South America, which it was the *Beagle's* mission to survey. For five years Darwin collected geological and biological specimens, made geological observations, absorbed Lyell's *Principles of Geology,* took voluminous notes, and speculated about everything from geology to anthropology. He sent such massive collections of specimens back to England that by the time he returned he had already gained a substantial reputation as a naturalist.

Shortly after his return, Darwin married and settled into an estate at Down where he remained, hardly traveling even to London, for the rest of his life. Despite continual ill health, he pursued an extraordinary range of biological studies: classifying barnacles, breeding pigeons, experimenting with plant growth, and much more. He wrote no fewer than sixteen books and many papers, read voraciously, corresponded extensively with everyone, from pigeon breeders to the most eminent scientists, whose ideas or information might bear on his theories, and kept detailed notes on an amazing variety of subjects. Few people have written authoritatively on so many different topics: his books include not only *The Voyage of the Beagle, The Origin of Species,* and *The Descent of Man,* but also *The Structure and Distribution of Coral Reefs* (containing a novel theory of the formation of coral atolls which is still regarded as correct), *A Monograph on the Sub-class Cirripedia* (the definitive study of barnacle classification), *The Various Contrivances by Which Orchids are Fertilised by Insects, The Variation of Animals and Plants Under Domestication* (an exhaustive summary of information on variation, so crucial to his evolutionary theory), *The Effects of Cross and Self Fertilisation in the Vegetable Kingdom* (an analysis of sexual reproduction and the sterility of hybrids between species), *The Expression of the Emotions in Man and Animals* (on the evolution of human behavior from animal behavior), and *The Formation of Vegetable Mould Through the Action of Worms.* There is every reason to believe that almost all these books bear, in one way or another, on the principles and ideas that were inherent in Darwin's theory of evolution. The worm book, for example, is devoted to showing how great the impact of a seemingly trivial process like worm burrowing may be on ecology and geology if it persists for a long time. The idea of such cumulative slight effects is, of course, inherent in Darwin's view of evolution: successive slight modifications of a species, if continued long enough, can transform it radically.

When Darwin embarked on his voyage, he was a devout Christian who did not doubt the literal truth of the Bible, and did not believe in evolution any more than did Lyell and the other English scientists he had met or whose books he had read. By the time he returned to England in 1836 he had made numerous observations that would later convince him of evolution. It seems likely, however, that the idea itself did not occur to him until the spring of 1837, when the ornithologist John Gould, who was working on some of Darwin's collections, pointed out to him

that each of the Galápagos Islands, off the coast of Ecuador, had a different kind of mockingbird. It was quite unclear whether they were different varieties of the same species, or different species. From this, Darwin quickly realized that species are not the discrete, clear-cut entities everyone seemed to imagine. The possibility of transformation entered his mind, and it applied to more than the mockingbirds: "When comparing . . . the birds from the separate islands of the Galápagos archipelago, both with one another and with those from the American mainland, I was much struck how entirely vague and arbitrary is the distinction between species and varieties."

In July 1837 he began his first notebook on the "Transmutation of Species." He later said that the Galápagos species and the similarity between South American fossils and living species were at the origin of all his views.

> During the voyage of the *Beagle* I had been deeply impressed by discovering in the Pampean formation great fossil animals covered with armour like that on the existing armadillos; secondly, by the manner in which closely allied animals replace one another in proceeding southward over the continent; and thirdly, by the South American character of most of the productions of the Galápagos archipelago, and more especially by the manner in which they differ slightly on each island of the group; none of these islands appearing to be very ancient in a geological sense. It was evident that such facts as these, as well as many others, could be explained on the supposition that species gradually become modified; and the subject has haunted me.

The first great step in Darwin's thought was the realization that evolution had occurred. The second was his brilliant insight into the possible cause of evolutionary change. Lamarck's theory of "felt needs" had not been convincing. A better one was required. It came on September 18, 1838, when after grappling with the problem for fifteen months, "I happened to read for amusement Malthus on Population, and being well prepared to appreciate the struggle for existence which everywhere goes on from long- continued observa-

tion of the habits of animals and plants, it at once struck me that under these circumstances favorable variations would tend to be preserved, and unfavorable ones to be destroyed. The result of this would be the formation of new species. Here, then, I had at last got a theory by which to work."

Malthus, an economist, had developed the pessimistic thesis that the exponential growth of human populations must inevitably lead to famine, unless it were checked by war, disease, or "moral restraint." This emphasis on exponential population growth was apparently the catalyst for Darwin, who then realized that since most natural populations of animals and plants remain fairly stable in numbers, many more individuals are born than survive. Because individuals vary in their characteristics, the struggle to survive must favor some variant individuals over others. These survivors would then pass on their characteristics to future generations. Repetition of this process generation after generation would gradually transform the species.

Darwin clearly knew that he could not afford to publish a rash speculation on so important a subject without developing the best possible case. The world of science was not hospitable to speculation, and besides, Darwin was dealing with a highly volatile issue. Not only was he affirming that evolution had occurred, he was proposing a purely material explanation for it, one that demolished the argument from design in a single thrust. Instead of publishing his theory, he patiently amassed a mountain of evidence, and finally, in 1844, collected his thoughts in an essay on natural selection. But he still didn't publish. Not until 1856, almost twenty years after he became an evolutionist, did he begin what he planned to be a massive work on the subject, tentatively titled *Natural Selection.*

Then, in June 1858, the unthinkable happened. Alfred Russel Wallace (1823–1913), a young naturalist who had traveled in the Amazon Basin and in the Malay Archipelago, had also become interested in evolution. Like Darwin, he was struck by the fact that "the most closely allied species are found in the same locality or in closely adjoining lo-

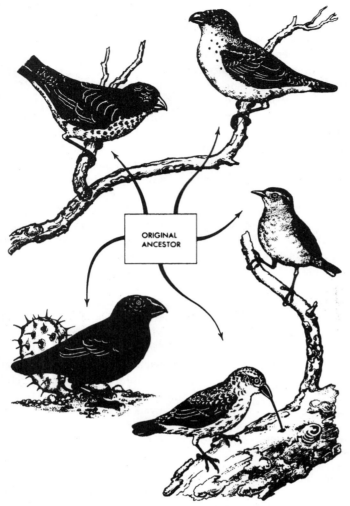

**Figure 1.** *Some species of Galápagos finches. Several of the most different species are represented here; intermediate species also exist. Clockwise from lower left are a male ground-finch (the plumage of the female resembles that of the tree-finches); the vegetarian tree-finch; the insectivorous tree-finch; the warbler-finch; and the woodpecker-finch, which uses a cactus spine to extricate insects from crevices. The slight differences among these species, and among species in other groups of Galápagos animals such as giant tortoises, were one of the observations that led Darwin to formulate his hypothesis of evolution. (From D. Lack, Darwin's Finches [Oxford: Oxford University Press, 1944].)*

calities and . . . therefore the natural sequence of the species by affinity is also geographical." In the throes of a malarial fever in Malaya, Wallace conceived of the same idea of natural selection as Darwin had, and sent Darwin a manuscript "On the Tendency of Varieties to Depart Indefinitely from the Original Type." Darwin's friends Charles Lyell and Joseph Hooker, a botanist, rushed in to help Darwin establish the priority of his ideas, and on July 1, 1858, they presented to the Linnean Society of London both Wallace's paper and extracts from Darwin's 1844 essay. Darwin abandoned his big book on natural selection and condensed the argument into a 490-page "abstract" that was published on November 24, 1859, under the title *The Origin of Species by Means of Natural Selection; or, the Preservation of Favored Races in the Struggle for Life.* Because it was an abstract, he had to leave out many of the detailed observations and references to the literature that he had amassed, but these were later provided in his other books, many of which are voluminous expansions on the contents of *The Origin of Species.*

The first five chapters of the *Origin* lay out the theory that Darwin had conceived. He shows that both domesticated and wild species are variable, that much of that variation is hereditary, and that breeders, by conscious selection of desirable varieties, can develop breeds of pigeons, dogs, and other forms that are more different from each other than species or even families of wild animals and plants are from each other. The differences between related species then are no more than an exaggerated form of the kinds of variations one can find in a single species; indeed, it is often extremely difficult to tell if natural populations are distinct species or merely well-marked varieties.

Darwin then shows that in nature there is competition, predation, and a struggle for life.

> Owing to this struggle, variations, however slight and from whatever cause proceeding, if they be in any degree profitable to the individuals of a species, in their infinitely complex relations to other organic beings and to their physical conditions of life, will tend to the preservation of such individuals, and will generally be inherited by the offspring. The offspring, also, will thus have a better chance of surviving, for, of the many individuals of any species which are periodically born, but a small number can survive. I have called this principle, by which each slight variation, if useful, is preserved, by the term natural selection, in order to mark its relation to man's power of selection.

Darwin goes on to give examples of how even slight variations promote survival, and argues that when populations are exposed to different conditions, different variations will be favored, so that the descendants of a species become diversified in structure, and each ancestral species can give rise to several new ones. Although "it is probable that each form remains for long periods unaltered," successive evolutionary modifications will ultimately alter the different species so greatly that they will be classified as different genera, families, or orders.

Competition between species will impel them to become more different, for "the more diversified the descendants from any one species become in structure, constitution and habits, by so much will they be better enabled to seize on many and widely diversified places in the polity of nature, and so be enabled to increase in numbers." Thus different adaptations arise, and "the ultimate result is that each creature tends to become more and more improved in relation to its conditions. This improvement inevitably leads to the greater advancement of the organization of the greater number of living beings throughout the world." But lowly organisms continue to persist, for "natural selection, or the survival of the fittest, does not necessarily include progressive development—it only takes advantage of such variations as arise and are beneficial to each creature under its complex relations of life." Probably no organism has reached a peak of perfection, and many lowly forms of life continue to exist, for "in some cases variations or individual differences of a favorable nature may never have arisen for natural selection to act on or accumulate. In no case, probably, has time sufficed for the utmost possible amount of development. In some few cases there has been what we must call retrogression of organization. But the main cause lies in the fact that under very simple conditions of life a high organization would be of no service. . . ."

In the rest of *The Origin of Species,* Darwin considers all the objections that might be raised against his theory; discusses the evolution of a great array of phenomena—hybrid sterility, the slave-making instinct of ants, the similarity of vertebrate embryos; and presents an enormous body of evidence for evolution. He draws his evidence from comparative anatomy, embryology, behavior, geographic variation, the geographic distribution of species, the study of rudimentary organs, atavistic variations ("throwbacks"), and the geological record to show how all of biology provides testimony that species have descended with modification from common ancestors.

Darwin's triumph was in synthesizing ideas and information in ways that no one had quite imagined before. From Lyell and the geologists he learned uniformitarianism: the cause of past events must be found in natural forces that operate today; and these, in the vastness of time, can accomplish great change. From Malthus and the nineteenth-century economists he learned of competition and the struggle for existence. From

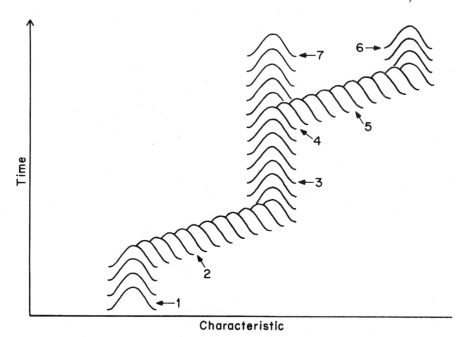

**Figure 2.** *Processes of evolutionary change. A characteristic that is variable (1) often shows a bell-shaped distribution—individuals vary on either side of the average. Evolutionary change (2) consists of a shift in successive generations, after which the characteristic may reach a new equilibrium (3). When the species splits into two different species (4), one of the species may undergo further evolutionary change (5) and reach a new equilibrium (6). The other may remain unchanged (7) or not. Each population usually remains variable throughout this process, but the average is shifted, ordinarily by natural selection.*

his work on barnacles, his travels, and his knowledge of domesticated varieties he learned that species do not have immutable essences but are variable in all their properties and blend into one another gradually. From his familiarity with the works of Whewell, Herschel, and other philosophers of science he developed a powerful method of pursuing science, the "hypothetico-deductive" method, which consists of formulating a hypothesis or speculation, deducing the logical predictions that must follow from the hypothesis, and then testing the hypothesis by seeing whether or not the predictions are verified. This was by no means the prevalent philosophy of science in Darwin's time.[5]

Darwin brought biology out of the Middle Ages. For divine design and unknowable supernatural forces he substituted natural material causes that could be studied by the methods of science. Instead of catastrophes unknown to physical science he invoked forces that could be studied in anyone's laboratory or garden. He replaced a young, static world by one in which there had been constant change for countless aeons. He established that life had a history, and

this proved the essential view that differentiated evolutionary thought from all that had gone before.

For the British naturalist John Ray, writing in 1701, organisms had no history—they were the same at that moment, and lived in the same places, doing the same things, as when they were first created. For Darwin, organisms spoke of historical change. If there has indeed been such a history, then fossils in the oldest rocks must differ from those in younger rocks: trilobites, dinosaurs, and mammoths will not be mixed together but will appear in some temporal sequence. If species come from common ancestors, they will have the same characteristics, modified for different functions: the same bones used by bats for flying will be used by horses for running. If species come from ancestors that lived in different environments, they will carry the evidence of their history with them in the form of similar patterns of embryonic development and in vestigial, rudimentary organs that no longer serve any function. If species have a history, their geographical distribution will reflect it: oceanic islands won't have elephants because they wouldn't have been able to get there.

Once the earth and its living inhabitants are seen as the products of historical change, the theological philosophy embodied in the great chain of being ceases to make sense; the plenitude, or fullness, of the world becomes not an eternal manifestation of God's bountiful creativity but an illusion. For most of earth's history, most of the present species have not existed; and many of those that did exist do so no longer. But the scientific challenge to medieval philosophy goes even deeper. If evolution has occurred, and if it has proceeded from the natural causes that Darwin envisioned, then the adaptations of organisms to their environment, the intricate construction of the bird's wing and the orchid's flower, are evidence not of divine design but of the struggle for existence. Moreover, and this may be the deepest implication of all, Darwin brought to biology, as his predecessors had brought to astronomy and geology, the sufficiency of efficient causes. No longer was there any reason to look for final causes or goals. To the questions "What purpose does this species serve? Why did God make tapeworms?" the answer is "To no purpose." Tapeworms were not put here to serve a purpose, nor were planets, nor plants, nor people. They came into existence not by design but by the action of impersonal natural laws.

By providing materialistic, mechanistic explanations, instead of miraculous ones, for the characteristics of plants and animals, Darwin brought biology out of the realm of theology and into the realm of science. For miraculous spiritual forces fall outside the province of science; all of science is the study of material causation.

Of course, *The Origin of Species* didn't convince everyone immediately. Evolution and its material cause, natural selection, evoked strong protests from ecclesiastical circles, and even from scientists.[6] The eminent geologist Adam Sedgwick, for example, wrote in 1860 that species must come into existence by creation,

> a power I cannot imitate or comprehend; but in which I can believe, by a legitimate conclusion of sound rea-

son drawn from the laws and harmonies of Nature. For I can see in all around me a design and purpose, and a mutual adaptation of parts which I *can* comprehend, and which prove that there is exterior to, and above, the mere phenomena of Nature a great prescient and designing cause.... The pretended physical philosophy of modern days strips man of all his moral attributes, or holds them of no account in the estimate of his origin and place in the created world. A cold atheistical materialism is the tendency of the so-called material philosophy of the present day.

Among the more scientific objections were those posed by the French paleontologist François Pictet, and they were echoed by many others. Since Darwin supposes that species change gradually over the course of thousands of generations, then, asked Pictet, "Why don't we find these gradations in the fossil record ... and why, instead of collecting thousands of identical individuals, do we not find more intermediary forms? ... How is it that the most ancient fossil beds are rich in a variety of diverse forms of life, instead of the few early types Darwin's theory leads us to expect? How is it that no species has been seen to evolve during human history, and that the 4000 years which separates us from the mummies of Egypt have been insufficient to modify the crocodile and the ibis?" Pictet protested that, although slight variations might in time alter a species slightly, "all known facts demonstrate ... that the prolonged influence of modifying causes has an action which is constantly restrained within sufficiently confined limits."

The anatomist Richard Owen likewise denied "that ... variability is progressive and unlimited, so as, in the course of generations, to change the species, the genus, the order, or the class." The paleontologist Louis Agassiz insisted that organisms fall into discrete groups, based on uniquely different created plans, between which no intermediates could exist. He chose the birds as a group that showed the sharpest of boundaries. Only a few years later, in 1868, the fossil *Archaeopteryx,* an exquisite intermediate between birds and reptiles, demolished Agassiz's argument,

and he had no more to say on the unique character of the birds.

Within twelve years of *The Origin of Species,* the evidence for evolution had been so thoroughly accepted that philosopher and mathematician Chauncey Wright could point out that among the students of science, "orthodoxy has been won over to the doctrine of evolution." However, Wright continued, "While the general doctrine of evolution has thus been successfully redeemed from theological condemnation, this is not yet true of the subordinate hypothesis of Natural Selection."

Natural selection turned out to be an extraordinarily difficult concept for people to grasp. St. George Mivart, a Catholic scholar and scientist, was not unusual in equating natural selection with chance. "The theory of Natural Selection may (though it need not) be taken in such a way as to lead man to regard the present organic world as formed, so to speak, *accidentally,* beautiful and wonderful as is the confessedly haphazard result." Many like him simply refused to understand that natural selection is the antithesis of chance and consequently could not see how selection might cause adaptation or any kind of progressive evolutionary change. Even in the 1940s there were those, especially among paleontologists, who felt that the progressive evolution of groups like the horses, as revealed by the fossil record, must have had some unknown cause other than natural selection. Paradoxically, then, Darwin had convinced the scientific world of evolution where his predecessors had failed; but he had not convinced all biologists of his truly original theory, the theory of natural selection.

Natural selection fell into particular disrepute in the early part of the twentieth century because of the rise of genetics—which, as it happened, eventually became the foundation of the modern theory of evolution. Darwin's supposition that variation was unlimited, and so in time could give rise to strikingly different organisms, was not entirely convincing because he had no good idea of where variation came from. In 1865, the Austrian monk Gregor Mendel discovered, from his crosses of pea plants, that discretely different characteristics such as wrinkled versus smooth seeds were inherited from generation to generation without being altered, as if they were caused by particles that passed from parent to offspring. Mendel's work was ignored for thirty-five years, until, in 1900, three biologists discovered his paper and realized that it held the key to the mystery of heredity. One of the three, Hugo de Vries, set about to explore the problem as Mendel had, and in the course of his studies of evening primroses observed strikingly different variations arise, *de novo.* The new forms were so different that de Vries believed they represented new species, which had arisen in a single step by alteration or, as he called it, mutation, of the hereditary material.

In the next few decades, geneticists working with a great variety of organisms observed many other drastic changes arise by mutation: fruit flies (Drosophila), for example, with white instead of red eyes or curled instead of straight wings. These laboratory geneticists, especially Thomas Hunt Morgan, an outstanding geneticist at Columbia University, asserted that evolution must proceed by major mutational steps, and that mutation, not natural selection, was the cause of evolution. In their eyes, Darwin's theory was dead on two counts: evolution was not gradual, and it was not caused by natural selection. Meanwhile, naturalists, taxonomists, and breeders of domesticated plants and animals continued to believe in Darwinism, because they saw that populations and species differed quantitatively and gradually rather than in big jumps, that most variation was continuous (like height in humans) rather than discrete, and that domesticated species could be altered by artificial selection from continuous variation.

The bitter conflict between the Mendelian geneticists and the Darwinians was resolved in the 1930s in a "New Synthesis" that brought the opposing views into a "neo-Darwinian" theory of evolution.[7] Slight variations in height, wing length, and other characteristics proved, under careful genetic analysis, to be inherited as particles, in the same way as the discrete variations studied by the Mendelians. Thus a large animal

simply has inherited more particles, or genes, for large size than a smaller member of the species has. The Mendelians were simply studying particularly well marked variations, while the naturalists were studying more subtle ones. Variations could be very slight, or fairly pronounced, or very substantial, but all were inherited in the same manner. All these variations, it was shown, arose by a process of mutation of the genes.

Three mathematical theoreticians, Ronald Fisher and J. B. S. Haldane in England and Sewall Wright in the United States, proved that a newly mutated gene would not automatically form a new species. Nor would it automatically replace the preexisting form of the gene, and so transform the species. Replacement of one gene by a mutant form of the gene, they said, could happen in two ways. The mutation could enable its possessors to survive or reproduce more effectively than the old form; if so, it would increase by natural selection, just as Darwin had said. The new characteristic that evolved in this way would ordinarily be considered an improved adaptation.

Sewall Wright pointed out, however, that not all genetic changes in species need be adaptive. A new mutation might be no better or worse than the preexisting gene—it might simply be "neutral." In small populations such a mutation could replace the previous gene purely by chance—a process he called random genetic drift. The idea, put crudely, is this. Suppose there is a small population of land snails in a cow pasture, and that 5 percent of them are brown and the rest are yellow. Purely by chance, a greater percentage of yellow snails than of brown ones get crushed by cows' hooves in one generation. The snails breed, and there will now be a slightly greater percentage of yellow snails in the next generation than there had been. But in the next generation, the yellow ones may suffer more trampling, purely by chance. The proportion of yellow offspring will then be lower again. These random events cause fluctuations in the percentage of the two types. Wright proved mathematically that eventually, if no other factors intervene, these fluctuations will bring the population either to 100 percent yellow or 100 percent

brown, purely by chance. The population will have evolved, then, but not by natural selection; and there is no improvement of adaptation.

During the period of the New Synthesis, though, genetic drift was emphasized less than natural selection, for which abundant evidence was discovered. Sergei Chetverikov in Russia, and later Theodosius Dobzhansky working in the United States, showed that wild populations of fruit flies contained an immense amount of genetic variation, including the same kinds of mutations that the geneticists had found arising in their laboratories. Dobzhansky and other workers went on to show that these variations affected survival and reproduction: that natural selection was a reality. They showed, moreover, that the genetic differences among related species were indeed compounded of the same kinds of slight genetic variations that they found within species. Thus the taxonomists and the geneticists converged onto a neo-Darwinian theory of evolution: evolution is due not to mutation *or* natural selection, but to both. Random mutations provide abundant genetic variation; natural selection, the antithesis of randomness, sorts out the useful from the deleterious, and transforms the species.

In the following two decades, the paleontologist George Gaylord Simpson showed that this theory was completely adequate to explain the fossil record, and the ornithologists Bernhard Rensch and Ernst Mayr, the botanist G. Ledyard Stebbins, and many other taxonomists showed that the similarities and differences among living species could be fully explained by neo-Darwinism. They also clarified the meaning of "species." Organisms belong to different species if they do not interbreed when the opportunity presents itself, thus remaining genetically distinct. An ancestral species splits into two descendant species when different populations of the ancestor, living in different geographic regions, become so genetically different from each other that they will not or cannot interbreed when they have the chance to do so. As a result, evolution can happen without the formation of new species: a single species can be genetically transformed without splitting into several descendants. Conversely, new species can be formed without much genetic change. If one population becomes different from the rest of its species in, for example, its mating behavior, it will not interbreed with the other populations. Thus it has become a new species, even though it may be identical to its "sister species" in every respect except its behavior. Such a new species is free to follow a new path of genetic change, since it does not become homogenized with its sister species by interbreeding. With time, therefore, it can diverge and develop different adaptations.

The conflict between the geneticists and the Darwinians that was resolved in the New Synthesis was the last major conflict in evolutionary science. Since that time, an enormous amount of research has confirmed most of the major conclusions of neo-Darwinism. We now know that populations contain very extensive genetic variation that continually arises by mutation of pre-existing genes. We also know what genes are and how they become mutated. Many instances of the reality of natural selection in wild populations have been documented, and there is extensive evidence that many species form by the divergence of different populations of an ancestral species.

The major questions in evolutionary biology now tend to be of the form, "All right, factors $x$ and $y$ both operate in evolution, but how important is $x$ compared to $y$?" For example, studies of biochemical genetic variation have raised the possibility that nonadaptive, random change (genetic drift) may be the major reason for many biochemical differences among species. How important, then, is genetic drift compared to natural selection? Another major question has to do with rates of evolution: Do species usually diverge very slowly, as Darwin thought, or does evolution consist mostly of rapid spurts, interspersed with long periods of constancy? Still another question is raised by mutations, which range all the way from gross changes of the kind Morgan studied to very slight alterations. Does evolution consist entirely of the substitution of mutations that have very slight effects, or are major mutations sometimes important too? Partisans on each side of all these questions argue vigorously for their interpretation of the evidence, but they don't doubt that the major factors of evolution are known. They simply emphasize one factor or another. Minor battles of precisely this kind go on continually in every field of science; without them there would be very little advancement in our knowledge.

Within a decade or two of *The Origin of Species,* the belief that living organisms had evolved over the ages was firmly entrenched in biology. As of 1982, the historical existence of evolution is viewed as fact by almost all biologists. To explain how the fact of evolution has been brought about, a theory of evolutionary mechanisms—mutation, natural selection, genetic drift, and isolation—has been developed.[8] But exactly what is the evidence for the fact of evolution?

## Notes

1. Andrew Dickson White, *A History of the Warfare of Science with Theology in Christendom* vol. I (London: Macmillan, 1896; reprint ed., New York: Dover, 1960).
2. A. O. Lovejoy, *The Great Chain of Being* (Cambridge, Mass.: Harvard University Press, 1936).
3. Much of this history is provided by J. C. Greene, *The Death of Adam: Evolution and its Impact on Western Thought* (Ames: Iowa State University Press, 1959).
4. A detailed history of this and other developments in evolutionary biology is given by Ernst Mayr, *The Growth of Biological Thought: Diversity, Evolution, Inheritance* (Cambridge, Mass.: Harvard University Press, 1982).
5. See D. L. Hull, *Darwin and His Critics* (Cambridge, Mass.: Harvard University Press, 1973).
6. Ibid.
7. E. Mayr and W. B. Provine, *The Evolutionary Synthesis* (Cambridge, Mass.: Harvard University Press, 1980).
8. Our modern understanding of the mechanisms of evolution is described in many books. Elementary textbooks include G. L. Stebbins, *Processes of Organic Evolution,* (Englewood Cliffs, N.J.: Prentice-Hall, 1971), and J. Maynard Smith, *The Theory of Evolution* (New York: Penguin Books, 1975). More advanced textbooks include Th. Dobzhansky, F. J. Ayala, G. L. Stebbins, and J. W. Valentine, *Evolution* (San Francisco: Freeman, 1977), and D. J. Futuyma, *Evolutionary Biology* (Sunderland, Mass.: Sinauer, 1979). Unreferenced facts and theories described in the text are familiar enough to most evolutionary biologists that they will be found in most or all of the references cited above.

# Darwin's Influence on Modern Thought

*Great minds shape the thinking of successive historical periods.
Luther and Calvin inspired the Reformation; Locke, Leibniz,
Voltaire and Rousseau, the Enlightenment. Modern thought is most
dependent on the influence of Charles Darwin*

## by Ernst Mayr

*ERNEST MAYR is one of the towering figures in the history of evolutionary biology. Following his graduation from the University of Berlin in 1926, ornithological expeditions to New Guinea fueled his interest in theoretical evolutionary biology. Mayr emigrated to the U.S. in 1931 and in 1953 joined the faculty of Harvard University, where he is now Alexander Agassiz Professor of Zoology, Emeritus. His conception of rapid speciation of isolated populations formed the basis for the well-known neoevolutionary concept of punctuated equilibrium. The author of some of the 20th century's most influential volumes on evolution, Mayr is the recipient of numerous awards, including the National Medal of Science.*

Clearly, our conception of the world and our place in it is, at the beginning of the 21st century, drastically different from the zeitgeist at the beginning of the 19th century. But no consensus exists as to the source of this revolutionary change. Karl Marx is often mentioned; Sigmund Freud has been in and out of favor; Albert Einstein's biographer Abraham Pais made the exuberant claim that Einstein's theories "have profoundly changed the way modern men and women think about the phenomena of inanimate nature." No sooner had Pais said this, though, than he recognized the exaggeration. "It would actually be better to say 'modern scientists' than 'modern men and women,'" he wrote, because one needs schooling in the physicist's style of thought and mathematical techniques to appreciate Einstein's contributions in their fullness. Indeed, this limitation is true for all the extraordinary theories of modern physics, which have had little impact on the way the average person apprehends the world.

The situation differs dramatically with regard to concepts in biology. Many biological ideas proposed during the past 150 years stood in stark conflict with what everybody assumed to be true. The acceptance of these ideas required an ideological revolution. And no biologist has been responsible for more—and for more drastic—modifications of the average person's worldview than Charles Darwin.

Darwin's accomplishments were so many and so diverse that it is useful to distinguish three fields to which he made major contributions: evolutionary biology; the philosophy of science; and the modern zeitgeist. Although I will be focusing on this last domain, for the sake of completeness I will put forth a short overview of his contributions—particularly as they inform his later ideas—to the first two areas.

## A SECULAR VIEW OF LIFE

Darwin founded a new branch of life science, evolutionary biology. Four of his contributions to evolutionary biology are especially important, as they held considerable sway beyond that discipline. The first is the non-constancy of species, or the modern conception of evolution itself. The second is the notion of branching evolution, implying the common descent of all species of living things on earth from a single unique origin. Up until 1859, all evolutionary proposals, such as that of naturalist Jean-Baptiste Lamarck, instead endorsed linear evolution, a teleological march toward greater perfection that had been in vogue since Aristotle's concept of *Scala Naturae,* the chain of being. Darwin further noted that evolution must be gradual, with no major breaks or discontinuities. Finally, he reasoned that the mechanism of evolution was natural selection.

These four insights served as the foundation for Darwin's founding of a new branch of the philosophy of science, a philosophy of biology. Despite the passing of a century before this new branch of philosophy fully developed, its eventual form is based on Darwinian concepts. For example, Darwin introduced historicity into science. Evolutionary biology, in contrast with physics and chemistry, is a historical science—the evolutionist attempts to explain events and processes that have already taken place. Laws and experiments are inappropriate techniques for the explication of such events and processes. Instead one constructs a historical narrative, consisting of a tentative reconstruction of the particular scenario that led to the events one is trying to explain.

For example, three different scenarios have been proposed for the sudden extinction of the dinosaurs at the end of the Cretaceous: a devastating epidemic; a catastrophic change of climate; and the impact of an asteroid, known as the Alvarez theory. The first two narratives were ultimately refuted by evidence incompatible with them. All the known facts, however, fit the Alvarez theory, which is now widely accepted. The testing of historical narratives implies that the wide gap between science and the humanities that so troubled physicist C. P. Snow is actually nonexistent—by virtue of its methodology and its acceptance of the time factor that makes change possible, evolutionary biology serves as a bridge.

The discovery of natural selection, by Darwin and Alfred Russell Wallace, must itself be counted as an extraordinary philosophical advance. The principle remained unknown throughout the more than 2,000-year history of philosophy ranging from the Greeks to Hume, Kant and the Victorian era. The concept of natural selection had remarkable power for explaining directional and adaptive changes. Its nature is simplicity itself. It is not a force like the forces described in the laws of physics; its mechanism is simply the elimination of inferior individuals. This process of nonrandom elimination impelled Darwin's contemporary, philosopher Herbert Spencer, to describe evolution with the now familiar term "survival of the fittest." (This description was long ridiculed as circular reasoning: "Who are

the fittest? Those who survive." In reality, a careful analysis can usually determine why certain individuals fail to thrive in a given set of conditions.)

The truly outstanding achievement of the principle of natural selection is that it makes unnecessary the invocation of "final causes"—that is, any teleological forces leading to a particular end. In fact, nothing is predetermined. Furthermore, the objective of selection even may change from one generation to the next, as environmental circumstances vary.

A diverse population is a necessity for the proper working of natural selection. (Darwin's success meant that typologists, for whom all members of a class are essentially identical, were left with an untenable viewpoint.) Because of the importance of variation, natural selection should be considered a two-step process: the production of abundant variation is followed by the elimination of inferior individuals. This latter step is directional. By adopting natural selection, Darwin settled the several-thousand-year-old argument among philosophers over chance or necessity. Change on the earth is the result of both, the first step being dominated by randomness, the second by necessity.

Darwin was a holist: for him the object, or target, of selection was primarily the individual as a whole. The geneticists, almost from 1900 on, in a rather reductionist spirit preferred to consider the gene the target of evolution. In the past 25 years, however, they have largely returned to the Darwinian view that the individual is the principal target.

For 80 years after 1859, bitter controversy raged as to which of four competing evolutionary theories was valid. "Transmutation" was the establishment of a new species or new type through a single mutation, or saltation. "Orthogenesis" held that intrinsic teleological tendencies led to transformation. Lamarckian evolution relied on the inheritance of acquired characteristics. And now there was Darwin's variational evolution, through natural selection. Darwin's theory clearly emerged as the victor during the evolutionary synthesis of the 1940s, when the new discoveries in genetics were married with taxonomic observations concerning systematics,

the classification of organisms by their relationships. Darwinism is now almost unanimously accepted by knowledgeable evolutionists. In addition, it has become the basic component of the new philosophy of biology.

A most important principle of the new biological philosophy, undiscovered for almost a century after the publication of *On the Origin of Species,* is the dual nature of biological processes. These activities are governed both by the universal laws of physics and chemistry and by a genetic program, itself the result of natural selection, which has molded the genotype for millions of generations. The causal factor of the possession of a genetic program is unique to living organisms, and it is totally absent in the inanimate world. Because of the backward state of molecular and genetic knowledge in his time, Darwin was unaware of this vital factor.

Another aspect of the new philosophy of biology concerns the role of laws. Laws give way to concepts in Darwinism. In the physical sciences, as a rule, theories are based on laws; for example, the laws of motion led to the theory of gravitation. In evolutionary biology, however, theories are largely based on concepts such as competition, female choice, selection, succession and dominance. These biological concepts, and the theories based on them, cannot be reduced to the laws and theories of the physical sciences. Darwin himself never stated this idea plainly. My assertion of Darwin's importance to modern thought is the result of an analysis of Darwinian theory over the past century. During this period, a pronounced change in the methodology of biology took place. This transformation was not caused exclusively by Darwin, but it was greatly strengthened by developments in evolutionary biology. Observation, comparison and classification, as well as the testing of competing historical narratives, became the methods of evolutionary biology, outweighing experimentation.

I do not claim that Darwin was single-handedly responsible for all the intellectual developments in this period. Much of it, like the refutation of French mathematician and physicist Pierre-Simon Laplace's determinism, was "in the air." But Darwin in most cases either had priority or promoted the new views most vigorously.

## THE DARWINIAN ZEITGEIST

A 21st-century person looks at the world quite differently than a citizen of the Victorian era did. This shift had multiple sources, particularly the incredible advances in technology. But what is not at all appreciated is the great extent to which this shift in thinking indeed resulted from Darwin's ideas.

Remember that in 1850 virtually all leading scientists and philosophers were Christian men. The world they inhabited had been created by God, and as the natural theologians claimed, He had instituted wise laws that brought about the perfect adaptation of all organisms to one another and to their environment. At the same time, the architects of the scientific revolution had constructed a worldview based on physicalism (a reduction to spatiotemporal things or events or their properties), teleology, determinism and other basic principles. Such was the thinking of Western man prior to the 1859 publication of *On the Origin of Species*. The basic principles proposed by Darwin would stand in total conflict with these prevailing ideas.

First, Darwinism rejects all supernatural phenomena and causations. The theory of evolution by natural selection explains the adaptedness and diversity of the world solely materialistically. It no longer requires God as creator or designer (although one is certainly still free to believe in God even if one accepts evolution). Darwin pointed out that creation, as described in the Bible and the origin accounts of other cultures, was contradicted by almost any aspect of the natural world. Every aspect of the "wonderful design" so admired by the natural theologians could be explained by natural selection. (A closer look also reveals that design is often not so wonderful—see "Evolution and the Origins of Disease," by Randolph M. Nesse and George C. Williams; SCIEN-TIFIC AMERICAN, November 1998). Eliminating God from science made room for strictly scientific explanations of all natural phenomena; it gave rise to positivism; it produced a powerful intellectual and spiritual revolution, the effects of which have lasted to this day.

Second, Darwinism refutes typology. From the time of the Pythagoreans and Plato, the general concept of the diversity of the world emphasized its invariance and stability. This viewpoint is called typology, or essentialism. The seeming variety, it was said, consisted of a limited number of natural kinds (essences or types), each one forming a class. The members of each class were thought to be identical, constant, and sharply separated from the members of other essences.

Variation, in contrast, is nonessential and accidental. A triangle illustrates essentialism: all triangles have the same fundamental characteristics and are sharply delimited against quadrangles or any other geometric figures. An intermediate between a triangle and a quadrangle is inconceivable. Typological thinking, therefore, is unable to accommodate variation and gives rise to a misleading conception of human races. For the typologist, Caucasians, Africans, Asians or Inuits are types that conspicuously differ from other human ethnic groups. This mode of thinking leads to racism. (Although the ignorant misapplication of evolutionary theory known as "social Darwinism" often gets blamed for justifications of racism, adherence to the disproved essentialism preceding Darwin in fact can lead to a racist viewpoint.)

Darwin completely rejected typological thinking and introduced instead the entirely different concept now called population thinking. All groupings of living organisms, including humanity, are populations that consist of uniquely different individuals. No two of the six billion humans are the same. Populations vary not by their essences but only by mean statistical differences. By rejecting the constancy of populations, Darwin helped to introduce history into scientific thinking and to promote a distinctly new approach to explanatory interpretation in science.

Third, Darwin's theory of natural selection made any invocation of teleology unnecessary. From the Greeks onward, there existed a universal belief in the existence of a teleological force in the world that led to ever greater perfection. This "final cause" was one of the causes specified by Aristotle. After Kant, in the *Critique of Judgment,* had unsuccessfully attempted to describe biological phenomena with the help of a physicalist Newtonian explanation, he then invoked teleological forces. Even after 1859, teleological explanations (orthogenesis) continued to be quite popular in evolutionary biology. The acceptance of the *Scala Naturae* and the explanations of natural theology were other manifestations of the popularity of teleology. Darwinism swept such considerations away.

(The designation "teleological" actually applied to various different phenomena. Many seemingly end-directed processes in inorganic nature are the simple consequence of natural laws—a stone falls or a heated piece of metal cools because of laws of physics, not some end-directed process. Processes in living organisms owe their apparent goal-directedness to the operation of an inborn genetic or acquired program. Adapted systems, such as the heart or kidneys, may engage in activities that can be considered goal seeking, but the systems themselves were acquired during evolution and are continuously fine-tuned by natural selection. Finally, there was a belief in cosmic teleology, with a purpose and predetermined goal ascribed to everything in nature. Modern science, however, is unable to substantiate the existence of any such cosmic teleology.)

Fourth, Darwin does away with determinism. Laplace notoriously boasted that a complete knowledge of the current world and all its processes would enable him to predict the future to infinity. Darwin, by comparison, accepted the universality of randomness and chance throughout the process of natural selection. (Astronomer and philosopher John Herschel referred to natural selection contemptuously as "the law of the higgledy-piggledy.") That chance should play an important role in natural processes has been an unpalatable thought for many physicists. Einstein expressed this distaste in his statement, "God does not play dice." Of course, as previously mentioned, only the first step in natural selection, the production of variation, is a matter of chance. The character of the second step, the actual selection, is to be directional.

Despite the initial resistance by physicists and philosophers, the role of contingency and chance in natural processes is now almost universally acknowledged. Many biologists and philosophers deny the existence of universal laws in biology and suggest that all regularities be stated in probabilistic terms, as nearly all so-called biological laws have exceptions. Philosopher of science Karl Popper's famous test of falsification therefore cannot be applied in these cases.

Fifth, Darwin developed a new view of humanity and, in turn, a new anthropocentrism. Of all of Darwin's proposals, the one his contemporaries found most difficult to accept was that the theory of common descent applied to Man. For the theologians and philosophers alike, Man was a creature above and apart from other living beings. Aristotle, Descartes and Kant agreed on this sentiment, no matter how else their thinking diverged. But biologists Thomas Huxley and Ernst Haeckel revealed through rigorous comparative anatomical study that humans and living apes clearly had common ancestry, an assessment that has never again been seriously questioned in science. The application of the theory of common descent to Man deprived man of his former unique position.

Ironically, though, these events did not lead to an end to anthropocentrism. The study of man showed that, in spite of his descent, he is indeed unique among all organisms. Human intelligence is unmatched by that of any other creature. Humans are the only animals with true language, including grammar and syntax. Only humanity, as Darwin emphasized, has developed genuine ethical systems. In addition, through high intelligence, language and long parental care, humans are the only creatures to have created a rich culture. And by these means, humanity has attained, for better or worse, an unprecedented dominance over the entire globe.

Sixth, Darwin provided a scientific foundation for ethics. The question is frequently raised—and usually rebuffed—as to whether evolution adequately explains healthy human ethics. Many wonder how, if selection rewards the individual only for behavior that enhances his own survival and reproductive success, such pure selfishness can lead to any sound ethics. The widespread thesis of social Darwinism, promoted at the end of the 19th century by Spencer, was that evolutionary explanations were at odds with the development of ethics.

We now know, however, that in a social species not only the individual must be considered—an entire social group can be the target of selection. Darwin applied this reasoning to the human species in 1871 in *The Descent of Man*. The survival and prosperity of a social group depends to a large extent on the harmonious cooperation of the members of the group, and this behavior must be based on altruism. Such altruism, by furthering the survival and prosperity of the group, also indirectly benefits the fitness of the group's individuals. The result amounts to selection favoring altruistic behavior.

Kin selection and reciprocal helpfulness in particular will be greatly favored in a social group. Such selection for altruism has been demonstrated in recent years to be widespread among many other social animals. One can then perhaps encapsulate the relation between ethics and evolution by saying that a propensity for altruism and harmonious cooperation in social groups *is* favored by natural selection. The old thesis of social Darwinism—strict selfishness—was based on an incomplete understanding of animals, particularly social species.

## THE INFLUENCE OF NEW CONCEPTS

Let me now try to summarize my major findings. No educated person any longer questions the validity of the so-called theory of evolution, which we now know to be a simple fact. Likewise, most of Darwin's particular theses have been fully confirmed, such as that of common descent, the gradualism of evolution, and his explanatory theory of natural selection.

I hope I have successfully illustrated the wide reach of Darwin's ideas. Yes, he established a philosophy of biology by introducing the time factor, by demonstrating the importance of chance and contingency, and by showing that theories in evolutionary biology are based on concepts rather than laws. But furthermore—and this is perhaps Darwin's greatest contribution—he developed a set of new principles that influence the thinking of every person: the living world, through evolution, can be explained without recourse to supernaturalism; essentialism or typology is invalid, and we must adopt population thinking, in which all individuals are unique (vital for education and the refutation of racism); natural selection, applied to social groups, is indeed sufficient to account for the origin and maintenance of altruistic ethical systems; cosmic teleology, an intrinsic process leading life automatically to ever greater perfection, is fallacious, with all seemingly teleological phenomena explicable by purely material processes; and determinism is thus repudiated, which places our fate squarely in our own evolved hands.

To borrow Darwin's phrase, there is grandeur in this view of life. New modes of thinking have been, and are being, evolved. Almost every component in modern man's belief system is somehow affected by Darwinian principles.

*This article is based on the September 23, 1999, lecture that Mayr delivered in Stockholm on receiving the Crafoord Prize from the Royal Swedish Academy of Science.*

## FURTHER INFORMATION

DARWIN ON MAN: A PSYCHOLOGICAL STUDY OF SCIENTIFIC CREATIVITY. Second edition. Howard E. Gruber. University of Chicago Press, 1981.

ONE LONG ARGUMENT: CHARLES DARWIN AND THE GENESIS OF MODERN EVOLUTIONARY THOUGHT. Ernst Mayr. Harvard University Press, 1993.

CHARLES DARWIN: VOYAGING: A BIOGRAPHY. Janet Browne. Princeton University Press, 1996.

THE DESCENT OF MAN. Charles Darwin. Popular current edition. Prometheus Books, 1997.

THE ORIGIN OF SPECIES. Charles Darwin. Popular current edition. Bantam Classic, 1999.

# Curse and Blessing of the Ghetto

*Tay-Sachs disease is a choosy killer, one that for centuries targeted Eastern European Jews above all others. By decoding its lethal logic, we can learn a lot about how genetic diseases evolve— and how they can be conquered.*

## Jared Diamond

*Contributing editor Jared Diamond is a professor of physiology at the UCLA School of Medicine.*

Marie and I hated her at first sight, even though she was trying hard to be helpful. As our obstetrician's genetics counselor, she was just doing her job, explaining to us the unpleasant results that might come out of the genetic tests we were about to have performed. As a

scientist, though, I already knew all I wanted to know about Tay-Sachs disease, and I didn't need to be reminded that the baby sentenced to death by it could be my own.

Fortunately, the tests would reveal that my wife and I were not carriers of the Tay-Sachs gene, and our preparenthood fears on that matter at least could be put to rest. But at the time I didn't yet know that. As I glared angrily at that

poor genetics counselor, so strong was my anxiety that now, four years later, I can still clearly remember what was going through my mind: If I were an evil deity, I thought, trying to devise exquisite tortures for babies and their parents, I would be proud to have designed Tay-Sachs disease.

Tay-Sachs is completely incurable, unpreventable, and preprogrammed in the genes. A Tay-Sachs infant usually appears normal for the first few months after birth, just long enough for the parents to grow to love him. An exaggerated "startle reaction" to sounds is the first ominous sign. At about six months the baby starts to lose control of his head and can't roll over or sit without support. Later he begins to drool, breaks out into unmotivated bouts of laughter, and suffers convulsions. Then his head grows abnormally large, and he becomes blind. Perhaps what's most frightening for the parents is that their baby loses all contact with his environment and becomes virtually a vegetable. By the child's third birthday, if he's still alive, his skin will turn yellow and his hands pudgy. Most likely he will die before he's four years old.

My wife and I were tested for the Tay-Sachs gene because at the time we rated as high-risk candidates, for two reasons. First, Marie was carrying twins, so we had double the usual chance to bear a Tay-Sachs baby. Second, both she and I are of Eastern European Jewish ancestry, the population with by far the world's highest Tay-Sachs frequency.

In peoples around the world Tay-Sachs appears once in every 400,000 births. But it appears a hundred times more frequently—about once in 3,600 births—among descendants of Eastern European Jews, people known as Ashkenazim. For descendants of most other groups of Jews—Oriental Jews, chiefly from the Middle East, or Sephardic Jews, from Spain and other Mediterranean countries—the frequency of Tay-Sachs disease is no higher than in non-Jews. Faced with such a clear correlation, one cannot help but wonder: What is it about this one group of people that produces such an extraordinarily high risk of this disease?

Finding the answer to this question concerns all of us, regardless of our ancestry. Every human population is especially susceptible to certain diseases, not only because of its life-style but also because of its genetic inheritance. For example, genes put European whites at high risk for cystic fibrosis, African blacks for sickle-cell disease, Pacific Islanders for diabetes—and Eastern European Jews for ten different diseases, including Tay-Sachs. It's not that Jews

are notably susceptible to genetic diseases in general; but a combination of historical factors has led to Jews' being intensively studied, and so their susceptibilities are far better known than those of, say, Pacific Islanders.

Tay-Sachs exemplifies how we can deal with such diseases; it has been the object of the most successful screening program to date. Moreover, Tay-Sachs is helping us understand how ethnic diseases evolve. Within the past couple of years discoveries by molecular biologists have provided tantalizing clues to precisely how a deadly gene can persist and spread over the centuries. Tay-Sachs may be primarily a disease of Eastern European Jews, but through this affliction of one group of people, we gain a window on how our genes simultaneously curse and bless us all.

---

*It seems unlikely that genetic accidents would have pumped up the frequency of the same gene not once but twice in the same population.*

---

The disease's hyphenated name comes from the two physicians—British ophthalmologist W. Tay and New York neurologist B. Sachs—who independently first recognized the disease, in 1881 and 1887, respectively. By 1896 Sachs had

seen enough cases to realize that the disease was most common among Jewish children.

Not until 1962, however, were researchers able to trace the cause of the affliction to a single biochemical abnormality: the excessive accumulation in nerve cells of a fatty substance called $G_{M2}$ ganglioside. Normally $G_{M2}$ ganglioside is present at only modest levels in cell membranes, because it is constantly being broken down as well as synthesized. The breakdown depends on the enzyme hexosaminidase A, which is found in the tiny structures within our cells known as lysosomes. In the unfortunate Tay-Sachs victims this enzyme is lacking, and without it the ganglioside piles up and produces all the symptoms of the disease.

We have two copies of the gene that programs our supply of hexosaminidase A, one inherited from our father, the other from our mother; each of our parents, in turn, has two copies derived from their own parents. As long as we have one good copy of the gene, we can produce enough hexosaminidase A to prevent a buildup of $G_{M2}$ ganglioside and we won't get Tay-Sachs. This genetic disease is of the sort termed recessive rather than dominant—meaning that to get it, a child must inherit a defective gene not just from one parent but from both of them. Clearly, each parent must have had one good copy of the gene along with the defective copy—if either had had two defective genes, he or she would have died of the disease long before reaching the age of reproduction. In genetic terms the diseased child is homozygous for the defective gene and both parents are heterozygous for it.

None of this yet gives any hint as to why the Tay-Sachs gene should be most common among Eastern European Jews. To come to grips with that question, we must take a short detour into history.

From their biblical home of ancient Israel, Jews spread peacefully to other Mediterranean lands, Yemen, and India. They were also dispersed violently through conquest by Assyrians, Babylonians, and Romans. Under the Carolingian kings of the eighth and ninth centuries Jews were invited to settle in

France and Germany as traders and financiers. In subsequent centuries, however, persecutions triggered by the Crusades gradually drove Jews out of Western Europe; the process culminated in their total expulsion from Spain in 1492. Those Spanish Jews—called Sephardim—fled to other lands around the Mediterranean. Jews of France and Germany—the Ashkenazim—fled east to Poland and from there to Lithuania and western Russia, where they settled mostly in towns, as businessmen engaged in whatever pursuit they were allowed.

There the Jews stayed for centuries, through periods of both tolerance and oppression. But toward the end of the nineteenth century and the beginning of the twentieth, waves of murderous anti-Semitic attacks drove millions of Jews out of Eastern Europe, with most of them heading for the United States. My mother's parents, for example, fled to New York from Lithuanian pogroms of the 1880s, while my father's parents fled from the Ukrainian pogroms of 1903–6. The more modern history of Jewish migration is probably well known to you all: most Jews who remained in Eastern Europe were exterminated during World War II, while most the survivors immigrated to the United States and Israel. Of the 13 million Jews alive today, more than three-quarters are Ashkenazim, the descendants of the Eastern European Jews and the people most at risk for Tay-Sachs.

Have these Jews maintained their genetic distinctness through the thousands of years of wandering? Some scholars claim that there has been so much intermarriage and conversion that Ashkenazic Jews are now just Eastern Europeans who adopted Jewish culture. However, modern genetic studies refute that speculation.

First of all, there are those ten genetic diseases that the Ashkenazim have somehow acquired, by which they differ both from other Jews and from Eastern European non-Jews. In addition, many Ashkenazic genes turn out to be ones typical of Palestinian Arabs and other peoples of the Eastern Mediterranean areas where Jews originated. (In fact, by genetic standards the current Arab-Is-raeli conflict is an internecine civil war.) Other Ashkenazic genes have indeed diverged from Mediterranean ones (including genes of Sephardic and Oriental Jews) and have evolved to converge on genes of Eastern European non-Jews subject to the same local forces of natural selection. But the degree to which Ashkenazim prove to differ genetically from Eastern European non-Jews implies an intermarriage rate of only about 15 percent.

Can history help explain why the Tay-Sachs gene in particular is so much more common in Ashkenazim than in their non-Jewish neighbors or in other Jews? At the risk of spoiling a mystery, I'll tell you now that the answer is yes, but to appreciate it, you'll have to understand the four possible explanations for the persistence of the Tay-Sachs gene.

First, new copies of the gene might be arising by mutation as fast as existing copies disappear with the death of Tay-Sachs children. That's the most likely explanation for the gene's persistence in most of the world, where the disease frequency is only one in 400,000 births—that frequency reflects a typical human mutation rate. But for this explanation to apply to the Ashkenazim would require a mutation rate of at least one per 3,600 births—far above the frequency observed for any human gene. Furthermore, there would be no precedent for one particular gene mutating so much more often in one human population than in others.

As a second possibility, the Ashkenazim might have acquired the Tay-Sachs gene from some other people who already had the gene at high frequency. Arthur Koestler's controversial book *The Thirteenth Tribe*, for example, popularized the view that the Ashkenazim are really not a Semitic people but are instead descended from the Khazar, a Turkic tribe whose rulers converted to Judaism in the eighth century. Could the Khazar have brought the Tay-Sachs gene to Eastern Europe? This speculation makes good romantic reading, but there is no good evidence to support it. Moreover, it fails to explain why deaths of Tay-Sachs children didn't eliminate the gene by natural selection in the past 1,200 years, nor how the Khazar ac-quired high frequencies of the gene in the first place.

The third hypothesis was the one preferred by a good many geneticists until recently. It invokes two genetic processes, termed the founder effect and genetic drift, that may operate in small populations. To understand these concepts, imagine that 100 couples settle in a new land and found a population that then increases. Imagine further that one parent among those original 100 couples happens to have some rare gene, one, say, that normally occurs at a frequency of one in a million. The gene's frequency in the new population will now be one in 200 as a result of the accidental presence of that rare founder.

Or suppose again that 100 couples found a population, but that one of the 100 men happens to have lots of kids by his wife or that he is exceptionally popular with other women, while the other 99 men are childless or have few kids or are simply less popular. That one man may thereby father 10 percent rather than a more representative one percent of the next generation's babies, and their genes will disproportionately reflect that man's genes. In other words, gene frequencies will have drifted between the first and second generation.

Through these two types of genetic accidents a rare gene may occur with an unusually high frequency in a small expanding population. Eventually, if the gene is harmful, natural selection will bring its frequency back to normal by killing off gene bearers. But if the resultant disease is recessive—if heterozygous individuals don't get the disease and only the rare, homozygous individuals die of it—the gene's high frequency may persist for many generations.

These accidents do in fact account for the astonishingly high Tay-Sachs gene frequency found in one group of Pennsylvania Dutch: out of the 333 people in this group, 98 proved to carry the Tay-Sachs gene. Those 333 are all descended from one couple who settled in the United States in the eighteenth century and had 13 children. Clearly, one of that founding couple must have carried the gene. A similar accident may explain why Tay-Sachs is also relatively common among French Canadians, who number 5 million today but are descended from fewer than 6,000 French immigrants who arrived in the New World between 1638 and 1759. In the two or three centuries since both these founding events, the high Tay-Sachs gene frequency among Pennsylvania Dutch and French Canadians has not yet had enough time to decline to normal levels.

The same mechanisms were one proposed to explain the high rate of Tay-Sachs disease among the Ashkenazim. Perhaps, the reasoning went, the gene just happened to be overrepresented in the founding Jewish population that settled in Germany or Eastern Europe. Perhaps the gene just happened to drift up in frequency in the Jewish populations scattered among the isolated towns of Eastern Europe.

But geneticists have long questioned whether the Ashkenazim population's history was really suitable for these genetic accidents to have been significant. Remember, the founder effect and genetic drift become significant only in small populations, and the founding populations of Ashkenazim may have been quite large. Moreover, Ashkenazic communities were considerably widespread; drift would have sent gene frequencies up in some towns but down in others. And, finally, natural selection has by now had a thousand years to restore gene frequencies to normal.

Granted, those doubts are based on historical data, which are not always as precise or reliable as one might want. But within the past several years the case against those accidental explanations for Tay-Sachs disease in the Ashkenazim has been bolstered by discoveries by molecular biologists.

Like all proteins, the enzyme absent in Tay-Sachs children is coded for by a piece of our DNA. Along that particular stretch of DNA there are thousands of different sites where a mutation could occur that would result in no enzyme and hence in the same set of symptoms. If molecular biologists had discovered that all cases of Tay-Sachs in Ashkenazim involved damage to DNA at the same site, that would have been strong evidence that in Ashkenazim the disease stems from a single mutation that has been multiplied by the founder effect or

genetic drift—in other words, the high incidence of Tay-Sachs among Eastern European Jews is accidental.

In reality, though, several different mutations along this stretch of DNA have been identified in Ashkenazim, and two of them occur much more frequently than in non-Ashkenazim populations. It seems unlikely that genetic accidents would have pumped up the frequency of the same gene not once but twice in the same population.

---

*We're not a melting pot, and we won't be for a long time. Each ethnic group has some characteristic genes of its own, a legacy of its distinct history.*

---

And that's not the sole unlikely coincidence arguing against accidental explanations. Recall that Tay-Sachs is caused by the excessive accumulation of one fatty substance, $G_{M2}$ ganglioside, from a defect in one enzyme, hexosaminidase A. But Tay-Sachs is one of ten genetic diseases characteristic of Ashkenazim. Among those other nine, two—Gaucher's disease and Niemann-Pick disease—result from the accumulation of two other fatty substances similar to $G_{M2}$ ganglioside, as a result of defects in two other enzymes similar to hexosaminidase A. Yet our bodies contain thousands of different enzymes.

It would have been an incredible roll of the genetic dice if, by nothing more than chance, Ashkenazim had independently acquired mutations in three closely related enzymes—and had acquired mutations in one of those enzymes twice.

All these facts bring us to the fourth possible explanation of why the Tay-Sachs gene is so prevalent among Ashkenazim: namely, that something about them favored accumulation of $G_{M2}$ ganglioside and related fats.

For comparison, suppose that a friend doubles her money on one stock while you are getting wiped out with your investments. Taken alone, that could just mean she was lucky on that one occasion. But suppose that she doubles her money on each of two different stocks and at the same time rings up big profits in real estate while also making a killing in bonds. That implies more than lady luck; it suggests that something about your friend—like shrewd judgment—favors financial success.

What could be the blessings of fat accumulation in Eastern European Jews? At first this question sounds weird. After all, that fat accumulation was noticed only because of the curses it bestows: Tay-Sachs, Gaucher's, or Niemann-Pick disease. But many of our common genetic diseases may persist because they bring both blessings and curses (see "The Cruel Logic of Our Genes," *Discover,* November 1989). They kill or impair individuals who inherit two copies of the faulty gene, but they help those who receive only one defective gene by protecting them against other diseases. The best understood example is the sickle-cell gene of African blacks, which often kills homozygotes but protects heterozygotes against malaria. Natural selection sustains such genes because more heterozygotes than normal individuals survive to pass on their genes, and those extra gene copies offset the copies lost through the deaths of homozygotes.

So let us refine our question and ask, What blessing could the Tay-Sachs gene bring to those individuals who are heterozygous for it? A clue first emerged back in 1972, with the publication of the results of a questionnaire that had asked U.S. Ashkenzaic parents of Tay-Sachs children what their own Eastern European-born parents had died of. Keep in mind that since these unfortunate children had to be homozygotes, with two copies of the Tay-Sachs gene, all their parents had to be heterozygotes, with one copy, and half of the parents' parents also had to be heterozygotes.

As it turned out, most of those Tay-Sachs grandparents had died of the usual causes: heart disease, stroke, cancer, and diabetes. But strikingly, only one of the 306 grandparents had died of tuberculosis, even though TB was generally one of the big killers in these grandparents' time. Indeed, among the general population of large Eastern European cities in the early twentieth century, TB caused up to 20 percent of all deaths.

This big discrepancy suggested that Tay-Sachs heterozygotes might somehow have been protected against TB. Interestingly, it was already well known that Ashkenazim in general had some such protection: even when Jews and non-Jews were compared within the same European city, class, and occupational group (for example, Warsaw garment workers), Jews had only half the TB death rate of non-Jews, despite their being equally susceptible to infection. Perhaps, one could reason, the Tay-Sachs gene furnished part of that well-established Jewish resistance.

A second clue to a heterozygote advantage conveyed by the Tay-Sachs gene emerged in 1983, with a fresh look at the data concerning the distributions of TB and the Tay-Sachs gene within Europe. The statistics showed that the Tay-Sachs gene was nearly three times more frequent among Jews originating from Austria, Hungary, and Czechoslovakia—areas where an amazing 9 to 10 percent of the population were heterozygotes—than among Jews from Poland, Russia, and Germany. At the same time records from an old Jewish TB sanatorium in Denver in 1904 showed that among patients born in Europe between 1860 and 1910, Jews from Austria and Hungary were overrepresented.

Initially, in putting together these two pieces of information, you might be tempted to conclude that because the highest frequency of the Tay-Sachs gene appeared in the same geographic region that produced the most cases of TB, the gene in fact offers no protection whatsoever. Indeed, this was precisely the mistaken conclusion of many researchers who had looked at these data before. But you have to pay careful attention to the numbers here: even at its highest frequency the Tay-Sachs gene was carried by far fewer people than would be infected by TB. What the statistics really indicate is that where TB is the biggest threat, natural selection produces the biggest response.

Think of it this way: You arrive at an island where you find that all the inhabitants of the north end wear suits of armor, while all the inhabitants of the south end wear only cloth shirts. You'd be pretty safe in assuming that warfare is more prevalent in the north—and that war-related injuries account for far more deaths there than in the south. Thus, if the Tay-Sachs gene does indeed lend heterozygotes some protection against TB, you would expect to find the gene most often precisely where you find TB most often. Similarly, the sickle-cell gene reaches its highest frequencies in those parts of Africa where malaria is the biggest risk.

But you may believe there's still a hole in the argument: If Tay-Sachs heterozygotes are protected against TB, you may be asking, why is the gene common just in the Ashkenazim? Why did it not become common in the non-Jewish populations also exposed to TB in Austria, Hungary, and Czechoslovakia?

At this point we must recall the peculiar circumstances in which the Jews of Eastern Europe were forced to live. They were unique among the world's ethnic groups in having been virtually confined to towns for most of the past 2,000 years. Being forbidden to own land, Eastern European Jews were not peasant farmers living in the countryside, but businesspeople forced to live in crowded ghettos, in an environment where tuberculosis thrived.

Of course, until recent improvements in sanitation, these towns were not very healthy places for non-Jews either. Indeed, their populations couldn't sustain themselves: deaths exceeded births, and the number of dead had to be balanced by continued emigration from the countryside. For non-Jews, therefore, there was no genetically distinct urban population. For ghetto-bound Jews, however, there could be no emigration from the countryside; thus the Jewish population was under the strongest selection to evolve genetic resistance to TB.

Those are the conditions that probably led to Jewish TB resistance, whatever particular genetic factors prove to underlie it. I'd speculate that $G_{M2}$ and related fats accumulate at slightly higher-than-normal levels in heterozygotes, although not at the lethal levels seen in homozygotes. (The fat accumulation in heterozygotes probably takes place in the cell membrane, the cell's "armor.") I'd also speculate that the accumulation provides heterozygotes with some protection against TB, and that that's why the genes for Tay-Sachs, Gaucher's, and Niemann-Pick disease reached high frequencies in the Ashkenazim.

Having thus stated the case, let me make clear that I don't want to overstate it. The evidence is still speculative. Depending on how you do the calculation, the low frequency of TB deaths in Tay-Sachs grandparents either barely reaches or doesn't quite reach the level of proof that statisticians require to accept an effect as real rather than as one that's arisen by chance. Moreover, we have no idea of the biochemical mechanism by which fat accumulation might confer resistance against TB. For the moment, I'd say that the evidence points to some selective advantage of Tay-Sachs heterozygotes among the Ashkenazim, and that TB resistance is the only plausible hypothesis yet proposed.

For now Tay-Sachs remains a speculative model for the evolution of ethnic diseases. But it's already a proven model of what to do about them. Twenty years ago a test was developed to identify Tay-Sachs heterozygotes, based on their lower-than-normal levels of hexosaminidase A. The test is simple, cheap, and accurate: all I did was to donate a small sample of my blood, pay $35, and wait a few days to receive the results.

If that test shows that at least one member of a couple is not a Tay-Sachs heterozygote, then any child of theirs can't be a Tay-Sachs homozygote. If both parents prove to be heterozygotes, there's a one-in-four chance of their child being a homozygote; that can then be determined by other tests performed on the mother early in pregnancy. If the results are positive, it's early enough for her to abort, should she choose to. That critical bit of knowledge has enabled parents who had gone through the agony of bearing a Tay-Sachs baby and watching him die to find the courage to try again.

The Tay-Sachs screening program launched in the United States in 1971 was targeted at the high-risk population: Ashkenazic Jewish couples of childbearing age. So successful has this approach been that the number of Tay-Sachs babies born each year in this country has declined tenfold. Today, in fact, more Tay-Sachs cases appear here in non-Jews than in Jews, because only the latter couples are routinely tested. Thus, what used to be the classic genetic disease of Jews is so no longer.

There's also a broader message to the Tay-Sachs story. We commonly refer to the United States as a melting pot, and in many ways that metaphor is apt. But in other ways we're not a melting pot, and we won't be for a long time. Each ethnic group has some characteristic genes of its own, a legacy of its distinct history. Tuberculosis and malaria are not major causes of death in the United States, but the genes that some of us evolved to protect ourselves against them are still frequent. Those genes are frequent only in certain ethnic groups, though, and they'll be slow to melt through the population.

With modern advances in molecular genetics, we can expect to see more, not less, ethnically targeted practice of medicine. Genetic screening for cystic fibrosis in European whites, for example, is one program that has been much discussed recently; when it comes, it will surely be based on the Tay-Sachs experience. Of course, what that may mean someday is more anxiety-ridden parents-to-be glowering at more dedicated genetics counselors. It will also mean fewer babies doomed to the agonies of diseases we may understand but that we'll never be able to accept.

# The Saltshaker's Curse

*Physiological adaptations that helped American blacks
survive slavery may now be predisposing their
descendants to hypertension*

## Jared Diamond

Jared Diamond is a professor of physiology at UCLA Medical School.

On the walls of the main corridor at UCLA Medical School hang thirty-seven photographs that tell a moving story. They are the portraits of each graduating class, from the year that the school opened (Class of 1955) to the latest crop (Class of 1991). Throughout the 1950s and early 1960s the portraits are overwhelmingly of young white men, diluted by only a few white women and Asian men. The first black student graduated in 1961, an event not repeated for several more years. When I came to UCLA in 1966, I found myself lecturing to seventy-six students, of whom seventy-four were white. Thereafter the numbers of blacks, Hispanics, and Asians exploded, until the most recent photos show the number of white medical students declining toward a minority.

In these changes of racial composition, there is of course nothing unique about UCLA Medical School. While the shifts in its student body mirror those taking place, at varying rates, in other professional groups throughout American society, we still have a long way to go before professional groups truly mirror society itself. But ethnic diversity among physicians is especially impor-

tant because of the dangers inherent in a profession composed of white practitioners for whom white biology is the norm.

Different ethnic groups face different health problems, for reasons of genes as well as of life style. Familiar examples include the prevalence of skin cancer and cystic fibrosis in whites, stomach cancer and stroke in Japanese, and diabetes in Hispanics and Pacific islanders. Each year, when I teach a seminar course in ethnically varying disease patterns, these by-now-familiar textbook facts assume a gripping reality, as my various students choose to discuss some disease that affects themselves or their relatives. To read about the molecular biology of sickle-cell anemia is one thing. It's quite another thing when one of my students, a black man homozygous for the sickle-cell gene, describes the pain of his own sickling attacks and how they have affected his life.

Sickle-cell anemia is a case in which the evolutionary origins of medically important genetic differences among peoples are well understood. (It evolved only in malarial regions because it confers resistance against malaria.) But in many other cases the evolutionary origins are not nearly so transparent. Why is it, for example, that only some human populations have a high frequency of the Tay-Sachs gene or of diabetes? . . .

Compared with American whites of the same age and sex, American blacks have, on the average, higher blood pressure, double the risk of developing hypertension, and nearly ten times the risk of dying of it. By age fifty, nearly half of U.S. black men are hypertensive. For a given age and blood pressure, hypertension more often causes heart disease and especially kidney failure and strokes in U.S. blacks than whites. Because the frequency of kidney disease in U.S. blacks is eighteen times that in whites, blacks account for about two-thirds of U.S. patients with hypertensive kidney failure, even though they make up only about one-tenth of the population. Around the world, only Japanese exceed U.S. blacks in their risk of dying from stroke. Yet it was not until 1932 that the average difference in blood pressure between U.S. blacks and whites was clearly demonstrated, thereby exposing a major health problem outside the norms of white medicine.

What is it about American blacks that makes them disproportionately likely to develop hypertension and then to die of its consequences? While this question is of course especially "interesting" to black readers, it also concerns all Americans, because other ethnic groups in the United States are not so far behind blacks in their risk of hypertension. If

*Natural History* readers are a cross section of the United States, then about one-quarter of you now have high blood pressure, and more than half of you will die of a heart attack or stroke to which high blood pressure predisposes. Thus, we all have valid reasons for being interested in hypertension.

First, some background on what those numbers mean when your doctor inflates a rubber cuff about your arm, listens, deflates the cuff, and finally pronounces, "Your blood pressure is 120 over 80." The cuff device is called a sphygmomanometer, and it measures the pressure in your artery in units of millimeters of mercury (that's the height to which your blood pressure would force up a column of mercury in case, God forbid, your artery were suddenly connected to a vertical mercury column). Naturally, your blood pressure varies with each stroke of your heart, so the first and second numbers refer, respectively, to the peak pressure at each heartbeat (systolic pressure) and to the minimum pressure between beats (diastolic pressure). Blood pressure varies somewhat with position, activity, and anxiety level, so the measurement is usually made while you are resting flat on your back. Under those conditions, 120 over 80 is an average reading for Americans.

There is no magic cutoff between normal blood pressure and high blood pressure. Instead, the higher your blood pressure, the more likely you are to die of a heart attack, stroke, kidney failure, or ruptured aorta. Usually, a pressure reading higher than 140 over 90 is arbitrarily defined as constituting hypertension, but some people with lower readings will die of a stroke at age fifty, while others with higher readings will die in a car accident in good health at age ninety.

Why do some of us have much higher blood pressure than others? In about 5 percent of hypertensive patients there is an identifiable single cause, such as hormonal imbalance or use of oral contraceptives. In 95 percent of such cases, though, there is no such obvious cause. The clinical euphemism for our ignorance in such cases is "essential hypertension."

Nowadays, we know that there is a big genetic component in essential hypertension, although the particular genes involved have not yet been identified. Among people living in the same household, the correlation coefficient for blood pressure is 0.63 between identical twins, who share all of their genes. (A correlation coefficient of 1.00 would mean that the twins share identical blood pressures as well and would suggest that pressure is determined entirely by genes and not at all by environment.) Fraternal twins or ordinary siblings or a parent and child, who share half their genes and whose blood pressure would therefore show a correlation coefficient of 0.5 if purely determined genetically, actually have a coefficient of about 0.25. Finally, adopted siblings or a parent and adopted child, who have no direct genetic connection, have a correlation coefficient of only 0.05. Despite the shared household environment, their blood pressures are barely more similar than those of two people pulled randomly off the street. In agreement with this evidence for genetic factors underlying blood pressure itself, your risk of actually developing hypertensive disease increases from 4 percent to 20 percent to 35 percent if, respectively, none or one or both of your parents were hypertensive.

But these same facts suggest that environmental factors also contribute to high blood pressure, since identical twins have similar but not identical blood pressures. Many environmental or life style factors contributing to the risk of hypertension have been identified by epidemiological studies that compare hypertension's frequency in groups of people living under different conditions. Such contributing factors include obesity, high intake of salt or alcohol or saturated fats, and low calcium intake. The proof of this approach is that hypertensive patients who modify their life styles so as to minimize these putative factors often succeed in reducing their blood pressure. Patients are especially advised to reduce salt intake and stress, reduce intake of cholesterol and saturated fats and alcohol, lose weight, cut out smoking, and exercise regularly.

Here are some examples of the epidemiological studies pointing to these risk factors. Around the world, comparisons within and between populations show that both blood pressure and the frequency of hypertension increase hand in hand with salt intake. At the one extreme, Brazil's Yanomamö Indians have the world's lowest-known salt consumption (somewhat above 10 milligrams per day!), lowest average blood pressure (95 over 61!), and lowest incidence of hypertension (no cases!). At the opposite extreme, doctors regard Japan as the "land of apoplexy" because of the high frequency of fatal strokes (Japan's leading cause of death, five times more frequent than in the United States), linked with high blood pressure and notoriously salty food. Within Japan itself these factors reach their extremes in Akita Prefecture, famous for its tasty rice, which Akita farmers flavor with salt, wash down with salty miso soup, and alternate with salt pickles between meals. Of 300 Akita adults studied, not one consumed less than five grams of salt daily, the average consumption was twenty-seven grams, and the most salt-loving individual consumed an incredible sixty-one grams—enough to devour the contents of the usual twenty-six-ounce supermarket salt container in a mere twelve days. The average blood pressure in Akita by age fifty is 151 over 93, making hypertension (pressure higher than 140 over 90) the norm. Not surprisingly, Akitas' frequency of death by stroke is more than double even the Japanese average, and in some Akita villages 99 percent of the population dies before age seventy.

Why salt intake often (in about 60 percent of hypertensive patients) leads to high blood pressure is not fully understood. One possible interpretation is that salt intake triggers thirst, leading to an increase in blood volume. In response, the heart increases its output and blood pressure rises, causing the kidneys to filter more salt and water under that increased pressure. The result is a new steady state, in which salt and water excretion again equals intake, but more salt and water are stored in the body and blood pressure is raised.

At this point, let's contrast hypertension with a simple genetic disease like Tay-Sachs disease. Tay-Sachs is due to a defect in a single gene; every Tay Sachs patient has a defect in that same gene. Everybody in whom that gene is defective is certain to die of Tay-Sachs, regardless of their life style or environment. In contrast, hypertension involves several different genes whose molecular products remain to be identified. Because there are many causes of raised blood pressure, different hypertensive patients may owe their condition to different gene combinations. Furthermore, whether someone genetically predisposed to hypertension actually develops symptoms depends a lot on life style. Thus, hypertension is not one of those uncommon, homogeneous, and intellectually elegant diseases that geneticists prefer to study. Instead, like diabetes and ulcers, hypertension is a shared set of symptoms produced by heterogeneous causes, all involving an interaction between environmental agents and a susceptible genetic background.

Since U.S. blacks and whites differ on the average in the conditions under which they live, could those differences account for excess hypertension in U.S. blacks? Salt intake, the dietary factor that one thinks of first, turns out on the average not to differ between U.S. blacks and whites. Blacks do consume less potassium and calcium, do experience more stress associated with more difficult socioeconomic conditions, have much less access to medical care, and are therefore much less likely to be diagnosed or treated until it is too late. Those factors surely contribute to the frequency and severity of hypertension in blacks.

However, those factors don't seem to be the whole explanation: hypertensive blacks aren't merely like severely hypertensive whites. Instead, physiological differences seem to contribute as well. On consuming salt, blacks retain it on average far longer before excreting it into the urine, and they experience a greater rise in blood pressure on a high-salt diet. Hypertension is more likely to be "salt-sensitive" in blacks than in whites, meaning that blood pressure is more likely to rise and fall with rises

and falls in dietary salt intake. By the same token, black hypertension is more likely to be treated successfully by drugs that cause the kidneys to excrete salt (the so-called thiazide diuretics) and less likely to respond to those drugs that reduce heart rate and cardiac output (so-called beta blockers, such as propanolol). These facts suggest that there are some qualitative differences between the causes of black and white hypertension, with black hypertension more likely to involve how the kidneys handle salt.

Physicians often refer to this postulated feature as a "defect": for example, "kidneys of blacks have a genetic defect in excreting sodium." As an evolutionary biologist, though, I hear warning bells going off inside me whenever a seemingly harmful trait that occurs frequently in an old and large human population is dismissed as a "defect." Given enough generations, genes that greatly impede survival are extremely unlikely to spread, unless their net effect is to increase survival and reproductive success. Human medicine has furnished the best examples of seemingly defective genes being propelled to high frequency by counterbalancing benefits. For example, sickle-cell hemoglobin protects far more people against malaria than it kills of anemia, while the Tay-Sachs gene may have protected far more Jews against tuberculosis than it killed of neurological disease. Thus, to understand why U.S. blacks now are prone to die as a result of their kidneys' retaining salt, we need to ask under what conditions people might have benefited from kidneys good at retaining salt.

That question is hard to understand from the perspective of modern Western society, where saltshakers are on every dining table, salt (sodium chloride) is cheap, and our bodies' main problem is getting rid of it. But imagine what the world used to be like before saltshakers became ubiquitous. Most plants contain very little sodium, yet animals require sodium at high concentrations in all their extracellular fluids. As a result, carnivores readily obtain their needed sodium by eating herbivores, but herbivores themselves face big problems in acquiring that sodium. That's why the

animals that one sees coming to salt licks are deer and antelope, not lions and tigers. Similarly, some human hunter-gatherers obtained enough salt from the meat that they ate. But when we began to take up farming ten thousand years ago, we either had to evolve kidneys superefficient at conserving salt or learn to extract salt at great effort or trade for it at great expense.

Examples of these various solutions abound. I already mentioned Brazil's Yanomamö Indians, whose staple food is low-sodium bananas and who excrete on the average only 10 milligrams of salt daily—barely one-thousandth the salt excretion of the typical American. A single Big Mac hamburger analyzed by *Consumer Reports* contained 1.5 grams (1,500 milligrams) of salt, representing many weeks of intake for a Yanomamö. The New Guinea highlanders with whom I work, and whose diet consists up to 90 percent of low-sodium sweet potatoes, told me of the efforts to which they went to make salt a few decades ago, before Europeans brought it as trade goods. They gathered leaves of certain plant species, burned them, scraped up the ash, percolated water through it to dissolve the solids, and finally evaporated the water to obtain small amounts of bitter salt.

Thus, salt has been in very short supply for much of recent human evolutionary history. Those of us with efficient kidneys able to retain salt even on a low-sodium diet were better able to survive our inevitable episodes of sodium loss (of which more in a moment). Those kidneys proved to be a detriment only when salt became routinely available, leading to excessive salt retention and hypertension with its fatal consequences. That's why blood pressure and the frequency of hypertension have shot up recently in so many populations around the world as they have made the transition from being self-sufficient subsistence farmers to members of the cash economy and patrons of supermarkets.

This evolutionary argument has been advanced by historian-epidemiologist Thomas Wilson and others to explain the current prevalence of hypertension in American blacks in particular. Many West African blacks, from whom most

American blacks originated via the slave trade, must have faced the chronic problem of losing salt through sweating in their hot environment. Yet in West Africa, except on the coast and certain inland areas, salt was traditionally as scarce for African farmers as it has been for Yanomamö and New Guinea farmers. (Ironically, those Africans who sold other Africans as slaves often took payment in salt traded from the Sahara.) By this argument, the genetic basis for hypertension in U.S. blacks was already widespread in many of their West African ancestors. It required only the ubiquity of saltshakers in twentieth-century America for that genetic basis to express itself as hypertension. This argument also predicts that as Africa's life style becomes increasingly Westernized, hypertension could become as prevalent in West Africa as it now is among U.S. blacks. In this view, American blacks would be no different from the many Polynesian, Melanesian, Kenyan, Zulu, and other populations that have recently developed high blood pressure under a Westernized life style.

But there's an intriguing extension to this hypothesis, proposed by Wilson and physician Clarence Grim, collaborators at the Hypertension Research Center of Drew University in Los Angeles. They suggest a scenario in which New World blacks may now be at more risk for hypertension than their African ancestors. That scenario involves very recent selection for super-efficient kidneys, driven by massive mortality of black slaves from salt loss.

Grim and Wilson's argument goes as follows. Black slavery in the Americas began about 1517, with the first imports of slaves from West Africa, and did not end until Brazil freed its slaves barely a century ago in 1888. In the course of the slave trade an estimated 12 million Africans were brought to the Americas. But those imports were winnowed by deaths at many stages, from an even larger number of captives and exports.

First, slaves captured by raids in the interior of West Africa were chained together, loaded with heavy burdens, and marched for one or two months, with little food and water, to the coast. About 25 percent of the captives died en route.

While awaiting purchase by slave traders, the survivors were held on the coast in hot, crowded buildings called barracoons, where about 12 percent of them died. The traders went up and down the coast buying and loading slaves for a few weeks or months until a ship's cargo was full (5 percent more died). The dreaded Middle Passage across the Atlantic killed 10 percent of the slaves, chained together in a hot, crowded, unventilated hold without sanitation. (Picture to yourself the result of those toilet "arrangements.") Of those who lived to land in the New World, 5 percent died while awaiting sale, and 12 percent died while being marched or shipped from the sale yard to the plantation. Finally, of those who survived, between 10 and 40 percent died during the first three years of plantation life, in a process euphemistically called seasoning. At that stage, about 70 percent of the slaves initially captured were dead, leaving 30 percent as seasoned survivors.

Even the end of seasoning, however, was not the end of excessive mortality. About half of slave infants died within a year of birth because of the poor nutrition and heavy workload of their mothers. In plantation terminology, slave women were viewed as either "breeding units" or "work units," with a built-in conflict between those uses: "These Negroes breed the best, whose labour is least," as an eighteenth-century observer put it. As a result, many New World slave populations depended on continuing slave imports and couldn't maintain their own numbers because death rates exceeded birth rates. Since buying new slaves cost less than rearing slave children for twenty years until they were adults, slave owners lacked economic incentive to change this state of affairs.

Recall that Darwin discussed natural selection and survival of the fittest with respect to animals. Since many more animals die than survive to produce offspring, each generation becomes enriched in the genes of those of the preceding generation that were among the survivors. It should now be clear that slavery represented a tragedy of unnatural selection in humans on a gigantic scale. From examining accounts of slave

mortality, Grim and Wilson argue that death was indeed selective: much of it was related to unbalanced salt loss, which quickly brings on collapse. We think immediately of salt loss by sweating under hot conditions: while slaves were working, marching, or confined in unventilated barracoons or ships' holds. More body salt may have been spilled with vomiting from seasickness. But the biggest salt loss at every stage was from diarrhea due to crowding and lack of sanitation—ideal conditions for the spread of gastrointestinal infections. Cholera and other bacterial diarrheas kill us by causing sudden massive loss of salt and water. (Picture your most recent bout of *turista,* multiplied to a diarrheal fluid output of twenty quarts in one day, and you'll understand why.) All contemporary accounts of slave ships and plantation life emphasized diarrhea, or "fluxes" in eighteenth-century terminology, as one of the leading killers of slaves.

Grim and Wilson reason, then, that slavery suddenly selected for superefficient kidneys surpassing the efficient kidneys already selected by thousands of years of West African history. Only those slaves who were best able to retain salt could survive the periodic risk of high salt loss to which they were exposed. Salt supersavers would have had the further advantage of building up, under normal conditions, more of a salt reserve in their body fluids and bones, thereby enabling them to survive longer or more frequent bouts of diarrhea. Those superkidneys became a disadvantage only when modern medicine began to reduce diarrhea's lethal impact, thereby transforming a blessing into a curse.

Thus, we have two possible evolutionary explanations for salt retention by New World blacks. One involves slow selection by conditions operating in Africa for millennia; the other, rapid recent selection by slave conditions within the past few centuries. The result in either case would make New World blacks more susceptible than whites to hypertension, but the second explanation would, in addition, make them more susceptible than African blacks. At present, we don't know the relative importance of these two explanations. Grim and Wilson's provocative hypothesis is likely to stimulate medical and physiological comparisons of American blacks with African blacks and thereby to help resolve the question.

While this piece has focused on one medical problem in one human population, it has several larger morals. One, of course, is that our differing genetic heritages predispose us to different diseases, depending on the part of the world where our ancestors lived. Another is that our genetic differences reflect not only ancient conditions in different parts of the world but also recent episodes of migration and mortality. A well-established example is the decrease in the frequency of the sickle-cell hemoglobin gene in U.S. blacks compared with African blacks, because selection for resistance to malaria is now unimportant in the United States. The example of black hypertension that Grim and Wilson discuss opens the door to considering other possible selective effects of the slave experience. They note that occasional periods of starvation might have selected slaves for superefficient sugar metabolism, leading under modern conditions to a propensity for diabetes.

Finally, consider a still more universal moral. Almost all people alive today exist under very different conditions from those under which every human lived 10,000 years ago. It's remarkable that our old genetic heritage now permits us to survive at all under such different circumstances. But our heritage still catches up with most of us, who will die of life style related diseases such as cancer, heart attack, stroke, and diabetes. The risk factors for these diseases are the strange new conditions prevailing in modern Western society. One of the hardest challenges for modern medicine will be to identify for us which among all those strange new features of diet, life style, and environment are the ones getting us into trouble. For each of us, the answers will depend on our particular genes, hence on our ancestry. Only with such individually tailored advice can we hope to reap the benefits of modern living while still housed in bodies designed for life before saltshakers.

## FIELD NOTES

# The Fortune Teller

*Will the secrets of genetic destiny bring comfort or only more sorrow to a remote land ravaged by violence?*

## KENNETH S. KOSIK

THE LOCALS OF MEDELLÍN, COLOMBIA, joke that when God created the world, one of the angels asked him why he was putting so many natural wonders in one place. God replied, "It will even out. Wait till you see the character of the people I'm going to put there." Self-effacement aside, among the people of Colombia there is a curious mixture of pride and bafflement, sorrow and theatricality, regret and resignation about their unusually bloody history—a history from which the country has not yet emerged. Violence and beauty intertwine in Colombia in complicated ways, just as the folk saying implies; that much I have learned during the many trips I have made there to conduct research and genetic testing on a rare form of Alzheimer's disease.

The lush valley of the Cordillera Central, the range of the Andes where Medellín is situated, is striking. From the airport, it is an hour-long winding descent to the city on a mountain road bordered by verdant slopes. At night, the soft lights in the valley suggest the mythical golden city of El Dorado, the way the first Spanish settlers must have pictured it some 400 years go. But daylight exposes the urban sprawl that extends well up the sides of the surrounding mountains, and the cruel poverty that penetrates the choked streets. On the far outskirts of Medellín, a few swimming pools and enormous mansions dot the landscape. Some of them are the vast estates of the drug lords, who can be identified in the city by their powerful four-wheel-drive vehicles, and whose pursuits a few years ago gave Medellín one of the highest murder rates of any city not at war.

This highly insular world, where Internet access coexists with ancient folk beliefs, opened to me in 1991. A neurologist at Brigham and Women's Hospital in Boston, I visited Colombia that year with the support of the Fogarty International Center, a branch of the National Institutes of Health, to help develop neuroscience in Latin America. In October 1992 I traveled to the University of Antioquia School of Medicine in Medellín, where I gave a talk on the biology of Alzheimer's disease—the degenerative brain disorder that strikes so many people at the end of their lives. There I was introduced to the neurologist Francisco Lopera.

Lopera told me of a fascinating find he had made. About a decade earlier, while evaluating a forty-four-year-old man complaining of memory loss, he had been struck by how closely the man's symptoms resembled Alzheimer's disease, except for the patient's young age. More disturbing was the man's family history: he mentioned many relatives with similar problems back in his village. Beginning with mildly annoying symptoms such as asking the same question repeatedly, the affected people later developed personality changes, became disoriented, and about a decade later died, usually of pneumonia after a prolonged vegetative period.

Lopera began investigating, and by the time I met him he had developed a series of detailed genealogies that tracked twelve interrelated families. Intrigued by this mysterious early-onset form of dementia, I agreed to help Lopera try to find the gene mutation at work and unlock its secrets.

But genes are not isolated entities that live only in laboratory test tubes; they are part of the fabric of a person's individual and cultural identity. Thus our quest turned out to be more than a scientific search for a snippet of mutant DNA: it became, for me, an odyssey both geographical and personal. The work has connected me to people whose lives would otherwise be quite foreign—Spanish-speaking farmers who are provincial and unsophisticated, yet uncannily wise. Their fates are enmeshed in that microscopic skein of genetic material, the human genome—a tangled scroll that I know how to read, but whose dictates they will have to live with.

LIKE MANY NEUROLOGISTS, LOPERA brings a depth of scholarly and esoteric knowledge to his work, though his patients usually suffer from commonplace maladies such as headaches and epilepsy. He has a nearly fixed smile that conveys his genuine good nature, but that can shift with ease

This article is reprinted by permission of *The Sciences* and is from the July/August 1999 issue, pp. 13-17. Individual subscriptions are $28 per year. Write to: The Sciences, 2 East 63rd Street, New York, NY 10021.

to an ironic grin. Our collaboration has included many earnest discussions over late-night bottles of wine, and has led to several articles written for professional journals.

The task that brought us together was a classic one. Geneticists are always on the lookout for inherited diseases that show up within a single extended family. Such case studies offer exceptional opportunities to isolate the faulty gene responsible, because family members tend to share certain idiosyncratic stretches of DNA that reappear through the generations. When investigators find that one of those unusual stretches of DNA always occurs in the family members who have the disease, but is not present in the other family members, they can assume the faulty gene is nearby, and zero in on it.

When Lopera and I began working together, our first task was to make certain the disease in question was Alzheimer's. A definitive diagnosis requires the microscopic study of brain tissue after death. But because funeral rites in Colombia invoke so many local traditions and superstitions, no one had yet been able to conduct a postmortem examination, even years after the afflicted families had come to light.

Nearly all the families live in a region of the country called Antioquia, of which Medellín is the capital, in a few rural pueblos: Angostura, Belmira, Caldas, Ituango, Sabanalarga, Santa Rosa de Osos and Sopetrán; San José de la Montaña, perched high in the mountains; and Yarumal—by far the largest, with paved streets and a sizable town square. About a year after I met Lopera, he learned that a middle-aged woman who had had early-onset dementia for eleven years had died in Angostura. Quickly he enlisted Juan Carlos Arango, a neuropathologist colleague at the University of Antioquia School of Medicine, to accompany him on the five-hour drive from Medellín.

When they arrived, the lloronas, professional mourners, had already joined family and friends around the body, which was laid out in the sitting room. People cried and talked, and some drank to excess through the night. Gradually one of the dead woman's sons became

suspicious about why the city doctors wanted his mother's brain tissue. Perhaps they planned to sell it to the gringos. All the other children agreed to have the brain examined, but this son lent a sinister tone to the negotiations. People whispered that he was connected to the narcotrafficantes as a sicario, or hit man, because he had been a member of the local police, a common route to the mafia. His gold chains, his remoteness from the townspeople and the bullyish way he carried himself enhanced that impression. He made the situation tense, and as he drank, the possibilities for trouble increased.

The mayor of Angostura came to the house, followed by the vaccine man, a village medical worker known to be very simpático, and both attempted to resolve the situation. Finally, with further entreaties from Lopera and other family members, the angry son relented. In a brief stop at the local infirmary on the way to the church, Lopera and Arango removed the dead woman's brain. Arango flew with it straight to Boston; there, in my laboratory, he proved the case was Alzheimer's disease.

LOPERA, MEANWHILE, CONTINUED TO labor over the genealogies. What had come to his attention as a few cases of early-onset dementia turned out to be a concealed epidemic involving nearly 4,000 people. Lopera's handwritten family trees began to fill large rolls of paper, enough to cover a huge wall. Each entry distilled an entire life story into a few spare symbols—age, gender, affected or non-affected, alive or dead. The names read like a dark, enchanted poem—Gilma, Resfa, María, Epifanía, Altagracia, Rosa, Fabiola. Lopera was struck by the inexorable appearance of the disease in one generation after the next. When one parent was affected, about half the children, regardless of gender, later developed the disease. In genetics that pattern of inheritance is called autosomal dominance, and it strongly suggested that a single mutation was responsible.

The gene involved was discovered—by someone else—a couple of years after we began the project. In 1995 the molecular geneticist Gerard D. Schel-

lenberg of the Veterans Affairs Medical Center in Seattle identified an approximate site on chromosome 14 where one of the mutant genes for early-onset Alzheimer's resided. Within months the geneticist Peter S. George Hyslop of the University of Toronto zeroed in on the gene and named it presenilin 1.

When the presenilin 1 gene is intact, it causes no problems for its bearer. But more than fifty different mutations—misspellings of DNA—can exist in presenilin 1, and wherever they occur, they lead to early-onset Alzheimer's. (In addition to presenilin 1, two other genes are known to cause early-onset Alzheimer's, and workers think there are still others waiting to be found.) Later in 1995, I enlisted the help of Alison M. Goate, a geneticist at Washington University in Saint Louis, and together we were able to identify the specific mutation responsible for the Colombian families' disease.

It is important to understand that Alzheimer's disease comes in two distinct flavors. The most common type, afflicting about four million elderly Americans, is not caused by a genetic mutation, though some people may have a gene that makes them more than usually susceptible. That form of Alzheimer's generally strikes people sixty-five or older; no one knows why. But in about 1 percent of cases—including those among the families in Colombia—Alzheimer's strikes the young and the cause is clearly a faulty gene. Both kinds of Alzheimer's leave the same telltale marks in the brain: knotty clumps of a protein called beta-amyloid. As investigators, we hope that an understanding of the relatively rare, genetic form of Alzheimer's will lead to a treatment for the more common type.

SHORTLY BEFORE OUR TEAM LEARNED the precise location of the Alzheimer's mutation, we invited the families involved to a meeting at the hospital in Yarumal. There we were greeted by the mayor, who assigned me two bodyguards: he said he had no fears about the people in his town, but could not be sure about people from other villages. Nearly a hundred people came—in donkey carts, on horseback and by bus. We gathered them together in an open auditorium, told them about our work and invited questions. They asked about a local superstition that the disease could be contracted by touching a tree, though they were unsure which tree was the contagious one. They also asked about marrying their first cousins. Although they were aware of the risk posed by intermarriage, still, the limited choice of a mate in their small villages meant that sometimes love outweighed more abstract concerns.

To the people gathered there, most of whom had no more than a first- or second-grade education, some genetic principles seemed to make intuitive sense, whereas others did not. No one had trouble, for instance, understanding that traits can be inherited. But the fact that the probability of inheriting a trait is unrelated to the previous births was more difficult to grasp. If one parent has the Alzheimer's mutation, there is a 50 percent risk that each child will have it too. But, just as parents who have had three girls in a row may expect their chance of having a boy to increase, the villagers endorsed a logical fallacy. One man announced to the assembled group: "We the families in which there are only a few affecteds must be grateful to those families with many affecteds." Local ideas of guilt and collective burden were deeply ingrained, and clashed with the principles of population genetics.

Where did the Colombian Alzheimer's mutation come from? *Paisas,* as the people of Antioquia call themselves, are generally regarded as different from other Colombians. Some say they are related to the Basques; others consider them a lost tribe of Israel. Various indigenous groups once ruled their land—principal among them the Chibchas, who originated the legend of El Dorado. Excellent goldsmiths, the Chibchas anointed their chiefs by rolling them in gold dust, which the new leaders then washed off in Lake Guatavita. In the sixteenth century Spain conquered the area, and for three centuries governed it with a harsh grip.

Even tracing back seven generations, it is impossible to find a common ancestor who links any of the twelve extended families that carry the Alz-

heimer's gene. Yet undoubtedly they are all related to a single individual, the first person in whom the deadly mutation occurred. Perhaps that person was a pre-Columbian, whose own people are now extinct, and whose only legacy is the defective Alzheimer's gene propagating in retribution among the Spanish usurpers of her land. Or perhaps the curse originated with a Spaniard—a sailor whose forgettable fling left an indelible genetic memory. Indeed, the mutation may have spread by any of the myriad entanglements through which human beings accomplish genetic recombination.

AFTER THE DISCOVERY OF THE MUTA-tion it became possible to predict, from a simple blood test, who within the Colombian families would get Alzheimer's—even whether a pregnant woman's fetus would one day contract the disease. We then were ethically bound to find out how such powerful information, if made available, would affect the local people. There is no known way to dodge the illness or even to postpone it. If someone carries the mutation, early-onset Alzheimer's is inevitable—unless another cause of early death makes a pre-emptive strike.

The village of Caldas is not far from Medellín. To get there we turned off the road onto a dirt path that runs along an abandoned railroad track. Near the end of a row of houses a smiling señora, her face lined with creases, greeted us with a litany of salutations. Her middle-aged daughter, a ruddy, dough-faced woman, stood beside her. We sat in their simple living room while the daughter brought out the Colombian coffee they call *tinto.* After chatting a bit, the señora Autila asked whether we would like to see her son, Rodrigo.

She told us Rodrigo's disease had begun five years earlier, at age forty-four, when they had found him lost and wandering in a field. It was the same field where another of her sons had been shot dead. The murder was not unusual. Nearly every family we visited had been touched by the violence that permeates Colombian society, and often it struck me that the biological disease my colleagues and I were trying to defeat was dwarfed by another, equally deadly con-

dition—one that had none of the predictability of an inherited gene defect, and about which we understood almost nothing.

In a small room next to the dining area, Rodrigo was neatly tucked into white sheets, unconscious and, except for his breathing, quite still. Occasionally this peaceful picture was interrupted by the gnashing of teeth and quick jerking movements that are typical of late-stage Alzheimer's. The room, bare of ornament, resembled a mortuary, with its white walls and the small cross at the head of the iron-railed bed—as if to ease Rodrigo's transition to the next world.

OUR NEXT STOP WAS MANRIQUE, A poor and violent barrio in Medellín. That was where Nubia lived with her demented mother and an unclear number of other family members. To reach the house we had to drive deep into what felt like a Brueghel painting. Blackened, distorted human faces looked out from dingy garages and the platforms of abandoned warehouses; vultures perched patiently overhead. Nubia's front door opened directly onto a busy street. Only a thin wall separated the inhabitants of the house from the noise and squalor outside.

Here was none of the tranquillity that surrounded Rodrigo in his whitewashed room. Nubia's mama was on display, visible to every passerby through the open front door. Emaciated, she sat contorted, her hands gnarled and stuck in an unnatural position, a feeding tube protruding from her nose. Motionless except for her aimlessly roving eyes, she was a constant reminder to her children of the fate that lay ahead for those among them who carried the mutant gene.

I told the grown children that we could now determine which of them would get the disease, and I asked whether they would want to take the test. "Before answering," I told them, "remember that there is no treatment." All the children said they would want to take the test. What would they do differently, once they knew the result? I asked. At that point no one had an answer, except twenty-three-year-old González, who later told our nurse that if his test were positive, he would shoot himself.

ONCE THE PROVINCE OF SHAMANS and *curanderos,* revealing the future of an otherwise healthy person is a very modern responsibility for physicians. When the genes tell a cruel story, we must be prepared for the power and danger of that information. In the United States, genetic counselors are trained to help people make sense of such news. Faced with someone like González, a counselor would sympathize with his despair while reminding him that many more worthwhile years lay ahead. But Colombia has no genetic counselors, and so, adhering to well-established ethical guidelines, Lopera and I have decided that the gene test will be given for research purposes only: the results will not be made available to the person tested or to anyone else. I am not fully comfortable with that arrangement, however, because I know there are, among the Colombians, people who might limit the number of children they chose to have if they knew they carried the mutation.

CURIOUSLY, THE *PRESENILIN 1* mutation found among the Colombians does not strike all its victims at the same age. Some people with the mutation get Alzheimer's in their early thirties, and others are not stricken until their late fifties. The question is, Why? One possibility is that something in the environment triggers the disease. But if that were the case, one would expect family members with different onset ages to have divergent lifestyles. Instead, the affected people have similar habits and occupations: the men work on coffee plantations, and the women are housewives.

A more likely explanation, therefore, is a modifier gene—a second gene that controls when the *presenilin 1* mutation begins to do its damage. It is not unusual for two genes to work in tandem—one doing damage, the other dictating when the damage will occur and how bad it will be. Modifier genes are among a growing group of known "risk factor" genes, genes that increase a person's chances of getting a disease.

For example, a specific variant of the *APOE* gene predisposes people to the more common kind of Alzheimer's (the kind that strikes elderly people), and may cause them to contract it earlier.

So the hunt is on among the Colombians. We have obtained blood samples from siblings who developed the disease at widely disparate ages, and we have begun the tedious search among the billions of nucleotides that make up the enormous stretches of human DNA. If a modifier gene exists, we will find it in two or three years. And the payoff could be enormous: if, for instance, a drug could be developed that inhibited the protein made by the modifier gene, physicians could delay the onset of Alzheimer's by as many as twenty years—not only in the Colombian families, but potentially also among the people who suffer from the more common version of the disease. Pushing back the age at which the widespread form of Alzheimer's strikes—from, say, age seventy to age ninety—would be nearly tantamount to a cure.

AT ONE POINT IN THE NOVEL *ONE Hundred Years of Solitude,* by the Nobel-prize-winning Colombian writer Gabriel García Márquez, the inhabitants of the fictional village of Macondo mysteriously begin to lose their memories. In a haunting parallel to the real disease that afflicts the families in Antioquia, the novel describes how the villagers first forget the names of objects, and then lose the ability to use them. The cure comes eventually in the form of "a drink of a gentle color," brought to town by a traveling gypsy.

Armed with the tools of modern genetics, are we biologists the gypsies who bring the campesinos the cure? Or are we dangerous intruders instead, one more band of exploiters in a long line of outsiders who, beginning with Cortés, have invaded and betrayed Latin America? Just as foreigners have historically plundered the continent's natural resources, so we, the prospectors of the late twentieth century, come to harvest genes.

Our work, however, has the feel of something predestined. Whether because of a Faustian pact or naïve curi-

osity, knowledge cannot be denied. Sooner or later we will know our genes; if we do not, our children will. We stand poised to be expelled from an Eden of genetic ignorance into a society where every talent and weakness, every wrinkle and freckle may be predicted from our genomes. More disturbing is the possibility that our genomes will become public property, that employers and insurance companies will peer into our DNA and then discriminate against us as a result—that the knowledge of our genetic destiny will rob us first of opportunity, and later of all hope.

Like magical concoctions from a Márquez novel, geneticists' devices can predict a tragic fate for children playing along the railroad tracks of Caldas or in the sunny church square of Yarumal. I worry particularly about the impact of newfound genetic knowledge in a land far from the microtiter plates, DNA chips and fluorescent gel bands of my laboratory. Ultimately, however, such qualms are pointless.

Scientific revolutions derive from small, incremental discoveries. Lopera and I, and other neurologists, who contribute a jigsaw piece here or there, cannot envision the completed puzzle. My experiences in Colombia have helped me put the genetic enterprise in perspective. What I have learned in that colorful yet tortured land, where the threat of violence is constant and senseless murder is accepted as a fact of life, is that no matter how much progress we scientists make toward understanding the present and controlling the future, destiny will always hold the trump card. We cannot know, in advance, the eventual impact of genetic knowledge. We can only strive to untangle its secrets with a sense of responsibility toward the communities that hold the precious genetic clues.

*KENNETH S. KOSIK is a professor of neurology at Harvard Medical School and an attending physician at Brigham and Women's Hospital in Boston, where he was a cofounder of the Memory Disorders Clinic.*

# The Five Sexes, Revisited

*The emerging recognition that people come in bewildering
sexual varieties is testing medical values and social norms*

## By Anne Fausto-Sterling

As Cheryl Chase stepped to the front of the packed meeting room in the Sheraton Boston Hotel, nervous coughs made the tension audible. Chase, an activist for intersexual rights, had been invited to address the May 2000 meeting of the Lawson Wilkins Pediatric Endocrine Society (LWPES), the largest organization in the United States for specialists in children's hormones. Her talk would be the grand finale to a four-hour symposium on the treatment of genital ambiguity in newborns, infants born with a mixture of both male and female anatomy, or genitals that appear to differ from their chromosomal sex. The topic was hardly a novel one to the assembled physicians.

Yet Chase's appearance before the group was remarkable. Three and a half years earlier, the American Academy of Pediatrics had refused her request for a chance to present the patients' viewpoint on the treatment of genital ambiguity, dismissing Chase and her supporters as "zealots." About two dozen intersex people had responded by throwing up a picket line. The Intersex Society of North America (ISNA) even issued a press release: "Hermaphrodites Target Kiddie Docs."

It had done my 1960s street-activist heart good. In the short run, I said to Chase at the time, the picketing would make people angry. But eventually, I assured her, the doors then closed would open. Now, as Chase began to address the physicians at their own convention,

*Much has changed since 1993. Intersexuals have materialized before our very eyes.*

that prediction was coming true. Her talk, titled "Sexual Ambiguity: The Patient-Centered Approach," was a measured critique of the near-universal practice of performing immediate, "corrective" surgery on thousands of infants born each year with ambiguous genitalia. Chase herself lives with the consequences of such surgery. Yet her audience, the very endocrinologists and surgeons Chase was accusing of reacting with "surgery and shame," received her with respect. Even more remarkably, many of the speakers who preceded her at the session had already spoken of the need to scrap current practices in favor of treatments more centered on psychological counseling.

What led to such a dramatic reversal of fortune? Certainly, Chase's talk at the LWPES symposium was a vindication of her persistence in seeking attention for her cause. But her invitation to speak was also a watershed in the evolving discussion about how to treat children with ambiguous genitalia. And that discussion, in turn, is the tip of a biocultural iceberg—the gender iceberg—that

continues to rock both medicine and our culture at large.

Chase made her first national appearance in 1993, in these very pages, announcing the formation of ISNA in a letter responding to an essay I had written for *The Sciences,* titled "The Five Sexes" [March/April 1993]. In that article I argued that the two-sex system embedded in our society is not adequate to encompass the full spectrum of human sexuality. In its place, I suggested a five-sex system. In addition to males and females, I included "herms" (named after true hermaphrodites, people born with both a testis and an ovary); "merms" (male pseudohermaphrodites, who are born with testes and some aspect of female genitalia); and "ferms" (female pseudohermaphrodites, who have ovaries combined with some aspect of male genitalia).

I had intended to be provocative, but I had also written with tongue firmly in cheek. So I was surprised by the extent of the controversy the article unleashed. Right-wing Christians were outraged, and connected my idea of five sexes with the United Nations–sponsored Fourth World Conference on Women, held in Beijing in September 1995. At the same time, the article delighted others who felt constrained by the current sex and gender system.

Clearly, I had struck a nerve. The fact that so many people could get riled up by my proposal to revamp our sex and gender system suggested that change—as well as resistance to it—might be in the offing.

Indeed, a lot has changed since 1993, and I like to think that my article was an important stimulus. As if from nowhere, intersexuals are materializing before our very eyes. Like Chase, many have become political organizers, who lobby physicians and politicians to change current treatment practices. But more generally, though perhaps no less provocatively, the boundaries separating masculine and feminine seem harder than ever to define.

Some find the changes under way deeply disturbing. Others find them liberating.

WHO IS AN INTERSEXUAL—AND how many intersexuals are there? the concept of intersexuality is rooted in the very ideas of male and female. In the idealized, Platonic, biological world, human beings are divided into two kinds: a perfectly dimorphic species. Males have an X and a Y chromosome, testes, a penis and all of the appropriate internal plumbing for delivering urine and semen to the outside world. They also have well-known secondary sexual characteristics, including a muscular build and facial hair. Women have two X chromosomes, ovaries, all of the internal plumbing to transport urine and ova to the outside world, a system to support pregnancy and fetal development, as well as a variety of recognizable secondary sexual characteristics.

That idealized story papers over many obvious caveats: some women have facial hair, some men have none; some women speak with deep voices, some men veritably squeak. Less well known is the fact that, on close inspection, absolute dimorphism disintegrates even at the level of basic biology. Chromosomes, hormones, the internal sex structures, the gonads and the external genitalia all vary more than most people realize. Those born outside of the Platonic dimorphic mold are called intersexuals.

In "The Five Sexes" I reported an estimate by a psychologist expert in the treatment of intersexuals, suggesting that some 4 percent of all live births are intersexual. Then, together with a group of Brown University undergraduates, I

set out to conduct the first systematic assessment of the available data on intersexual birthrates. We scoured the medical literature for estimates of the frequency of various categories of intersexuality, from additional chromosomes to mixed gonads, hormones and genitalia. For some conditions we could find only anecdotal evidence; for most, however, numbers exist. On the basis of that evidence, we calculated that for every 1,000 children born, seventeen are intersexual in some form. That number—1.7 percent—is a ballpark estimate, not a precise count, though we believe it is more accurate than the 4 percent I reported.

Our figure represents all chromosomal, anatomical and hormonal exceptions to the dimorphic ideal; the number of intersexuals who might, potentially, be subject to surgery as infants is smaller—probably between one in 1,000 and one in 2,000 live births. Furthermore, because some populations possess the relevant genes at high frequency, the intersexual birthrate is not uniform throughout the world.

Consider, for instance, the gene for congenital adrenal hyperplasia (CAH). When the CAH gene is inherited from both parents, it leads to a baby with masculinized external genitalia who possesses two X chromosomes and the internal reproductive organs of a potentially fertile woman. The frequency of the gene varies widely around the world: in New Zealand it occurs in only forty-three children per million; among the Yupik Eskimo of southwestern Alaska, its frequency is 3,500 per million.

INTERSEXUALITY HAS ALWAYS BEEN to some extent a matter of definition, and in the past century physicians have been the ones who defined children as intersexual—and provided the remedies. When only the chromosomes are unusual, but the external genitalia and gonads clearly indicate either a male or a female, physicians do not advocate intervention. Indeed, it is not clear what kind of intervention could be advocated in such cases. But the story is quite different when infants are born with mixed genitalia, or with external

genitals that seem at odds with the baby's gonads.

Most clinics now specializing in the treatment of intersex babies rely on case-management principles developed in the 1950s by the psychologist John Money and the psychiatrists Joan G. Hampson and John L. Hampson, all of Johns Hopkins University in Baltimore, Maryland. Money believed that gender identity is completely malleable for about eighteen months after birth. Thus, he argued, when a treatment team is presented with an infant who has ambiguous genitalia, the team could make a gender assignment solely on the basis of what made the best surgical sense. The physicians could then simply encourage the parents to raise the child according to the surgically assigned gender. Following that course, most physicians maintained, would eliminate psychological distress for both the patient and the parents. Indeed, treatment teams were never to use such words as "intersex" or "hermaphrodite"; instead, they were to tell parents that nature intended the baby to be the boy or the girl that the physicians had determined it was. Through surgery, the physicians were merely completing nature's intention.

Although Money and the Hampsons published detailed case studies of intersex children who they said had adjusted well to their gender assignments, Money thought one case in particular proved his theory. It was a dramatic example, inasmuch as it did not involve intersexuality at all: one of a pair of identical twin boys lost his penis as a result of a circumcision accident. Money recommended that "John" (as he came to be known in a later case study) be surgically turned into "Joan" and raised as a girl. In time, Joan grew to love wearing dresses and having her hair done. Money proudly proclaimed the sex reassignment a success.

But as recently chronicled by John Colapinto, in his book As Nature Made Him, Joan—now known to be an adult male named David Reimer—eventually rejected his female assignment. Even without a functioning penis and testes (which had been removed as part of the reassignment) John/Joan sought masculinizing medication, and married a woman with children (whom he adopted).

Since the full conclusion to the John/Joan story came to light, other individuals who were reassigned as males or females shortly after birth but who later rejected their early assignments have come forward. So, too, have cases in which the reassignment has worked—at least into the subject's mid-twenties. But even then the aftermath of the surgery can be problematic. Genital surgery often leaves scars that reduce sexual sensitivity. Chase herself had a complete clitoridectomy, a procedure that is less frequently performed on intersexuals today. But the newer surgeries, which reduce the size of the clitoral shaft, still greatly reduce sensitivity.

THE REVELATION OF CASES OF failed reassignments and the emergence of intersex activism have led an increasing number of pediatric endocrinologists, urologists and psychologists to reexamine the wisdom of early genital surgery. For example, in a talk that preceded Chase's at the LWPES meeting, the medical ethicist Laurence B. McCullough of the Center for Medical Ethics and Health Policy at Baylor College of Medicine in Houston, Texas, introduced an ethical framework for the treatment of children with ambiguous genitalia. Because sex phenotype (the manifestation of genetically and embryologically determined sexual characteristics) and gender presentation (the sex role projected by the individual in society) are highly variable, McCullough argues, the various forms of intersexuality should be defined as normal. All of them fall within the statistically expected variability of sex and gender. Furthermore, though certain disease states may accompany some forms of intersexuality, and may require medical intervention, intersexual conditions are not themselves diseases.

McCullough also contends that in the process of assigning gender, physicians should minimize what he calls irreversible assignments: taking steps such as the surgical removal or modification of gonads or genitalia that the patient may one day want to have reversed. Finally, McCullough urges physicians to

abandon their practice of treating the birth of a child with genital ambiguity as a medical or social emergency. Instead, they should take the time to perform a thorough medical workup and should disclose everything to the parents, including the uncertainties about the final outcome. The treatment mantra, in other words, should be therapy, not surgery.

I believe a new treatment protocol for intersex infants, similar to the one outlined by McCullough, is close at hand. Treatment should combine some basic medical and ethical principles with a practical but less drastic approach to the birth of a mixed-sex child. As a first step, surgery on infants should be performed only to save the child's life or to substantially improve the child's physical well-being. Physicians may assign a sex—male or female—to an intersex infant on the basis of the probability that the child's particular condition will lead to the formation of a particular gender identity. At the same time, though, practitioners ought to be humble enough to recognize that as the child grows, he or she may reject the assignment—and they should be wise enough to listen to what the child has to say. Most important, parents should have access to the full range of information and options available to them.

Sex assignments made shortly after birth are only the beginning of a long journey. Consider, for instance, the life of Max Beck: Born intersexual, Max was surgically assigned as a female and consistently raised as such. Had her medical team followed her into her early twenties, they would have deemed her assignment a success because she was married to a man. (It should be noted that success in gender assignment has traditionally been defined as living in that gender as a heterosexual.) Within a few years, however, Beck had come out as a butch lesbian; now in her mid-thirties, Beck has become a man and married his lesbian partner, who (through the miracles of modern reproductive technology) recently gave birth to a girl.

Transsexuals, people who have an emotional gender at odds with their physical sex, once described themselves in terms of dimorphic absolutes—males

trapped in female bodies, or vice versa. As such, they sought psychological relief through surgery. Although many still do, some so-called transgendered people today are content to inhabit a more ambiguous zone. A male-to-female transsexual, for instance, may come out as a lesbian. Jane, born a physiological male, is now in her late thirties and living with her wife, whom she married when her name was still John. Jane takes hormones to feminize herself, but they have not yet interfered with her ability to engage in intercourse as a man. In her mind Jane has a lesbian relationship with her wife, though she views their intimate moments as a cross between lesbian and heterosexual sex.

---

*A person who projects a social gender at odds with his or her genitals may die for the transgression.*

---

It might seem natural to regard intersexuals and transgendered people as living midway between the poles of male and female. But male and female, masculine and feminine, cannot be parsed as some kind of continuum. Rather, sex and gender are best conceptualized as points in a multidimensional space. For some time, experts on gender development have distinguished between sex at the genetic level and at the cellular level (sex-specific gene expression, X and Y chromosomes); at the hormonal level (in the fetus, during childhood and after puberty); and at the anatomical level (genitals and secondary sexual characteristics). Gender identity presumably emerges from all of those corporeal aspects via some poorly understood interaction with environment and experience. What has become increasingly clear is that one can find levels of masculinity and femininity in almost every possible permutation. A chromosomal, hormonal and genital male (or female) may emerge with a female (or male) gender identity. Or a chromosomal female with male fetal hormones and masculinized genitalia— but with female pubertal hormones— may develop a female gender identity.

THE MEDICAL AND SCIENTIFIC communities have yet to adopt a language that is capable of describing such diversity. In her book *Hermaphrodites and the Medical Invention of Sex,* the historian and medical ethicist Alice Domurat Dreger of Michigan State University in East Lansing documents the emergence of current medical systems for classifying gender ambiguity. The current usage remains rooted in the Victorian approach to sex. The logical structure of the commonly used terms "true hermaphrodite," "male pseudohermaphrodite" and "female pseudohermaphrodite" indicates that only the so-called true hermaphrodite is a genuine mix of male and female. The others, no matter how confusing their body parts, are really hidden males or females. Because true hermaphrodites are rare—possibly only one in 100,000— such a classification system supports the idea that human beings are an absolutely dimorphic species.

At the dawn of the twenty-first century, when the variability of gender seems so visible, such a position is hard to maintain. And here, too, the old medical consensus has begun to crumble. Last fall the pediatric urologist Ian A. Aaronson of the Medical University of South Carolina in Charleston organized the North American Task Force on Intersexuality (NATFI) to review the clinical responses to genital ambiguity in infants. Key medical associations, such as the American Academy of Pediatrics, have endorsed NATFI. Specialists in surgery, endocrinology, psychology, ethics, psychiatry, genetics and public health, as well as intersex patient-advocate groups, have joined its ranks.

One of the goals of NATFI is to establish a new sex nomenclature. One proposal under consideration replaces the current system with emotionally neutral terminology that emphasizes developmental processes rather than preconceived gender categories. For example, Type I intersexes develop out of anomalous virilizing influences; Type II result from some interruption of virilization; and in Type III intersexes the gonads themselves may not have developed in the expected fashion.

WHAT IS CLEAR IS THAT SINCE 1993, modern society has moved beyond five sexes to a recognition that gender variation is normal and, for some people, an arena for playful exploration. Discussing my "five sexes" proposal in her book *Lessons from the Intersexed,* the psychologist Suzanne J. Kessler of the State University of New York at Purchase drives this point home with great effect:

> The limitation with Fausto-Sterling's proposal is that . . . [it] still gives genitals . . . primary signifying status and ignores the fact that in the everyday world gender attributions are made without access to genital inspection. . . . What has primacy in everyday life is the gender that is performed, regardless of the flesh's configuration under the clothes.

I now agree with Kessler's assessment. It would be better for intersexuals and their supporters to turn everyone's focus away from genitals. Instead, as she suggests, one should acknowledge that people come in an even wider assortment of sexual identities and characteristics than mere genitals can distinguish. Some women may have "large clitorises or fused labia," whereas some men may have "small penises or misshapen scrota," as Kessler puts it, "phenotypes with no particular clinical or identity meaning."

As clearheaded as Kessler's program is—and despite the progress made in the 1990s—our society is still far from that ideal. The intersexual or transgendered person who projects a social gender— what Kessler calls "cultural genitals"— that conflicts with his or her physical genitals still may die for the transgression. Hence legal protection for people whose cultural and physical genitals do not match is needed during the current transition to a more gender-diverse world. One easy step would be to eliminate the category of "gender" from official documents, such as driver's licenses and passports. Surely attributes both more visible (such as height, build and eye color) and less visible (fingerprints and genetic profiles) would be more expedient.

A more far-ranging agenda is presented in the International Bill of Gender Rights, adopted in 1995 at the fourth annual International Conference on Transgender Law and Employment Policy in Houston, Texas. It lists ten "gender rights," including the right to define one's own gender, the right to change one's physical gender if one so chooses and the right to marry whomever one wishes. The legal bases for such rights are being hammered out in the courts as I write and, most recently, through the establishment, in the state of Vermont, of legal same-sex domestic partnerships.

NO ONE COULD HAVE FORESEEN such changes in 1993. And the idea that I played some role, however small, in reducing the pressure—from the medical community as well as from society at large—to flatten the diversity of human sexes into two diametrically opposed camps gives me pleasure.

Sometimes people suggest to me, with not a little horror, that I am arguing for a pastel world in which androgyny reigns and men and women are boringly the same. In my vision, however, strong colors coexist with pastels. There are and will continue to be highly masculine people out there; it's just that some of them are women. And some of the most feminine people I know happen to be men.

*Anne Fausto-Sterling is a professor of biology and women's studies at Brown University. Portions of this article were adapted from her recent book SEXING THE BODY (Basic Books, 2000).*

# Unit 2

7. **Machiavellian Monkeys,** James Shreeve
8. **What Are Friends For?** Barbara Smuts
9. **Dian Fossey and Digit,** Sy Montgomery
10. **The Mind of the Chimpanzee,** Jane Goodall
11. **Dim Forest, Bright Chimps,** Christophe Boesch and Hedwige Boesch-Achermann
12. **To Catch a Colobus,** Craig B. Stanford
13. **Coping With Crowding,** Frans B. M. de Waal, Filippo Aureli, and Peter G. Judge
14. **Are We in Anthropodenial?** Frans de Waal

## Key Points to Consider

❖ What is the role of deception among primates, and how might it have led to greater intelligence?

❖ Why is friendship important to olive baboons? What implications does this have for the origins of pair-bonding in hominid evolution?

❖ How is it possible to study objectively and assess emotional and mental states of nonhuman primates?

❖ What are the implications for human evolution of tool use, social hunting, and food sharing among Ivory Coast chimpanzees?

❖ Why is the mountain gorilla in danger of extinction?

❖ How do primates cope with crowding? Under what circumstances do they turn to violence?

❖ Are we in anthropodenial? Explain your answer.

 **Links**   **www.dushkin.com/online/**

15. **African Primates at Home**
    *http://www.indiana.edu/~primate/primates.html*
16. **Chimpanzee and Great Ape Language Resources—Anthropology**
    *http://www.brown.edu/Departments/Anthropology/apelang.html*
17. **Electronic Zoo/NetVet-Primate Page**
    *http://netvet.wustl.edu/primates.htm*
18. **Jane Goodall Research Center**
    *http://www.usc.edu/dept/elab/anth/goodall.html*

These sites are annotated on pages 4 and 5.

Primates are fun. They are active, intelligent, colorful, emotionally expressive, and unpredictable. In other words, observing them is like holding up an opaque mirror to ourselves. The image may not be crystal-clear or, indeed, what some would consider flattering, but it is certainly familiar enough to be illuminating.

Primates are, of course, but one of many orders of mammals that adaptively radiated into the variety of ecological niches vacated at the end of the Age of Reptiles about 65 million years ago. Whereas some mammals took to the sea (cetaceans), and some took to the air (chiroptera, or bats), primates are characterized by an arboreal or forested adaptation. Whereas some mammals can be identified by their food-getting habits, such as the meat-eating carnivores, primates have a penchant for eating almost anything and are best described as omnivorous. In taking to the trees, primates did not simply develop a full-blown set of distinguishing characteristics that set them off easily from other orders of mammals the way the rodent order can be readily identified by its gnawing set of front teeth. Rather, each primate seems to represent degrees of anatomical, biological, and behavioral characteristics on a continuum of progress with respect to the particular traits we humans happen to be interested in.

None of this is meant to imply, of course, that the living primates are our ancestors. Since the prosimians, monkeys, and apes are our contemporaries, they are no more our ancestors than we are theirs, and, as living end-products of evolution, we have all descended from a common stock in the distant past. So, if we are interested primarily in our own evolutionary past, why study primates at all? Because, by the criteria we have set up as significant milestones in the evolution of humanity, an inherent reflection of our own bias, primates have not evolved as far as we have. They and their environments, therefore, may represent glimmerings of the evolutionary stages and ecological circumstances through which our own ancestors may have gone. What we stand to gain, for instance, is an educated guess as to how our own ancestors might have appeared and behaved as semierect creatures before becoming bipedal. Aside from being a pleasure to observe, then, living primates can teach us something about our past.

Another reason for studying primates is that they allow us to test certain notions too often taken for granted. For instance, in "Coping With Crowding," Frans de Waal, Filippo Aureli, and Peter Judge call into question the notion that high population densities in primates neces- sarily lead to violence. In another example, Barbara Smuts, in "What Are Friends For?" reveals that friend- ship bonds, as illustrated by the olive baboons of East Africa, have little if anything to do with a sexual division of labor or even sexual exclusivity between a pair-bonded male and female. Smuts challenges the traditional male-oriented idea that primate societies are dominated solely by males for males.

This unit demonstrates that relationships between the sexes are subject to wide variation, that the kinds of answers obtained depend upon the kinds of questions asked, and that we have to be very careful in making inferences about human beings from any one particular primate study. We may, if we are not careful, draw conclusions that say more about our own skewed perspectives than about that which we claim to understand. Still another benefit of primate field research is that it provides us with perspectives that the bones and stones of the fossil hunters will never reveal: a sense of the richness and variety of social patterns that must have existed in the primate order for many tens of millions of years. (See James Shreeve's report "Machiavellian Monkeys," Sy Montgomery's essay, "Dian Fossey and Digit," and Jane Goodall's "The Mind of the Chimpanzee.")

Even if we had the physical remains of the earliest hominids in front of us, which we do not have, there is no way such evidence could thoroughly answer the questions that physical anthropologists care most deeply about: How did these creatures move about and get their food? Did they cooperate and share? On what levels did they think and communicate? Did they have a sense of family, let alone a sense of self? In one way or another, all of the previously mentioned articles on primates relate to these issues, as do some of the subsequent ones on the fossil evidence. But what sets off this unit from the others is how some of the authors attempt to deal with these matters head-on, even in the absence of direct fossil evidence. Christophe Boesch and Hedwige Boesch-Achermann, in "Dim Forest, Bright Chimps," indicate that some aspects of "hominization" (the acquisition of such humanlike qualities as cooperative hunting and food sharing) actually may have begun in the African rain forest rather than in the dry savanna, as has usually been proposed. They base their suggestions on some remarkable first-hand observations of forest-dwelling chimpanzees.

As if to show that chimpanzee behavior may vary according to local circumstances, just as we know human behavior does, Craig Stanford, in "To Catch a Colobus," contrasts his observations of chimpanzees' hunting in Gombe National Park with the findings of the Boesches.

Recent research has shown some striking resemblances between apes and humans, hinting that such qualities might have been characteristic of our common ancestors. Following this line of reasoning, Frans de Waal ("Are We in Anthropodenial?") argues that we can make educated guesses as to the mental and physical processes of our hominid predecessors.

Taken collectively, the articles in this section show how far anthropologists are willing to go to construct theoretical formulations based upon limited data. Although making so much out of so little may be seen as a fault and may generate irreconcilable differences among theorists, a readiness to entertain new ideas should be welcomed for what it is—a stimulus for more intensive and meticulous research.

# Machiavellian Monkeys

*The sneaky skills of our primate cousins suggest that we may owe our great intelligence to an inherited need to deceive.*

## James Shreeve

This is a story about frauds, cheats, liars, faithless lovers, incorrigible con artists, and downright thieves. You're gonna love 'em.

Let's start with a young rascal named Paul. You'll remember his type from your days back in the playground. You're minding your own business, playing on the new swing set, when along comes Paul, such a little runt that you hardly notice him sidle up to you. All of a sudden he lets out a scream like you've run him through with a white-hot barbed harpoon or something. Of course the teacher comes running, and the next thing you know you're being whisked inside with an angry finger shaking in your face. That's the end of recess for you. But look out the window: there's Paul, having a great time on *your* swing. Cute kid.

Okay, you're a little older now and a little smarter. You've got a bag of chips stashed away in your closet, where for once your older brother won't be able to find them. You're about to open the closet door when he pokes his head in the room. Quickly you pretend to be fetching your high tops; he gives you a look but he leaves. You wait a couple of minutes, lacing up the sneakers in case he walks back in, then you dive for the chips. Before you can get the bag open, he's over your shoulder, snatching it out of your hands. "Nice try, punk," he says through a mouthful, "but I was hiding outside your room the whole time."

This sort of trickery is such a common part of human interaction that we hardly notice how much time we spend defending ourselves against it or perpetrating it ourselves. What's so special about the fakes and cheaters here, however, is that they're not human. Paul is a young baboon, and your big brother is, well, a chimpanzee. With some admittedly deceptive alterations of scenery and props, the situations have been lifted from a recent issue of *Primate Report.* The journal is the work of Richard Byrne and Andrew Whiten, two psychologists at the University of St. Andrews in Scotland, and it is devoted to cataloging the petty betrayals of monkeys and apes as witnessed by primatologists around the world. It is a testament to the evolutionary importance of what Byrne and Whiten call Machiavellian intelligence—a facility named for the famed sixteenth-century author of *The Prince,* the ultimate how-to guide to prevailing in a complex society through the judicious application of cleverness, deceit, and political acumen.

Deception is rife in the natural world. Stick bugs mimic sticks. Harmless snakes resemble deadly poisonous ones. When threatened, blowfish puff themselves up and cats arch their backs and bristle their hair to seem bigger than they really are. All these animals could be said to practice deception because they fool other animals—usually members of other species—into thinking they are something that they patently are not. Even so, it would be overreading the situation to attribute Machiavellian cunning to a blowfish, or to accuse a stick bug of being a lying scoundrel. Their deceptions, whether in their looks or in their actions, are programmed genetic responses. Biology leaves them no choice but to dissemble: they are just being true to themselves.

The kind of deception that interests Byrne and Whiten—what they call tactical deception—is a different kettle of blowfish altogether. Here an animal has the mental flexibility to take an "honest" behavior and use it in such a way that another animal—usually a member of the deceiver's own social group—is misled, thinking that a normal, familiar state of affairs is under way, while, in fact, something quite different is happening.

Take Paul, for example. The real Paul is a young chacma baboon that caught Whiten's attention in 1983, while he and Byrne were studying foraging among the chacma in the Drakensberg Mountains of southern Africa. Whiten saw a member of Paul's group, an adult female named Mel, digging in the ground, trying to extract a nutritious plant bulb. Paul approached and looked around. There were no other baboons within sight. Suddenly he let out a yell, and within seconds his mother came running, chasing the startled Mel over a small cliff. Paul then took the bulb for himself.

In this case the deceived party was Paul's mother, who was misled by his scream into believing that Paul was being attacked, when actually no such attack was taking place. As a result of her apparent misinterpretation Paul was left alone to eat the bulb that Mel had carefully extracted—a morsel, by the way, that he would not have had the strength to dig out on his own.

If Paul's ruse had been an isolated case, Whiten might have gone on with his foraging studies and never given it a second thought. But when he compared his field notes with Byrne's, he noticed that both their notebooks were sprinkled with similar incidents and had been so all summer long. After they returned home to Scotland, they boasted about their "dead smart" baboons to their colleagues in pubs after conferences, expecting them to be suitably impressed. Instead the other researchers countered with tales about their own shrewd vervets or Machiavellian macaques.

"That's when we realized that a whole phenomenon might be slipping through a sieve," says Whiten. Researchers had assumed that this sort of complex trickery was a product of the sophisticated human brain. After all, deceitful behavior seemed unique to humans, and the human brain is unusually large, even for primates—"three times as big as you would expect for a primate of our size," notes Whiten, if you're plotting brain size against body weight.

But if primates other than humans deceived one another on a regular basis, the two psychologists reasoned, then it raised the extremely provocative possibility that the primate brain, and ultimately the human brain, is an instrument crafted for social manipulation. Humans evolved from the same evolutionary stock as apes, and if tactical deception was an important part of the lives of our evolutionary ancestors, then the sneakiness and subterfuge that human beings are so manifestly capable of might not be simply a result of our great intelligence and oversize brain, but a driving force behind their development.

To Byrne and Whiten these were ideas worth pursuing. They fit in with a theory put forth some years earlier by English psychologist Nicholas Humphrey. In 1976 Humphrey had eloquently suggested that the evolution of primate intelligence might have been spurred not by the challenges of environment, as was generally thought, but rather by the complex cognitive demands of living with one's own companions. Since then a number of primatologists had begun to flesh out his theory with field observations of politically astute monkeys and apes.

---

*Suddenly Paul let out a yell, and his mother came running, chasing Mel over a small cliff.*

---

Deception, however, had rarely been reported. And no wonder: If chimps, baboons, and higher primates generally are skilled deceivers, how could one ever know it? The best deceptions would by their very nature go undetected by the other members of the primate group, not to mention by a human stranger. Even those ruses that an observer could see through would have to be rare, for if used too often, they would lose their effectiveness. If Paul always cried wolf, for example, his mother would soon learn to ignore his ersatz distress. So while the monkey stories swapped over beers certainly suggested that deception was widespread among higher primates, it seemed unlikely that one or even a few researchers could observe enough instances of it to scientifically quantify how much, by whom, when, and to what effect.

Byrne and Whiten's solution was to extend their pub-derived data base with a more formal survey. In 1985 they sent a questionnaire to more than 100 primatologists working both in the field and in labs, asking them to report back any incidents in which they felt their subjects had perpetrated deception on one another. The questionnaire netted a promising assortment of deceptive tactics used by a variety of monkeys and all the great apes. Only the relatively small-brained and socially simple lemur family, which includes bush babies and lorises, failed to elicit a single instance. This supported the notion that society, sneakiness, brain size, and intelligence are intimately bound up with one another. The sneakier the primate, it seemed, the bigger the brain.

Byrne and Whiten drew up a second, much more comprehensive questionnaire in 1989 and sent it to hundreds more primatologists and animal behaviorists, greatly increasing the data base. Once again, when the results were tallied, only the lemur family failed to register a single case of deception.

All the other species, however, represented a simian rogues' gallery of liars and frauds. Often deception was used to distract another animal's attention. In one cartoonish example, a young baboon, chased by some angry elders, suddenly stopped, stood on his hind legs, and stared at a spot on the horizon, as if he noticed the presence of a predator or a foreign troop of baboons. His pursuers braked to a halt and looked in the same direction, giving up the chase. Powerful field binoculars revealed that no predator or baboon troop was anywhere in sight.

Sometimes the deception was simply a matter of one animal hiding a choice bit of food from the awareness of those strong enough to take it away. One of Jane Goodall's chimps, for example, named Figan, was once given some bananas after the more dominant members of the troop had wandered off. In the excitement, he uttered some loud "food barks"; the others quickly returned and took the bananas away. The next day Figan again waited behind the others and got some bananas. This time, however, he kept silent, even though the human observers, Goodall reported, "could hear faint choking sounds in his throat."

Concealment was a common ruse in sexual situations as well. Male monkeys and chimpanzees in groups have fairly strict hierarchies that control their access to females. Animals at the top of the order intimidate those lower down, forcing them away from females. Yet one researcher reported seeing a male stumptailed macaque of a middle rank leading a female out of sight of the more dominant males and then mating with her silently, his climax unaccompanied by the harsh, low-pitched grunts that the male stump-tailed normally makes. At one point during the tryst the female turned and stared into his face, then covered his mouth with her hand. In another case a subordinate chimpanzee, aroused by the presence of a female in estrus, covered his erect penis with his hand when a dominant male approached, thus avoiding a likely attack.

In one particularly provocative instance a female hamadryas baboon slowly shuffled toward a large rock, appearing to forage, all the time keeping an eye on the most dominant male in the group. After 20 minutes she ended up with her head and shoulders visible to the big, watchful male, but with her hands happily engaged in the elicit activity of grooming a favorite subordinate male, who was hidden from view behind the rock.

Baboons proved singularly adept at a form of deception that Byrne and Whiten call "using a social tool." Paul's scam is a perfect example: he fools his mother into acting as a lever to pry the plant bulb away from the adult female, Mel. But can it be said unequivocally that he intended to deceive her? Perhaps Paul had simply learned through trial and error that letting out a yell brought his mother running and left him with food, in which case there is no reason to endow his young baboon intellect with Machiavellian intent. How do we know that Mel didn't actually threaten Paul in some way that Byrne and Whiten, watching, could not comprehend? While we're at it, how do we know that any of the primate deceptions reported here were really deliberate, conscious acts?

"It has to be said that there is a whole school of psychology that would deny such behavior even to humans," says Byrne. The school in question—strict behaviorism—would seek an explanation for the baboons' behavior not by trying to crawl inside their head but by carefully analyzing observable behaviors and the stimuli that might be triggering them. Byrne and Whiten's strategy against such skepticism was to be hyperskeptical themselves. They accepted that trial-and-error learning or simple conditioning, in which an ani-

mal's actions are reinforced by a reward, might account for a majority of the incidents reported to them—even when they believed that tactical deception was really taking place. But when explaining things "simply" led to a maze of extraordinary coincidences and tortuous logic, the evidence for deliberate deception seemed hard to dismiss.

*Society, sneakiness, brain size, and intelligence are intimately bound up with one another.*

Paul, for instance, *might* have simply learned that screaming elicits the reward of food, via his mother's intervention. But Byrne witnessed him using the same tactic several times, and in each case his mother was out of sight, able to hear his yell but not able to see what was really going on. If Paul was simply conditioned to scream, why would he do so only when his mother could not see who was—or was not—attacking her son?

Still, it is possible that she was not intentionally deceived. But in at least one other, similar case there is virtually no doubt that the mother was responding to a bogus attack, because the alleged attacker was quite able to verbalize his innocence. A five-year-old male chimp named Katabi, in the process of weaning, had discovered that the best way to get his reluctant mother to suckle him was to convince her he needed reassurance. One day Katabi approached a human observer—Japanese primatologist Toshisada Nishida—and began to screech, circling around the researcher and waving an accusing hand at him. The chimp's mother and her escort immediately glared at Nishida, their hair erect. Only by slowly backing away from the screaming youngster did Nishida avoid a possible attack from the two adult chimps.

"In fact I did nothing to him," Nishida protested. It follows that the adults were indeed misled by Katabi's

hysterics—unless there was some threat in Nishida unknown even to himself.

"If you try hard enough," says Byrne, "you can explain every single case without endowing the animal with the ability to deceive. But if you look at the whole body of work, there comes a point where you have to strive officiously to deny it."

The cases most resistant to such officious denials are the rarest—and the most compelling. In these interactions the primate involved not only employed tactical deception but clearly understood the concept. Such comprehension would depend upon one animal's ability to "read the mind" of another: to attribute desires, intentions, or even beliefs to the other creature that do not necessarily correspond to its own view of the world. Such mind reading was clearly evident in only 16 out of 253 cases in the 1989 survey, all of them involving great apes.

For example, consider Figan again, the young chimp who suppressed his food barks in order to keep the bananas for himself. In his case, mind reading is not evident: he might simply have learned from experience that food barks in certain contexts result in a loss of food, and thus he might not understand the nature of his own ruse, even if the other chimps are in fact deceived.

But contrast Figan with come chimps observed by Dutch primatologist Frans Plooij. One of these chimps was alone in a feeding area when a metal box containing food was opened electronically. At the same moment another chimp happened to approach. (Sound familiar? It's your older brother again.) The first chimp quickly closed the metal box (that's you hiding your chips), walked away, and sat down, looking around as if nothing had happened. The second chimp departed, but after going some distance away he hid behind a tree and peeked back at the first chimp. When the first chimp thought the coast was clear, he opened the box. The second chimp ran out, pushed the other aside, and ate the bananas.

Chimp One might be a clever rogue, but Chimp Two, who counters his deception with a ruse of his own, is the true mind reader. The success of his ploy is based on his insight that Chimp One was trying to deceive *him* and on his ability to adjust his behavior accordingly. He has in fact performed a prodigious cognitive leap—proving himself capable of projecting himself into another's mental space, and becoming what Humphrey would call a natural psychologist.

Niccolò Machiavelli might have called him good raw material. It is certainly suggestive that only the great apes—our closest relatives—seem capable of deceits based on such mind reading, and chimpanzees most of all. This does not necessarily mean that chimps are inherently more intelligent: the difference may be a matter of social organization. Orangutans live most of their lives alone, and thus they would not have much reason to develop such a complex social skill. And gorillas live in close family groups, whose members would be more familiar, harder to fool, and more likely to punish an attempted swindle. Chimpanzees, on the other hand, spend their lives in a shifting swirl of friends and relations, where small groups constantly form and break apart and reform with new members.

"What an opportunity for lying and cheating!" muses Byrne. Many anthropologists now believe that the social life of early hominids—our first non-ape ancestors—was much like that of chimps today, with similar opportunities to hone their cognitive skills on one another. Byrne and Whiten stop just short of saying that mind reading is the key to understanding the growth of human intelligence. But it would be disingenuous to ignore the possibility. If you were an early hominid who could comprehend the subjective impressions of others and manipulate them to your own ends, you might well have a competitive advantage over those less psychosocially nimble, perhaps enjoying slightly easier access to food and to the mating opportunities that would ensure your genetic survival.

Consider too how much more important your social wits would be in a world where the targets of your deceptions were constantly trying to outsmart *you*. After millennia of intrigue and counterintrigue, a hominid species might well evolve a brain three times bigger than it "should" be—and capable of far more than deceiving other hominids. "The ability to attribute other intentions to other people could have been an enormous building block for many human achievements, including language," says Whiten. "That this leap seems to have been taken by chimps and possibly the other great apes puts that development in human mentality quite early."

So did our intellect rise to its present height on a tide of manipulation and deceit? Some psychologists, even those who support the notion that the evolution of intelligence was socially driven, think that Bryne and Whiten's choice of the loaded adjective *Machiavellian* might be unnecessarily harsh.

"In my opinion," says Humphrey, "the word gives too much weight to the hostile use of intelligence. One of the functions of intellect in higher primates and humans is to keep the social unit together and make it able to successfully exploit the environment. A lot of intelligence could better be seen as driven by the need for cooperation and compassion." To that, Byrne and Whiten only point out that cooperation is itself an excellent Machiavellian strategy—sometimes.

The Scottish researchers are not, of course, the first to have noticed this. "It is good to appear clement, trustworthy, humane, religious, and honest, and also to be so," Machiavelli advised his aspiring Borgia prince in 1513. "But always with the mind so disposed that, when the occasion arises not to be so, you can become the opposite."

# What Are Friends For?

*Among East African baboons, friendship means companions, health, safety . . .
and, sometimes, sex*

## Barbara Smuts

Virgil, a burly adult male olive baboon, closely followed Zizi, a middle-aged female easily distinguished by her grizzled coat and square muzzle. On her rump Zizi sported a bright pink swelling, indicating that she was sexually receptive and probably fertile. Virgil's extreme attentiveness to Zizi suggested to me—and all rival males in the troop—that he was her current and exclusive mate.

Zizi, however, apparently had something else in mind. She broke away from Virgil, moved rapidly through the troop, and presented her alluring sexual swelling to one male after another. Before Virgil caught up with her, she had managed to announce her receptive condition to several of his rivals. When Virgil tried to grab her, Zizi screamed and dashed into the bushes with Virgil in hot pursuit. I heard sounds of chasing and fighting coming from the thicket. Moments later Zizi emerged from the bushes with an older male named Cyclops. They remained together for several days, copulating often. In Cyclops's presence, Zizi no longer approached or even glanced at other males.

Primatologists describe Zizi and other olive baboons (*Papio cynocephalus anubis*) as promiscuous, meaning that both males and females usually mate with several members of the opposite sex within a short period of time. Promiscuous mating behavior characterizes many of the larger, more familiar primates, including chimpanzees, rhesus macaques, and gray langurs, as well as olive, yellow, and chacma baboons, the three subspecies of savanna baboon. In colloquial usage, promiscuity often connotes wanton and random sex, and several early studies of primates supported this stereotype. However, after years of laboriously recording thousands of copulations under natural conditions, the Peeping Toms of primate fieldwork have shown that, even in promiscuous species, sexual pairings are far from random.

Some adult males, for example, typically copulate much more often than others. Primatologists have explained these differences in terms of competition: the most dominant males monopolize females and prevent lower-ranking rivals from mating. But exceptions are frequent. Among baboons, the exceptions often involve scruffy, older males who mate in full view of younger, more dominant rivals.

A clue to the reason for these puzzling exceptions emerged when primatologists began to question an implicit assumption of the dominance hypothesis—that females were merely passive objects of male competition. But what if females were active arbiters in this system? If females preferred some males over others and were able to express these preferences, then models of mating activity based on male dominance alone would be far too simple.

Once researchers recognized the possibility of female choice, evidence for it turned up in species after species. The story of Zizi, Virgil, and Cyclops is one of hundreds of examples of female primates rejecting the sexual advances of particular males and enthusiastically cooperating with others. But what is the basis for female choice? Why might they prefer some males over others?

This question guided my research on the Eburru Cliffs troop of olive baboons, named after one of their favorite sleeping sites, a sheer rocky outcrop rising several hundred feet above the floor of the Great Rift Valley, about 100 miles northwest of Nairobi, Kenya. The 120 members of Eburru Cliffs spent their days wandering through open grassland studded with occasional acacia thorn trees. Each night they retired to one of a dozen sets of cliffs that provided protection from nocturnal predators such as leopards.

Most previous studies of baboon sexuality had focused on females who, like Zizi, were at the peak of sexual receptivity. A female baboon does not mate when she is pregnant or lactating, a period of abstinence lasting about eighteen months. The female then goes into estrus, and for about two weeks out of every thirty-five-day cycle, she mates. Toward the end of this two-week period she may ovulate, but usually the female undergoes four or five estrous cycles before she conceives. During pregnancy, she once again resumes a chaste existence. As a result, the typical female baboon is sexually active for less than 10 percent of her adult life. I thought that by focusing on the other 90 percent, I might learn something new. In particular, I suspected that routine, day-to-day

Reprinted with permission from *Natural History*, February 1987, pp. 36–44. © 1987 by the American Museum of Natural History.

relationships between males and pregnant or lactating (nonestrous) females might provide clues to female mating preferences.

Nearly every day for sixteen months, I joined the Eburru Cliffs baboons at their sleeping cliffs at dawn and traveled several miles with them while they foraged for roots, seeds, grass, and occasionally, small prey items, such as baby gazelles or hares (see "Predatory Baboons of Kekopey," *Natural History,* March 1976). Like all savanna baboon troops, Eburru Cliffs functioned as a cohesive unit organized around a core of related females, all of whom were born in the troop. Unlike the females, male savanna baboons leave their natal troop to join another where they may remain for many years, so most of the Eburru Cliffs adult males were immigrants. Since membership in the troop remained relatively constant during the period of my study, I learned to identify each individual. I relied on differences in size, posture, gait, and especially, facial features. To the practiced observer, baboons look as different from one another as human beings do.

As soon as I could recognize individuals, I noticed that particular females tended to turn up near particular males again and again. I came to think of these pairs as friends. Friendship among animals is not a well-documented phenomenon, so to convince skeptical colleagues that baboon friendship was real, I needed to develop objective criteria for distinguishing friendly pairs.

I began by investigating grooming, the amiable simian habit of picking through a companion's fur to remove dead skin and ectoparasites (see "Little Things That Tick Off Baboons," *Natural History,* February 1984). Baboons spend much more time grooming than is necessary for hygiene, and previous research had indicated that it is a good measure of social bonds.

Although eighteen adult males lived in the troop, each nonestrous female performed most of her grooming with just one, two, or occasionally, three males. For example, of Zizi's twenty-four grooming bouts with males, Cyclops accounted for thirteen, and a second male, Sherlock, accounted for all the rest. Different females tended to favor different males as grooming partners.

Another measure of social bonds was simply who was observed near whom. When foraging, traveling, or resting, each pregnant or lactating female spent a lot of time near a few males and associated with the others no more often than expected by chance. When I compared the identities of favorite grooming partners and frequent companions, they overlapped almost completely. This enabled me to develop a formal definition of friendship: any male that scored high on both grooming and proximity measures was considered a friend.

Virtually all baboons made friends; only one female and three males who had most recently joined the troop lacked such companions. Out of more than 600 possible adult female-adult male pairs in the troop, however, only about one in ten qualified as friends; these really were special relationships.

Several factors seemed to influence which baboons paired up. In most cases, friends were unrelated to each other, since the male had immigrated from another troop. (Four friendships, however, involved a female and an adolescent son who had not yet emigrated. Unlike other friends, these related pairs never mated.) Older females tended to be friends with older males; younger females with younger males. I witnessed occasional May–December romances, usually involving older females and young adult males. Adolescent males and females were strongly rule-bound, and with the exception of mother-son pairs, they formed friendships only with one another.

Regardless of age or dominance rank, most females had just one or two male friends. But among males, the number of female friends varied greatly from none to eight. Although high-ranking males enjoyed priority of access to food and sometimes mates, dominant males did not have more female friends than low-ranking males. Instead it was the older males who had lived in the troop for many years who had the most friends. When a male had several female friends, the females were often closely related to one another. Since female baboons spend a lot of time near their kin, it is probably easier for a male to maintain bonds with several related females at once.

When collecting data, I focused on one nonestrous female at a time and kept track of her every movement toward or away from any male; similarly, I noted every male who moved toward or away from her. Whenever the female and male moved close enough to exchange intimacies, I wrote down exactly what happened. When foraging together, friends tended to remain a few yards apart. Males more often wandered away from females than the reverse, and females, more often than males, closed the gap. The female behaved as if she wanted to keep the male within calling distance, in case she needed his protection. The male, however, was more likely to make approaches that brought them within actual touching distance. Often, he would plunk himself down right next to his friend and ask her to groom him by holding a pose with exaggerated stillness. The female sometimes responded by grooming, but more often, she exhibited the most reliable sign of true intimacy: she ignored her friend and simply continued whatever she was doing.

In sharp contrast, when a male who was not a friend moved close to a female, she dared not ignore him. She stopped whatever she was doing and held still, often glancing surreptitiously at the intruder. If he did not move away, she sometimes lifted her tail and presented her rump. When a female is not in estrus, this is a gesture of appeasement, not sexual enticement. Immediately after this respectful acknowledgement of his presence, the female would slip away. But such tense interactions with nonfriend males were rare, because females usually moved away before the males came too close.

These observations suggest that females were afraid of most of the males in their troop, which is not surprising: male baboons are twice the size of females, and their canines are longer and sharper than those of a lion. All Eburru Cliffs males directed both mild and severe aggression toward females. Mild aggression, which usually involved threats and chases but no body contact, occurred most often during feeding competition or when the male redirected aggression toward a female after losing a fight with another male. Females and juveniles showed aggression toward other females and juveniles in similar circumstances and occasionally inflicted superficial wounds. Severe aggression by males, which involved body contact and sometimes biting, was less common and also more puzzling, since there was no apparent cause.

An explanation for at least some of these attacks emerged one day when I was watching Pegasus, a young adult male, and his friend Cicily, sitting together in the middle of a small clearing. Cicily moved to the edge of the clearing to feed, and a higher-ranking female, Zora, suddenly attacked her. Pegasus stood up and looked as if he were about to intervene when both females disappeared into the bushes. He sat back down, and I remained with him. A full ten minutes later, Zora appeared at the edge of the clearing; this was the first time she had come into view since her attack on Cicily. Pegasus instantly pounced on Zora, repeatedly grabbed her neck in his mouth and lifted her off the ground, shook her whole body, and then dropped her. Zora screamed continuously and tried to escape. Each time, Pegasus caught her and continued his brutal attack. When he finally released her five minutes later she had a deep canine gash on the palm of her hand that made her limp for several days.

This attack was similar in form and intensity to those I had seen before and labeled "unprovoked." Certainly, had I come upon the scene after Zora's aggression toward Cicily, I would not have understood why Pegasus attacked Zora. This suggested that some, perhaps many, severe attacks by males actually represented punishment for actions that had occurred some time before.

Whatever the reasons for male attacks on females, they represent a serious threat. Records of fresh injuries indicated that Eburru Cliffs adult females received canine slash wounds from males at the rate of one for every female each year, and during my study, one female died of her injuries. Males probably pose an even greater threat to infants. Although only one infant was

killed during my study, observers in Botswana and Tanzania have seen recent male immigrants kill several young infants.

Protection from male aggression, and from the less injurious but more frequent aggression of other females and juveniles, seems to be one of the main advantages of friendship for a female baboon. Seventy times I observed an adult male defend a female or her offspring against aggression by another troop member, not infrequently a high-ranking male. In all but six of these cases, the defender was a friend. Very few of these confrontations involved actual fighting; no male baboon, subordinate or dominant, is anxious to risk injury by the sharp canines of another.

Males are particularly solicitous guardians of their friends' youngest infants. If another male gets too close to an infant or if a juvenile female plays with it too roughly, the friend may intervene. Other troop members soon learn to be cautious when the mother's friend is nearby, and his presence provides the mother with a welcome respite from the annoying pokes and prods of curious females and juveniles obsessed with the new baby. Male baboons at Gombe Park in Tanzania and Amboseli Park in Kenya have also been seen rescuing infants from chimpanzees and lions. These several forms of male protection help to explain why females in Eburru Cliffs stuck closer to their friends in the first few months after giving birth than at any other time.

The male-infant relationship develops out of the male's friendship with the mother, but as the infant matures, this new bond takes on a life of its own. My co-worker Nancy Nicolson found that by about nine months of age, infants actively sought out their male friends when the mother was a few yards away, suggesting that the male may function as an alternative caregiver. This seemed to be especially true for infants undergoing unusually early or severe weaning. (Weaning is generally a gradual, prolonged process, but there is tremendous variation among mothers in the timing and intensity of weaning. See "Mother Baboons," *Natural History,* September 1980). After being rejected by the mother, the crying infant often

approached the male friend and sat huddled against him until its whimpers subsided. Two of the infants in Eburru Cliffs lost their mothers when they were still quite young. In each case, their bond with the mother's friend subsequently intensified, and—perhaps as a result—both infants survived.

A close bond with a male may also improve the infant's nutrition. Larger than all other troop members, adult males monopolize the best feeding sites. In general, the personal space surrounding a feeding male is inviolate, but he usually tolerates intrusions by the infants of his female friends, giving them access to choice feeding spots.

Although infants follow their male friends around rather than the reverse, the males seem genuinely attached to their tiny companions. During feeding, the male and infant express their pleasure in each other's company by sharing spirited, antiphonal grunting duets. If the infant whimpers in distress, the male friend is likely to cease feeding, look at the infant, and grunt softly, as if in sympathy, until the whimpers cease. When the male rests, the infants of his female friends may huddle behind him, one after the other, forming a "train," or, if feeling energetic, they may use his body as a trampoline.

When I returned to Eburru Cliffs four years after my initial study ended, several of the bonds formed between males and the infants of their female friends were still intact (in other cases, either the male or the infant or both had disappeared). When these bonds involved recently matured females, their long-time male associates showed no sexual interest in them, even though the females mated with other adult males. Mothers and sons, and usually maternal siblings, show similar sexual inhibitions in baboons and many other primate species.

The development of an intimate relationship between a male and the infant of his female friend raises an obvious question: Is the male the infant's father? To answer this question definitely we would need to conduct genetic analysis, which was not possible for these baboons. Instead, I estimated paternity probabilities from observations of the temporary (a few hours or days) exclusive mating relationships, or consortships, that estrous females form with a series of different males. These estimates were apt to be fairly accurate, since changes in the female's sexual swelling allow one to pinpoint the timing of conception to within a few days. Most females consorted with only two or three males during this period, and these males were termed likely fathers.

In about half the friendships, the male was indeed likely to be the father of his friend's most recent infant, but in the other half he was not—in fact, he had never been seen mating with the female. Interestingly, males who were friends with the mother but not likely fathers nearly always developed a relationship with her infant, while males who had mated with the female but were not her friend usually did not. Thus friendship with the mother, rather than paternity, seems to mediate the development of male-infant bonds. Recently, a similar pattern was documented for South American capuchin monkeys in a laboratory study in which paternity was determined genetically.

These results fly in the face of a prominent theory that claims males will invest in infants only when they are closely related. If males are not fostering the survival of their own genes by caring for the infant, then why do they do so? I suspected that the key was female choice. If females preferred to mate with males who had already demonstrated friendly behavior, then friendships with mothers and their infants might pay off in the future when the mothers were ready to mate again.

To find out if this was the case, I examined each male's sexual behavior with females he had befriended before they resumed estrus. In most cases, males consorted considerably more often with their friends than with other females. Baboon females typically mate with several different males, including both friends and nonfriends, but prior friendship increased a male's probability of mating with a female above what it would have been otherwise.

This increased probability seemed to reflect female preferences. Females occasionally overtly advertised their disdain for certain males and their desire

for others. Zizi's behavior, described above, is a good example. Virgil was not one of her friends, but Cyclops was. Usually, however, females expressed preferences and aversions more subtly. For example, Delphi, a petite adolescent female, found herself pursued by Hector, a middle-aged adult male. She did not run away or refuse to mate with him, but whenever he wasn't watching, she looked around for her friend Homer, an adolescent male. When she succeeded in catching Homer's eye, she narrowed her eyes and flattened her ears against her skull, the friendliest face one baboon can send another. This told Homer she would rather be with him. Females expressed satisfaction with a current consort partner by staying close to him, initiating copulations, and not making advances toward other males. Baboons are very sensitive to such cues, as indicated by an experimental study in which rival hamadryas baboons rarely challenged a male-female pair if the female strongly preferred her current partner. Similarly, in Eburru Cliffs, males were less apt to challenge consorts involving a pair that shared a long-term friendship.

Even though females usually consorted with their friends, they also mated with other males, so it is not surprising that friendships were most vulnerable during periods of sexual activity. In a few cases, the female consorted with another male more often than with her friend, but the friendship survived nevertheless. One female, however, formed a strong sexual bond with a new male. This bond persisted after conception, replacing her previous friendship. My observations suggest that adolescent and young adult females tend to have shorter, less stable friendships than do older females. Some friendships, however, last a very long time. When I returned to Eburru Cliffs six years after my study began, five couples were still together. It is possible that friendships occasionally last for life (baboons probably live twenty to thirty years in the wild), but it will require longer studies, and some very patient scientists to find out.

By increasing both the male's chances of mating in the future and the likelihood that a female's infant will survive, friendship contributes to the repro-

ductive success of both partners. This clarifies the evolutionary basis of friendship-forming tendencies in baboons, but what does friendship mean to a baboon? To answer this question we need to view baboons as sentient beings with feelings and goals not unlike our own in similar circumstances. Consider, for example, the friendship between Thalia and Alexander.

The affair began one evening as Alex and Thalia sat about fifteen feet apart on the sleeping cliffs. It was like watching two novices in a singles bar. Alex stared at Thalia until she turned and almost caught him looking at her. He glanced away immediately, and then she stared at him until his head began to turn toward her. She suddenly became engrossed in grooming her toes. But as soon as Alex looked away, her gaze returned to him. They went on like this for more than fifteen minutes, always with split-second timing. Finally, Alex managed to catch Thalia looking at him. He made the friendly eyes-narrowed, ears-back face and smacked his lips together rhythmically. Thalia froze, and for a second she looked into his eyes. Alex approached, and Thalia, still nervous, groomed him. Soon she calmed down, and I found them still together on the cliffs the next morning. Looking back on this event months later, I realized that it marked the beginning of their friendship. Six years later, when I returned to Eburru Cliffs, they were still friends.

If flirtation forms an integral part of baboon friendship, so does jealousy. Overt displays of jealousy, such as chasing a friend away from a potential rival, occur occasionally, but like humans, baboons often express their emotions in more subtle ways. One evening a colleague and I climbed the cliffs and settled down near Sherlock, who was friends with Cybelle, a middle-aged female still foraging on the ground below the cliffs. I observed Cybelle while my colleague watched Sherlock, and we kept up a running commentary. As long as Cybelle was feeding or interacting with females, Sherlock was relaxed, but each time she approached another male, his body would stiffen, and he would stare intently at the scene below. When Cybelle presented politely to a male who had recently tried to befriend her, Sherlock even made threatening sounds under his breath. Cybelle was not in estrus at the time, indicating that male baboon jealousy extends beyond the sexual arena to include affiliative interactions between a female friend and other males.

Because baboon friendships are embedded in a network of friendly and antagonistic relationships, they inevitably lead to repercussions extending beyond the pair. For example, Virgil once provoked his weaker rival Cyclops into a fight by first attacking Cyclops's friend Phoebe. On another occasion, Sherlock chased Circe, Hector's best friend, just after Hector had chased Antigone, Sherlock's friend.

In another incident, the prime adult male Triton challenged Cyclops's possession of meat. Cyclops grew increasingly tense and seemed about to abandon the prey to the younger male. Then Cyclops's friend Phoebe appeared with her infant Phyllis. Phyllis wandered over to Cyclops. He immediately grabbed her, held her close, and threatened Triton away from the prey. Because any challenge to Cyclops now involved a threat to Phyllis as well, Triton risked being mobbed by Phoebe and her relatives and friends. For this reason, he backed down. Males frequently use the infants of their female friends as buffers in this way. Thus, friendship involves costs as well as benefits because it makes the participants vulnerable to social manipulation or redirected aggression by others.

Finally, as with humans, friendship seems to mean something different to each baboon. Several females in Eburru Cliffs had only one friend. They were devoted companions. Louise and Pandora, for example, groomed their friend Virgil and no other male. Then there was Leda, who, with five friends, spread herself more thinly than any other female. These contrasting patterns of friendship were associated with striking personality differences. Louise and Pandora were unobtrusive females who hung around quietly with Virgil and their close relatives. Leda seemed to be everywhere at once, playing with infants, fighting with juveniles, and making friends with males. Similar differences were apparent among the males. Some devoted a great deal of time and energy to cultivating friendships with females, while others focused more on challenging other males. Although we probably will never fully understand the basis of these individual differences, they contribute immeasurably to the richness and complexity of baboon society.

Male-female friendships may be widespread among primates. They have been reported for many other groups of savanna baboons, and they also occur in rhesus and Japanese Macaques, capuchin monkeys, and perhaps in bonobos (pygmy chimpanzees). These relationships should give us pause when considering popular scenarios for the evolution of male-female relationships in humans. Most of these scenarios assume that, except for mating, males and females had little to do with one another until the development of a sexual division of labor, when, the story goes, females began to rely on males to provide meat in exchange for gathered food. This, it has been argued, set up new selection pressures favoring the development of long-term bonds between individual males and females, female sexual fidelity, and as paternity certainty increased, greater male investment in the offspring of these unions. In other words, once women began to gather and men to hunt, presto—we had the nuclear family.

This scenario may have more to do with cultural biases about women's economic dependence on men and idealized views of the nuclear family than with the actual behavior of our hominid ancestors. The nonhuman primate evidence challenges this story in at least three ways.

First, long-term bonds between the sexes can evolve in the absence of a sexual division of labor of food sharing. In our primate relatives, such relationships rest on exchanges of social, not economic, benefits.

Second, primate research shows that highly differentiated, emotionally intense male-female relationships can occur without sexual exclusivity. Ancestral men and women may have experienced intimate friendships long before they invented marriage and norms of sexual fidelity.

Third, among our closest primate relatives, males clearly provide mothers and infants with social benefits even when they are unlikely to be the fathers of those infants. In return, females provide a variety of benefits to the friendly males, including acceptance into the group and, at least in baboons, increased mating opportunities in the future. This suggests that efforts to reconstruct the evolution of hominid societies may have overemphasized what the female must supposedly do (restrict her mating to just one male) in order to obtain male parental investment.

Maybe it is time to pay more attention to what the male must do (provide benefits to females and young) in order to obtain female cooperation. Perhaps among our ancestors, as in baboons today, sex and friendship went hand in hand. As for marriage—well, that's another story.

# Dian Fossey and Digit

## Sy Montgomery

Every breath was a battle to draw the ghost of her life back into her body. At age forty-two it hurt her even to breathe.

Dian Fossey had been asthmatic as a child and a heavy smoker since her teens; X-rays of her lungs taken when she graduated from college, she remembered, looked like "a road map of Los Angeles superimposed over a road map of New York." And now, after eight years of living in the oxygen-poor heights of Central Africa's Virunga Volcanoes, breathing the cold, sodden night air, her lungs were crippled. The hike to her research camp, Karisoke, at 10,000 feet, took her graduate students less than an hour; for Dian it was a gasping two-and-a-half-hour climb. She had suffered several bouts of pneumonia. Now she thought she was coming down with it again.

Earlier in the week she had broken her ankle. She heard the bone snap when she fell into a drainage ditch near her corrugated tin cabin. She had been avoiding a charging buffalo. Two days later she was bitten by a venomous spider on the other leg. Her right knee was swollen huge and red; her left ankle was black. But she would not leave the mountain for medical treatment in the small hospital down in Ruhengeri. She had been in worse shape before. Once, broken ribs punctured a lung; another time she was bitten by a dog thought to be rabid. Only when her temperature reached 105 and her symptoms clearly matched those described in her medical

book for rabies had she allowed her African staff to carry her down on a litter.

Dian was loath to leave the camp in charge of her graduate students, two of whom she had been fighting with bitterly. Kelly Steward and Sandy Harcourt, once her closest camp colleagues and confidantes, had committed the unforgivable error of falling in love with each other. Dian considered this a breach of loyalty. She yelled at them. Kelly cried and Sandy sulked.

But on this May day of 1974 Sandy felt sorry for Dian. As a gesture of conciliation, he offered to help her hobble out to visit Group 4. Splinted and steadied by a walking stick, she quickly accepted.

Group 4 was the first family of mountain gorillas Dian had contacted when she established her camp in Rwanda in September 1967. A political uprising had forced her to flee her earlier research station in Zaire. On the day she founded Karisoke—a name she coined by combining the names of the two volcanoes between which her camp nestled, Karisimbi and Visoke—poachers had led her to the group. The two Batwa tribesmen had been hunting antelope in the park—an illegal practice that had been tolerated for decades—and they offered to show her the gorillas they had encountered.

At that first contact, Dian watched the gorillas through binoculars for forty-five minutes. Across a ravine, ninety feet away, she could pick out three distinctive individuals in the fourteen-member

group. There was a majestic old male, his black form silvered from shoulder to hip. This 350-pound silverback was obviously the sultan of the harem of females, the leader of the family. One old female stood out, a glare in her eyes, her lips compressed as if she had swallowed vinegar. And one youngster was "a playful little ball of disorganized black fluff . . . full of mischief and curiosity," as Dian would later describe him in *Gorillas in the Mist*. She guessed then that he was about five years old. He tumbled about in the foliage like an animated black dustball. When the lead silverback spotted Dian behind a tree, the youngster obediently fled at his call, but Dian had the impression that the little male would rather have stayed for a longer look at the stranger. In a later contact she noticed the juvenile's swollen, extended middle finger. After many attempts at naming him, she finally called him Digit.

It was Digit, now twelve, who came over to Dian as she sat crumpled and coughing among the foliage with Sandy. Digit, a gaunt young silverback, served his family as sentry. He left the periphery of his group to knuckle over to her side. She inhaled his smell. A good smell, she noted with relief: for two years a draining wound in his neck had hunched his posture and sapped his spirit. Systemic infection had given his whole body a sour odor, not the normal, clean smell of fresh sweat. During that time Digit had become listless. Little would arouse his interest: not the sex play between the group's lead silverback and receptive females, not even visits from Dian. Digit would sit at the edge of the group for hours, probing the wound with his fingers, his eyes fixed on some distant spot as if dwelling on a sad memory.

But today Digit looked directly into Dian's eyes. He chose to remain beside her throughout the afternoon, like a quiet visitor to a shut-in, old friends with no need to talk. He turned his great domed head to her, looking at her solemnly with a brown, cognizant gaze. Normally a prolonged stare from a gorilla is a threat. But Digit's gaze bore no aggression. He seemed to say: I know. Dian would later write that she believed Digit understood she was sick. And she returned to camp that afternoon, still limping, still sick, still troubled, but whole.

"We all felt we shared something with the gorillas," one of her students would later recall of his months at Karisoke. And it is easy to feel that way after even a brief contact with these huge, solemn beings. "The face of a gorilla," wrote nature writer David Quammen after just looking at a picture of one, "offers a shock of what feels like total recognition." To be in the presence of a mountain gorilla for even one hour simply rips your soul open with awe. They are the largest of the great apes, the most hugely majestic and powerful; but it is the gaze of a gorilla that transfixes, when its eyes meet yours. The naturalist George Schaller, whose year-long study preceded Dian's, wrote that this is a look found in the eye of no other animal except, perhaps, a whale. It is not so much intelligence that strikes you, but understanding. You feel there has been an exchange.

The exchange between Digit and Dian that day was deep and long. By then Digit had known Dian for seven years. She had been a constant in his growing up from a juvenile to a young blackback and now to a silverback sentry. He had known her longer than he had known his own mother, who had died or left his group before he was five; he had known Dian longer than he had known his father, the old silverback who died of natural causes less than a year

after she first observed him. When Digit was nine, his three age-mates in Group 4 departed: his half sisters were "kidnaped" by rival silverbacks, as often happens with young females. Digit then adopted Dian as his playmate, and he would often leave the rest of the group to amble to her side, eager to examine her gear, sniff her gloves and jeans, tug gently at her long brown braid.

As for Dian, her relationship with Digit was stronger than her bonds with her mother, father, or stepfather. Though she longed for a husband and babies, she never married or bore children. Her relationship with Digit endured longer than that with any of her lovers and outlasted many of her human friendships.

In her slide lectures in the United States, Dian would refer to him as "my friend, Digit." "Friend," she admitted, was too weak a word, too casual; but she could find no other. Our words are something we share with other humans; but what Dian had with Digit was something she guarded as uniquely hers.

A mountain gorilla group is one of the most cohesive family units found among primates, a fact that impressed George Schaller. Adult orangutans live mostly alone, males and females meeting to mate. Chimpanzees' social groupings are so loosely organized, changing constantly in number and composition, that Jane Goodall couldn't make sense of them for nearly a decade. But gorillas live in tight-knit, clearly defined families. Typically a group contains a lead silverback, perhaps his adult brother, half brother, or nephew, and several adult females and their offspring.

A gorilla group travels, feeds, plays, and rests together. Seldom is an individual more than a hundred feet away from the others. The lead silverback slows his pace to that of the group's slowest, weakest member. All adults tolerate the babies and youngsters in the group, often with great tenderness. A wide-eyed baby, its fur still curly as black wool, may crawl over the great black bulk of any adult with impunity; a toddler may even step on the flat, leathery nose of a silverback. Usually the powerful male will gently set the baby aside

or even dangle it playfully from one of his immense fingers.

When Dian first discovered Group 4, she would watch them through binoculars from a hidden position, for if they saw her they would flee. She loved to observe the group's three infants toddle and tumble together. If one baby found the play too rough, it would make a coughing sound, and its mother would lumber over and cradle it tenderly to her breast. Dian watched Digit and his juvenile sisters play: wrestling, rolling, and chasing games often took them as far as fifty feet from the hulking adults. Sometimes a silverback led the youngsters in a sort of square dance. Loping from one palmlike *Senecio* tree to another, each gorilla would grab a trunk for a twirl, then spin off to embrace another trunk down the slope, until all the gorillas lay in a bouncing pileup of furry black bodies. And then the silverback would lead the youngsters up the slope again for another game.

Within a year, this cheerful silverback eventually took over leadership of the group, after the old leader died. Dian named him Uncle Bert, after her uncle Albert Chapin. With Dian's maternal aunt, Flossie (Dian named a Group 4 female after her as well), Uncle Bert had helped care for Dian after her father left the family when she was three. While Dian was in college Bert and Flossie gave her money to help with costs that her holiday, weekend, and summer jobs wouldn't cover. Naming the silverback after her uncle was the most tender tribute Dian could have offered Bert Chapin: his was the name given to the group's male magnet, its leader, protector—and the centerpiece of a family life whose tenderness and cohesion Dian, as a child, could not have imagined.

Dian was a lonely only child. Her father's drinking caused the divorce that took him out of her life; when her mother, Kitty, remarried when Dian was five, even the mention of George Fossey's name became taboo in the house. Richard Price never adopted Dian. Each night she ate supper in the kitchen with the housekeeper. Her stepfather did not allow her at the dinner table with him and her mother until she was ten. Though Dian's stepfather, a building contractor, seemed wealthy, she largely paid her own way through school. Once she worked as a machine operator in a factory.

Dian seldom spoke of her family to friends, and she carried a loathing for her childhood into her adult life. Long after Dian left the family home in California, she referred to her parents as "the Prices." She would spit on the ground whenever her stepfather's name was mentioned. When her Uncle Bert died, leaving Dian $50,000, Richard Price badgered her with cables to Rwanda, pressing her to contest the will for more money; after Dian's death he had her will overturned by a California court, claiming all her money for himself and his wife.

Her mother and stepfather tried desperately to thwart Dian's plans to go to Africa. They would not help her finance her lifelong dream to go on safari when she was twenty-eight. She borrowed against three years of her salary as an occupational therapist to go. And when she left the States three years later to begin her study of the mountain gorillas, her mother begged her not to go, and her stepfather threatened to stop her.

She chose to remain in the alpine rain forest, as alone as she had ever been. She chose to remain among the King Kong beasts whom the outside world still considered a symbol of savagery, watching their gentle, peaceful lives unfold.

Once Dian, watching Uncle Bert with his family, saw the gigantic male pluck a handful of white flowers with his huge black hands. As the young Digit ambled toward him, the silverback whisked the bouquet back and forth across the youngster's face. Digit chuckled and tumbled into Uncle Bert's lap, "much like a puppy wanting attention," Dian wrote. Digit rolled against the silverback, clutching himself in ecstasy as the big male tickled him with petals.

By the end of her first three months in Rwanda, Dian was following two gorilla groups regularly and observing another sporadically. She divided most of her time between Group 5's fifteen members, ranging on Visoke's southeastern slopes, and Group 4. Group 8, a family

of nine, all adult, shared Visoke's western slopes with Group 4.

Dian still could not approach them. Gorilla families guard carefully against intrusion. Each family has at least one member who serves as sentry, typically posted at the periphery of the group to watch for danger—a rival silverback or a human hunter. Gorilla groups seldom interact with other families, except when females transfer voluntarily out of their natal group to join the families of unrelated silverbacks or when rival silverbacks "raid" a neighboring family for females.

Adult gorillas will fight to the death defending their families. This is why poachers who may be seeking only one infant for the zoo trade must often kill all the adults in the family to capture the baby. Once Dian tracked one such poacher to his village; the man and his wives fled before her, leaving their small child behind.

At first Dian observed the animals from a distance, silently, hidden. Then slowly, over many months, she began to announce her presence. She imitated their contentment vocalizations, most of often the *naoom, naoom, naoom,* a sound like belching or deeply clearing the throat. She crunched wild celery stalks. She crouched, eyes averted, scratching herself loud and long, as gorillas do. Eventually she could come close enough to them to smell the scent of their bodies and see the ridges inside the roofs of their mouths when they yawned; at times she came close enough to distinguish, without binoculars, the cuticles of their black, humanlike fingernails.

She visited them daily; she learned to tell by the contour pressed into the leaves which animal had slept in a particular night nest, made from leaves woven into a bathtub shape on the ground. She knew the sound of each individual voice belching contentment when they were feeding. But it was more than two years before she knew the touch of their skin.

Peanuts, a young adult male in Group 8, was the first mountain gorilla to touch his fingers to hers. Dian was lying on her back among the foliage, her right arm outstretched, palm up. Peanuts looked at her hand intently; then he stood, extended his hand, and touched

her fingers for an instant. *National Geographic* photographer Bob Campbell snapped the shutter only a moment afterward: that the photo is blurry renders it dreamlike. The 250-pound gorilla's right hand still hangs in midair. Dian's eyes are open but unseeing, her lips parted, her left hand brought to her mouth, as if feeling for the lingering warmth of a kiss.

Peanuts pounded his chest with excitement and ran off to rejoin his group. Dian lingered after he left; she named the spot where they touched Fasi Ya Mkoni, "the Place of the Hands." With his touch, Peanuts opened his family to her; she became a part of the families she had observed so intimately for the past two years. Soon the gorillas would come forward and welcome her into their midst.

Digit was almost always the first member of Group 4 to greet her. "I received the impression that Digit really looked forward to the daily contacts," she wrote in her book. "If I was alone, he often invited play by flopping over on his back, waving stumpy legs in the air, and looking at me smilingly as if to say, 'How can you resist me?' "

At times she would be literally blanketed with gorillas, when a family would pull close around her like a black furry quilt. In one wonderful photo, Puck, a young female of Group 5, is reclining in back of Dian and, with the back of her left hand, touching Dian's cheek—the gesture of a mother caressing the cheek of a child.

Mothers let Dian hold their infants; silverbacks would groom her, parting her long dark hair with fingers thick as bananas, yet deft as a seamstress's touch. "I can't tell you how rewarding it is to be with them," Dian told a New York crowd gathered for a slide lecture in 1982. "Their trust, the cohesiveness, the tranquility . . ." Words failed her, and her hoarse, breathy voice broke. "It is really something."

Other field workers who joined Dian at Karisoke remember similar moments. Photographer Bob Campbell recalls how Digit would try to groom his sleeves and pants and, finding nothing groomable, would pluck at the hairs of his wrist; most of the people who worked there have pictures of themselves with young gorillas on their heads or in their laps.

But with Dian it was different. Ian Redmond, who first came to Karisoke in 1976, remembers one of the first times he accompanied Dian to observe Group 4. It was a reunion: Dian hadn't been out to visit the group for a while. "The animals filed past us, and each one paused and briefly looked into my face, just briefly. And then each one looked into Dian's eyes, at very close quarters, for half a minute or so. It seemed like each one was queuing up to stare into her face and remind themselves of her place with them. It was obvious they had a much deeper and stronger relationship with Dian than with any of the other workers."

In the early days Dian had the gorillas mostly to herself. It was in 1972 that Bob Campbell filmed what is arguably one of the most moving contacts between two species on record: Digit, though still a youngster, is huge. His head is more than twice the size of Dian's, his hands big enough to cover a dinner plate. He comes to her and with those enormous black hands gently takes her notebook, then her pen, and brings them to his flat, leathery nose. He gently puts them aside in the foliage and rolls over to snooze at Dian's side.

Once Dian spotted Group 4 on the opposite side of a steep ravine but knew she was not strong enough to cross it. Uncle Bert, seeing her, led the entire group across the ravine to her. This time Digit was last in line. "Then," wrote Dian, "he finally came right to me and gently touched my hair. . . . I wish I could have given them all something in return."

At times like these, Dian wept with joy. Hers was the triumph of one who has been chosen: wild gorillas would come to her.

The great intimacy of love is onlyness, of being the loved One. It is the kind of love most valued in Western culture; people choose only one "best" friend, one husband, one wife, one God. Even our God is a jealous one, demanding "Thou shalt have no other gods before Me."

This was a love Dian sought over and over again—as the only child of parents who did not place her first, as the paramour of a succession of married lovers. The love she sought most desperately was a jealous love, exclusive—not *agape*, the Godlike, spiritual love of all beings, not the uniform, brotherly love, *philia*. The love Dian sought was the love that singles out.

Digit singled Dian out. By the time he was nine he was more strongly attracted to her than were any of the other gorillas she knew. His only age-mates in his family, his half sisters, had left the group or been kidnaped. When Digit heard Dian belch-grunting a greeting, he would leave the company of his group to scamper to greet her. To Digit, Dian was the sibling playmate he lacked. And Dian recognized his longing as clearly as she knew her own image in a mirror.

Dian had had few playmates as a child. She had longed for a pet, but her stepfather wouldn't allow her to keep even a hamster a friend offered, because it was "dirty." He allowed her a single goldfish; she was devastated when it died and was never allowed another.

But Digit was no pet. "Dian's relationship with the gorillas is really the highest form of human-animal relationship," observed Ian Redmond. "With almost any other human-animal relationship, that involves feeding the animals or restraining the animals or putting them in an enclosure, or if you help an injured animal—you do something to the animal. Whereas Dian and the gorillas were on completely equal terms. It was nothing other than the desire to be together. And that's as pure as you can get."

When Digit was young, he and Dian played together like children. He would strut toward her, playfully whacking foliage; she would tickle him; he would chuckle and climb on her head. Digit was fascinated by any object Dian had with her: once she brought a chocolate bar to eat for lunch and accidentally dropped it into the hollow stump of a tree where she was sitting next to Digit. Half in jest, she asked him to get it back for her. "And according to script," she wrote her Louisville friend, Betty Schartzel, "Digit reached one long,

hairy arm into the hole and retrieved the candy bar." But the chocolate didn't appeal to him. "After one sniff he literally threw it back into the hole. The so-called 'wild gorillas' are really very discriminating in their tastes!"

Dian's thermoses, notebooks, gloves, and cameras were all worthy of investigation. Digit would handle these objects gently and with great concentration. Sometimes he handed them back to her. Once Dian brought Digit a hand mirror. He immediately approached it, propped up on his forearms, and sniffed the glass. Digit pursed his lips, cocked his head, and then uttered a long sigh. He reached behind the mirror in search of the body connected to the face. Finding nothing, he stared at his reflection for five minutes before moving away.

Dian took many photos of all the gorillas, but Digit was her favorite subject. When the Rwandan Office of Tourism asked Dian for a gorilla photo for a travel poster, the slide she selected was one of Digit. He is pictured holding a stick of wood he has been chewing, his shining eyes a mixture of innocence and inquiry. He looks directly into the camera, his lips parted and curved as if about to smile. "Come to meet him in Rwanda," exhorts the caption. When his poster began appearing in hotels, banks, and airports, "I could not help feeling that our privacy was on the verge of being invaded," Dian wrote.

Her relationship with Digit was one she did not intend to share. Hers was the loyalty and possessiveness of a silverback: what she felt for the gorillas, and especially Digit, was exclusive, passionate, and dangerous.

No animal, Dian believed, was truly safe in Africa. Africans see most animals as food, skins, money. "Dian had a compulsion to buy every animal she ever saw in Africa," remembers her friend Rosamond Carr, an American expatriate who lives in nearby Gisenyi, "to save it from torture." One day Dian, driving in her Combi van, saw some children on the roadside, swinging a rabbit by the ears. She took it from them, brought it back to camp, and built a spacious hutch for it. Another time it would be a chicken: visiting villagers sometimes brought one to camp, intending, of course, that it be eaten. Dian would keep it as a pet.

Dian felt compelled to protect the vulnerable, the innocent. Her first plan after high school had been to become a veterinarian; after failing chemistry and physics, she chose occupational therapy; with her degree, she worked for a decade with disabled children.

One day Dian came to the hotel in Gisenyi where Rosamond was working as a manager. Dian was holding a monkey. She had seen it at a market, packed in a carton. Rosamond remembers, "I look and see this rotten little face, this big ruff of hair, and I say, 'Dian. I'm sorry, you cannot have that monkey in this hotel!'" But Dian spent the night with the animal in her room anyway.

"Luckily for me, she left the next day. I have never seen anything like the mess. There were banana peels on the ceiling, sweet potatoes on the floor; it had broken the water bottle, the glasses had been smashed and had gone down the drain of the washbasin. And with that adorable animal she starts up the mountain."

Kima, as Dian named the monkey, proved no less destructive in camp. Full grown when Dian brought her, Kima bit people, urinated on Dian's typewriter, bit the head off all her matches, and terrorized students on their way to the latrine, leaping off the roof of Dian's cabin and biting them. Yet Dian loved her, built a hatchway allowing Kima free access to her cabin, bought her toys and dolls, and had her camp cook prepare special foods for her. Kima especially liked french fries, though she discarded the crunchy outsides and ate only the soft centers. "Everyone in camp absolutely hated that animal," Rosamond says. "But Dian loved her."

Another of Dian's rescue attempts occurred one day when she was driving down the main street of Gisenyi on a provisioning trip. Spotting a man walking a rack-ribbed dog on a leash, she slammed on the brakes. "I want to buy that dog," she announced. The Rwandan protested that it was not for sale. She got out of her Combi, lifted up the sickly animal, and drove off with it.

Rosamond learned of the incident from a friend named Rita who worked at the American embassy. For it was to Rita's home that the Rwandan man returned that afternoon to explain why the dog, which he had been taking to the vet for worming, had never made it to its destination. "Madame, a crazy woman stopped and stole your dog, and she went off with it in a gray van."

"Rita got her dog back," Rosamond continues. Dian had taken it to the hotel where she was staying overnight; when Rita tracked her down, she was feeding the dog steak in her room. "And that was typical of Dian. She had to save every animal she saw. And they loved her— every animal I ever saw her with simply loved her."

When Dian first came to Karisoke, elephants frequently visited her camp. Rosamond used to camp with Dian in those early days before the cabin was built. The elephants came so close that she remembers hearing their stomachs rumble at night. Once she asked Dian if she undressed at night. "Of course not, are you crazy?" Dian replied. "I go to bed in my blue jeans. I have to get up six times at night to see what's happening outside."

One night an elephant selected Dian's tent pole as a scratching post. Another time a wild elephant accepted a banana from Dian's hand. The tiny antelopes called duiker often wandered through camp; one became so tame it would follow Dian's laying hens around. A family of seven bushbucks adopted Karisoke as home, as did an ancient bull buffalo she named Mzee.

Dian's camp provided refuge from the poacher-infested, cattle-filled forest. For centuries the pygmylike Batwa had used these volcanic slopes as a hunting ground. And as Rwanda's human population exploded, the Virungas were the only source of bush meat left, and poaching pressure increased. Today you will find no elephants in these forests; they have all been killed by poachers seeking ivory.

If you look at the Parc National des Volcans from the air, the five volcanoes, their uppermost slopes puckered like the lips of an old woman, seem to be standing on tiptoe to withdraw from the flood of cultivation and people below. Rwanda is the most densely populated country in Africa, with more than 500 people per square mile. Almost every inch is cultivated, and more than 23,000 new families need new land each year. In rural Rwanda outside of the national parks, if you wander from a path you are more likely to step in human excrement than the scat of a wild animal. The Parc des Volcans is thoroughly ringed with *shambas*, little farm plots growing bananas, peanuts, beans, manioc, and with fields of pyrethrum, daisylike flowers cultivated as a natural insecticide for export. The red earth of the fields seems to bleed from all the human scraping.

The proud, tall Batutsi have few other areas to pasture their cattle, the pride of their existence; everywhere else are shambas. From the start Dian tried to evict the herders from the park, kidnaping their cows and sometimes even shooting them. On the Rwandan side of the mountain, cattle herds were so concentrated, she wrote, that "many areas were reduced to dustbowls." She felt guilty, but the cattle destroyed habitat for the gorillas and other wild animals the park was supposed to protect. Worse were the snares set by the Batwa. Many nights she stayed awake nursing a duiker or bushbuck whose leg had been mangled in a trap. Dian lived in fear that one of the gorillas would be next.

The Batwa do not eat gorillas; gorillas fall victim to their snares, set for antelope, by accident. But the Batwa have for centuries hunted gorillas, to use the fingers and genitals of silverbacks in magic rituals and potions. And now the hunters found a new reason to kill gorillas: they learned that Westerners would pay high prices for gorillas heads for trophies, gorilla hands for ashtrays, and gorilla youngsters for zoos.

In March 1969, only eighteen months into her study, a friend in Ruhengeri came to camp to tell Dian that a young gorilla had been captured from the southern slopes of Mount Karisimbi. All ten adults in the group had been killed so that the baby could be taken for display in the Cologne Zoo. The capture had been approved by the park conservator, who was paid handsomely for his cooperation. But something had gone wrong: the baby gorilla was dying.

Dian took the baby in, a three- to four-year-old female she named Coco. The gorilla's wrists and feet had been bound with wire to a pole when the hunters carried her away from the corpses of her family; she had spent two or three weeks in a coffinlike crate, fed only corn, bananas, and bread, before Dian came to her rescue. When Dian left the park conservator's office, she was sure the baby would die. She slept with Coco in her bed, awakening amid pools of the baby's watery feces.

A week later came another sick orphan, a four- to five-year-old female also intended for the zoo. Her family had shared Karisimbi's southern slope with Coco's; trying to defend the baby from capture, all eight members of her group had died. Dian named this baby Pucker for the huge sores that gave her face a puckered look.

It took Dian two months to nurse the babies back to health. She transformed half her cabin into a giant gorilla playpen filled with fresh foliage. She began to take them into the forest with her, encouraging them to climb trees and vines. She was making plans to release them into a wild group when the park conservator made the climb to camp. He and his porters descended with both gorillas in a box and shipped them to the zoo in West Germany. Coco and Pucker died there nine years later, within a month of one another, at an age when, in the wild, they would have been mothering youngsters the same age they had been when they were captured.

Thereafter Dian's antipoaching tactics became more elaborate. She learned from a friend in Ruhengeri that the trade in gorilla trophies was flourishing; he had counted twenty-three gorilla heads for sale in that town in one year. As loyal as a silverback, as wary as a sentry, Dian and her staff patrolled the forest for snares and destroyed the gear poachers left behind in their temporary shelters.

Yet each day dawned to the barking of poachers' dogs. A field report she submitted to the National Geographic Society in 1972 gave the results of the most recent gorilla census: though her study groups were still safe, the surrounding areas of the park's five volcanoes were literally under siege. On Mount Muhavura census workers saw convoys of smugglers leaving the park every forty-five minutes. Only thirteen gorillas were left on the slopes of Muhavura. On neighboring Mount Gahinga no gorillas were left. In the two previous years, census workers had found fresh remains of slain silverbacks. And even the slopes of Dian's beloved Karisimbi, she wrote, were covered with poachers' traps and scarred by heavily used cattle trails; "poachers and their dogs were heard throughout the region."

It was that same year, 1972, that a maturing Digit assumed the role of sentry of Group 4. In this role he usually stayed on the periphery of the group to watch for danger; he would be the first to defend his family if they were attacked. Once when Dian was walking behind her Rwandan tracker, the dark form of a gorilla burst from the bush. The male stood upright to his full height of five and a half feet; his jaw gaped open, exposing black gums and three-inch canines as he uttered two long, piercing screams at the terrified tracker. Dian stepped into view, shoving the tracker down behind her, and stared into the animal's face. They recognized each other immediately. Digit dropped to all fours and ran back to his group.

Dian wrote that Digit's new role made him more serious. No longer was he a youngster with the freedom to roll and wrestle with his playmate. But Dian was still special to him. Once when Dian went out to visit the group during a downpour, the young silverback emerged from the gloom and stood erect before his crouching human friend. He pulled a stalk of wild celery—a favorite gorilla food that Digit had seen Dian munch on many times—peeled it with his great hands, and dropped the stalk at her feet like an offering. Then he turned and left.

As sentry, Digit sustained the wound that sapped his strength for the next two years. Dian did not observe the fight, but she concluded from tracking clues that Digit had warded off a raid by the silverback leader of Group 8, who had previously kidnaped females from Group 4. Dian cringed each time she heard him coughing and retching. Digit sat alone, hunched and indifferent. Dian worried that his growth would be retarded. In her field notes she described his mood as one of deep dejection.

This was a time when Dian was nursing wounds of her own. She had hoped that Bob Campbell, the photographer, would marry her, as Hugo van Lawick had married Jane; but Bob left Karisoke for the last time at the end of May 1972, to return to his wife in Nairobi. Then she had a long affair with a Belgian doctor, who left her to marry the woman he had been living with. Dian's health worsened. Her trips overseas for primatology conferences and lecture tours were usually paired with hospital visits to repair broken bones and heal her fragile lungs. She feared she had tuberculosis. She noted her pain in her diary telegraphically: "Very lung-sick." "Coughing up blood." "Scum in urine."

When she was in her twenties, despite her asthma, Dian seemed as strong as an Amazon. Her large-boned but lanky six-foot frame had a coltish grace; one of her suitors, another man who nearly married her, described her as "one hell of an attractive woman," with masses of long dark hair and "eyes like a Spanish dancer." But now Dian felt old and ugly and weak. She used henna on her hair to try to cover the gray. (Dian told a friend that her mother's only comment about her first appearance on a National Geographic TV special was, "Why did you dye your hair that awful orange color?") In letters to friends Dian began to sign off as "The Fossil." She referred to her house as "the Mausoleum." In a cardboard album she made for friends from construction paper and magazine cutouts, titled "The Sage of Karisoke," she pasted a picture of a mummified corpse sitting upright on a bed. She realized that many of her students disliked her. Under the picture Dian printed a caption: "Despite their protests, she stays on."

By 1976 Dian was spending less and less time in the field. Her lungs and legs had grown too weak for daily contacts; she had hairline fractures on her feet. And she was overwhelmed with paperwork. She became increasingly testy with her staff, and her students feared to knock on her door. Her students wouldn't even see her for weeks at a time, but they would hear her pounding on her battered Olivetti, a task from which she would pause only to take another drag on an Impala *filtrée* or to munch sunflower seeds. Her students were taking the field data on the gorillas by this time: when Dian went out to see the groups, she simply visited with them.

One day, she ventured out along a trail as slippery as fresh buffalo dung to find Group 4. By the time she found them, the rain was driving. They were huddled against the downpour. She saw Digit sitting about thirty feet apart from the group. She wanted to join him but resisted; she now feared that her early contact with him had made him too human-oriented, more vulnerable to poachers. So she settled among the soaking foliage several yards from the main group. She could barely make

out the humped black forms in the heavy mist.

On sunny days there is no more beautiful place on earth than the Virungas; the sunlight makes the *Senecio* trees sparkle like fireworks in midexplosion; the gnarled old *Hagenias,* trailing lacy beards of gray-green lichen and epiphytic ferns, look like friendly wizards, and the leaves of palms seem like hands upraised in praise. But rain transforms the forest into a cold, gray hell. You stare out, tunnel-visioned, from the hood of a dripping raincape, at a wet landscape cloaked as if in evil enchantment. Each drop of rain sends a splintering chill into the flesh, and your muscles clench with cold; you can cut yourself badly on the razorlike cutty grass and not even feel it. Even the gorillas, with their thick black fur coats, look miserable and lonely in the rain.

Minutes after she arrived, Dian felt an arm around her shoulders. "I looked

up into Digit's warm, gentle brown eyes," she wrote in *Gorillas in the Mist.* He gazed at her thoughtfully and patted her head, then sat by her side. As the rain faded to mist, she laid her head down in Digit's lap.

On January 1, 1978, Dian's head tracker returned to camp late in the day. He had not been able to find Group 4. But he had found blood along their trail.

Ian Redmond found Digit's body the next day. His head and hands had been hacked off. There were five spear wounds in his body.

Ian did not see Dian cry that day. She was almost supercontrolled, he remembers. No amount of keening, no incantation or prayer could release the pain of her loss. But years later she filled a page of her diary with a single word, written over and over: "Digit Digit Digit Digit . . ."

# The Mind of the Chimpanzee

## Jane Goodall

Often I have gazed into a chimpanzee's eyes and wondered what was going on behind them. I used to look into Flo's, she so old, so wise. What did she remember of her young days? David Greybeard had the most beautiful eyes of them all, large and lustrous, set wide apart. They somehow expressed his whole personality, his serene self-assurance, his inherent dignity—and, from time to time, his utter determination to get his way. For a long time I never liked to look a chimpanzee straight in the eye—I assumed that, as is the case with most primates, this would be interpreted as a threat or at least as a breach of good manners. No so. As long as one looks with gentleness, without arrogance, a chimpanzee will understand, and may even return the look. And then—or such is my fantasy—it is as though the eyes are windows into the mind. Only the glass is opaque so that the mystery can never be fully revealed.

I shall never forget my meeting with Lucy, an eight-year-old home-raised chimpanzee. She came and sat beside me on the sofa and, with her face very close to mine, searched in my eyes—for what? Perhaps she was looking for signs of mistrust, dislike, or fear, since many people must have been somewhat disconcerted when, for the first time, they came face to face with a grown chimpanzee. Whatever Lucy read in my eyes clearly satisfied her for she suddenly put one arm round my neck and gave me a generous and very chimp-like kiss, her mouth wide open and laid over mine. I was accepted.

For a long time after that encounter I was profoundly disturbed. I had been at Gombe for about fifteen years then and I was quite familiar with chimpanzees in the wild. But Lucy, having grown up as a human child, was like a changeling, her essential chimpanzeeness overlaid by the various human behaviours she had acquired over the years. No longer purely chimp yet eons away from humanity, she was man-made, some other kind of being. I watched, amazed, as she opened the refrigerator and various cupboards, found bottles and a glass, then poured herself a gin and tonic. She took the drink to the TV, turned the set on, flipped from one channel to another then, as though in disgust, turned it off again. She selected a glossy magazine from the table and, still carrying her drink, settled in a comfortable chair. Occasionally, as she leafed through the magazine she identified something she saw, using the signs of ASL, the American Sign Language used by the deaf. I, of course, did not understand, but my hostess, Jane Temerlin (who was also Lucy's 'mother'), translated: 'That dog,' Lucy commented, pausing at a photo of a small white poodle. She turned the page. 'Blue,' she declared, pointing then signing as she gazed at a picture of a lady advertising some kind of soap powder and wearing a brilliant blue dress. And finally, after some vague hand movements—perhaps signed mutterings—'This Lucy's, this mine,' as she closed the magazine and laid it on her lap. She had just been taught, Jane told me, the use of the possessive pronouns during the thrice weekly ASL lessons she was receiving at the time.

The book written by Lucy's human 'father,' Maury Temerlin, was entitled *Lucy, Growing Up Human*. And in fact, the chimpanzee is more like us than is any other living creature. There is close resemblance in the physiology of our two species and genetically, in the structure of the DNA, chimpanzees and humans differ by only just over one per cent. This is why medical research uses chimpanzees as experimental animals when they need substitutes for humans in the testing of some drug or vaccine. Chimpanzees can be infected with just about all known human infectious diseases including those, such as hepatitis B and AIDS, to which other non-human animals (except gorillas, orangutans and gibbons) are immune. There are equally striking similarities between humans and chimpanzees in the anatomy and wiring of the brain and nervous system, and—although many scientists have been reluctant to admit to this—in social behaviour, intellectual ability, and the emotions. The notion of an evolutionary continuity in physical structure from pre-human ape to modern man has long been morally acceptable to most scientists. That the same might hold good for mind was generally considered an absurd hypothesis—particularly by those who used, and often misused, animals in their laboratories. It is, after all, convenient to believe that the creature you are using, while it may react in disturbingly human-like ways, is, in fact, merely a mindless and, above all, unfeeling, 'dumb' animal.

When I began my study at Gombe in 1960 it was not permissible—at least not in ethological circles—to talk about an animal's mind. Only humans had minds. Nor was it quite proper to talk about animal personality. Of course everyone knew that they *did* have their own unique characters—everyone who had ever owned a dog or other pet was aware of that. But ethologists, striving to make theirs a 'hard' science, shied away from the task of trying to explain such things objectively. One respected ethologist, while acknowledging that there was 'variability between individual animals,' wrote that it was best that this fact be 'swept under the carpet.' At that time ethological carpets fairly bulged with all that was hidden beneath them.

How naive I was. As I had not had an undergraduate science education I didn't realize that animals were not supposed to have personalities, or to think, or to feel emotions or pain. I had no idea that it would have been more appropriate to assign each of the chimpanzees a number rather than a name when I got to know him or her. I didn't realize that it was not scientific to discuss behaviour in terms of motivation or purpose. And no one had told me that terms such as *childhood* and *adolescence* were uniquely human phases of the life cycle, culturally determined, not to be used when referring to young chimpanzees. Not knowing, I freely made use of all those forbidden terms and concepts in my initial attempt to describe, to the best of my ability, the amazing things I had observed at Gombe.

I shall never forget the response of a group of ethologists to some remarks I made at an erudite seminar. I described how Figan, as an adolescent, had learned to stay behind in camp after senior males had left, so that we could give him a few bananas for himself. On the first occasion he had, upon seeing the fruits, uttered loud, delighted food calls: whereupon a couple of the older males had charged back, chased after Figan, and taken his bananas. And then, coming to the point of the story, I explained how, on the next occasion, Figan had actually suppressed his calls. We could hear little sounds, in his throat, but so quiet that none of the others could have heard them. Other young chimps, to whom we tried to smuggle fruit without the knowledge of their elders, never learned such self-control. With shrieks of glee they would fall to, only to be robbed of their booty when the big

males charged back. I had expected my audience to be as fascinated and impressed as I was. I had hoped for an exchange of views about the chimpanzee's undoubted intelligence. Instead there was a chill silence, after which the chairman hastily changed the subject. Needless to say, after being thus snubbed, I was very reluctant to contribute any comments, at any scientific gatherings, for a very long time. Looking back, I suspect that everyone was interested, but it was, of course, not permissible to present a mere 'anecdote' as evidence for anything.

The editorial comments on the first paper I wrote for publication demanded that every *he* or *she* be replaced with *it*, and every *who* be replaced with *which*. Incensed, I, in my turn, crossed out the *its* and *whichs* and scrawled back the original pronouns. As I had no desire to carve a niche for myself in the world of science, but simply wanted to go on living among and learning about chimpanzees, the possible reaction of the editor of the learned journal did not trouble me. In fact I won that round: the paper when finally published did confer upon the chimpanzees the dignity of their appropriate genders and properly upgraded them from the status of mere 'things' to essential Beingness.

However, despite my somewhat truculent attitude, I did want to learn, and I was sensible of my incredible good fortune in being admitted to Cambridge. I wanted to get my PhD, if only for the sake of Louis Leakey and the other people who had written letters in support of my admission. And how lucky I was to have, as my supervisor, Robert Hinde. Not only because I thereby benefitted from his brilliant mind and clear thinking, but also because I doubt that I could have found a teacher more suited to my particular needs and personality. Gradually he was able to cloak me with at least some of the trappings of a scientist. Thus although I continued to hold to most of my convictions—that animals had personalities; that they could feel happy or sad or fearful; that they could feel pain; that they could strive towards planned goals and achieve greater success if they were highly motivated—I soon realized

that these personal convictions were, indeed, difficult to prove. It was best to be circumspect—at least until I had gained some credentials and credibility. And Robert gave me wonderful advice on how best to tie up some of my more rebellious ideas with scientific ribbon. 'You can't *know* that Fifi was jealous,' had admonished on one occasion. We argued a little. And then: 'Why don't you just say *If Fifi were a human child we would say she was jealous.*' I did.

It is not easy to study emotions even when the subjects are human. I know how I feel if I am sad or happy or angry, and if a friend tells me that he is feeling sad, happy or angry, I assume that his feelings are similar to mine. But of course I cannot know. As we try to come to grips with the emotions of beings progressively more different from ourselves the task, obviously, becomes increasingly difficult. If we ascribe human emotions to non-human animals we are accused of being anthropomorphic—a cardinal sin in ethology. But is it so terrible? If we test the effect of drugs on chimpanzees because they are biologically so similar to ourselves, if we accept that there are dramatic similarities in chimpanzee and human brain and nervous system, is it not logical to assume that there will be similarities also in at least the more basic feelings, emotions, moods of the two species?

In fact, all those who have worked long and closely with chimpanzees have no hesitation in asserting that chimps experience emotions similar to those which in ourselves we label pleasure, joy, sorrow, anger, boredom and so on. Some of the emotional states of the chimpanzee are so obviously similar to ours that even an inexperienced observer can understand what is going on. An infant who hurls himself screaming to the ground, face contorted, hitting out with his arms at any nearby object, banging his head, is clearly having a tantrum. Another youngster, who gambols around his mother, turning somersaults, pirouetting and, every so often, rushing up to her and tumbling into her lap, patting her or pulling her hand towards him in a request for tickling, is obviously filled with *joie de vivre*. There are few observers who would not unhesitatingly ascribe his behaviour to a happy, care-free state of well-being. And one cannot watch chimpanzee infants for long without realizing that they have the same emotional need for affection and reassurance as human children. An adult male, reclining in the shade after a good meal, reaching benignly to play with an infant or idly groom an adult female, is clearly in a good mood. When he sits with bristling hair, glaring at his subordinates and threatening them, with irritated gestures, if they come too close, he is clearly feeling cross and grumpy. We make these judgements because the similarity of so much of a chimpanzee's behaviour to our own permits us to empathize.

It is hard to empathize with emotions we have not experienced. I can image, to some extent, the pleasure of a female chimpanzee during the act of procreation. The feelings of her male partner are beyond my knowledge—as are those of the human male in the same context. I have spent countless hours watching mother chimpanzees interacting with their infants. But not until I had an infant of my own did I begin to understand the basic, powerful instinct of mother-love. If someone accidentally did something to frighten Grub, or threaten his well-being in any way, I felt a surge of quite irrational anger. How much more easily could I then understand the feelings of the chimpanzee mother who furiously waves her arm and barks in threat at an individual who approaches her infant too closely, or at a playmate who inadvertently hurts her child. And it was not until I knew the numbing grief that gripped me after the death of my second husband that I could even begin to appreciate the despair and sense of loss that can cause young chimps to pine away and die when they lose their mothers.

Empathy and intuition can be of tremendous value as we attempt to understand certain complex behavioral interactions, provided that the behaviour, as it occurs, is recorded precisely and objectively. Fortunately I have seldom found it difficult to record facts in an orderly manner even during times of powerful emotional involvement. And "knowing" intuitively how a chimpanzee is feeling—after an attack,

for example—may help one to understand what happens next. We should not be afraid at least to try to make use of our close evolutionary relationship with the chimpanzees in our attempts to interpret complex behaviour.

Today, as in Darwin's time, it is once again fashionable to speak of and study the animal mind. This change came about gradually, and was, at least in part, due to the information collected during careful studies of animal societies in the field. As these observations became widely known, it was impossible to brush aside the complexities of social behaviour that were revealed in species after species. The untidy clutter under the ethological carpets was brought out and examined, piece by piece. Gradually it was realized that parsimonious explanations of apparently intelligent behaviours were often misleading. This led to a succession of experiments that, taken together, clearly prove that many intellectual abilities that had been thought unique to humans were actually present, though in a less highly developed form, in other, non-human beings. Particularly, of course, in the non-human primates and especially in chimpanzees.

When first I began to read about human evolution, I learned that one of the hallmarks of our own species was that we, and only we, were capable of making tools. *Man the Toolmaker* was an oft-cited definition—and this despite the careful and exhaustive research of Wolfgang Kohler and Robert Yerkes on the tool-using and tool-making abilities of chimpanzees. Those studies, carried out independently in the early twenties, were received with scepticism. Yet both Kohler and Yerkes were respected scientists, and both had a profound understanding of chimpanzee behaviour. Indeed, Kohler's descriptions of the personalities and behaviour of the various individuals in his colony, published in his book *The Mentality of Apes,* remain some of the most vivid and colourful ever written. And his experiments, showing how chimpanzees could stack boxes, then climb the unstable constructions to reach fruit suspended from the ceiling, or join two short sticks to make a pole long enough to rake in fruit otherwise out of reach, have become classic, ap-

pearing in almost all textbooks dealing with intelligent behaviour in non-human animals.

By the time systematic observations of tool-using came from Gombe those pioneering studies had been largely forgotten. Moreover, it was one thing to know that humanized chimpanzees in the lab could use implements: it was quite another to find that this was a naturally occurring skill in the wild. I well remember writing to Louis about my first observations, describing how David Greybeard not only used bits of straw to fish for termites but actually stripped leaves from a stem and thus *made* a tool. And I remember too receiving the now oft-quoted telegram he sent in response to my letter: "Now we must redefine *tool,* redefine *Man,* or accept chimpanzees as humans."

There were initially, a few scientists who attempted to write off the termiting observations, even suggesting that I had taught the chimps! By and large, though, people were fascinated by the information and by the subsequent observations of the other contexts in which the Gombe chimpanzees used objects as tools. And there were only a few anthropologists who objected when I suggested that the chimpanzees probably passed their tool-using traditions from one generation to the next, through observations, imitation and practice, so that each population might be expected to have its own unique tool-using culture. Which, incidentally, turns out to be quite true. And when I described how one chimpanzee, Mike, spontaneously solved a new problem by using a tool (he broke off a stick to knock a banana to the ground when he was too nervous to actually take it from my hand) I don't believe there were any raised eyebrows in the scientific community. Certainly I was not attacked viciously, as were Kohler and Yerkes, for suggesting that humans were not the only beings capable of reasoning and insight.

The mid-sixties saw the start of a project that, along with other similar research, was to teach us a great deal about the chimpanzee mind. This was Project Washoe, conceived by Trixie and Allen Gardner. They purchased an infant chimpanzee and began to teach her the signs of ASL, the American Sign Language used by the deaf. Twenty years earlier another husband and wife team, Richard and Cathy Hayes, had tried, with an almost total lack of success, to teach a young chimp, Vikki, to talk. The Hayes's undertaking taught us a lot about the chimpanzee mind, but Vikki, although she did well in IQ tests, and was clearly an intelligent youngster, could not learn human speech. The Gardners, however, achieved spectacular success with their pupil, Washoe. Not only did she learn signs easily, but she quickly began to string them together in meaningful ways. It was clear that each sign evoked, in her mind, a mental image of the object it represented. If, for example, she was asked, in sign language, to fetch an apple, she would go and locate an apple that was out of sight in another room.

Other chimps entered the project, some starting their lives in deaf signing families before joining Washoe. And finally Washoe adopted an infant, Loulis. He came from a lab where no thought of teaching signs had ever penetrated. When he was with Washoe he was given no lessons in language acquisition—not by humans, anyway. Yet by the time he was eight years old he had made fifty-eight signs in their correct contexts. How did he learn them? Mostly, it seems, by imitating the behaviour of Washoe and the other three signing chimps, Dar, Moja and Tatu. Sometimes, though, he received tuition from Washoe herself. One day, for example, she began to swagger about bipedally, hair bristling, signing *food! food! food!* in great excitement. She had seen a human approaching with a bar of chocolate. Loulis, only eighteen months old, watched passively. Suddenly Washoe stopped her swaggering, went over to him, took his hand, and moulded the sign for *food* (fingers pointing towards mouth). Another time, in a similar context, she made the sign for *chewing gum*—but with *her* hand on *his* body. On a third occasion Washoe, apropos of nothing, picked up a small chair, took it over to Loulis, set it down in front of him, and very distinctly made the *chair* sign three times, watching him closely as she did so. The two food signs be-

came incorporated into Loulis's vocabulary but the sign for chair did not. Obviously the priorities of a young chimp are similar to those of a human child!

When news of Washoe's accomplishments first hit the scientific community it immediately provoked a storm of bitter protest. It implied that chimpanzees were capable of mastering a human language, and this, in turn, indicated mental powers of generalization, abstraction and concept-formation as well as an ability to understand and use abstract symbols. And these intellectual skills were surely the prerogatives of *Homo sapiens*. Although there were many who were fascinated and excited by the Gardners' findings, there were many more who denounced the whole project, holding that the data was suspect, the methodology sloppy, and the conclusions not only misleading, but quite preposterous. The controversy inspired all sorts of other language projects. And, whether the investigators were sceptical to start with and hoped to disprove the Gardners' work, or whether they were attempting to demonstrate the same thing in a new way, their research provided additional information about the chimpanzee's mind.

And so, with new incentive, psychologists began to test the mental abilities of chimpanzees in a variety of different ways; again and again the results confirmed that their minds are uncannily like our own. It had long been held that only humans were capable of what is called 'cross-modal transfer of information'—in other words, if you shut your eyes and someone allows you to feel a strangely shaped potato, you will subsequently be able to pick it out from other differently shaped potatoes simply by looking at them. And vice versa. It turned out that chimpanzees can 'know' with their eyes what they 'feel' with their fingers in just the same way. In fact, we now know that some other non-human primates can do the same thing. I expect all kinds of creatures have the same ability.

Then it was proved, experimentally and beyond doubt, that chimpanzees could recognize themselves in mirrors—that they had, therefore, some kind of self-concept. In fact, Washoe, some

years previously, had already demonstrated the ability when she spontaneously identified herself in the mirror, staring at her image and making her name sign. But that observation was merely anecdotal. The proof came when chimpanzees who had been allowed to play with mirrors were, while anaesthetized, dabbed with spots of odourless paint in places, such as the ears or the top of the head, that they could see only in the mirror. When they woke they were not only fascinated by their spotted images, but immediately investigated, with their fingers, the dabs of paint.

The fact that chimpanzees have excellent memories surprised no one. Everyone, after all, has been brought up to believe that 'an elephant never forgets' so why should a chimpanzee be any different? The fact that Washoe spontaneously gave the name-sign of Beatrice Gardner, her surrogate mother, when she saw her after a separation of eleven years was no greater an accomplishment than the amazing memory shown by dogs who recognize their owners after separations of almost as long—and the chimpanzee has a much longer life span than a dog. Chimpanzees can plan ahead, too, at least as regards the immediate future. This, in fact, is well illustrated at Gombe, during the termiting season: often an individual prepares a tool for use on a termite mound that is several hundred yards away and absolutely out of sight.

This is not the place to describe in detail the other cognitive abilities that have been studied in laboratory chimpanzees. Among other accomplishments chimpanzees possess pre-mathematical skills: they can, for example, readily differentiate between *more* and *less*. They can classify things into specific categories according to a given criterion—thus they have no difficulty in separating a pile of food into *fruits* and *vegetables* on one occasion, and, on another, dividing the same pile of food into *large* versus *small* items, even though this requires putting some vegetables with some fruits. Chimpanzees who have been taught a language can combine signs creatively in order to describe objects for which they have no symbol. Washoe, for example, puzzled her caretakers by asking, repeatedly, for a *rock berry*. Eventually it transpired that she was referring to Brazil nuts which she had encountered for the first time a while before. Another language-trained chimp described a cucumber as a *green banana*, and another referred to an Alka-Seltzer as a *listen drink*. They can even invent signs. Lucy, as she got older, had to be put on a leash for her outings. One day, eager to set off but having no sign for *leash*, she signalled her wishes by holding a crooked index finger to the ring on her collar. This sign became part of her vocabulary. Some chimpanzees love to draw, and especially to paint. Those who have learned sign language sometimes spontaneously label their works, 'This [is] apple'—or bird, or sweetcorn, or whatever. The fact that the paintings often look, to our eyes, remarkably unlike the objects depicted by the artists either means that the chimpanzees are poor draughtsmen or that we have much to learn regarding ape-style representational art!

People sometimes ask why chimpanzees have evolved such complex intellectual powers when their lives in the wild are so simple. The answer is, of course, that their lives in the wild are not so simple! They use—and need—all their mental skills during normal day-to-day life in their complex society. They are always having to make choices—where to go, or with whom to travel. They need highly developed social skills—particularly those males who are ambitious to attain high positions in the dominance hierarchy. Low-ranking chimpanzees must learn deception—to conceal their intentions or to do things in secret—if they are to get their way in the presence of their superiors. Indeed, the study of chimpanzees in the wild suggests that their intellectual abilities evolved, over the millennia, to help them cope with daily life. And now, the solid core of data concerning chimpanzee intellect collected so carefully in the lab setting provides a background against which to evaluate the many examples of intelligent, rational behaviour that we see in the wild.

It is easier to study intellectual prowess in the lab where, through carefully devised tests and judicious use of rewards, the chimpanzees can be encouraged to exert themselves, to stretch their minds to the limit. It is more meaningful to study the subject in the wild, but much harder. It is more meaningful because we can better understand the environmental pressures that led to the evolution of intellectual skills in chimpanzee societies. It is harder because, in the wild, almost all behaviours are confounded by countless variables; years of observing, recording and analysing take the place of contrived testing; sample size can often be counted on the fingers of one hand; the only experiments are nature's own, and only time— eventually—may replicate them.

In the wild a single observation may prove of utmost significance, providing a clue to some hitherto puzzling aspect of behaviour, a key to the understanding of, for example, a changed relationship. Obviously it is crucial to see as many incidents of this sort as possible. During the early years of my study at Gombe it became apparent that one person alone could never learn more than a fraction of what was going on in a chimpanzee community at any given time. And so, from 1964 onwards, I gradually built up a research team to help in the gathering of information about the behaviour of our closest living relatives.

# Dim Forest, Bright Chimps

*In the rain forest of Ivory Coast, chimpanzees meet
the challenge of life by hunting cooperatively
and using crude tools*

**Christophe Boesch and
Hedwige Boesch-Achermann**

Taï National Park, Ivory Coast, December 3, 1985. Drumming, barking, and screaming, chimps rush through the undergrowth, little more than black shadows. Their goal is to join a group of other chimps noisily clustering around Brutus, the dominant male of this seventy-member chimpanzee community. For a few moments, Brutus, proud and self-confident, stands fairly still, holding a shocked, barely moving red colobus monkey in his hand. Then he begins to move through the group, followed closely by his favorite females and most of the adult males. He seems to savor this moment of uncontested superiority, the culmination of a hunt high up in the canopy. But the victory is not his alone. Cooperation is essential to capturing one of these monkeys, and Brutus will break apart and share this highly prized delicacy with most of the main participants of the hunt and with the females. Recipients of large portions will, in turn, share more or less generously with their offspring, relatives, and friends.

In 1979, we began a long-term study of the previously unknown chimpanzees of Taï National Park, 1,600 square miles of tropical rain forest in the Republic of the Ivory Coast (Côte d'Ivoire). Early

on, we were most interested in the chimps' use of natural hammers—branches and stones—to crack open the five species of hard-shelled nuts that are abundant here. A sea otter lying on its back, cracking an abalone shell with a rock, is a familiar picture, but no primate had ever before been observed in the wild using stones as hammers. East Africa's savanna chimps, studied for decades by Jane Goodall in Gombe, Tanzania, use twigs to extract ants and termites from their nests or honey from a bees' nest, but they have never been seen using hammerstones.

As our work progressed, we were surprised by the many ways in which the life of the Taï forest chimpanzees differs from that of their savanna counterparts, and as evidence accumulated, differences in how the two populations hunt proved the most intriguing. Jane Goodall had found that chimpanzees hunt monkeys, antelope, and wild pigs, findings confirmed by Japanese biologist Toshida Nishida, who conducted a long-term study 120 miles south of Gombe, in the Mahale Mountains. So we were not surprised to discover that the Taï chimps eat meat. What intrigued us was the degree to which they hunt cooperatively. In 1953 Raymond Dart proposed

that group hunting and cooperation were key ingredients in the evolution of *Homo sapiens*. The argument has been modified considerably since Dart first put it forward, and group hunting has also been observed in some social carnivores (lions and African wild dogs, for instance), and even some birds of prey. Nevertheless, many anthropologists still hold that hunting cooperatively and sharing food played a central role in the drama that enabled early hominids, some 1.8 million years ago, to develop the social systems that are so typically human.

We hoped that what we learned about the behavior of forest chimpanzees would shed new light on prevailing theories of human evolution. Before we could even begin, however, we had to habituate a community of chimps to our presence. Five long years passed before we were able to move with them on their daily trips through the forest, of which "our" group appeared to claim some twelve square miles. Chimpanzees are alert and shy animals, and the limited field of view in the rain forest—about sixty-five feet at best—made finding them more difficult. We had to rely on sound, mostly their vocalizations and drumming on trees. Males often drum regularly while moving through the forest: pant-hooting, they draw near a big buttress tree; then, at full speed they fly over the buttress, hitting it repeatedly with their hands and feet. Such drumming may resound more than half a mile in the forest. In the beginning, our ignorance about how they moved and who was drumming led to failure more often than not, but eventually we learned that the dominant males drummed during the day to let other group members know the direction of travel. On some days, however, intermittent drumming about dawn was the only signal for the whole day. If we were out of earshot at the time, we were often reduced to guessing.

During these difficult early days, one feature of the chimps' routine proved to be our salvation: nut cracking is a noisy business. So noisy, in fact, that in the early days of French colonial rule, one officer apparently even proposed the theory that some unknown tribe was forging iron in the impenetrable and dangerous jungle.

Guided by the sounds made by the chimps as they cracked open nuts, which they often did for hours at a time, we were gradually able to get within sixty feet of the animals. We still seldom saw the chimps themselves (they fled if we came too close), but even so, the evidence left after a session of nut cracking taught us a great deal about what types of nuts they were eating, what sorts of hammer and anvil tools they were using, and—thanks to the very distinctive noise a nut makes when it finally splits open—how many hits were needed to crack a nut and how many nuts could be opened per minute.

After some months, we began catching glimpses of the chimpanzees before they fled, and after a little more time, we were able to draw close enough to watch them at work. The chimps gather nuts from the ground. Some nuts are tougher to crack than others. Nuts of the *Panda oleosa* tree are the most demanding, harder than any of the foods processed by present-day hunter-gatherers and breaking open only when a force of 3,500 pounds is applied. The stone hammers used by the Taï chimps range from stones of ten ounces to granite blocks of four to forty-five pounds. Stones of any size, however, are a rarity in the forest and are seldom conveniently placed near a nut-bearing tree. By observing closely, and in some cases imitating the way the chimps handle hammerstones, we learned that they have an impressive ability to find just the right tool for the job at hand. Taï chimps could remember the positions of many of the stones scattered, often out of sight, around a panda tree. Without having to run around rechecking the stones, they would select one of appropriate size that was closest to the tree. These mental abilities in spatial representation compare with some of those of nine-year-old humans.

To extract the four kernels from inside a panda nut, a chimp must use a hammer with extreme precision. Time and time again, we have been impressed to see a chimpanzee raise a twenty-pound stone above its head, strike a nut with ten or more powerful blows, and then, using the same hammer, switch to delicate little taps from a height of only four inches. To finish the job, the chimps often break off a small piece of twig and use it to extract the last tiny fragments of kernel from the shell. Intriguingly, females crack panda nuts more often than males, a gender difference in tool use that seems to be more pronounced in the forest chimps than in their savanna counterparts.

After five years of fieldwork, we were finally able to follow the chimpanzees at close range, and gradually, we gained insights into their way of hunting. One morning, for example, we followed a group of six male chimps on a three-hour patrol that had taken them into foreign territory to the north. (Our study group is one of five chimpanzee groups more or less evenly distributed in the Taï forest.) As always during these approximately monthly incursions, which seem to be for the purpose of territorial defense, the chimps were totally silent, clearly on edge and on the lookout for trouble. Once the patrol was over, however, and they were back within their own borders, the chimps shifted their attention to hunting. They were after monkeys, the most abundant mammals in the forest. Traveling in large, multi-species groups, some of the forest's ten species of monkeys are more apt than others to wind up as a meal for the chimps. The relatively sluggish and large (almost thirty pounds) red colobus monkeys are the chimps' usual fare. (Antelope also live in the forest, but in our ten years at Taï, we have never seen a chimp catch, or even pursue, one. In contrast, Gombe chimps at times do come across fawns, and when they do, they seize the opportunity—and the fawn.)

The six males moved on silently, peering up into the vegetation and stopping from time to time to listen for the sound of monkeys. None fed or groomed; all focused on the hunt. We followed one old male, Falstaff, closely, for he tolerates us completely and is one of the keenest and most experienced hunters. Even from the rear, Falstaff set the pace; whenever he stopped, the others paused to wait for him. After thirty minutes, we heard the unmistakable noises of monkeys jumping from branch to branch. Silently, the chimps turned in the direction of the sounds, scanning the canopy. Just then, a diana monkey spotted them and gave an alarm call. Dianas are very alert and fast; they are also about half the weight of colobus monkeys. The chimps quickly gave up and continued their search for easier, meatier prey.

Shortly after, we heard the characteristic cough of a red colobus monkey. Suddenly Rousseau and Macho, two twenty-year-olds, burst into action, running toward the cough. Falstaff seemed surprised by their precipitousness, but after a moment's hesitation, he also ran. Now the hunting barks of the chimps mixed with the sharp alarm calls of the monkeys. Hurrying behind Falstaff, we saw him climb up a conveniently situated tree. His position, combined with those of Schubert and Ulysse, two mature chimps in their prime, effectively blocked off three of the monkeys' possible escape routes. But in another tree, nowhere near any escape route and thus useless, waited the last of the hunters, Kendo, eighteen years old and the least experienced of the group. The monkeys, taking advantage of Falstaff's delay and Kendo's error, escaped.

The six males moved on and within five minutes picked up the sounds of another group of red colobus. This time, the chimps approached cautiously, nobody hurrying. They screened the canopy intently to locate the monkeys, which were still unaware of the approaching danger. Macho and Schubert chose two adjacent trees, both full of monkeys, and started climbing very quietly, taking care not to move any branches. Meanwhile, the other four chimps blocked off anticipated escape routes. When Schubert was halfway up, the monkeys finally detected the two chimps. As we watched the colobus monkeys take off in literal panic, the appropriateness of the chimpanzees' scientific name—*Pan* came to mind: with a certain stretch of the imagination, the fleeing monkeys could be shepherds and shepherdesses frightened at the sudden appearance of Pan, the wild Greek god of the woods, shepherds, and their flocks.

Taking off in the expected direction, the monkeys were trailed by Macho and Schubert. The chimps let go with loud hunting barks. Trying to escape, two colobus monkeys jumped into smaller trees lower in the canopy. With this, Rousseau and Kendo, who had been watching from the ground, sped up into the trees and tried to grab them. Only a third of the weight of the chimps, however, the monkeys managed to make it to the next tree along branches too small for their pursuers. But Falstaff had anticipated this move and was waiting for them. In the following confusion, Falstaff seized a juvenile and killed it with a bite to the neck. As the chimps met in a rush on the ground, Falstaff began to eat, sharing with Schubert and Rousseau. A juvenile colobus does not provide much meat, however, and this time, not all the chimps got a share. Frustrated individuals soon started off on another hunt, and relative calm returned fairly quickly: this sort of hunt, by a small band of chimps acting on their own at the edge of their territory, does not generate the kind of high excitement that prevails when more members of the community are involved.

So far we have observed some 200 monkey hunts and have concluded that success requires a minimum of three motivated hunters acting cooperatively.

Alone or in pairs, chimps succeed less than 15 percent of the time, but when three or four act as a group, more than half the hunts result in a kill. The chimps seem well aware of the odds: 92 percent of all the hunts we observed were group affairs.

Gombe chimps also hunt red colobus monkeys, but the percentage of group hunts is much lower: only 36 percent. In addition, we learned from Jane Goodall that even when Gombe chimps do hunt in groups, their strategies are different. When Taï chimps arrive under a group of monkeys, the hunters scatter, often silently, usually out of sight of one another but each aware of the others' positions. As the hunt progresses, they gradually close in, encircling the quarry. Such movements require that each chimp coordinate his movements with those of the other hunters, as well as with those of the prey, at all times.

Coordinated hunts account for 63 percent of all those observed at Taï but only 7 percent of those at Gombe. Jane Goodall says that in a Gombe group hunt, the chimpanzees typically travel together until they arrive at a tree with monkeys. Then, as the chimps begin climbing nearby trees, they scatter as each pursues a different target. Goodall gained the impression that Gombe chimps boost their success by hunting independently but simultaneously, thereby disorganizing their prey; our impression is that the Taï chimps owe their success to being organized themselves.

Just why the Gombe and Taï chimps have developed such different hunting strategies is difficult to explain, and we plan to spend some time at Gombe in the hope of finding out. In the meantime, the mere existence of differences is interesting enough and may perhaps force changes in our understanding of human evolution. Most currently accepted theories propose that some three million years ago, a dramatic climate change in Africa east of the Rift Valley turned dense forest into open, drier habitat. Adapting to the difficulties of life under these new conditions, our ancestors supposedly evolved into cooperative hunters and began sharing food they caught. Supporters of this idea point out that plant and animal remains indicative

of dry, open environments have been found at all early hominid excavation sites in Tanzania, Kenya, South Africa, and Ethiopia. That the large majority of apes in Africa today live west of the Rift Valley appears to many anthropologists to lend further support to the idea that a change in environment caused the common ancestor of apes and humans to evolve along a different line from those remaining in the forest.

Our observations, however, suggest quite another line of thought. Life in dense, dim forest may require more sophisticated behavior than is commonly assumed: compared with their savanna relatives, Taï chimps show greater complexity in both hunting and tool use. Taï chimps use tools in nineteen different ways and have six different ways of making them, compared with sixteen uses and three methods of manufacture at Gombe.

Anthropologist colleagues of mine have told me that the discovery that some chimpanzees are accomplished users of hammerstones forces them to look with a fresh eye at stone tools turned up at excavation sites. The important role played by female Taï chimps in tool use also raises the possibility that in the course of human evolution, women may have been decisive in the development of many of the sophisticated manipulative skills characteristic of our species. Taï mothers also appear to pass on their skills by actively teaching their offspring. We have observed mothers providing their young with hammers and then stepping in to help when the inexperienced youngsters encounter difficulty. This help may include carefully showing how to position the nut or hold the hammer properly. Such behavior has never been observed at Gombe.

Similarly, food sharing, for a long time said to be unique to humans, seems more general in forest than in savanna chimpanzees. Taï chimp mothers share with their young up to 60 percent of the nuts they open, at least until the latter become sufficiently adept, generally at about six years old. They also share other foods acquired with tools, including honey, ants, and bone marrow. Gombe mothers share such foods much less often, even with their infants. Taï chimps also share meat more frequently than do their Gombe relatives, sometimes dividing a chunk up and giving portions away, sometimes simply allowing beggars to grab pieces.

Any comparison between chimpanzees and our hominid ancestors can only be suggestive, not definitive. But our studies lead us to believe that the process of hominization may have begun independently of the drying of the environment. Savanna life could even have delayed the process; many anthropologists have been struck by how slowly hominid-associated remains, such as the hand ax, changed after their first appearance in the Olduvai age.

Will we have the time to discover more about the hunting strategies or other, perhaps as yet undiscovered abilities of these forest chimpanzees? Africa's tropical rain forests, and their inhabitants, are threatened with extinction by extensive logging, largely to provide the Western world with tropical timber and such products as coffee, cocoa, and rubber. Ivory Coast has lost 90 percent of its original forest, and less than 5 percent of the remainder can be considered pristine. The climate has changed dramatically. The harmattan, a cold, dry wind from the Sahara previously unknown in the forest, has now swept through the Taï forest every year since 1986. Rainfall has diminished; all the rivulets in our study region are now dry for several months of the year.

In addition, the chimpanzee, biologically very close to humans, is in demand for research on AIDS and hepatitis vaccines. Captive-bred chimps are available, but they cost about twenty times more than wild-caught animals. Chimps taken from the wild for these purposes are generally young, their mothers having been shot during capture. For every chimp arriving at its sad destination, nine others may well have died in the forest or on the way. Such priorities—cheap coffee and cocoa and chimpanzees—do not do the economies of Third World countries any good in the long run, and they bring suffering and death to innocent victims in the forest. Our hope is that Brutus, Falstaff, and their families will survive, and that we and others will have the opportunity to learn about them well into the future. But there is no denying that modern times work against them and us.

# To Catch a Colobus

**Chimpanzees in Gombe National Park band together to kill nearly a fifth of the red colobus monkeys in their range**

## Craig B. Stanford

*Craig B. Stanford is an assistant professor of anthropology at the University of Southern California. His first fieldwork on primates was in Peru, where he studied tamarins. For his Ph.D. at the University of California, Berkeley, Stanford traveled to India and Bangladesh to investigate ecological influences on social behavior in capped langur monkeys. Stanford hopes to expand his research to the evolution of hunting behavior in primates, including humans.*

On a sunny July morning, I am sitting on the bank of Kakombe Stream in Gombe National Park, Tanzania. Forty feet above my head, scattered through large fig trees, is a group of red colobus monkeys. This is J group, whose twenty-five members I have come to know as individuals during several seasons of fieldwork. Gombe red colobus are large, long-tailed monkeys, with males sometimes weighing more than twenty pounds. Both sexes have a crown of red hair, a gray back, and buff underparts. The highlight of this particular morning has been the sighting of a new infant, born sometime in the previous two days. As the group feeds noisily on fruit and leaves overhead, I mull over the options for possible names for the infant.

While I watch the colobus monkeys, my attention is caught by the loud and excited pant-hoots of a party of chimpanzees farther down the valley. I judge the group to be of considerable size and

traveling in my direction. As the calls come closer, the colobus males begin to give high-pitched alarm calls, and mothers gather up their infants and climb higher into the tree crowns.

A moment later, a wild chorus of panthoots erupts just behind me, followed by a cacophony of colobus alarm calls, and it is obvious to both J group and to me that the chimps have arrived. The male chimps immediately climb up to the higher limbs of the tall albizia tree into which most of the colobus group have retreated. Colobus females and their offspring huddle high in the crown, while a phalanx of five adult males descends to meet the advancing ranks of four adult male chimpanzees, led by seventeen-year-old, 115-pound Frodo. Frodo is the most accomplished hunter of colobus monkeys at Gombe and the only one willing to take on several colobus males simultaneously in order to catch his prey. The other hunters keep their distance while Frodo first scans the group of monkeys, then advances upon the colobus defenders. Time and again he lunges at the colobus males, attempting to race past them and into the cluster of terrified females and infants. Each time he is driven back; at one point, the two largest males of J group leap onto Frodo's back until he retreats, screaming, a few yards away.

A brief lull in the hunt follows, during which the colobus males run to one another and embrace for reassurance, then part to renew their defense. Frodo

soon charges again into the midst of the colobus males, and this time manages to scatter them long enough to pluck the newborn from its mother's abdomen. In spite of fierce opposition, Frodo has caught his quarry, and he now sits calmly and eats it while the other hunters and two female chimps—their swollen pink rumps a sign that they are in estrus, a period of sexual receptivity—sit nearby begging for meat. The surviving colobus monkeys watch nervously from a few feet away. Minutes later, the mother of the dead infant attempts to approach, perhaps to try to rescue her nearly consumed offspring. She is chased, falls from the tree to the forest floor, and is pounced upon and killed by juvenile chimpanzees that have been watching the hunt from below. Seconds later, before these would-be hunters have had a chance to begin their meal, Wilkie, the chimpanzee group's dominant male, races down the tree and steals the carcass from them. He shows off his prize by charging across the forest floor, dead colobus in hand, and then, amid a frenzy of chimps eager for a morsel, he sits down to share the meat with his ally Prof and two females from the hunting party.

Until Jane Goodall observed chimpanzees eating meat in the early 1960s, they were thought to be complete vegetarians. We now know that a small but regular portion of the diet of wild chimps consists of the meat of such mammals as bush pigs, small antelopes, and a variety of monkey species. For example, chimpanzees in the Mahale Mountains of Tanzania, the Taï forest of Ivory Coast, and in Gombe all regularly hunt red colobus monkeys. Documenting the effect of such predation on wild primate populations, however, is extremely difficult because predators—whether chimps, leopards, or eagles—are generally too shy to hunt in the presence of people. The result is that even if predation is a regular occurrence, researchers are not likely to see it, let alone study it systematically.

Gombe is one of the few primate study sites where both predators and their prey have been habituated to human observers, making it possible to witness hunts. I have spent the past four field seasons at Gombe, studying the predator-prey relationship between the 45-member Kasakela chimpanzee community and the 500 red colobus monkeys that share the same twelve square miles of Gombe National Park. Gombe's rugged terrain is composed of steep slopes of open woodland, rising above stream valleys lush with riverine forest. The chimpanzees roam across these hills in territorial communities, which divide up each day into foraging parties of from one to forty animals. So far, I have clocked in more than a thousand hours with red colobus monkeys and have regularly followed the chimps on their daily rounds, observing some 150 encounters between the monkeys and chimps and more than 75 hunts. My records, together with those of my colleagues, show that the Gombe chimps may kill more than 100 red colobus each year, or nearly one-fifth of the colobus inhabiting their range. Most of the victims are immature monkeys under two years old. Also invaluable have been the data gathered daily on the chimps for the past two decades by a team of Tanzanian research assistants.

One odd outcome of my work has been that I am in the unique position of knowing both the hunters and their victims as individuals, which makes my research intriguing but a bit heart-wrenching. In October 1992, for example, a party of thirty-three chimpanzees encountered my main study group, J, in upper Kakombe valley. The result was

devastating from the monkeys' viewpoint. During the hour-long hunt, seven were killed; three were caught and torn apart right in front of me. Nearly four hours later, the hunters were still sharing and eating the meat they had caught, while I sat staring in disbelief at the remains of many of my study subjects.

Determined to learn more about the chimp-colobus relationship, however, I continued watching, that day and many others like it. I will need several more field seasons before I can measure the full impact of chimpanzee hunting on the Gombe red colobus, but several facts about hunting and its effects on the monkeys have already emerged. One major factor that determines the outcome of a hunt in Gombe is the number of male chimps involved. (Although females also hunt, the males are responsible for more than 90 percent of all colobus kills.) Red colobus males launch a courageous counterattack in response to their chimpanzee predators, but their ability to defend their group is directly proportional to the number of attackers and does not seem to be related to the number of defenders. The outcome of a hunt is thus almost always in the hands of the chimps, and in most instances, the best the monkeys can hope to do is limit the damage to a single group member rather than several. Chimpanzees have a highly fluid social grouping pattern in which males tend to travel together while females travel alone with their infants. At times, however, twenty or more male and female chimpanzees forage together. When ten or more male chimps hunt together, they are successful nine times out of ten, and the colobus have little hope of escape.

Hunting success depends on other factors as well. Unlike the shy red-tailed and blue monkeys with which they share the forest (and which are rarely hunted by the chimps), red colobus do not flee the moment they hear or see chimps approaching. Instead, the red colobus give alarm calls and adopt a vigilant wait-and-see strategy, with males positioned nearest the potential attackers. The alarm calls increase in frequency and intensity as the chimpanzees draw closer and cease only when the chimps are sighted beneath the tree. Then, the

colobus sit quietly, watching intently, and only if the chimps decide to hunt do the colobus males launch a counterattack. The monkeys' decision to stand and fight rather than flee may seem maladaptive given their low rate of successful defense. I observed, however, that when the monkeys scatter or try to flee, the chimps nearly always pursue and catch one or more of them.

Fleeing red colobus monkeys are most likely to be caught when they have been feeding on the tasty new leaves of the tallest trees, the "emergents," which rise above the canopy. When these trees are surrounded by low plant growth, they frequently become death traps because the only way colobus can escape from attacking chimps is to leap out of the tree—often into the waiting arms of more chimpanzees on the ground below.

One of my primary goals has been to learn why a party of chimps will eagerly hunt a colobus group one day while ignoring the same group under seemingly identical circumstances on another. One determinant is the number of males in the chimp party: the more males, the more likely the group will hunt. Hunts are also undertaken mainly when a mother colobus carrying a small infant is visible, probably because of the Gombe chimps' preference for baby red colobus, which make up 75 percent of all kills. The situation is quite different in the Taï forest, where half of the chimp kills are adult colobus males (see "Dim Forest, Bright Chimps," *Natural History,* September 1991). Christophe and Hedwige Boesch have shown that the Taï chimps hunt cooperatively, perhaps because red colobus monkeys are harder to catch in the much taller canopy of the Taï rainforest. Successful Taï chimp hunters also regularly share the spoils. In contrast, each chimp in Gombe appears to have his own hunting strategy.

The single best predictor of when Gombe chimps will hunt is the presence of one or more estrous females in the party. This finding, together with the earlier observation by Geza Teleki (formerly of George Washington University) that male hunters tend to give meat preferentially to swollen females traveling with the group, indicates that Gombe chimps sometimes hunt in order to obtain meat to offer a sexually receptive female. Since hunts also occur when no estrous females are present, this trade of sex for meat cannot be the exclusive explanation, but the implications are nonetheless intriguing. Gombe chimps use meat not only for nutrition; they also share it with their allies and withhold it from their rivals. Meat is thus a social, political, and even reproductive tool. These "selfish" goals may help explain why the Gombe chimps do not cooperate during a hunt as often as do Taï chimps.

Whatever the chimps want the monkey meat for, their predation has a severe effect on the red colobus population. Part of my work involves taking repeated censuses of the red colobus groups living in the different valleys that form the hunting range of our chimpanzees. In the core area of the range, where hunting is most intense, predation by chimps is certainly the limiting factor on colobus population growth: red colobus group size in this area is half that at the periphery of the chimps' hunting range. The number of infant and juvenile red colobus monkeys is particularly low in the core area; most of the babies there are destined to become chimpanzee food.

The proportion of the red colobus population eaten by chimps appears to fluctuate greatly from year to year, and probably from decade to decade, as the number of male hunters in the chimpanzee community changes. In the early 1980s, for instance, there were five adult and adolescent males in the Kasakela chimp community, while today there are eleven; the number of colobus kills per year has risen as the number of hunters in the community has grown.

Furthermore, a single avid hunter may have a dramatic effect. I estimate that Frodo has single-handedly killed up to 10 percent of the entire red colobus population within his hunting range. I now want to learn if chimps living in forests elsewhere in Africa are also taking a heavy toll of red colobus monkeys. If they are, then they will add support to the theory that predation is an important limiting factor on wild primate populations and may also influence some aspects of behavior. Meanwhile, I will continue to watch in awe as Frodo and his fellow hunters attack my colobus monkeys and to marvel at the courageousness of the colobus males that risk their lives to protect the other members of their group.

# Coping with CROWDING

*A persistent and popular view holds that high population density inevitably leads to violence. This myth, which is based on rat research, applies neither to us nor to other primates*

## by Frans B. M. de Waal, Filippo Aureli and Peter G. Judge

*FRANS B. M. DE WAAL, FILIPPO AURELI and PETER G. JUDGE share a research interest in the social relationships and behavioral strategies of nonhuman primates. Their work on aspects of this topic will appear in* Natural Conflict Resolution, *to be published by the University of California Press. De Waal, author of* Chimpanzee Politics *and* Good Natured, *worked for many years at the Arnhem zoo in the Netherlands before coming to the U.S., where he is now director of the Living Links Center at the Yerkes Regional Primate Research Center in Atlanta and professor of psychology at Emory University. Aureli is a senior lecturer in biological and earth sciences at Liverpool John Moores University in England. Judge is an assistant professor at Bloomsburg University in Pennsylvania and a research associate at Yerkes.*

In 1962 this magazine published a seminal paper by experimental psychologist John B. Calhoun entitled "Population Density and Social Pathology." The article opened dramatically with an observation by the late-18th-century English demographer Thomas Malthus that human population growth is automatically followed by increased vice and misery. Calhoun went on to note that although we know overpopulation causes disease and food shortage, we understand virtually nothing about its behavioral impact.

This reflection had inspired Calhoun to conduct a nightmarish experiment. He placed an expanding rat population in a crammed room and observed that the rats soon set about killing, sexually assaulting and, eventually, cannibalizing one another. Much of this activity happened among the occupants of a central feeding section. Despite the presence of food elsewhere in the room, the rats were irresistibly drawn to the social stimulation—even though many of them could not reach the central food dispensers. This pathological togetherness, as Calhoun described it, as well as the attendant chaos and behavioral deviancy, led him to coin the phrase "behavioral sink."

In no time, popularizers were comparing politically motivated street riots to rat packs, inner cities to behavioral sinks and urban areas to zoos. Warning that society was heading for either anarchy or dictatorship, Robert Ardrey, an American science journalist, remarked in 1970 on the voluntary nature of human crowding: "Just as Calhoun's rats freely chose to eat in the middle pens, we freely enter the city." Calhoun's views soon became a central tenet of the voluminous literature on aggression.

In extrapolating from rodents to people, however, these thinkers and writers were making a gigantic leap of faith. A look at human populations suggests why such a simple extrapolation is so problematic. Compare, for instance, per capita murder rates with the number of people per square kilometer in different nations—as we did, using data from the United Nation's *1996 Demographic Yearbook*. If things were straightforward, the two ought to vary in tandem. Instead there is no statistically meaningful relation.

But, one could argue, perhaps such a relation is obscured by variation in national income level, political organization or some other variable. Apparently not, at least for income. We divided the nations into three categories—free-market, former East Block and Third World—and did the analysis again. This time we did find one significant correlation, but it was in the other direction: it showed more violent crime in the least crowded countries of the former East Block. A similar trend existed for free-market nations, among which the U.S.

FRANS B. M. DE WAAL

RHESUS MONKEYS from three different settings show different rates of grooming—that is, of calming one another. The monkeys seem to adapt to crowded conditions by grooming more frequently. Among the males, grooming of each other and of females was more common when they lived in crowded conditions than when they lived in more spacious quarters. Among female non-kin, aggression was common and increased further with crowding but was accompanied by increased grooming, which served to reduce conflicts.

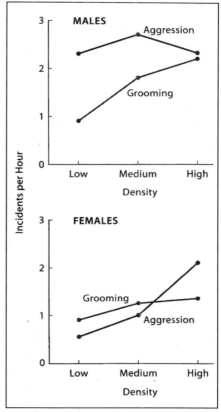

BRYAN CHRISTIE

SOURCE: Peter G. Judge and Frans B. M. de Waal

had by far the highest homicide rate despite its low overall population density. The Netherlands had a population density 13 times as high, but its homicide rate was eight times lower.

Knowing that crime is generally more common in urban areas than it is in the countryside, we factored in the proportion of each nation's population that lives in large cities and controlled for it. But this correction did nothing to bring about a positive correlation between population density and homicide. Perhaps because of the overriding effects of history and culture, the link between available space and human aggression—if it exists at all—is decidedly not clear-cut.

Even if we look at small-scale human experiments, we find no supporting evidence. Crowding of children and college students, for instance, sometimes produced irritation and mild aggression, but in general, people seemed adept at avoiding conflict. Andrew S. Baum and his co-workers in the psychiatry depart-

ment at the Uniformed Services University found that dormitory residents who shared facilities with many people spent less time socializing and kept the doors to their rooms closed more often than did students who had more space. Baum concluded that the effects of crowding are not nearly as overwhelming as originally presumed. Published in the 1980s, these and other findings began to undermine, at least in the scientific community, the idea that people and rats react in the same ways to being packed together. In modern society, people commonly assemble in large masses—during their daily commute to work or during holiday-season shopping expeditions— and most of the time they control their behavior extraordinarily well.

Calhoun's model, we must conclude, does not generally apply to human behavior. Is this because our culture and intelligence makes us unique, or is the management of crowding part of an older heritage? To answer this question, we turn to the primates.

## PRIMATES ARE NOT RATS

Primate research initially appeared to support the harrowing scenario that had been presented for rats. In the 1960s scientists reported that city-dwelling monkeys in India were more aggressive than were those living in forests. Others claimed that monkeys in zoos were excessively violent. Those monkeys were apparently ruled by terrifying bullies who dominated a social hierarchy that was considered an artifact of captivity—in other words, in the wild, peace and egalitarianism prevailed. Borrowing from the hyperbole of popularizers, one study of crowding in small captive groups of baboons even went so far as to report a "ghetto riot."

As research progressed, however, conflicting evidence accumulated. Higher population density seemed to increase aggression occasionally—but the opposite was also true. One report, for instance, described intense fighting and killing when a group of macaques were released into a corral 73 times *larger* than their previous quarters had been. Then, after two and a half years in the corral, a similar increase in aggression occurred when the monkeys were crowded back into a small pen.

Whereas the macaque study manipulated population density through environmental change, other early research did so by adding new monkeys to existing groups. Given the xenophobic nature of monkeys, these tests mainly measured their hostile attitude toward strangers, which is quite different from the effect of density. The better controlled the studies became, the less clear-cut the picture turned out to be. Increased population density led to increased aggression in only 11 of the 17 best-designed studies of the past few decades.

In the meantime, the view of wild primates was changing. They were no longer the purely peaceful, egalitarian creatures people had presumed them to be. In the 1970s field-workers began reporting sporadic but lethal violence in a wide range of species—from macaques to chimpanzees—as well as strict and well-defined hierarchies that remained stable for decades. This view of an often anxiety-filled existence was confirmed when researchers found high levels of the stress hormone cortisol in the blood of wild monkeys [see "Stress in the Wild," by Robert M. Sapolsky; SCIENTIFIC AMERICAN, JANUARY 1990.

As the view of primates became more complex, and as the rat scenario was weakened by counterexamples, researchers began to wonder whether primates had developed a means to reduce conflict in crowded situations. We saw the first hint of this possibility in a study of the world's largest zoo colony of chimpanzees in Arnhem, the Netherlands. The apes lived on a spacious, forested island in the summer but were packed together in a heated building during the winter. Despite a 20-fold reduction in space, aggression increased only slightly. In fact, the effect of crowding was not entirely negative: friendly grooming and greetings, such as kissing and submissive bowing, increased as well.

We wondered if this conciliatory behavior mitigated tension and proposed a way to test this possibility. Without ig-

FRANS B. M. DE WAAL

CHIMPANZEES IN THE WILD have hostile territorial relations with other groups, and in captivity they are bothered by the presence of noisy neighboring chimps. By examining apes under three conditions—those living in a crowded space and able to hear their neighbors, those living in a crowded space without such worrisome sounds, and those living in isolated large compounds (*photograph below*)—we were able to measure the association between aggression, space and stress. Aggression (*photograph at left*) remained the same, but stress varied with neighbors' noise. Chimpanzees in small spaces exposed to vocalizations from other groups showed the highest levels of the stress hormone cortisol.

FRANS B. M. DE WAAL

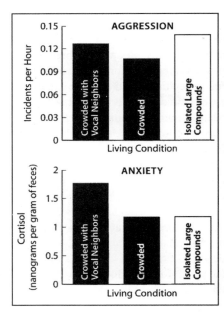

BRYAN CHRISTIE

*SOURCE: Filippo Aureli and Frans B. M. de Waal*

noring the fact that crowding increases the potential for conflict, we predicted that primates employ counterstrategies—including avoiding potential aggressors and offering appeasement or reassuring body contact. Because some of the skills involved are probably acquired, the most effective coping responses would be expected in animals who have experienced high density for a long time. Perhaps they develop a different "social culture" in the same way that people in different places have varying standards of privacy and interpersonal comfort zones. For example, studies show that white North Americans and the British keep greater distances from others during conversations than Latin Americans and Arabs do.

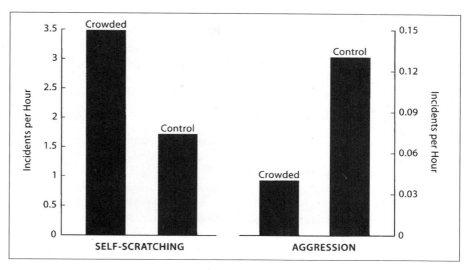

BRYAN CHRISTIE

SOURCE: Filippo Aureli and Frans B. M. de Waal

During brief periods of crowding, people often limit social interaction—a way of avoiding any conflict. Chimpanzees do the same, reducing their aggressive interactions. This doesn't mean that crowded situations do not induce anxiety. Chimpanzees packed together tend to scratch themselves more often—a sign of stress.

## COPING CULTURE

We set about finding several populations of monkeys that were of the same species but that had been living in different conditions to see if their behavior varied in discernible ways. We collected detailed data on 122 individual rhesus monkeys at three different sites in the U.S.: in relatively cramped outdoor pens at the Wisconsin primate center in Madison, in large open corrals at the Yerkes primate center in Atlanta and on Morgan Island off the coast of South Carolina. These last monkeys had approximately 2,000 times more space per individual than the highest-density groups. All three groups had lived together for many years, often for generations, and included individuals of both sexes. All the groups had also been in human care, receiving food and veterinary treatment, making them comparable in that regard as well.

Rhesus society typically consists of a number of subgroups, known as matrilines, of related females and their offspring. Females remain together for life, whereas males leave their natal group at puberty. Rhesus monkeys make a sharp distinction between kin and non-kin: by far the most friendly contact, such as grooming, takes place within the matrilines. Females of one matriline also fiercely support one another in fights against other matrilines. Because of

their strict hierarchy and pugnacious temperament, rhesus seemed to be ideal subjects. We figured that if this aggressive primate showed coping responses, our hypothesis would have withstood its most rigorous test.

Our first finding was, surprisingly, that density did not affect male aggressiveness. Adult males increasingly engaged in friendly contact under crowded conditions. They groomed females more, and likewise the females groomed the males more frequently. (Grooming is a calming behavior. In another study, we demonstrated that a monkey's heart rate slows down when it is being groomed.) Females also bared their teeth more often to the males—the rhesus way of communicating low status and appeasing potentially aggressive dominant monkeys.

Females showed a different response with other females, however. Within their own matrilines they fought more but did not change the already high level of friendly interaction. In their dealings with other matrilines, they also showed more aggression—but here it was coupled with more grooming and submissive grinning.

These findings make sense in light of the differences between kin and non-kin

relationships. Related females—such as sisters and mothers and daughters—are so strongly bonded that their relationships are unlikely to be disrupted by antagonism. Rhesus monkeys are used to managing intrafamilial conflict, cycling through fights and reconciliations, followed by comforting contact. Crowding does little to change this, except that they may have to repair frayed family ties more often. Between matrilines, on the other hand, crowding poses a serious challenge. Normally, friendly contact between matrilines is rare and antagonism common. But reduced escape opportunities make the risk of escalated conflict greater in a confined space. And our data indicated that female rhesus monkeys make a concerted effort at improving these potentially volatile relationships.

## EMOTIONS IN CHECK

In a second project, we turned our attention to chimpanzees. As our closest animal relatives, chimpanzees resemble us in appearance, psychology and cognition. Their social organization is also humanlike, with well-developed male bonding—which is rare in nature—reciprocal exchange and a long dependency of offspring on the mother. In the wild, male chimpanzees are extremely territorial, sometimes invading neighboring territories and killing enemy males. In captivity such encounters are, of course, prevented.

We collected data on more than 100 chimpanzees in various groups at the Yerkes primate center. Although some groups had only a tenth the space of others, cramped quarters had no measurable impact on aggression. In contrast to the monkeys, chimpanzees maintained their grooming and appeasement behavior—no matter the situation. If crowding did induce social tensions, our chimpanzees seemed to control them directly.

We usually do not think of animals as holding in their emotions, but chimpanzees may be different. These apes are known for deceptive behavior—for instance, they will hide hostile intentions behind a friendly face until an adversary has come within reach. In our study, emotional control was reflected in the way chimpanzees responded to the vocalizations of neighboring groups. Such noises commonly provoke hooting and charging displays, which in wild chimpanzees serve to ward off territorial intrusion.

In a confined space, however, excited reactions trigger turmoil within the group. We found that chimpanzees in the most crowded situations had a three times *lower* tendency to react to neighbors' vocalizations than chimpanzees with more space did. Chimpanzees may be smart enough to suppress responses to external stimuli if those tend to get them into trouble. Indeed, field-workers report that chimpanzee males on territorial patrol suppress all noise if being detected by their neighbors is to their disadvantage.

The inhibition of natural responses is not without cost. We know that continuous stress has the potential to suppress the immune system and therefore has important implications for health and longevity. We developed two noninvasive techniques to measure stress in our chimpanzees. One was to record the rate of self-scratching. Just as with college students who scratch their heads when faced with a tough exam question, self-scratching indicates anxiety in other primates. Our second technique was to collect fecal samples and analyze them for cortisol. Both measures showed that groups of chimpanzees who had little space and heard neighbors' vocalizations experienced more stress. Space by itself was not a negative factor, because in the absence of noisy neighbors, chimpanzees in small spaces showed the same stress level as those with a good deal of space.

So even though chimpanzees fail to show a rise in aggression when crowded, this does not necessarily mean that they are happy and relaxed. They may be working hard to maintain the peace. Given a choice, they would prefer more room. Every spring, when the chimpanzees at the Arnhem zoo hear the door to their outdoor island being opened for the first time, they fill the building with a chorus of ecstasy. They then rush outside to engage in a pandemonium in which all of the apes, young and old, embrace and kiss and thump one another excitedly on the back.

The picture is even more complex if we also consider short periods of acute crowding. This is a daily experience in human society, whether we find ourselves on a city bus or in a movie theater. During acute crowding, rhesus monkeys show a rise in mild aggression, such as threats, but not violence. Threats serve to keep others at a distance, forestalling unwanted contact. The monkeys also avoid one another and limit active social engagement, as if they are trying to stay out of trouble by lying low.

Chimpanzees take this withdrawal tactic one step further: they are actually less aggressive when briefly crowded. Again, this reflects greater emotional restraint. Their reaction is reminiscent of people on an elevator, who reduce frictions by minimizing large body movements, eye contact and loud verbalizations. We speak of the elevator effect, therefore, as a way in which both people and other primates handle the risks of temporary closeness.

Our research leads us to conclude that we come from a long lineage of social animals capable of flexibly adjusting to all kinds of conditions, including unnatural ones such as crowded pens and city streets. The adjustment may not be without cost, but it is certainly preferable to the frightening alternative predicted on the basis of rodent studies.

We should add, though, that even the behavioral sink of Calhoun's rats may not have been entirely the product of crowding. Food competition seemed to play a role as well. This possibility contains a serious warning for our own species in an ever more populous world: the doomsayers who predict that crowding will inevitably rip the social fabric may have the wrong variable in mind. We have a natural, underappreciated talent to deal with crowding, but crowding combined with scarcity of resources is something else.

## Further Information

THE HIDDEN DIMENSION. E. T. Hall. Doubleday, 1966.

CROWDING. A. Baum in *Handbook of Environmental Psychology*, Vol. 1. Edited by D. Stokols and I. Altman. Wiley, 1987.

THE MYTH OF A SIMPLE RELATION BETWEEN SPACE AND AGGRESSION IN CAPTIVE PRIMATES. F. B. M. de Waal in *Zoo Biology* supplement, Vol. 1, pages 141–148; 1989.

INHIBITION OF SOCIAL BEHAVIOR IN CHIMPANZEES UNDER HIGH-DENSITY CONDITIONS. F. Aureli and F. B. M. de Waal in *American Journal of Primatology*, Vol. 41, No. 3, pages 213–228; March 1997.

RHESUS MONKEY BEHAVIOUR UNDER DIVERSE POPULATION DENSITIES: COPING WITH LONG-TERM CROWDING. P. G. Judge and F. B. M. de Waal in *Animal Behaviour*, Vol. 54, no. 3, pages 643–662; September 1997.

COMMENTARY

# Are We in Anthropodenial?

## BY FRANS DE WAAL

WHEN GUESTS ARRIVE AT THE Yerkes Regional Primate Research Center in Georgia, where I work, they usually pay a visit to the chimpanzees. And often, when she sees them approaching the compound, an adult female chimpanzee named Georgia will hurry to the spigot to collect a mouthful of water. She'll then casually mingle with the rest of the colony behind the mesh fence, and not even the sharpest observer will notice anything unusual. If necessary, Georgia will wait minutes, with her lips closed, until the visitors come near. Then there will be shrieks, laughs, jumps—and sometimes falls—when she suddenly sprays them.

I have known quite a few apes that are good at surprising people, naive and otherwise. Heini Hediger, the great Swiss zoo biologist, recounts how he—being prepared to meet the challenge and paying attention to the ape's every move—got drenched by an experienced chimpanzee. I once found myself in a similar situation with Georgia; she had taken a drink from the spigot and was sneaking up to me. I looked her straight in the eye and pointed my finger at her, warning in Dutch, "I have seen you!" She immediately stepped back, let some of the water dribble from her mouth, and swallowed the rest. I certainly do not wish to claim that she understands Dutch, but she must have sensed that I knew what she was up to, and that I was not going to be an easy target.

Now, no doubt even a casual reader will have noticed that in describing Georgia's actions, I've implied human qualities such as intentions, the ability to interpret my own awareness, and a tendency toward mischief. Yet scientific tradition says I should avoid such language—I am committing the sin of anthropomorphism, of turning nonhumans into humans. The word comes from the Greek, meaning "human form," and it was the ancient Greeks who first gave the practice a bad reputation. They did not have chimpanzees in mind: the philosopher Xenophanes objected to Homer's poetry because it treated Zeus and the other gods as if they were people. How could we be so arrogant, Xenophanes asked, as to think that the gods should look like us? If horses could draw pictures, he suggested mockingly, they would no doubt make their gods look like horses.

Nowadays the intellectual descendants of Xenophanes warn against perceiving animals to be like ourselves. There are, for example, the behaviorists, who follow psychologist B. F. Skinner in viewing the actions of animals as responses shaped by rewards and punishments rather than the result of internal decision making, emotions, or intentions. They would say that Georgia was not "up to" anything when she sprayed water on her victims. Far from planning and executing a naughty plot, Georgia merely fell for the irresistible reward of human surprise and annoyance. Whereas any person acting like her would be scolded, arrested, or held accountable, Georgia is somehow innocent.

Behaviorists are not the only scientists who have avoided thinking about the inner life of animals. Some sociobiologists—researchers who look for the roots of behavior in evolution—depict animals as "survival machines" and "pre-programmed robots" put on Earth to serve their "selfish" genes. There is a certain metaphorical value to these concepts, but is has been negated by the misunderstanding they've created. Such language can give the impression that only genes are entitled to an inner life. No more delusively anthropomorphizing idea has been put forward since the pet-rock craze of the 1970s. In fact, during evolution, genes—a mere batch of molecules—simply multiply at different rates, depending on the traits they produce in an individual. To say that genes are selfish is like saying a snowball growing in

*To endow animals with human emotions has long been a scientific taboo. But if we do not, we risk missing something fundamental, about both animals and us.*

size as it rolls down a hill is greedy for snow.

Logically, these agnostic attitudes toward a mental life in animals can be valid only if they're applied to our own species as well. Yet it's uncommon to find researchers who try to study human behavior as purely a matter of reward and punishment. Describe a person as having intentions, feelings, and thoughts and you most likely won't encounter much resistance. Our own familiarity with our inner lives overrules whatever some school of thought might claim about us. Yet despite this double standard toward behavior in humans and animals, modern biology leaves us no choice other than to conclude that we *are* animals. In terms of anatomy, physiology, and neurology we are really no more exceptional than, say, an elephant or a platypus is in its own way. Even such presumed hallmarks of humanity as warfare, politics, culture, morality, and language may not be completely unprecedented. For example, different groups of wild chimpanzees employ different technologies—some fish for termites with sticks, others crack nuts with stones—that are transmitted from one generation to the next through a process reminiscent of human culture.

Given these discoveries, we must be very careful not to exaggerate the uniqueness of our species. The ancients apparently never gave much thought to this practice, the opposite of anthropomorphism, and so we lack a word for it. I will call it anthropodenial: a blindness to the humanlike characteristics of other animals, or the animal-like characteristics of ourselves.

Those who are in anthropodenial try to build a brick wall to separate humans from the rest of the animal kingdom. They carry on the tradition of René Descartes, who declared that while humans possessed souls, animals were mere automatons. This produced a serious dilemma when Charles Darwin came along: If we descended from such automatons, were we not automatons ourselves? If not, how did we get to be so different?

Each time we must ask such a question, another brick is pulled out of the dividing wall, and to me this wall is beginning to look like a slice of Swiss cheese. I work on a daily basis with animals from which it is about as hard to distance yourself as from "Lucy," the famed 3.2-million-year-old fossil australopithecine. If we owe Lucy the respect of an ancestor, does this not force a different look at the apes? After all, as far as we can tell, the most significant difference between Lucy and modern chimpanzees is found in their hips, not their craniums.

As soon as we admit that animals are far more like our relatives than like machines, then anthropodenial becomes impossible and anthropomorphism becomes inevitable—and scientifically acceptable. But not *all* forms of anthropomorphism, of course. Popular culture bombards us with examples of animals being humanized for all sorts of purposes, ranging from education to entertainment to satire to propaganda. Walt Disney, for example, made us forget that Mickey is a mouse, and Donald a duck. George Orwell laid a cover of human societal ills over a population of livestock. I was once struck by an advertisement for an oil company that claimed its propane saved the environment, in which a grizzly bear enjoying a pristine landscape had his arm around his mate's shoulders. In fact, bears are nearsighted and do not form pair-bonds, so the image says more about our own behavior than theirs.

Perhaps that was the intent. The problem is, we do not always remember that, when used in this way, anthropomorphism can provide insight only into human affairs and not into the affairs of animals. When my book *Chimpanzee Politics* came out in France, in 1987, my publisher decided (unbeknownst to me) to put François Mitterrand and Jacques Chirac on the cover with a chimpanzee between them. I can only assume he wanted to imply that these politicians acted like "mere" apes. Yet by doing so he went completely against the whole point of my book, which was not to ridicule people but to show that chimpanzees live in complex societies full of alliances and power plays that in some ways mirror our own.

*Bonobos have been known to assist companions new to their quarters in zoos, taking them by the hand to guide them through the maze of corridors connecting parts of their building.*

You can often hear similar attempts at anthropomorphic humor in the crowds that form around the monkey exhibit at a typical zoo. Isn't it interesting that antelopes, lions, and giraffes rarely elicit hilarity? But people who watch primates end up hooting and yelling, scratching themselves in exaggeration, and pointing at the animals while shouting, "I had to look twice, Larry. I thought it was you!" In my mind, the laughter reflects anthropodenial: it is a nervous reaction caused by an uncomfortable resemblance.

That very resemblance, however, can allow us to make better use of anthropomorphism, but for this we must view it as a means rather than an end. It should not be our goal to find some quality in an animal that is precisely equivalent to an aspect of our own inner lives. Rather, we should use the fact that we are similar to animals to develop ideas we can test. For example, after observing a group of chimpanzees at length, we begin to suspect that some individuals are attempting to "deceive" others—by giving false alarms to distract unwanted attention from the theft of food or from forbidden sexual activity. Once we frame the observation in such terms, we can devise testable predictions. We can figure out just what it would take to demonstrate deception on the part of chimpanzees. In this way, a speculation is turned into a challenge.

Naturally, we must always be on guard. To avoid making silly interpretations based on anthropomorphism, one must always interpret animal behavior in the wider context of a species' habits and natural history. Without experience with primates, one could imagine that a grinning rhesus monkey must be delighted, or that a chimpanzee running toward another with loud grunts must be in an aggressive mood. But primatologists know from many hours of observation that rhesus monkeys bare their teeth when intimidated, and that chimpanzees often grunt when they meet and embrace. In other words, a grinning rhesus monkey signals submission, and a chimpanzee's grunting often serves as a greeting. A careful observer may thus arrive at an informed anthropomorphism that is at odds with extrapolations from human behavior.

One must also always be aware that some animals are more like ourselves than others. The problem of sharing the experiences of organisms that rely on different senses is a profound one. It was expressed most famously by the philosopher Thomas Nagel when he asked, "What is it like to be a bat?" A bat perceives its world in pulses of reflected sound, something we creatures of vision would have a hard time imagining. Perhaps even more alien would be the experience of an animal such as the star-nosed mole. With 22 pink, writhing tentacles around its nostrils, it is able to feel microscopic textures on small objects in the mud with the keenest sense of touch of any animal on Earth.

Humans can barely imagine a star-nosed mole's *Umwelt*—a German term for the environment as perceived by the animal. Obviously, the closer a species is to us, the easier it is to enter its *Umwelt*. This is why anthropomorphism is not only tempting in the case of apes but also hard to reject on the grounds that we cannot know how they perceive the world. Their sensory systems are essentially the same as ours.

LAST SUMMER, AN APE SAVED A three-year-old boy. The child, who had fallen 20 feet into the primate exhibit at Chicago's Brookfield Zoo, was scooped up and carried to safety by Binti Jua, an eight-year-old western lowland female gorilla. The go-rilla sat down on a log in a stream, cradling the boy in her lap and patting his back, and then carried him to one of the exhibit doorways before laying him down and continuing on her way.

Binti became a celebrity overnight, figuring in the speeches of leading politicians who held her up as an example of much-needed compassion. Some scientists were less lyrical, however. They cautioned that Binti's motives might have been less noble than they appeared, pointing out that this gorilla had been raised by people and had been taught parental skills with a stuffed animal. The whole affair might have been one of a confused maternal instinct, they claimed.

The intriguing thing about this flurry of alternative explanations was that nobody would think of raising similar doubts when a person saves a dog hit by a car. The rescuer might have grown up around a kennel, have been praised for being kind to animals, have a nurturing personality, yet we would still see his behavior as an act of caring. Whey then, in Binti's case, was her background held against her? I am not saying that I know what went through Binti's head, but I do know that no one had prepared her for this kind of emergency and that it is unlikely that, with her own 17-month-old infant on her back, she was "maternally confused." How in the world could such a highly intelligent animal mistake a blond boy in sneakers and a red T-shirt for a juvenile gorilla? Actually, the biggest surprise was how surprised most people were. Students of ape behavior did not feel that Binti had done anything unusual. Jörg Hess, a Swiss gorilla expert, put it most bluntly, "The incident can be sensational only for people who don't know a thing about gorillas."

Binti's action made a deep impression mainly because it benefited a member of our own species, but in my work on the evolution of morality and empathy, I have encountered numerous instances of animals caring for one another. For example, a chimpanzee consoles a victim after a violent attack, placing an arm around him and patting his back. And bonobos (or pygmy chimpanzees) have been known to as-sist companions new to their quarters in zoos, taking them by the hand to guide them through the maze of corridors connecting parts of their building. These kinds of cases don't reach the newspapers but are consistent with Binti's assistance to the unfortunate boy and the idea that apes have a capacity for sympathy.

The traditional bulwark against this sort of cognitive interpretation is the principle of parsimony—that we must make as few assumptions as possible when trying to construct a scientific explanation, and that assuming an ape is capable of something like sympathy is too great a leap. But doesn't that same principle of parsimony argue against assuming a huge cognitive gap when the evolutionary distance between humans and apes is so small? If two closely related species act in the same manner, their underlying mental processes are probably the same, too. The incident at the Brookfield Zoo shows how hard it is to avoid anthropodenial and anthropomorphism at the same time: in trying to avoid thinking of Binti as a human being, we run straight into the realization that Binti's actions make little sense if we refuse to assume intentions and feelings.

In the end we must ask: What kind of risk we are willing to take—the risk of underestimating animal mental life or the risk of overestimating it? There is no simple answer. But from an evolutionary perspective, Binti's kindness, like Georgia's mischief, is most parsimoniously explained in the same way we explain our own behavior—as the result of a complex, and familiar, inner life.

---

FRANS DE WAAL is a professor of psychology at Emory University and research professor at the Yerkes Regional Primate Research Center in Atlanta. He is the author of several books, including *Chimpanzee Politics* and *Good Natured: The Origins of Right and Wrong in Humans and Other Animals*. His latest book, in collaboration with acclaimed wildlife photographer Frans Lanting, is *Bonobo: The Forgotten Ape,* published by the University of California Press (1997).

# Unit 3

## Key Points to Consider

❖ How can the muriqui monkeys be sexually competitive and yet gregarious and cooperative?

❖ How do human males and females differ in their reproductive goals?

❖ How does human sexuality differ from that of other creatures?

❖ What implications does bonobo sexual behavior have for understanding human evolution?

❖ Why do many cultures the world over treat menstruating women as taboo?

❖ How do social bonds provide females with protection against abusive males?

 **Links**    **www.dushkin.com/online/**

These sites are annotated on pages 4 and 5.

Any account of hominid evolution would be remiss if it did not at least attempt to explain that most mystifying of all human experiences—our sexuality.

No other aspect of our humanity—whether it be upright posture, tool-making ability, or intelligence in general—seems to elude our intellectual grasp at least as much as it dominates our subjective consciousness. While we are a long way from reaching a consensus as to why it arose and what it is all about, there is widespread agreement that our very preoccupation with sex is in itself one of the hallmarks of being human. Even as we experience it and analyze it, we exalt it and condemn it. Beyond seemingly irrational fixations, however, there is the further tendency to project our own values upon the observations we make and the data we collect.

There are many who argue quite reasonably that the human bias has been more male- than female-oriented and that the recent "feminization" of anthropology has resulted in new kinds of research and refreshingly new theoretical perspectives. (See "The Myth of the Coy Female" by Carol Tavris and "A Woman's Curse?" by Meredith Small. Not only should we consider the source when evaluating the old theories, so goes the reasoning, but we should also welcome the source when considering the new. To take one example, traditional theory would have

predicted that the reproductive competitiveness of muriqui monkeys, as described in "These Are Real Swinging Primates" by Shannon Brownlee, would be associated with greater size and aggression among males. That this is not so, that making love can be more important than making war, and that females do not necessarily have to live in fear of competitive males, just goes to show that, even among monkeys, nothing can be taken for granted. The very idea that females are helpless in the face of male aggression is called into question by Barbara Smuts in "Apes of Wrath." There is even evidence that males and females have conflicting evolutionary goals, as discussed in "The War Between Men and Women" by Robert Sapolsky.

Finally, there is the question of the social significance of sexuality in humans. In "What's Love Got to Do With It?" Meredith Small shows that the chimp-like bonobos of Zaire use sex to reduce tensions and cement social relations and, in so doing, have achieved a high degree of equality between the sexes. Whether we see parallels in the human species, says Small, depends on our willingness to interpret bonobo behavior as a "modern version of our own ancestors' sex play," and this, in turn, may depend on our prior theoretical commitments.

# These Are Real Swinging Primates

*There's a good evolutionary reason why the rare muriqui of Brazil should heed the dictum 'Make love, not war'*

## Shannon Brownlee

When I first heard of the muriqui four years ago, I knew right away that I had to see one. This is an unusual monkey, to say the least. To begin with, it's the largest primate in South America; beyond that, the males have very large testicles. We're talking gigantic, the size of billiard balls, which means that the 30-pound muriqui has *cojones* that would look more fitting on a 400-pound gorilla.

But it wasn't prurience that lured me to Brazil. My interest in the muriqui was intellectual, because more than this monkey's anatomy is extraordinary. Muriqui society is untroubled by conflict: troops have no obvious pecking order; males don't compete overtly for females; and, most un-monkeylike, these monkeys almost never fight.

The muriqui is also one of the rarest monkeys in the world. It lives in a single habitat, the Atlantic forest of southeastern Brazil. This mountainous region was once blanketed with forest from São Paulo to Salvador (*see map*), but several centuries of slash-and-burn agriculture have reduced it to fragments.

In 1969 Brazilian conservationist Alvaro Coutinho Aguirre surveyed the remaining pockets of forest and estimated that 2,000 to 3,000 muriquis survived. His data were all but ignored until Russell Mittermeier, a biologist, trained his sights on the muriquis ten years later. Known as Russel of the Apes to his colleagues, Mittermeier, an American, directs the primate program for the World Wildlife Fund. He hopscotches from forest to forest around the world looking for monkeys in trouble and setting up conservation plans for them. In 1979 he and Brazilian zoologist Celio Valle retraced Aguirre's steps and found even fewer muriquis. Today only 350 to 500 are left, scattered among four state and national parks and six other privately held plots.

In 1981 Karen Strier, then a graduate student at Harvard, approached Mittermeier for help in getting permission to observe the muriqui. He took her to a coffee plantation called Montes Claros, near the town of Caratinga, 250 miles north of Rio de Janeiro. Over the next four years she studied the social behavior of the muriqui there—and came up with a provocative theory about how the monkey's unconventional behavior, as well as its colossal testicles, evolved. She reasoned that the evolution of both could be explained, at least in part, by the muriquis' need to avoid falling out of trees.

Last June I joined Strier, now a professor at Beloit (Wis.) College, on one of her periodic journeys to Montes Claros—clear mountains, in Portuguese. We arrived there after a disagreeable overnight bus trip over bad roads. As we neared the plantation, I found it difficult to believe there was a forest—much less a monkey—within miles. Through the grimy windows of the bus I saw hillsides stripped down to russet dirt and dotted with spindly coffee plants and stucco farmhouses. There wasn't anything taller than a banana tree in sight. As the bus lurched around the last curve before our stop the forest finally appeared, an island of green amid thousands of acres of coffee trees and brown pastures.

Strier was eager to start looking for the muriquis—"There's a chance we won't see them the whole four days you're here," she said—so no sooner had we dropped our bags off at a cottage on the plantation than we set out along a dirt road into the forest. The trees closed around us—and above us, where they gracefully arched to form a vault of green filigree. Parrots screeched; leaves rustled; a large butterfly flew erratically by on transparent wings. By this time Strier had guided me onto a steep trail, along which she stopped from time to time to listen for the monkeys.

They appeared soon enough, but our first meeting was less than felicitous. After we had climbed half a mile, Strier motioned for me to stop. A muffled sound, like that of a small pig grunting contentedly, came from up ahead. We moved forward a hundred yards. Putting a finger to her lips, Strier sank to her haunches and looked up.

I did the same; twelve round black eyes stared back at me. A group of six muriquis squatted, silent, 15 feet above in the branches, watching us intently. They began to grunt again. A sharp smell with undertones of cinnamon permeated the air. A light rain began to fall. I held out my palm to catch a drop. It was warm.

"Hey, this isn't rain!" I said.

Strier grinned and pointed to her head. "That's why I wear a hat," she said.

My enthusiasm for the muriquis waned slightly after that. We left them at dusk and retired to the cottage, where Strier described her arrival at Montes Claros four years earlier. Mittermeier acted as guide and interpreter during the first few days of her pilot study. He introduced her to the owner of the 5,000-acre plantation, Feliciano Miguel Abdala, then 73, who had preserved the 2,000-acre forest for more than 40 years. His is one of the only remaining tracts of Atlantic forest, and he agreed to let Strier use it as the site of her study. Then Mittermeier introduced her to the muriquis, assuring her they would be easy to see.

They weren't, and observing them closely is a little like stargazing on a rainy night: not only do you run the risk of getting wet, but you can also spend a lot of time looking up and never see a thing. Mittermeier was adept at spotting the monkeys in the forest, and helped Strier acquire this skill.

But brief glimpses of the monkeys weren't enough. "My strategy was to treat them like baboons, the only other species I'd ever studied," she says. "I thought I couldn't let them out of my sight." She tried to follow on the ground as they swung along in the trees. "They went berserk," she says. They threw branches, shrieked, urinated on her—or worse—and fled.

Even after the muriquis grew accustomed to her, keeping up with them wasn't easy. They travel as much as two miles a day, which is tough for someone picking her way through thick growth on the forest floor. As Strier and a Brazilian assistant learned the muriquis' habitual routes and daily patterns, they cleared trails. These helped, but the muriquis could still travel much faster than she could. "I've often thought the thing to have would be a jet pack," Strier says. "It would revolutionize primatology. Your National Science Foundation grant would include binoculars, pencils, and a jet pack."

The monkeys move by brachiating, swinging hand over hand from branch to branch, much like a child on a jungle gym. Only one other group of monkeys brachiates; the rest clamber along branches on all fours. The muriquis' closest relatives are two other Latin American genera, the woolly monkeys and the spider monkeys—hence woolly spider monkey, its English name. But the muriqui is so unlike them that it has its own genus, *Brachyteles,* which refers to its diminutive thumb, an adaptation for swinging through the trees. Its species name is *arachnoides,* from the Greek for spider, which the muriqui resembles when its long arms, legs, and tail are outstretched.

Brachiating is a specialization that's thought to have evolved because it enables primates to range widely to feed on fruit. Curiously, though, muriquis have a stomach designed for digesting leaves. Strier found that their diet consists of a combination of the two foods. They eat mostly foliage, low-quality food for a monkey, but prefer flowers and fruits, like figs and the *caja manga,* which is similar to the mango. Year after year they return to certain trees when they bloom and bear fruit. The rest of the time the muriquis survive on leaves by passing huge quantities of them through their elongated guts, which contain special bacteria to help them digest the foliage. By the end of the day their bellies are so distended with greenery that even the males look pregnant.

We returned to the trail the next morning just after dawn. Condensation trickled from leaves; howler monkeys roared and capuchins cooed and squeaked; a bird sang with the sweet, piercing voice of a piccolo. Then Strier had to mention snakes. "Watch out for snakes," she said blithely, scrambling on all fours up a steep bank. I followed her, treading cautiously.

The muriquis weren't where we had left them the day before. Strier led me along a ridge through a stand of bamboo, where a whisper of movement drifted up from the slope below. Maybe it was just the wind, but she thought it was the muriquis, so we sat down to wait. After a couple of hours, she confessed, "This part of research can get kind of boring."

By noon the faint noise became a distinct crashing. "That's definitely them," she said. "It's a good thing they're so noisy, or I'd never be able to find them." The monkeys, perhaps a dozen of them, swarmed uphill, breaking branches, chattering, uttering their porcine grunts as they swung along. At the crest of the ridge they paused, teetering in indecision while they peered back and forth before settling in some legume trees on the ridgetop. We crept down out of the bamboo to within a few feet of them, so close I noticed the cinnamon scent again—only this time I kept out of range.

Each monkey had its own feeding style. One hung upside down by its tail and drew the tip of a branch to its mouth; it delicately plucked the tenderest shoots with its rubbery lips. Another sat upright, grabbing leaves by the handful and stuffing its face. A female with twins—"Twins have never been seen in this species," Strier whispered as she excitedly scribbled notes—ate with one hand while hanging by the other and her tail. Her babies clung to the fur on her belly.

I had no trouble spotting the males. Their nether parts bulged unmistakably—blue-black or pink-freckled, absurd-looking monuments to monkey virility. I asked Strier what sort of obscene joke evolution was playing on the muriquis when it endowed them thus.

We were about to consider this question when a high-pitched whinnying began a few hundred yards away. Immediately a monkey just overhead pulled itself erect and let out an ear-splitting shriek, which set the entire troop to neighing like a herd of nervous horses. Then they took off down into the valley.

Strier and I had to plunge pell-mell into the underbrush or risk losing them for the rest of the day. "They're chasing the other troop," she said as we galloped downhill. A group of muriquis living on the opposite side of the forest had made a rare foray across the valley.

The monkeys we were observing swung effortlessly from tree to tree; we wrestled with thorny vines, and fell farther and farther behind. An impenetrable thicket forced us to backtrack in search of another route. By the time we caught up to the muriquis, they were lounging in a tree, chewing on unripe fruit and chuckling in a self-satisfied sort of way. The intruding troop was nowhere to be seen. "They must have scared the hell out of those other guys," said Strier, laughing.

Such confrontations occur infrequently; muriquis ordinarily tolerate another troop's incursions. Strier thinks they challenge intruders only when there's a valuable resource to defend—like the fruit tree they were sitting in.

Tolerance of another troop is odd behavior for monkeys, but not as odd as the fact that members of a muriqui troop never fight among themselves. "They're remarkably placid," said Strier. "They wait in line to dip their hands into water collected in the bole of a tree. They have no apparent pecking order or dominance hierarchy. Males and females are equal in status, and males don't squabble over females." No other primate society is known to be so free of competition, not even that of gorillas, which have lately gained a reputation for being the gentle giants of the primate world.

Strier's portrayal of the muriqui brought to mind a bizarre episode that Katharine Milton, an anthropologist at the University of California at Berkeley, once described. While studying a troop of muriquis in another patch of the Atlantic forest, she observed a female mating with a half a dozen males in succession; that a female monkey would entertain so many suitors came as no surprise, but Milton was astonished at the sight of the males lining up behind the female "like a choo-choo train" and politely taking turns copulating. They continued in this manner for two days, stopping only to rest and eat, and never even so much as bared their teeth.

Primates aren't known for their graciousness in such matters, and I found Milton's report almost unbelievable. But Strier confirms it. She says that female muriquis come into heat about every two and a half years, after weaning their latest offspring, and repeatedly copulate during that five- to seven-day period with a number of males. Copulations, "cops" in animal-behavior lingo, last as long as 18 minutes, and average six, which for most primates (including the genus *Homo,* if Masters and Johnson are correct) would be a marathon. Yet no mat-

ter how long a male muriqui takes, he's never harassed by suitors-in-waiting.

Strier has a theory to explain the muriqui's benignity, based on a paper published in 1980 by Richard Wrangham, a primatologist at the University of Michigan. He proposed that the social behavior of primates could in large part be predicted by what the females eat.

This isn't a completely new idea. For years primatologists sought correlations between ecological conditions and social structure, but few patterns emerged—until Wrangham's ingenious insight that environment constrains the behavior of each sex differently. Specifically, food affects the sociability of females more than males.

Wrangham started with the generally accepted premise that both sexes in every species have a common aim: to leave as many offspring as possible. But each sex pursues this goal in its own way. The best strategy for a male primate is to impregnate as many females as he can. All he needs, as Wrangham points out, is plenty of sperm and plenty of females. As for the female, no matter how promiscuous she is, she can't match a male's fecundity. On average, she's able to give birth to only one offspring every two years, and her success in bearing and rearing it depends in part upon the quality of food she eats. Therefore, all other things being equal, male primates will spend their time cruising for babes, while females will look for something good to eat.

Wrangham perceived that the distribution of food—that is, whether it's plentiful or scarce, clumped or evenly dispersed—will determine how gregarious the females of a particular species are. He looked at the behavior of 28 species and found that, in general, females forage together when food is plentiful and found in large clumps—conditions under which there's enough for all the members of the group and the clumps can be defended against outsiders. When clumps become temporarily depleted, the females supplement their diet with what Wrangham calls subsistence foods. He suggests that female savanna baboons, for example, live in groups because their favorite foods, fruits and flowers, grow in large clumps that are easy to defend. When these are exhausted

they switch to seeds, insects, and grasses. The females form long-lasting relationships within their groups, and establish stable dominance hierarchies.

Chimpanzees provide an illustration of how females behave when their food isn't in clumps big enough to feed everybody. Female chimps eat flowers, shoots, leaves, and insects, but their diet is composed largely of fruits that are widely scattered and often not very plentiful. They may occasionally gather at a particularly abundant fruit tree, but when the fruit is gone they disperse to forage individually for other foods. Members of the troop are constantly meeting at fruit trees, splitting up, and gathering again.

These two types of female groups, the "bonded" savanna baboons and "fissioning" chimps, as Wrangham calls them, pose very different mating opportunities for the males of their species. As a consequence, the social behavior of the two species is different. For a male baboon, groups of females represent the perfect opportunity for him to get cops. All he has to do is exclude other males. A baboon troop includes a clan of females accompanied by a number of males, which compete fiercely for access to them. For baboons there are few advantages to fraternal cooperation, and many to competition.

Male chimpanzees fight far less over females than male baboons do, principally because there's little point—the females don't stick together. Instead, the males form strong alliances with their fellows. They roam in gangs looking for females in heat, and patrol their troop's borders against male interlopers.

Wrangham's theory made so much sense, Strier says, that it inspired researchers to go back into the field with a new perspective. She saw the muriqui as an excellent species for evaluating the model, since Wrangham had constructed it before anyone knew the first thing about this monkey. His idea would seem all the more reasonable if it could predict the muriqui's behavior.

It couldn't, at least not entirely. Strier has found that the females fit Wrangham's predictions: they stick together and eat a combination of preferred and subsistence foods, defending the preferred from other troops. But the males don't conform to the theory. "Considering that the females are foraging together, there should be relatively low pressure on the males to cooperate," she says. "It's odd: the males should compete, but they don't."

She thinks that limitations on male competition may explain muriqui behavior. First, the muriquis are too big to fight in trees. "I think these monkeys are at about the limit of size for rapid brachiation," she says. "If they were bigger, they couldn't travel rapidly through the trees. They fall a lot as it is, and it really shakes them up. I've seen an adult fall about sixty feet, nearly to the ground, before catching hold of a branch. That means that whatever they fight about has got to be worth the risk of falling out of a tree."

Moreover, fighting may require more energy than the muriquis can afford. Milton has estimated the caloric value of the food eaten by a muriqui each day and compared it to the amount of energy she would expect a monkey of that size to need. She concluded that the muriqui had little excess energy to burn on combat.

The restriction that rapid brachiation sets on the muriqui's size discourages competition in more subtle ways, as well.

Given that muriquis are polygynous, the male should be bigger than the female, as is almost invariably the case among other polygynous species—but he's not. The link between larger males and polygyny is created by sexual selection, an evolutionary force that Darwin first recognized, and which he distinguished from natural selection by the fact that it acts exclusively on one sex. Sexual selection is responsible for the manes of male lions, for instance, and for the large canines of male baboons.

In a polygynous society, the advantages to being a large male are obvious: he who's biggest is most likely to win the battles over females—and pass on his genes for size. But sexual selections' push toward large males has been thwarted in the muriqui, says Strier. Any competitive benefits greater size might bring a male would be offset in part by the excessive demands on his energy and the costs of falling out of trees.

She believes that the constraints on the males' size have had a profound effect on the muriquis' social behavior. Most important, says Strier, with males and females being the same size, the females can't be dominated, which means they can pick their mates. Most female

primates aren't so fortunate: if they copulate with subordinate males, they risk being attacked by dominant ones. But a female muriqui in heat can easily refuse a suitor, simply by sitting down or by moving away. Fighting not only doesn't help the male muriqui in his quest for cops; it may even harm his chances, since females can shun an aggressive male. Strier believes that females may also be responsible for the male muriquis' canine teeth not being oversized. As a rule, the male's canines are the same size as the female's only in monogamous primate species, but over the generations female muriquis may have mated more readily with males whose teeth were no bigger than their own. In sum, Strier thinks, for a male muriqui the costs of competing are far outweighted by the benefits of avoiding it.

But he has the means to vie for reproductive success and still come across as Mr. Nice Guy: his sperm. Sperm competition, as it's called, is a hot new idea in sociobiology, originally proposed to explain male bonding in chimpanzees, and, as Milton was the first to suggest, it may explain why the muriqui has such enormous testicles.

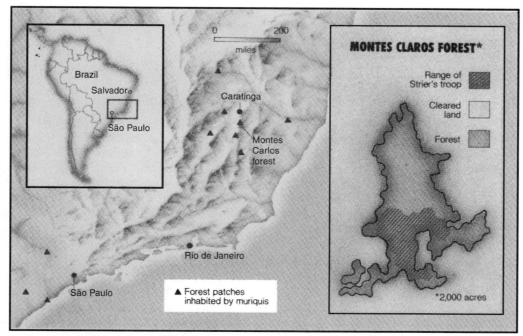

JOE LEMONNIER

**The 350 to 500 surviving muriquis live in ten patches of the Atlantic forest of southeastern Brazil.**

The competition is something like a game of chance. Imagine a bucket with a hole in the bottom just big enough for a marble to pass through. People gather round, each with a handful of marbles. They drop their marbles in the bucket, mix them up, and one comes out the bottom. Whoever owns that marble is the winner.

In the sperm competition among male muriquis, the bucket is a female, the marbles are sperm, and winning means becoming a father. No male can be sure it will be his sperm that impregnates a female, since she mates with a number of his fellows. His chances are further complicated by the fact that the female muriqui, like all New World monkeys, gives no visible indication of ovulation; there may be nothing that signals the male (or the female) when during her heat that occurs. So it's to the male's advantage to continue mating as often as the female will have him.

This may sound like monkey heaven, but it puts the male on the horns of a dilemma. If he copulates as often as possible, he could run low on sperm just when the female is ovulating. On the other hand, if he refrains from copulating to save sperm, he may miss his chance at procreating altogether. Selection may have come to his aid, Strier reasons, by acting on his testicles.

Here's a plausible scenario. Suppose a male came along that could produce more sperm than the average muriqui because his testicles were bigger than average. That male would clean up in the reproductive arena. The ratio of testicle size to body weight has been correlated with high sperm count and repeated copulation over a short period in other mammals, and bigger testicles probably also increase the percentage of viable and motile sperm.

If the muriqui's testicles are anything like those of other species, then a male with extra big ones has a slight reproductive advantage. Like a player with more marbles to put in the bucket, a male that can produce more and better sperm has a better than average chance of impregnating females and passing on this advantageous trait to his sons. Just as important, the outsized organs probably don't cost him much in metabolic

energy. Thus, over generations, the muriqui's testicles have grown larger and larger.

Strier's theory has five years of data behind it, and it's the kind of theory that will stimulate researchers to reexamine their ideas about other species. Yet it isn't her only concern; she concentrates equally on the muriqui's uncertain future. On our last day in the forest we watched the monkeys cross a six-foot gap in the canopy 60 feet above us. One by one they stood poised for a moment on the end of a branch before launching themselves. Strier counted them as they appeared in silhouette against a grey sky. The total was 33, including the twins. "They're up from twenty-two in 1982," she said. "That's a very fast increase."

The muriquis at Montes Claros make up almost one-tenth of the total population of the species, and they're critical to its survival—as are all the other isolated and widely separated troops. Each groups's genetic pool is limited, and eventually the troops could suffer inbreeding depression, a decline in fecundity that often appears in populations with little genetic variability.

Strier and Mittermeier predict that one day muriquis will have to be managed, the way game species are in the U.S. They may be transported between patches of forest to provide some gene flow. But that's a dangerous proposition now. There are too few muriquis to risk it, and none has ever bred or survived for long in captivity. "Before my study, conservationists would probably have moved males between forests," Strier says. "That would've been a mistake. I have tentative evidence that in a natural situation the females may be the ones that do the transferring between groups."

For now, though, she thinks the biggest concern isn't managing the monkeys but preventing their habitat from disappearing. Preserving what remains of the Atlantic forest won't be easy, and no one knows this better than Feliciano Miguel Abdala, the man responsible for there being any forest at all at Montes Claros.

Abdala has little formal education, but he's rich; he owns nine plantations beside Montes Claros. His family lives

in relative splendor in Caratinga, but he likes to spend the weekdays here. His house is just beyond the edge of the forest, and sunlight filters through the bougainvillea vine entwining the front porch. Chickens can be seen through the cracks in the floorboards, scratching in the dirt under the house. Electric cords are strung crazily from the rafters, and a bare bulb dangles in the center of his office. Abdala removes his straw hat decorously and places it on a chair before sitting at his desk.

Abdala bought the 5,000 acres of Montes Claros in 1944. The region was barely settled then, and smoke still rose from the great burning heaps of slash left from clearing the forest. Abdala's land included one of the last stands of trees. I ask him why he saved it. "I am a conservationist," he says. "For a long time the local people thought I was crazy because I wouldn't cut the forest. I told them not to shoot the monkeys, and they stopped. Now all my workers are crazy, too."

I ask Abdala about his plans for his forest. He rubs his head distractedly and says, vaguely. "I hope it will continue."

Abdala believes the government should buy Montes Claros—plantation and rain forest—to create a nature reserve. He'll probably maintain the forest as long as he lives, but the land is quite valuable, and his heirs might not share his lofty sentiments.

As important as the muriquis have become to understanding social systems, and as much as U.S. conservationists may wish to see these monkeys preserved, Strier thinks that in the end it's up to the Brazilians to save them. She's expecting a three-year grant from the National Science Foundation; part of the money will go toward allowing her to observe the monkeys in other forest patches, watching for variation in their behavior as a test of her ideas. Studies like hers will be critical not only for proving theories but also for ensuring that plans for managing the muriquis will work. The rest of the money will permit her to train seven Brazilian graduate students, because she says, "the future of the muriqui lies with the Brazilians."

# The WAR BETWEEN MEN AND WOMEN

## By Robert Sapolsky

## What do you do if a lot of the struggle takes place at a molecular level and neither person knows it?

As most newlyweds quickly learn, intimate relationships, even the most blissful, can buzz with tension. Couples typically find themselves struggling over money, in-laws, ex-lovers, and how much the woman's placenta should grow when she gets pregnant. That last one is a killer. The guy wants his woman to have a fast-growing placenta, while the woman does all she can to keep it down to a reasonable size.

Of course, the fight over the placenta doesn't exactly take place out in the open. The average man, if asked what he thinks of his wife's placenta, would probably say he hasn't given it a thought. Instead the placenta conflict gets played out, unbeknownst to either person, inside the woman's body. A

strange genetic process called genomic imprinting is responsible. And its existence is only one small example of how males and females have conflicting evolutionary goals. Understanding that the struggle takes place can explain a lot of strange behavior and physiology. And it can even explain how we came to be susceptible to certain horrific diseases.

At first it might seem unlikely that men and women do have conflicting evolutionary goals. The point of life, according to evolutionary theorists, is for organisms to pass on copies of their genes to succeeding generations. Some organisms, such as cockroaches, do this by producing as many offspring as possible, hoping some will survive. Others, such as elephants and humans, have

many fewer young but shower them with care.

So yes, both mom and dad want their kid to survive. And in monogamous species, when the father can be pretty sure it really is his kid, he may well cooperate with the mother. But that's not quite the way it is in more polygamous animal species such as orangutans, nor was it that way, say many evolutionary biologists, among our own ancestors. Those males want their offspring to survive at any cost—even at the cost of the female's health and future fertility with other males. For example, if the male can figure out a way to make the female spend most of her food energy making the offspring grow big and strong, that's okay, even if she starves. That's where

# Males want their offspring to survive at any cost

the struggle over the placenta comes in: men and other male mammals pass on genes to their unborn children that encourage the mother's placenta to grow big, nourishing the fetus at the mother's expense and at the expense of her future kids with other guys.

Females want their offspring to survive too, but not at the risk of their future fertility. For example, in mammals, nursing inhibits ovulation. So a mammal mom wouldn't nurse her young for the rest of her life, even if doing so greatly increased its chances of survival. Otherwise, she might never again ovulate, become pregnant, and bear more young.

This conflict is played out viciously among fruit flies. Rather than growing old in each other's arms, drosophila mate with multiple partners, none of whom stick around for a second date.

males compete against each other. After 40 generations, the evolutionary winners were males with the strongest toxic punch in their semen. Females who mated with them had a shorter life expectancy.

The same sort of coevolutionary arms race happens in humans and other mammals. As a result, we have developed a bizarre set of genes called imprinted genes, that seem to violate the basic tenets of genetics.

Think back to Gregor Mendel, high school biology, and dominant and recessive traits. That most monkish of monks taught that genetic traits are coded for by pairs of genes, one from each parent. He figured out how the pairs of genes interact to influence the organism, depending on whether the pair have identical or differing messages. According to Mendel, it doesn't matter which parent

placenta, the fetus, or the newborn. And the genes derived from the father favor greater, faster, more expensive growth, while the maternally derived genes counter that exuberance. As the evolutionist David Haig of Harvard first suggested in 1989, imprinted genes—including these genes in humans—are a case of intersexual competition, fruit fly sperm wars redux.

The first battleground is the placenta, a tissue that can seem more than a little creepy. It's only partially related to the female, but it invades (a term used in obstetrics) her body, sending tentacles toward her blood vessels to divert nutrients for the benefit of a growing fetus. The placenta is also the scene of a pitched battle, with paternally derived genes pushing it to invade more aggressively while maternally derived genes

# Imprinted genes can turn the placenta into a cancer

And look at what they've come up with: male semen contains toxins that kill the sperm of other males. When a male fly mates with a female who has recently had sex with someone else, his spermicide goes to work, killing competitors' sperm. That's a great adaptation, but unfortunately the stuff is toxic to the female and gradually harms her health. This doesn't bother the male at all. It increases his evolutionary fitness, and he's never going to see her again.

William Rice, an evolutionary geneticist then at the University of California at Santa Cruz, did a wonderfully slick experiment in which he kept female fruit flies from evolving while letting the

contributed which genetic message. Whether the offspring gets the vanilla version of a gene from the mother and the chocolate version from the father or the other way around, the trait coded for by the pair of genes will look the same.

Imprinted genes violate Mendel's rules. With these genes, only the gene from one parent has input—the matching gene from the other parent is silenced, losing its influence over the trait expressed. Most experts in this new field believe that there are only a couple hundred of these genes in humans, but they can be quite influential.

About half the genes in question have something to do with growth—of the

try to hold it back. How do we know? In rare diseases, maternal or paternal genes related to placental growth are knocked out of action. Lose the paternal input and the anti-growth maternal component is left unopposed—the placenta never invades the mother's endometrium, so the fetus has no chance to grow. In contrast, remove the maternal input, leaving those paternal genes unopposed, and the placenta grows into a stupendously aggressive cancer called choriocarcinoma.

The imprinting struggle continues during fetal development. One gene, which codes for a powerful growth-stimulating hormone in mice and hu-

# Stay-at-Home Dads

Conflict between males and females takes a complicated turn in the rare species with high "male parental investment." In such species, a male instinctually takes care of youngsters he thinks are his own. He mates with someone, and babies appear an appropriate

length of time later, so he protects them from predators and takes them to ice-skating lessons. A lot of bird species fit this profile. Sometimes the male does more parenting than the female. At the moment when the egg hatches, she has invested far more energy in the gestation than he

has, but afterward the tide gradually turns. In those cases, what should a heartlessly practical female do if she wants to maximize her reproductive success? She should figure out the exact moment when he's spent more cumulative energy than she has on passing on copies

of his genes via these offspring. When that moment arrives, she should abandon the youngsters. He will likely continue taking care of them, guaranteeing her reproductive success and leaving her free to start a new round of reproduction with someone else.

—R. S.

# Reports of human monogamy are greatly exaggerated

mans, is expressed only by paternally derived genes. This is a classic case of dad pushing for maximal fetal development. In mice (though not in people), the mother counteracts the pro-growth tumult by expressing a gene for a cellular receptor that regulates the growth hormone's effectiveness. Thrust and parry.

Once a baby is born, imprinted genes take a particularly impressive turn. Certain paternally expressed genes help make kids active nursers. On the surface, this looks like another example of the usual picture: faster development at the cost of mom's lactational calories. But now we're talking about imprinted genes that influence behavior. Other genes influence brain development in even stranger ways (*See* Brain Genes, below).

The discovery of imprinted genes may pave the way for curing a number of unpleasant diseases involving tumors, infertility, and fetal overgrowth or underdevelopment. But philosophically, the findings are disturbing. They appear to have some deflating implications about human nature. Among fruit flies, sperm-war genes show that males care little about the females' future. What about us? "In sickness and in health," we promise, "until death do us part." We're the species that came up with Paul Newman and Joanne Woodward. For monogamous animals, the future health and fertility of the female is as much in the male's interest as hers. So what are these imprinted genes doing in a human couple pondering which appetizers to serve at their golden wedding anniversary?

## Self-Conscious Scrub Jays

When biologists talk about male orangutans "realizing" that they have less to lose in mating than females, or female scrub jays "calculating" exactly when to abandon their young to a caring father, they're speaking metaphorically. Except for the most cognitively sophisticated primates, animals don't sit there with an evolution textbook and a calculator, strategizing consciously. Instead phrases like "the scrub jay wants to do this, decides that this is the right time," and so on are shorthand for the more correct but cumbersome, "Over the course of evolution, scrub jays who, at least in part through genetically influenced mechanisms, are better able to optimize the timing of their behavior leave more copies of their genes, thus making this attribute more prevalent in the population." Personifying the animals is just an expository device agreed upon to keep everyone from falling asleep during conferences.—*R. S.*

The answer is that reports of our monogamy are greatly exaggerated. Features of human anatomy and physiology argue against it. Most human cultures allow polygamy. And most studies, ranging from genetic paternity tests to *Cosmo* questionnaires, suggest that there's a lot of action going on outside the pair-bond, even in monogamous societies. We have more in common with fruit flies than commonly believed. (Mind you, we're not one of the more polygamous species around. Even the busiest patriarchs weigh in with only a few hundred kids.)

Does nature have to be so bloody in tooth and claw and gene? Must everything be based on competition? Why can't we all just get along? Here's where the evolutionary biologists, with Bogart-esque weariness, pull out the great

clichés of their field. Biology isn't about what should be, they explain, but what is. It's a tough evolutionary world out there. It's dog outreproduce dog. But a recent experiment by Rice and evolutionary behaviorist Brett Holland hints that intersexual competition needn't be inevitable. With careful manipulation, it can be derailed. The researchers isolated pairs of mating flies, forcing them to be monogamous. They then bred the offspring with the offspring of other such enforced monogamous pairs, continuing to maintain the monogamy. And after only 40 generations, the monogamous descendants produced less harmful seminal fluid.

They also treated their mates with unusual courtesy—normal fruit-fly courtship looks like sexual harassment. Once competition between males was no

## Brain Genes

Mom wants you to be clever, but dad cares more about your metabolism. At least, that's the way the evidence of genomic imprinting points. Experiments with mice show that some maternally expressed genes favor a bigger cortex, the intellectual part of the brain. Mutations that knock out those genes cause retardation. In contrast,

some paternally expressed genes favor growth of the hypothalamus, which controls many unconscious body functions.

How do these imprinted genes related to brain function fit into the scheme of intersexual warfare? Instead of the usual scenario, in which dad wants more growth while mom wants less, each par-

ent's genes favor a different kind of growth. Does a female enhance her future health and fertility by supplying her young with a thick cortex and super SAT scores? Does a bigger hypothalamus produce a kid who is able to sap more of mom's resources? No one knows, but Eric B. Keverne of the University of Cambridge, Eng-

land, who has done much of the work on brain-related imprinted genes, continues to wrestle with these intriguing findings, trying to fit them into the framework of intersexual warfare. Meanwhile, some evolutionary biologists speculate that the traits might have evolved for entirely different reasons.
—*R. S.*

# Monogamous flies treat their mates with courtesy

longer a selective force, producing toxic chemicals apparently became a maladaptive waste of energy. Freed of the cost of intersexual warfare, these monogamous flies actually outbred the usual competitive flies.

Just imagine carrying out the same experiment in people. Isolate some humans and force them and their descendants into monogamy for a millennium, and we would probably begin to disarm our mammalian weapons of intersexual warfare, namely imprinted genes. They are an evolutionary burden, making possible some truly horrendous cancers. Remove their advantages by eliminating polygamy, and natural selection should edit them out.

Having arrived at what sounds like a surreal moral—an exhortation to remember the Sixth Commandment as part of the "Let's Whip Choriocarcinoma by the Year 3000" campaign—it's time to take a step back. Understanding how intersexual competition started with flies is relatively easy. Thanks to random genetic variability, some male flies stumbled into ever so slightly toxic sperm, which the females had to detoxify or die. And from there, the competition spiraled upward. The story of imprinted genes is a bit more complicated, but once paternally derived genes began pushing for the-hell-with-the-mom growth, the battle inevitably escalated. If the tribe next door shows up at the Paleolithic watering hole with clubs that seem just a wee bit on the big side for the purpose of bonking prey animals over the head, the home team will naturally respond by getting even bigger clubs, just in case. And soon we have a world with choriocarcinoma, toxic fruit-fly semen, and umpteen times the education budget buying $600 toilet seats for the military. As in so many other arenas of conflict, it's easier to ratchet up than down.

# The Myth of the Coy Female

## Carol Tavris

[Thus] we arrived at the important conclusion that polygamy is the natural order among human beings, just as it is in most species of the animal kingdom . . . monogamy is responsible for the high incidence of divorce and female grievances in modern society, as well as the genetic deevolution and behavioral degeneration of civilization as a whole. . . . Culture is to blame, and fortunately *culture can be changed*. Mating is the key. [Emphasis in original.]

—Sam Kash Kachigan,
*The Sexual Matrix*

Sam Kash Kachigan is not a social scientist; he's just a regular fellow who thinks that the theories of sociobiology offer the best hope of improving relations between women and men. "Mating is the key," he argues. The mating he has in mind, it turns out, would (if we were truly to follow our evolutionary heritage) occur between rich old men and beautiful young girls. Among the annoying contemporary practices that Kachigan laments is the habit of beautiful young girls marrying boys their own age. To Kachigan, in any truly civilized society—that is, one in which our practices fit our sociobiological natures—girls would marry men who were old enough to demonstrate their "true potential":

In every respect, then, it makes much more sense for young women to mate with *older* men, who will have *proven* their genetic endowment as well as their financial and emotional capacity for raising children. [Emphasis in original.]

Why do I suspect that Kachigan is such a man?

The basic ideas behind sociobiology date back to Charles Darwin, who in 1871 described what he considered to be a basic dichotomy in the sexual natures of males and females of all species. Males actively pursue females; they are promiscuous; and those who are strongest, most fit in evolutionary terms, succeed in their sexual conquest. Females, said Darwin, are "comparatively passive"; they may choose their preferred suitor, but then remain monogamous and faithful. That this dichotomy conveniently fit Victorian dating and mating patterns was, naturally, pure coincidence.

For a century after Darwin, research on sexual selection and sexual behavior was based on the belief that males are passionate and undiscriminating (any female in a storm will do), whereas females are restrained, cautious, and highly discriminating in their choice of partner (only a male who meets her shopping list of qualifications will do). According to primatologist Sarah Blaffer Hrdy, this stereotype of "the coy female" has persisted in the public mind—and she adds a phrase that by now should be familiar to us—*"despite the accumulation of abundant openly available evidence contradicting it"* [my emphasis].

The stereotype of the coy female got a major boost in an important paper published in 1948 by Angus John Bateman. Bateman was a distinguished plant geneticist who did dozens of experiments with Drosophila, the tiny fruit fly

that many people remember from science experiments in junior high school. Bateman found that successful male fruit flies could, with multiple matings, produce nearly three times as many offspring as the most reproductively successful female. As Hrdy explains, "whereas a male could always gain by mating just one more time, and hence benefit from a nature that made him undiscriminatingly eager to mate, a female, already breeding near capacity after just one copulation, could gain little from multiple mating and should be quite uninterested in mating more than once or twice."

What, you may ask, does a human man have in common with a fruit fly? When it comes to sexual strategies, said Bateman, the answer is everything. Generalizing from his sixty-four experiments with Drosophila to all species, Bateman concluded that there is a universally lopsided division in the sexual natures of all creatures, apart from "a few very primitive organisms." Quite simply, males profit, evolutionarily speaking, from frequent mating, and females do not. This is why, said Bateman, "there is nearly always a combination of an undiscriminating eagerness in the males and a discriminating passivity in the females."

The modern field of sociobiology took this idea still further, attempting to account for complex human social arrangements and customs—warfare and corporate raiding, feeding infants and giving children karate lessons—in terms of the individual's basic need to reproduce his or her genes. Women and men, sociobiologists believe, adopt highly different strategies in order to do this. Males compete with other males for access to desirable females, and their goal is to inseminate as many females as possible. Females, in contrast, are motivated to attach themselves to genetically "superior" males because of the female's greater "investment" in terms of time and energy in her offspring; this, according to sociobiologists, is why females are more faithful and nurturant than males. As biologist Ruth Hubbard observes, "Thus, from the seemingly innocent asymmetries between eggs and sperm [say the sociobiologists] flow such major social consequences as female fidelity, male promiscuity, women's disproportional contribution to the care of children, and the unequal distribution of labor by sex."

Sociobiological explanations of competitive, promiscuous men and choosy, inhibited but flirtatious women fit right in with many elements within the popular culture. "And so it was," Hrdy says, "that 'coyness' came to be the single most commonly mentioned attribute of females in the literature on sociobiology."

It all seems a cruel joke of nature. Certainly many people are convinced, as the King of Siam sings in *The King and I,* that the male is like the honeybee, flitting from flower to flower, "gathering all he can," whereas the female has "honey for just one man." But notice that it is the King who sings that song; until relatively recently, no one was asking Queens for their view of things. Nor were male observers asking why, if human females were so naturally chaste, coy, and monogamous, social taboos from ostracism to death had to be placed on females who indulged in forbidden sexual relationships. For that matter, why did non-marital affairs need to be forbidden anyway, if females have "honey for just one man"?

Sociobiologists attempt to explain human social customs by drawing on research on nonhuman animals, from the fields of primatology, evolutionary biology, anthropology, and related disciplines. In the last two decades, however, there has been an explosion of new research that casts doubt on many socio-

biological assumptions, a change that is largely a result of the growing numbers of women who have entered these fields. Most of the women saw animal behavior in a different light from most of the male observers who had preceded them. Male primatologists, for example, had tended to observe and emphasize male-male competition and the number of times the male animals "got lucky"; the female animals, to the human men observing them, seemed mysterious and unpredictable. This is not unlike the ways in which human females have seemed mysterious and unpredictable to the human males who have observed *them.*

At first, women who went into these research fields saw the world as they had been taught to see it, through the academic perspective of their mentors. But after a while, they began to ask different questions and to bring different expectations to their observations. Hrdy recalls her own first glimpse of a female langur

> . . . moving away from her natal group to approach and solicit males in an all-male band. At the time, I had no context for interpreting behavior that merely seemed strange and incomprehensible to my Harvard-trained eyes. Only in time, did I come to realize that such wandering and such seemingly "wanton" behavior were recurring events in the lives of langurs.

Eventually, Hrdy learned that female langurs often leave their troops to join up with bands of males; and she also found that often a female, for reasons unknown, "simply takes a shine to the resident male of a neighboring troop." In fact, female langurs (and many other primate species) are able to shift from being in heat once a month to being continuously receptive for weeks at a time, a state not unlike the first phase of (human) love. In many primates, female receptivity is often *situation specific,* rather than being dependent exclusively on cyclical periods of being in heat.

As a result of the efforts of many pioneers like Hrdy, we now know that the females of many animal species do not behave like the patient, coy fruit fly. On the contrary, the females are sexually ar-

dent and can even be called polyandrous (having many male partners). Further, their sexual behavior does not depend simply on the goal of being fertilized by the male, because in many cases females actively solicit males when they are not ovulating, and even when they are already pregnant. Here are a few illustrations from hundreds of research studies:

- Many species of female birds are promiscuous. In one study, researchers vasectomized the "master" of a blackbird harem . . . but the females nevertheless conceived.
- Many species of female fish are promiscuous. A female shiner perch who is not ovulating will nevertheless mate with many males, collecting sperm and storing them internally until she is ready to ovulate.
- Many species of female cats, notably leopards, lions, and pumas, are promiscuous. A lioness may mate dozens of times with many different partners during the week she is in estrus.
- Many species of female primates are promiscuous. Among savanna baboons and Barbary macaques, females initiate many different brief sexual encounters. Among chimpanzees, Hrdy reports, some females form partnerships with one male, but others engage in communal mating with all males in the vicinity. And among wild tamarin monkeys, a species long thought to be monogamous (at least in captivity), supposedly faithful females will mate with several males. So do female Hanuman langurs, blue monkeys, and redtail monkeys, all primates that were formerly believed to be one-man women. The old notion that primate females typically form "one-male breeding units," as primatologists would say, is now seriously called into question.

In spite of rapidly accumulating evidence that females of many different and varied species do mate "promiscuously" (a word that itself has evaluative overtones), it was not until 1980 or so that researchers realized that this fact threw, well, a monkey wrench into traditional evolutionary theories. Why would females have more copulations than are necessary for conception? Why would they go off with some guy from a neighboring town, whom none of her friends approves of? Why risk losing the genetic father's support by joining the baboon equivalent of Hell's Angels? And the brooding question over all of them, why did female primates develop continuous sexual receptivity?

These questions stimulated a flurry of new theories to explain why female philandering would make as much survival sense as its male counterpart. Most of these new explanations directly resulted from considering the world from the female's point of view. Traditional theories of sexual selection, after all, were based exclusively on the perspective of the male: Males compete for *access* to the female, who apparently is just hanging around waiting to go out and party with the winner. And it's only from a male point of view that multiple female matings can be considered "excessive," or that female sexual interest is even described as her time of "receptivity." Is she passively "receptive" to the active intentions of the male? The word implies that she's just putting up with his annoying lustfulness yet again.

New hypotheses argue that there are genetic benefits for the offspring of sexually adventurous mothers. According to Hrdy's review of these explanations, the "fertility backup" hypothesis assumes that females need sperm from a number of males in order to assure conception by the healthiest sperm. The "inferior cuckold" hypothesis suggests that a female who has a genetically inferior mate will sneak off with a genetically superior male when she is likely to conceive. (I suppose she knows this by the size of his income.) And the "diverse paternity" hypothesis argues that when the environment is unpredictable, females diversify. Over a reproductive lifetime, females who have numerous partners, and thus different fathers for their offspring, improve their offspring's chances for survival.

Other theories look for the social and environmental benefits of female promiscuity to the mother and her infants. The "therapeutic hypothesis" suggests that having lots of partners and multiple orgasms (in some species) makes intercourse and conception more pleasurable, and therefore more likely to occur. The

"keep 'em around" hypothesis maintains that females actively solicit lower-status males (with the tacit approval of dominant males), a behavior that prevents weaker males from leaving the group. Hrdy's own favored theory is what she calls the "manipulation hypothesis," the idea that females mate with numerous males precisely because paternity becomes uncertain. The result is that male partners will be more invested in, and tolerant of, the female's infants. This idea, Hrdy explains,

> grew out of a dawning awareness that, first of all, individual females could do a great deal that would affect the survival of their offspring, and second, that males, far from mere dispensers of sperm, were critical features on the landscape where infants died or survived. That is, females were more political, males more nurturing (or at least not neutral), than some earlier versions of sexual selection theory would lead us to suppose.

Both of these points are essential: Not only are females more than passive receptacles of sperm, but also males are more than "mere dispensers of sperm." They don't just mate and run. They have a key role in determining whether infants survive or die. Among primates, there is enormous variation in the extent to which males nurture and protect offspring:

- Among the ruffed lemur, the male tends the nest while the female forages for food.
- Among New World monkeys, males directly care for offspring in half of all species; often, the male is the primary caretaker, carrying the infant on his back, sharing food with it.
- In a rare study of a monogamous species of night money, an observer found that during one infant's first week of life, the mother carried it 33 percent of the time, the father 51 percent of the time, and a juvenile member of the troop the remaining time.
- Among baboons, males do not have much direct contact with infants, but they hover nearby protectively and offer what Hrdy calls "quality" time in a very real sense: They increase the infant's chances of survival. They discourage attacks on the infant from

males who are unknown, in both the literal and the Biblical sense, to the mother.

Hrdy's "manipulation hypothesis" assumes that primate males respond more benevolently to the offspring of females with whom they have mated, so the females derive obvious benefits from mating with more than one male. In numerous primate species, the mother's multiple sexual partners act like godfathers to the infant, as primatologist Jeanne Altmann calls them. Each of these males will help care for the female's offspring. Baboon males, many of whom could have served as the model for *Three Men and a Baby,* develop special relationships with the infant, carrying it on their backs on times of danger and protecting it from strangers and hazards. These affectionate bonds are possible because of the mother's closeness to the males, says Hrdy, and because the infant comes to trust these males and seek them out.

The manipulation hypothesis may or may not hold up with further research, as Hrdy acknowledges. It certainly does not apply to most human societies, where husbands do not look too kindly on their wives' "special relationships" with other men, let alone their previous lovers, husbands, and wooers. Hrdy's work, nonetheless, shows that theories depend, first and foremost, on what an observer *observes,* and then on how those observations can be blurred by unconscious expectations. Hrdy initially regarded those "wanton" female langurs as aberrations because their behavior did not fit the established theory. Not until researchers began to speculate on the potential benefits of female promiscuity did they come up with different questions and answers about female sexual behavior than had sociobiologists.

In evolutionary biology, if not in the popular press, the myth of the coy female (and, for that matter, the myth of the absent father) is dead. Hrdy is encouraged by the speed with which primatologists, once aware of the male bias that permeated their discipline, have produced "a small stampede by members of both sexes to study female reproductive strategies." This she takes to be a healthy sign, as I do. But Hrdy cautions against "substituting a new set of biases for the old ones":

> That is, among feminist scholars it is now permissible to say that males and females are different, provided one also stipulates that females are more cooperative, more nurturing, more supportive—not to mention equipped with unique moral sensibilities. . . .

Perhaps it is impossible, as biologist Donna Haraway suggests, for any of us to observe the behavior of other species, let alone our own, in a way that does not mirror the assumptions of our own way of life. It is disconcerting, says Hrdy wryly, that primatologists were finding "politically motivated females and nurturing males at roughly the same time that a woman runs for vice president of the United States and [Garry] Trudeau starts to poke fun at 'caring males' in his cartoons." Informally, scientists admit that their prejudices—such as the tendency to identify with the same sex of the species they are studying—affect their research. One woman primatologist told Hrdy, "I sometimes identify with female baboons more than I do with males of my own species."

The recognition of a male-centered bias in primatology and biology proved to be an enormous step forward, allowing scientists of both sexes to revise their theories of animal behavior. Sociobiologists (and their fans like Sam Kash Kachigan) can no longer justify traditional sex roles, particularly male dominance and female nurturance and chastity, by appealing to the universality of such behavior in other species. Other species aren't cooperating.

But that is not the only moral of the Parable of the Primates. The female perspective is invaluable, but, as Hrdy warns, a female-centered bias will provide its own set of distortions. Cultural feminists who look to evolutionary biology to explain women's allegedly sweeter, more cooperative ways are on as shaky ground as the antifeminists they would replace.

If the sociobiological heroine is the coy female who is so different from males, the heroine of modern sexology is the lusty female who is just like them. I like her better, but I'm afraid that she, too, is (as a student of mine once inadvertently said) a fig leaf of the imagination. . . .

# A Woman's Curse?

*Why do cultures the world over treat menstruating women as taboo?
An anthropologist offers a new answer—and a challenge to Western
ideas about contraception*

## By Meredith F. Small

THE PASSAGE FROM GIRLHOOD TO WOM-anhood is marked by a flow of blood from the uterus. Without elaborate ceremony, often without discussion, girls know that when they begin to menstruate, their world is changed forever. For the next thirty years or so, they will spend much energy having babies, or trying not to, reminded at each menstruation that either way, the biology of reproduction has a major impact on their lives.

Anthropologists have underscored the universal importance of menstruation by documenting how the event is interwoven into the ideology as well as the daily activities of cultures around the world. The customs attached to menstruation take peculiarly negative forms: the so-called menstrual taboos. Those taboos may prohibit a woman from having sex with her husband or from cooking for him. They may bar her from visiting sacred places or taking part in sacred activities. They may forbid her to touch certain items used by men, such as hunting gear or weapons, or to eat certain foods or to wash at certain times. They may also require that a woman paint her face red or wear a red hip cord, or that she segregate herself in a special hut while she is menstruating. In short, the taboos set menstruating women apart from the rest of their society, marking them as impure and polluting.

Anthropologists have studied menstrual taboos for decades, focusing on the negative symbolism of the rituals as a cultural phenomenon. Perhaps, sug-gested one investigator, taking a Freudian perspective, such taboos reflect the anxiety that men feel about castration, an anxiety that would be prompted by women's genital bleeding. Others have suggested that the taboos serve to prevent menstrual odor from interfering with hunting, or that they protect men from microorganisms that might otherwise be transferred during sexual intercourse with a menstruating woman. Until recently, few investigators had considered the possibility that the taboos—and the very fact of menstruation—might instead exist because they conferred an evolutionary advantage.

In the mid-1980s the anthropologist Beverly I. Strassmann of the University of Michigan in Ann Arbor began to study the ways men and women have evolved to accomplish (and regulate) reproduction. Unlike traditional anthropologists, who focus on how culture affects human behavior, Strassmann was convinced that the important role played by biology was being neglected. Menstruation, she suspected, would be a key for observing and understanding the interplay of biology and culture in human reproductive behavior.

To address the issue, Strassmann decided to seek a culture in which making babies was an ongoing part of adult life. For that she had to get away from industrialized countries, with their bias toward contraception and low birthrates. In a "natural-fertility population," she reasoned, she could more clearly see the connection between the physiology of women and the strategies men and women use to exploit that physiology for their own reproductive ends.

Strassmann ended up in a remote corner of West Africa, living in close quarters with the Dogon, a traditional society whose indigenous religion of ancestor worship requires that menstruating women spend their nights at a small hut. For more than two years Strassmann kept track of the women staying at the hut, and she confirmed the menstruations by testing urine samples for the appropriate hormonal changes. In so doing, she amassed the first long-term data describing how a traditional society appropriates a physi-ological event—menstruation—and re-fracts that event through a prism of behaviors and beliefs.

What she found explicitly challenges the conclusions of earlier investigators about the cultural function of menstrual taboos. For the Dogon men, she discov-ered, enforcing visits to the menstrual hut serves to channel parental resources into the upbringing of their own chil-dren. But more, Strassmann, who also had training as a reproductive physiolo-gist, proposed a new theory of why menstruation itself evolved as it did—and again, the answer is essentially a story of conserving resources. Finally, her observations pose provocative ques-tions about women's health in industri-alized societies, raising serious doubts about the tactics favored by Western medicine for developing contraceptive technology.

MENSTRUATION IS THE VISIBLE stage of the ovarian cycle, orchestrated primarily by hormones secreted by the ovaries: progesterone and a family of hormones called estrogens. At the beginning of each cycle (by convention, the first day of a woman's period) the levels of the estrogens begin to rise. After about five days, as their concentrations increase, they cause the blood- and nutrient-rich inner lining of the uterus, called the endometrium, to thicken and acquire a densely branching network of blood vessels. At about the middle of the cycle, ovulation takes place, and an egg makes its way from one of the two ovaries down one of the paired fallopian tubes to the uterus. The follicle from which the egg was released in the ovary now begins to secrete progesterone as well as estrogens, and the progesterone causes the endometrium to swell and become even richer with blood vessels—in short, fully ready for a pregnancy, should conception take place and the fertilized egg become implanted.

If conception does take place, the levels of estrogens and progesterone continue to rise throughout the pregnancy. That keeps the endometrium thick enough to support the quickening life inside the uterus. When the baby is born and the new mother begins nursing, the estrogens and progesterone fall to their initial levels, and lactation hormones keep them suppressed. The uterus thus lies quiescent until frequent lactation ends, which triggers the return to ovulation.

If conception does not take place after ovulation, all the ovarian hormones also drop to their initial levels, and menstruation—the shedding of part of the uterine lining—begins. The lining is divided into three layers: a basal layer that is constantly maintained, and two superficial layers, which shed and regrow with each menstrual cycle. All mammals undergo cyclical changes in the state of the endometrium. In most mammals the sloughed-off layers are resorbed into the body if fertilization does not take place. But in some higher primates, including humans, some of the shed endometrium is not resorbed. The shed lining, along with some blood, flows from the body through the vaginal opening, a process that in humans typically lasts from three to five days.

OF COURSE, PHYSIOLOGICAL FACTS alone do not explain why so many human groups have infused a bodily function with symbolic meaning. And so in 1986 Strassmann found herself driving through the Sahel region of West Africa at the peak of the hot season, heading for a sandstone cliff called the Bandiagara Escarpment, in Mali. There, permanent Dogon villages of mud or stone houses dotted the rocky plateau. The menstrual huts were obvious: round, low-roofed buildings set apart from the rectangular dwellings of the rest of the village.

The Dogon are a society of millet and onion farmers who endorse polygyny, and they maintain their traditional culture despite the occasional visits of outsiders. In a few Dogon villages, in fact, tourists are fairly common, and ethnographers had frequently studied the Dogon language, religion and social structure before Strassmann's arrival. But her visit was the first time someone from the outside wanted to delve into an intimate issue in such detail.

It took Strassmann a series of hikes among villages, and long talks with male elders under the thatched-roof shelters where they typically gather, to find the appropriate sites for her research. She gained permission for her study in fourteen villages, eventually choosing two. That exceptional welcome, she thinks, emphasized the universality of her interests. "I'm working on all the things that really matter to [the Dogon]—fertility, economics—so they never questioned my motives or wondered why I would be interested in these things," she says. "It seemed obvious to them." She set up shop for the next two and a half years in a stone house in the village, with no running water or electricity. Eating the daily fare of the Dogon, millet porridge, she and a research assistant began to integrate themselves into village life, learning the language, getting to know people and tracking visits to the menstrual huts.

Following the movements of menstruating women was surprisingly easy. The menstrual huts are situated outside the walled compounds of the village, but in full view of the men's thatched-roof shelters. As the men relax under their shelters, they can readily see who leaves the huts in the morning and returns to them in the evening. And as nonmenstruating women pass the huts on their way to and from the fields or to other compounds, they too can see who is spending the night there. Strassmann found that when she left her house in the evening to take data, any of the villagers could accurately predict whom she would find in the menstrual huts.

THE HUTS THEMSELVES ARE CRAMPED, dark buildings—hardly places where a woman might go to escape the drudgery of work or to avoid an argument with her husband or a co-wife. The huts sometimes become so crowded that some occupants are forced outside—making the women even more conspicuous. Although babies and toddlers can go with their mothers to the huts, the women consigned there are not allowed to spend time with the rest of their families. They must cook with special pots, not their usual household possessions. Yet they are still expected to do their usual jobs, such as working in the fields.

Why, Strassmann wondered, would anyone put up with such conditions?

The answer, for the Dogon, is that a menstruating woman is a threat to the sanctity of religious altars, where men pray and make sacrifices for the protection of their fields, their families and their village. If menstruating women come near the altars, which are situated both indoors and outdoors, the Dogon believe that their aura of pollution will ruin the altars and bring calamities upon the village. The belief is so ingrained that the women themselves have internalized it, feeling its burden of responsibility and potential guilt. Thus violations of the taboo are rare, because a menstruating woman who breaks the rules knows that she is personally responsible if calamities occur.

NEVERTHELESS, STRASSMANN STILL thought a more functional explanation for menstrual taboos might also exist, one closely related to reproduction. As she was well aware, even before her studies among the Dogon, people around the world have a fairly sophisticated view of how reproduction works. In general, people everywhere know full well that menstruation signals the absence of a pregnancy and the possibility of another one. More precisely, Strassmann could frame her hypothesis by reasoning as follows: Across cultures, men and women recognize that a lack of menstrual cycling in a woman implies she is either pregnant, lactating or menopausal. Moreover, at least among natural-fertility cultures that do not practice birth control, continual cycles during peak reproductive years imply to people in those cultures that a woman is sterile. Thus, even though people might not be able to pinpoint ovulation, they can easily identify whether a woman will soon be ready to conceive on the basis of whether she is menstruating. And that leads straight to Strassmann's insightful hypothesis about the role of menstrual taboos: information about menstruation can be a means of tracking paternity.

"There are two important pieces of information for assessing paternity," Strassmann notes: timing of intercourse and timing of menstruation. "By forcing women to signal menstruation, men are trying to gain equal access to one part of that critical information." Such information, she explains, is crucial to Dogon men, because they invest so many resources in their own offspring. Descent is marked through the male line; land and the food that comes from the land is passed down from fathers to sons. Information about paternity is thus crucial to a man's entire lineage. And because each man has as many as four wives, he cannot possibly track them all. So forcing women to signal their menstrual periods, or lack thereof, helps men avoid cuckoldry.

TO TEST HER HYPOTHESIS, Strassmann tracked residence in the menstrual huts for 736 consecutive days, collecting data on 477 com-

plete cycles. She noted who was at each hut and how long each woman stayed. She also collected urine from ninety-three women over a ten-week period, to check the correlation between residence in the menstrual hut and the fact of menstruation.

The combination of ethnographic records and urinalyses showed that the Dogon women mostly play by the rules. In 86 percent of the hormonally detected menstruations, women went to the hut. Moreover, none of the tested women went to the hut when they were not menstruating. In the remaining 14 percent of the tested menstruations, women stayed home from the hut, in violation of the taboo, but some were near menopause and so not at high risk for pregnancy. More important, none of the women who violated the taboo did it twice in a row. Even they were largely willing to comply.

Thus, Strassmann concluded, the huts do indeed convey a fairly reliable signal, to men and to everyone else, about the status of a woman's fertility. When she leaves the hut, she is considered ready to conceive. When she stops going to the hut, she is evidently pregnant or menopausal. And women of prime reproductive age who visit the hut on a regular basis are clearly infertile.

It also became clear to Strassmann that the Dogon do indeed use that information to make paternity decisions. In several cases a man was forced to marry a pregnant woman, simply because everyone knew that the man had been the woman's first sexual partner after her last visit to the menstrual hut. Strassmann followed one case in which a child was being brought up by a man because he was the mother's first sexual partner after a hut visit, even though the woman soon married a different man. (The woman already knew she was pregnant by the first man at the time of her marriage, and she did not visit the menstrual hut before she married. Thus the truth was obvious to everyone, and the real father took the child.)

In general, women are cooperative players in the game because without a man, a woman has no way to support herself or her children. But women follow the taboo reluctantly. They com-

plain about going to the hut. And if their husbands convert from the traditional religion of the Dogon to a religion that does not impose menstrual taboos, such as Islam or Christianity, the women quickly cease visiting the hut. Not that such a religious conversion quells a man's interest in his wife's fidelity: far from it. But the rules change. Perhaps the sanctions of the new religion against infidelity help keep women faithful, so the men can relax their guard. Or perhaps the men are willing to trade the reproductive advantages of the menstrual taboo for the economic benefits gained by converting to the new religion. Whatever the case, Strassmann found an almost perfect correlation between a husband's religion and his wives' attendance at the hut. In sum, the taboo is established by men, backed by supernatural forces, and internalized and accepted by women until the men release them from the belief.

BUT BEYOND THE CULTURAL MACHINA-tions OF men and women that Strassmann expected to find, her data show something even more fundamental—and surprising—about female biology. On average, she calculates, a woman in a natural-fertility population such as the Dogon has only about 110 menstrual periods in her lifetime. The rest of the time she will be prepubescent, pregnant, lactating or menopausal. Women in industrialized cultures, by contrast, have more than three times as many cycles: 350 to 400, on average, in a lifetime. They reach menarche (their first menstruation) earlier—at age twelve and a half, compared with the onset age of sixteen in natural-fertility cultures. They have fewer babies, and they lactate hardly at all. All those factors lead women in the industrialized world to a lifetime of nearly continuous menstrual cycling.

The big contrast in cycling profiles during the reproductive years can be traced specifically to lactation. Women in more traditional societies spend most of their reproductive years in lactation amenorrhea, the state in which the hormonal changes required for nursing suppress ovulation and inhibit menstruation. And it is not just that the Dogon bear more children (eight to nine on average); they also nurse each child on demand rather than in scheduled bouts, all through the night as well as the day, and intensely enough that ovulation simply stops for about twenty months per child. Women in industrialized societies typically do not breast-feed as intensely (or at all), and rarely breast-feed each child for as long as the Dogon women do. (The average for American women is four months.)

The Dogon experience with menstruation may be far more typical of the human condition over most of evolutionary history than is the standard menstrual experience in industrialized nations. If so, Strassmann's findings alter some of the most closely held beliefs about female biology. Contrary to what the Western medical establishment might think, it is not particularly "normal" to menstruate each month. The female body, according to Strassmann, is biologically designed to spend much more time in lactation amenorrhea than in menstrual cycling. That in itself suggests that oral contraceptives, which alter hormone levels to suppress ovulation and produce a bleeding, could be forcing a continual state of cycling for which the body is ill-prepared. Women might be better protected against reproductive cancers if their contraceptives mimicked lactation amenorrhea and depressed the female reproductive hormones, rather than forcing the continual ebb and flow of menstrual cycles.

Strassmann's data also call into question a recently popularized idea about menstruation: that regular menstrual cycles might be immunologically beneficial for women. In 1993 the controversial writer Margie Profet, whose ideas about evolutionary and reproductive biology have received vast media attention, proposed in *The Quarterly Review of Biology* that menstruation could have such an adaptive value. She noted that viruses and bacteria regularly enter the female body on the backs of sperm, and she hypothesized that the best way to get them out is to flush them out. Here, then, was a positive, adaptive role for something unpleasant, an evolutionary reason for suffering cramps each month. Menstruation, according to

Profet, had evolved to rid the body of pathogens. The "anti-pathogen" theory was an exciting hypothesis, and it helped win Profet a MacArthur Foundation award. But Strassmann's work soon showed that Profet's ideas could not be supported because of one simple fact: under less-industrialized conditions, women menstruate relatively rarely.

Instead, Strassmann notes, if there is an adaptive value to menstruation, it is ultimately a strategy to conserve the body's resources. She estimates that maintaining the endometrial lining during the second half of the ovarian cycle takes substantial metabolic energy. Once the endometrium is built up and ready to receive a fertilized egg, the tissue requires a sevenfold metabolic increase to remain rich in blood and ready to support a pregnancy. Hence, if no pregnancy is forthcoming, it makes a lot of sense for the body to let part of the endometrium slough off and then regenerate itself, instead of maintaining that rather costly but unneeded tissue. Such energy conservation is common among vertebrates: male rhesus monkeys have shrunken testes during their nonbreeding season, Burmese pythons shrink their guts when they are not digesting, and hibernating animals put their metabolisms on hold.

Strassmann also suggests that periodically ridding oneself of the endometrium could make a difference to a woman's long-term survival. Because female reproductive hormones affect the brain and other tissues, the metabolism of the entire body is involved during cycling. Strassmann estimates that by keeping hormonal low through half the cycle, a woman can save about six days' worth of energy for every four nonconceptive cycles. Such caloric conservation might have proved useful to early hominids who lived by hunting and gathering, and even today it might be helpful for women living in less affluent circumstances than the ones common in the industrialized West.

**B**UT PERHAPS THE MOST PROVOCATIVE implications of Strassmann's work have to do with women's health. In 1994 a group of physicians and anthropologists published a paper, also in

*The Quarterly Review of Biology,* suggesting that the reproductive histories and lifestyles of women in industrialized cultures are at odds with women's naturally evolved biology, and that the differences lead to greater risks of reproductive cancers. For example, the investigators estimated that women in affluent cultures may have a hundredfold greater risk of breast cancer than do women who subsist by hunting and gathering. The increased risk is probably caused not only by low levels of exercise and a high-fat diet, but also by a relatively high number of menstrual cycles over a lifetime. Repeated exposure to the hormones of the ovarian cycle—because of early menarche, late menopause, lack of pregnancy and little or no breast-feeding—is implicated in other reproductive cancers as well.

Those of us in industrialized cultures have been running an experiment on ourselves. The body evolved over millions of years to move across the landscape looking for food, to live in small kin-based groups, to make babies at intervals of four years or so and to invest heavily in each child by nursing intensely for years. How many women now follow those traditional patterns? We move little, we rely on others to get our food, and we rarely reproduce or lactate. Those culturally initiated shifts in lifestyles may pose biological risks.

Our task is not to overcome that biology, but to work with it. Now that we have a better idea of how the female body was designed, it may be time to rework our lifestyles and change some of our expectations. It may be time to borrow from our distant past or from our contemporaries in distant cultures, and treat our bodies more as nature intended.

*MERIDITH F. SMALL is a professor of anthropology at Cornell University in Ithaca, New York. Her latest book,* OUR BABIES, OURSELVES: HOW BIOLOGY AND CULTURE SHAPE THE WAY WE PARENT, *was published in May 1998 [see Laurence A. Marschall's review in Books in Brief, November/December 1998].*

# What's Love Got to Do With It?

## Sex Among Our Closest Relatives Is a Rather Open Affair

## Meredith F. Small

Maiko and Lana are having sex. Maiko is on top, and Lana's arms and legs are wrapped tightly around his waist. Lina, a friend of Lana's, approaches from the right and taps Maiko on the back, nudging him to finish. As he moves away, Lina enfolds Lana in her arms, and they roll over so that Lana is now on top. The two females rub their genitals together, grinning and screaming in pleasure.

This is no orgy staged for an X-rated movie. It doesn't even involve people—or rather, it involves them only as observers. Lana, Maiko, and Lina are bonobos, a rare species of chimplike ape in which frequent couplings and casual sex play characterize every social relationship—between males and females, members of the same sex, closely related animals, and total strangers. Primatologists are beginning to study the bonobos' unrestrained sexual behavior for tantalizing clues to the origins of our own sexuality.

In reconstructing how early man and woman behaved, researchers have generally looked not to bonobos but to common chimpanzees. Only about 5 million years ago human beings and chimps shared a common ancestor, and we still have much behavior in common: namely, a long period of infant dependency, a reliance on learning what to eat and how to obtain food, social bonds that persist over generations, and the need to deal as a

group with many everyday conflicts. The assumption has been that chimp behavior today may be similar to the behavior of human ancestors.

Bonobo behavior, however, offers another window on the past because they, too, shared our 5-million-year-old ancestor, diverging from chimps just 2 million years ago. Bonobos have been less studied than chimps for the simple reason that they are difficult to find. They live only on a small patch of land in Zaire, in central Africa. They were first identified, on the basis of skeletal material, in the 1920s, but it wasn't until the 1970s that their behavior in the wild was studied, and then only sporadically.

Bonobos, also known as pygmy chimpanzees, are not really pygmies but welterweights. The largest males are as big as chimps, and the females of the two species are the same size. But bonobos are more delicate in build, and their arms and legs are long and slender.

On the ground, moving from fruit tree to fruit tree, bonobos often stand and walk on two legs—behavior that makes them seem more like humans than chimps. In some ways their sexual behavior seems more human as well, suggesting that in the sexual arena, at least, bonobos are the more appropriate ancestral model. Males and females frequently copulate face-to-face,

which is an uncommon position in animals other than humans. Males usually mount females from behind, but females seem to prefer sex face-to-face. "Sometimes the female will let a male start to mount from behind," says Amy Parish, a graduate student at the University of California at Davis who's been watching female bonobo sexual behavior in several zoo colonies around the world. "And then she'll stop, and of course he's really excited, and then she continues face-to-face." Primatologists assume the female preference is dictated by her anatomy: her enlarged clitoris and sexual swellings are oriented far forward. Females presumably prefer face-to-face contact because it feels better.

---

*"Sex is fun. Sex makes them feel good and keeps the group together."*

---

Like humans but unlike chimps and most other animals, bonobos separate sex from reproduction. They seem to treat sex as a pleasurable activity, and they rely on it as a sort of social glue, to make or break all sorts of relationships. "Ancestral humans behaved like this," proposes Frans de Waal, an ethologist at the Yerkes Regional Primate Research Center at Emory University. "Later, when we developed the family system, the use of sex for this sort of purpose became more limited, mainly occurring within families. A lot of the things we see, like pedophilia and homosexuality, may be leftovers that some now consider unacceptable in our particular society."

Depending on your morals, watching bonobo sex play may be like watching humans at their most extreme and perverse. Bonobos seem to have sex more often and in more combinations than the average person in any culture, and most of the time bonobo sex has nothing to do with making babies. Males mount females and females sometimes mount them back; females rub against other females just for fun; males stand rump to rump and press their scrotal areas together. Even juveniles participate by rubbing their genital areas against adults, although ethologists don't think that males actually insert their penises into juvenile females. Very young animals also have sex with each other: little males suck on each other's penises or French-kiss. When two animals initiate sex, others freely join in by poking their fingers and toes into the moving parts.

One thing sex does for bonobos is decrease tensions caused by potential competition, often competition for food. Japanese primatologists observing bonobos in Zaire were the first to notice that when bonobos come across a large fruiting tree or encounter piles of provisioned sugarcane, the sight of food triggers a binge of sex. The atmosphere of this sexual free-for-all is decidedly friendly, and it eventually calms the group down. "What's striking is how rapidly the sex drops off," says Nancy Thompson-Handler of the State University of New York at Stony Brook, who has observed bonobos at a site in Zaire called Lomako. "After ten minutes, sexual behavior decreases by fifty percent." Soon the group turns from sex to feeding.

But it's tension rather than food that causes the sexual excitement. "I'm sure the more food you give them, the more sex you'll get," says De Waal. "But it's not really the food, it's competition that triggers this. You can throw in a card-board box and you'll get sexual behavior." Sex is just the way bonobos deal with competition over limited resources and with the normal tensions caused by living in a group. Anthropologist Frances White of Duke University, a bonobo observer at Lomako since 1983, puts it simply: "Sex is fun. Sex makes them feel good and therefore keeps the group together."

---

*"Females rule the business. It's a good species for feminists, I think."*

---

Sexual behavior also occurs after aggressive encounters, especially among males. After two males fight, one may reconcile with his opponent by presenting his rump and backing up against the other's testicles. He might grab the penis of the other male and stroke it. It's the male bonobo's way of shaking hands and letting everyone know that the conflict has ended amicably.

Researchers also note that female bonobo sexuality, like the sexuality of female humans, isn't locked into a monthly cycle. In most other animals, including chimps, the female's interest in sex is tied to her ovulation cycle. Chimp females sport pink swellings on their hind ends for about two weeks, signaling their fertility, and they're only approachable for sex during that time. That's not the case with humans, who show no outward signs that they are ovulating, and can mate at all phases of the cycle. Female bonobos take the reverse tack, but with similar results. Their large swellings are visible for weeks before and after their fertile periods, and there is never any discernibly wrong time to mate. Like humans, they have sex whether or not they are ovulating.

What's fascinating is that female bonobos use this boundless sexuality in all their relationships. "Females rule the business—sex and food," says De Waal. "It's a good species for feminists, I think." For instance, females regularly use sex to cement relationships with other females. A genital-genital rub, bet-ter known as GG-rubbing by observers, is the most frequent behavior used by bonobo females to reinforce social ties or relieve tension. GG-rubbing takes a variety of forms. Often one female rolls on her back and extends her arms and legs. The other female mounts her and they rub their swellings right and left for several seconds, massaging their clitorises against each other. GG-rubbing occurs in the presence of food because food causes tension and excitement, but the intimate contact has the effect of making close friends.

Sometimes females would rather GG-rub with each other than copulate with a male. Parish filmed a 15-minute scene at a bonobo colony at the San Diego Wild Animal Park in which a male, Vernon, repeatedly solicited two females, Lisa and Loretta. Again and again he arched his back and displayed his erect penis—the bonobo request for sex. The females moved away from him, tactfully turning him down until they crept behind a tree and GG-rubbed with each other.

Unlike most primate species, in which males usually take on the dangerous task of leaving home, among bonobos females are the ones who leave the group when they reach sexual maturity, around the age of eight, and work their way into unfamiliar groups. To aid in their assimilation into a new community, the female bonobos make good use of their endless sexual favors. While watching a bonobo group at a feeding tree, White saw a young female systematically have sex with each member before feeding. "An adolescent female, presumably a recent transfer female, came up to the tree, mated with all five males, went into the tree, and solicited GG-rubbing from all the females present," says White.

Once inside the new group, a female bonobo must build a sisterhood from scratch. In groups of humans or chimps, unrelated females construct friendships through the rituals of shopping together or grooming. Bonobos do it sexually. Although pleasure may be the motivation behind a female-female assignation, the function is to form an alliance.

These alliances are serious business, because they determine the pecking order at food sites. Females with powerful friends eat first, and subordinate females may not get any food at all if the resource is small. When times are rough, then, it pays to have close female friends. White describes a scene at Lomako in which an adolescent female, Blanche, benefited from her established friendship with Freda. "I was following Freda and her boyfriend, and they found a tree that they didn't expect to be there. It was a small tree, heavily in fruit with one of their favorites. Freda went straight up the tree and made a food call to Blanche. Blanche came tearing over—she was quite far away—and went tearing up the tree to join Freda, and they GG-rubbed like crazy."

Alliances also give females leverage over larger, stronger males who otherwise would push them around. Females have discovered there is strength in numbers. Unlike other species of primates, such as chimpanzees or baboons (or, all too often, humans), where tensions run high between males and females, bonobo females are not afraid of males, and the sexes mingle peacefully. "What is consistently different from chimps," says Thompson-Handler, "is the composition of parties. The vast majority are mixed, so there are males and females of all different ages."

Female bonobos cannot be coerced into anything, including sex. Parish recounts an interaction between Lana and

a male called Akili at the San Diego Wild Animal Park. "Lana had just been introduced into the group. For a long time she lay on the grass with a huge swelling. Akili would approach her with a big erection and hover over her. It would have been easy for him to do a mount. But he wouldn't. He just kept trying to catch her eye, hovering around her, and she would scoot around the ground, avoiding him. And then he'd try again. She went around full circle." Akili was big enough to force himself on her. Yet he refrained.

In another encounter, a male bonobo was carrying a large clump of branches. He moved up to a female and presented his erect penis by spreading his legs and

## HIDDEN HEAT

Standing upright is not a position usually—or easily—associated with sex. Among people, at least, anatomy and gravity prove to be forbidding obstacles. Yet our two-legged stance may be the key to a distinctive aspect of human sexuality: the independence of women's sexual desires from a monthly calendar.

Males in the two species most closely related to us, chimpanzees and bonobos, don't spend a lot of time worrying, "Is she interested or not?" The answer is obvious. When ovulatory hormones reach a monthly peak in female chimps and bonobos, and their eggs are primed for fertilization, their genital area swells up, and both sexes appear to have just one thing on their mind. "These animals really turn on when this happens. Everything else is dropped," says primatologist Frederick Szalay of Hunter College in New York.

Women, however, don't go into heat. And this departure from our relatives' sexual behavior has long puzzled researchers. Clear signals of fertility and the willingness to do something about it bring major evolutionary advantages: ripe eggs lead to healthier pregnancies, which leads to more of your genes in succeeding generations, which is what evolution is all about. In addition, male chimps give females that are waving these red flags of fertility first chance at high-protein food such as meat.

So why would our ancestors give this up? Szalay and graduate student Robert Costello have a simple explanation. Women gave heat up, they say, because our ancestors stood up. Fossil footprints

indicate that somewhere around 3.5 million years ago hominids—non-ape primates—began walking on two legs. "In hominids, something dictated getting up. We don't know what it was," Szalay says. "But once it did, there was a problem with the signaling system." The problem was that it didn't work. Swollen genital areas that were visible when their owners were down on all fours became hidden between the legs. The mating signal was lost.

"Uprightness meant very tough times for females working with the old ovarian cycle," Szalay says. Males wouldn't notice them, and the swellings themselves, which get quite large, must have made it hard for two-legged creatures to walk around.

Those who found a way out of this quandary, Szalay suggests, were females with small swellings but with a little less hair on their rears and a little extra fat. It would have looked a bit like the time-honored mating signal. They got more attention, and produced more offspring. "You don't start a completely new trend in signaling," Szalay says. "You have a little extra fat, a little nakedness to mimic the ancestors. If there was an ever-so-little advantage because, quite simply, you look good, it would be selected for."

And if a little nakedness and a little fat worked well, Szalay speculates, then a lot of both would work even better. "Once you start a trend in sexual signaling, crazy things happen," he notes. "It's almost like: let's escalate, let's add more. That's what happens in horns with sheep. It's a particular part of the body that brings an ad-

vantage." In a few million years human ancestors were more naked than ever, with fleshy rears not found in any other primate. Since these features were permanent, unlike the monthly ups and downs of swellings, sex was free to become a part of daily life.

It's a provocative notion, say Szalay's colleagues, but like any attempt to conjure up the past from the present, there's no real proof of cause and effect. Anthropologist Helen Fisher of the American Museum of Natural History notes that Szalay is merely assuming that fleshy buttocks evolved because they were sex signals. Yet their mass really comes from muscles, which chimps don't have, that are associated with walking. And anthropologist Sarah Blaffer Hrdy of the University of California at Davis points to a more fundamental problem: our ancestors may not have had chimplike swellings that they needed to dispense with. Chimps and bonobos are only two of about 200 primate species, and the vast majority of those species don't have big swellings. Though they are our closest relatives, chimps and bonobos have been evolving during the last 5 million years just as we have, and swollen genitals may be a recent development. The current unswollen human pattern may be the ancestral one.

"Nobody really knows what happened," says Fisher. "Everybody has an idea. You pays your money and you takes your choice."

—Joshua Fischman

arching his back. She rolled onto her back and they copulated. In the midst of their joint ecstasy, she reached out and grabbed a branch from the male. When he pulled back, finished and satisfied, she moved away, clutching the branch to her chest. There was no tension between them, and she essentially traded copulation for food. But the key here is that the male allowed her to move away with the branch—it didn't occur to him to threaten her, because their status was virtually equal.

Although the results of sexual liberation are clear among bonobos, no one is sure why sex has been elevated to such a high position in this species and why it is restricted merely to reproduction among chimpanzees. "The puzzle for me," says De Waal, "is that chimps do all this bonding with kissing and embracing, with body contact. Why do bonobos do it in a sexual manner?" He speculates that the use of sex as a standard way to underscore relationships began between adult males and adult females as an extension of the mating process and later spread to all members of the group. But no one is sure exactly how this happened.

It is also unclear whether bonobo sexually became exaggerated only after their split from the human lineage or whether the behavior they exhibit today is the modern version of our common ancestor's sex play. Anthropologist Adrienne Zihlman of the University of California at Santa Cruz, who has used the evidence of fossil bones to argue that our earliest known non-ape ancestors, the australopithecines, had body proportions similar to those of bonobos, says, "The path of evolution is not a straight line from either species, but what I think is important is that the bonobo information gives us more possibilities for looking at human origins."

Some anthropologists, however, are reluctant to include the details of bonobo life, such as wide-ranging sexuality and a strong sisterhood, into scenarios of human evolution. "The researchers have all these commitments to male dominance [as in chimpanzees], and yet bonobos have egalitarian relationships," says De Waal. "They also want to see humans as unique, yet bonobos fit very nicely into many of the scenarios, making humans appear less unique."

Our divergent, non-ape path has led us away from sex and toward a culture that denies the connection between sex and social cohesion. But bonobos, with their versatile sexuality, are here to remind us that our heritage may very well include a primordial urge to make love, not war.

# Apes of Wrath

## Barbara Smuts

*Barbara Smuts is a professor of psychology and anthropology at the University of Michigan. She has been doing fieldwork in animal behavior since the early 1970s, studying baboons, chimps, and dolphins. "In my work I combine research in animal behavior with an abiding interest in feminist perspectives on science," says Smuts. She is the author of* Sex and Friendship in Baboons.

Nearly 20 years ago I spent a morning dashing up and down the hills of Gombe National Park in Tanzania, trying to keep up with an energetic young female chimpanzee, the focus of my observations for the day. On her rear end she sported the small, bright pink swelling characteristic of the early stages of estrus, the period when female mammals are fertile and sexually receptive. For some hours our run through the park

*Some female primates use social bonds to escape male aggression. Can women?*

was conducted in quiet, but then, suddenly, a chorus of male chimpanzee pant hoots shattered the tranquility of the forest. My female rushed forward to join the males. She greeted each of them, bowing and then turning to present her swelling for inspection. The males examined her perfunctorily and resumed grooming one another, showing no further interest.

At first I was surprised by their indifference to a potential mate. Then I re-

alized that it would be many days before the female's swelling blossomed into the large, shiny sphere that signals ovulation. In a week or two, I thought, these same males will be vying intensely for a chance to mate with her.

The attack came without warning. One of the males charged toward us, hair on end, looking twice as large as my small female and enraged. As he rushed by he picked her up, hurled her to the ground, and pummeled her. She cringed and screamed. He ran off, rejoining the other males seconds later as if nothing had happened. It was not so easy for the female to return to normal. She whimpered and darted nervous glances at her attacker, as if worried that he might renew his assault.

In the years that followed I witnessed many similar attacks by males against females, among a variety of Old World primates, and eventually I found this sort of aggression against females so puzzling that I began to study it systematically—something that has rarely been done. My long-term research on olive baboons in Kenya showed that, on average, each pregnant or lactating female was attacked by an adult male about once a week and seriously injured about once a year. Estrous females were the target of even more aggression. The obvious question was, Why?

In the late 1970s, while I was in Africa among the baboons, feminists back in the United States were turning their attention to male violence against women. Their concern stimulated a wave of research documenting disturbingly high levels of battering, rape, sexual harassment, and murder. But although scientists investigated this kind of behavior from many perspec-

tives, they mostly ignored the existence of similar behavior in other animals. My observations over the years have convinced me that a deeper understanding of male aggression against females in other species can help us understand its counterpart in our own.

Researchers have observed various male animals—including insects, birds, and mammals—chasing, threatening, and attacking females. Unfortunately, because scientists have rarely studied such aggression in detail, we do not know exactly how common it is. But the males of many of these species are most aggressive toward potential mates, which suggests that they sometimes use violence to gain sexual access.

Jane Goodall provides us with a compelling example of how males use violence to get sex. In her 1986 book, *The Chimpanzees of Gombe,* Goodall describes the chimpanzee dating game. In one of several scenarios, males gather around attractive estrous females and try to lure them away from other males for a one-on-one sexual expedition that may last for days or weeks. But females find some suitors more appealing than others and often resist the advances of less desirable males. Males often rely on aggression to counter female resistance. For example, Goodall describes how Evered, in "persuading" a reluctant Winkle to accompany him into the forest, attacked her six times over the course of five hours, twice severely.

Sometimes, as I saw in Gombe, a male chimpanzee even attacks an estrous female days before he tries to mate with her. Goodall thinks that a male uses such aggression to train a female to fear him so that she will be more likely to surrender to his subsequent sexual advances. Similarly, male hamadryas baboons, who form small harems by kidnapping child brides, maintain a tight rein over their females through threats and intimidation. If, when another male is nearby, a hamadryas female strays even a few feet from her mate, he shoots her a threatening stare and raises his brows. She usually responds by rushing to his side; if not, he bites the back of her neck. The neck bite is ritualized—the male does not actually sink his razor-sharp canines into her flesh—but the threat of injury is clear. By repeating this behavior hundreds of times, the male lays claim to particular females months or even years before mating with them. When a female comes into estrus, she solicits sex only from her harem master, and other males rarely challenge his sexual rights to her.

---

*In some species, females remain in their birth communities their whole lives, joining forces with related females to defend vital food resources against other females.*

---

These chimpanzee and hamadryas males are practicing sexual coercion: male use of force to increase the chances that a female victim will mate with him, or to decrease the chances that she will mate with someone else. But sexual coercion is much more common in some primate species than in others. Orangutans and chimpanzees are the only nonhuman primates whose males in the wild force females to copulate, while males of several other species, such as vervet monkeys and bonobos (pygmy chimpanzees), rarely if ever try to coerce females sexually. Between the two extremes lie many species, like hamadryas baboons, in which males do not force

copulation but nonetheless use threats and intimidation to get sex.

These dramatic differences between species provide an opportunity to investigate which factors promote or inhibit sexual coercion. For example, we might expect to find more of it in species in which males are much larger than females—and we do. However, size differences between the sexes are far from the whole story. Chimpanzee and bonobo males both have only a slight size advantage, yet while male chimps frequently resort to force, male bonobos treat the fair sex with more respect. Clearly, then, although size matters, so do other factors. In particular, the social relationships females form with other females and with males appear to be as important.

In some species, females remain in their birth communities their whole lives, joining forces with related females to defend vital food resources against other females. In such "female bonded" species, females also form alliances against aggressive males. Vervet monkeys are one such species, and among these small and exceptionally feisty African monkeys, related females gang up against males. High-ranking females use their dense network of female alliances to rule the troop; although smaller than males, they slap persistent suitors away like annoying flies. Researchers have observed similar alliances in many other female-bonded species, including other Old World monkeys such as macaques, olive baboons, patas and rhesus monkeys, and gray langurs; New World monkeys such as the capuchin; and prosimians such as the ring-tailed lemur.

Females in other species leave their birth communities at adolescence and spend the rest of their lives cut off from their female kin. In most such species, females do not form strong bonds with other females and rarely support one another against males. Both chimpanzees and hamadryas baboons exhibit this pattern, and, as we saw earlier, in both species females submit to sexual control by males.

This contrast between female-bonded species, in which related females gang together to thwart males, and non-female-bonded species, in which they don't, breaks down when we come to the bonobo. Female bonobos, like their close

relatives the chimpanzees, leave their kin and live as adults with unrelated females. Recent field studies show that these unrelated females hang out together and engage in frequent homoerotic behavior, in which they embrace face-to-face and rapidly rub their genitals together; sex seems to cement their bonds. Examining these studies in the context of my own research has convinced me that one way females use these bonds is to form alliances against males, and that, as a consequence, male bonobos do not dominate females or attempt to coerce them sexually. How and why female bonobos, but not chimpanzees, came up with this solution to male violence remains a mystery.

Female primates also use relationships with males to help protect themselves against sexual coercion. Among olive baboons, each adult female typically forms long-lasting "friendships" with a few of the many males in her troop. When a male baboon assaults a female, another male often comes to her rescue; in my troop, nine times out of ten the protector was a friend of the female's. In return for his protection, the defender may enjoy her sexual favors the next time she comes into

---

*Some of the factors that influence female vulnerability to male sexual coercion in different species may also help explain such variation among different groups in the same species.*

---

estrus. There is a dark side to this picture, however. Male baboons frequently threaten or attack their female friends—when, for example, one tries to form a friendship with a new male. Other males apparently recognize friendships and rarely intervene. The female, then, becomes less vulnerable to aggression from males in general, but more vulnerable to aggression from her male friends.

As a final example, consider orangutans. Because their food grows so sparsely adult females rarely travel with anyone but their dependent offspring. But orangutan females routinely fall victim to forced copulation. Female orangutans, it seems, pay a high price for their solitude.

Some of the factors that influence female vulnerability to male sexual coercion in different species may also help explain such variation among different groups in the same species. For example, in a group of chimpanzees in the Taï Forest in the Ivory Coast, females form closer bonds with one another than do females at Gombe. Taï females may consequently have more egalitarian relationships with males than their Gombe counterparts do.

Such differences between groups especially characterize humans. Among the South American Yanomamö, for instance, men frequently abduct and rape women from neighboring villages and severely beat their wives for suspected adultery. However, among the Aka people of the Central African Republic, male aggression against women has never been observed. Most human societies, of course, fall between these two extremes.

How are we to account for such variation? The same social factors that help explain how sexual coercion differs among nonhuman primates may deepen our understanding of how it varies across different groups of people. In most traditional human societies, a woman leaves her birth community when she marries and goes to live with her husband and his relatives. Without strong bonds to close female kin, she will probably be in danger of sexual coercion. The presence of close female kin, though, may protect her. For example, in a community in Belize, women live near their female relatives. A man will sometimes beat his wife if he becomes jealous or suspects her of infidelity, but when this happens, onlookers run to tell her female kin. Their arrival on the scene, combined with the presence of other glaring women, usually shames the man enough to stop his aggression.

Even in societies in which women live away from their families, kin may provide protection against abusive husbands, though how much protection varies dramatically from one society to the next. In some societies a woman's kin, including her father and brothers, consistently support her against an abusive husband, while in others they rarely help her. Why?

The key may lie in patterns of male-male relationships. Alliances between males are much more highly developed in humans than in other primates, and men frequently rely on such alliances to compete successfully against other men. They often gain more by supporting their male allies than they do by supporting female kin. In addition, men often use their alliances to defeat rivals and abduct or rape their women, as painfully illustrated by recent events in Bosnia. When women live far from close kin, among men who value their alliances with other men more than their bonds with women, they may be even more vulnerable to sexual coercion than many nonhuman primate females.

---

*Even in societies in which women live away from their families, kin may provide protection against abusive husbands.*

---

Like nonhuman primate females, many women form bonds with unrelated males who may protect them from other males. However, reliance on men exacts a cost—women and other primate females often must submit to control by their protectors. Such control is more elaborate in humans because allied men agree to honor one another's proprietary rights over women. In most of the world's cultures, marriage involves not only the exclusion of other men from sexual access to a man's wife—which protects the woman against rape by other men—but also entails the husband's right to complete control over his wife's sexual life, including the right to punish her for real or suspected adultery, to have sex with her whenever he wants, and even to restrict her contact with other people, especially men.

In modern industrial society, many men—perhaps most—maintain such traditional notions of marriage. At the same time, many of the traditional sources of support for women, including censure of abusive husbands by the woman's kinfolk or other community members, are eroding as more and more people end up without nearby kin or long-term neighbors. The increased vulnerability of women isolated from their birth communities, however, is not just a by-product of modern living. Historically, in highly patriarchal societies like those found in China and northern India, married women lived in households ruled by their husband's mother and male kin, and their ties with their own kin were virtually severed. In these societies, today as in the past, the husband's female kin often view the wife as a competitor for resources. Not only do they fail to support her against male coercive control, but they sometimes actively encourage it. This scenario illustrates an important point: women do not invariably support other women against men, in part because women may perceive their interests as best served through alliances with men, not with other women. When men have most of the power and control most of the resources, this looks like a realistic assessment.

Decreasing women's vulnerability to sexual coercion, then, may require fundamental changes in social alliances. Women gave voice to this essential truth with the slogan SISTERHOOD IS POWERFUL—a reference to the importance of women's ability to cooperate with unrelated women as if they were indeed sisters. However, among humans, the male-dominant social system derives support from political, economic, legal, and ideological institutions that other primates can't even dream of. Freedom from male control—including male sexual coercion—therefore requires women to form alliances with one another (and with like-minded men) on a scale beyond that shown by nonhuman primates and humans in the past. Although knowledge of other primates can provide inspiration for this task, its achievement depends on the uniquely human ability to envision a future different from anything that has gone before.

# Unit 4

## Key Points to Consider

❖ Under what circumstances did bipedalism evolve?

❖ What is the "man the hunter" hypothesis, and how might the "scavenging theory" better suit the early hominid data?

❖ How would you draw the early hominid family tree?

 **Links**

## www.dushkin.com/online/

These sites are annotated on pages 4 and 5.

A primary focal point of this book, as well as of the whole of biological anthropology, is the search for and interpretation of fossil evidence for hominid (meaning human or humanlike) evolution. Paleo- anthropologists are those who carry out this task by conducting the painstaking excavations and detailed analyses that serve as a basis for understanding our past. Every fragment found is cherished like a ray of light that may help to illuminate the path taken by our ancestors in the process of becoming "us." At

least, that is what we would like to believe.

In reality, each discovery leads to further mystery, and for every fossil-hunting paleoanthropologist who thinks his or her find supports a particular theory, there are many others anxious to express their disagreement. (See "Early Hominid Fossils From Africa" by Meave Leakey and Alan Walker and "A New Human Ancestor?" by Elizabeth Culotta.)

How wonderful it would be, we sometimes think in moments of frustration over inconclusive data, if the fossils would just speak for themselves, and every primordial piece of humanity were to carry with it a self-evident explanation for its place in the evolutionary story. Paleoanthropology would then be more a quantitative problem of amassing enough material to reconstruct our ancestral development than a qualitative problem of interpreting what it all means. It would certainly be a simpler process, but would it be as interesting?

Most scientists tolerate, welcome, or even (dare it be said?) thrive on controversy, recognizing that diversity of opinion refreshes the mind, rouses students, and captures the imagination of the general public. After all, where would paleo-anthropology be without the gadflies, the near-mythic heroes, and, lest we forget, the research funds they generate? Consider, for example, the issue of the differing roles played by males and females in the transition to humanity and all that it implies with regard to bipedalism, tool making, and the origin of the family. Did bipedalism really evolve in the grasslands? (See James Shreeve's "Sunset on the Savanna.") Should the primary theme of human evolution be summed up as "man the hunter" or "woman the gatherer?"

Not all the research and theoretical speculation taking place in the field of paleoanthropology is so controversial. Most scientists, in fact, go about their work quietly and methodically, generating hypotheses that are much less explosive and yet have the cumulative effect of enriching our understanding of the details of human evolution. In "Scavenger Hunt," for instance, Pat Shipman tells how modern technology, in the form of the scanning electron microscope, combined with meticulous detailed analysis of cut marks on fossil animal bones, can help us better understand the locomotor and food-getting adaptations of our early hominid ancestors. In one stroke, she is able to challenge the traditional "man the hunter" theme that has pervaded most early hominid research and writing and to simultaneously set forth an alternative hypothesis that will, in turn, inspire further research.

As we mull over the controversies outlined in this unit, we should not take them as reflecting an inherent weakness of the field of paleoanthropology, but rather as symbolic of its strength: the ability and willingness to scrutinize, question, and reflect (seemingly endlessly) on every bit of evidence.

Contrary to the way that the creationists would have it, an admission of doubt is not an expression of ignorance but simply a frank recognition of the imperfect state of our knowledge. If we are to increase our understanding of ourselves, we must maintain an atmosphere of free inquiry without preconceived notions and an unquestioning commitment to a particular point of view.

To paraphrase anthropologist Ashley Montagu, whereas creationism seeks certainty without proof, science seeks proof without certainty.

# Sunset on the Savanna

*Why do we walk? For decades anthropologists said that we became bipedal to survive on the African savanna. But a slew of new fossils have destroyed that appealing notion and left researchers groping for a new paradigm.*

## James Shreeve

*James Shreeve is a contributing editor of DISCOVER. He is co-author, with anthropologist Donald Johanson, of* Lucy's Child: The Discovery of a Human Ancestor. *His latest book is* The Neandertal Enigma. *Shreeve is currently at work on his first novel.*

**IT'S A WONDERFUL STORY.** *Once upon a time, there was an ape who lived in the middle of a dark forest. It spent most of its days in the trees, munching languidly on fruits and berries. But then one day the ape decided to leave the forest for the savanna nearby. Or perhaps it was the savanna that moved, licking away at the edge of the forest one tree at a time until the fruits and berries all the apes had found so easily weren't so easy to find anymore.*

In either case, the venturesome ape found itself out in the open, where the air felt dry and crisp in its lungs. Life was harder on the savanna: there might be miles between one meal and another, there were seasons of drought to contend with, and large, fierce animals who didn't mind a little ape for lunch. But the ape did not run back into the forest. Instead it learned to adapt, walking from one place to another on two legs. And it learned to live by its wits. As the years passed, the ape grew smarter and smarter until it was too smart to be called an ape anymore. It lived anywhere it wanted and gradually made the whole world turn to its own purposes. Meanwhile, back in the forest, the other apes went on doing the same old thing, lazily munching on leaves and fruit. Which is why they are still just apes, even to this day.

The tale of the ape who stood up on two legs has been told many times over the past century, not in storybooks or nursery rhymes but in anthropology texts and learned scientific journals. The retellings have differed from one another in many respects: the name of the protagonist, for instance, the location in the world where his transformation took place, and the immediate cause of his metamorphosis. One part of the story, however, has remained remarkably constant: the belief that it was the shift from life in the forest to life in a more open habitat that set the ape apart by forcing it onto two legs. Bipedalism allowed hominids to see over tall savanna grass, perhaps, or escape predators, or walk more efficiently over long distances. In other scenarios, it freed the hands to make tools for hunting or gathering plants. A more recent hypothesis suggests that an erect posture exposes less skin to the sun, keeping body temperature lower in open terrain. Like the painted backdrop to a puppet theater, the savanna can accommodate any number of dramatic scenarios and possible plots.

But now that familiar stage set has come crashing down under the weight of a spectacular crop of new hominid fossils from Africa, combined with revelations about the environment of our earliest ancestors. The classic savanna hypothesis is clearly wrong, and while some still argue that the open grasslands played some role in the origins of bipedalism, a growing number of researchers are beginning to think the once unthinkable: the savanna may have had little or nothing to do with the origins of bipedalism.

"The savanna paradigm has been overthrown," says Phillip Tobias, a distinguished paleoanthropologist at the University of Witwatersrand in Johannesburg and formerly a supporter of the hypothesis. "We have to look now for some other explanation for bipedalism."

The roots of the savanna hypothesis run deep. More than 100 years ago, Charles Darwin thought that mankind's early ancestor moved from "some warm, forest-clad land" owing to "a change in its manner of procuring subsistence, or to a change in the surrounding conditions." In his view, the progenitor assumed a two-legged posture to free the hands for fashioning tools and performing other activities that in turn nourished the development of an increasingly refined intelligence. Darwin believed that this seminal event happened in Africa, where mankind's closest relatives, the African apes, still lived.

By the turn of this century, however, most anthropologists believed that the critical move to the grasslands had occurred in Asia. Though the bones of a primitive hominid—which later came to be called *Homo erectus*—had been discovered on the Southeast Asian island of Java, the change of venue had more to do with cultural values and racist reasoning than with hard evidence. Africa

African apes

Homo

Present

1

A. africanus

2

3

Millions of years ago

Ardipithecus
ramidus

A. afarensis

4

Australopithecus
anamensis

5

Common ancestor of African apes and hominids

Nenad Jakesevic

New hominid fossils have filled out our evolutionary tree, but the question of exactly how they are related to one another (and ourselves) remains unanswered.

was the "dark continent," where progress was slowed by heat, disease, and biotic excess. In such a place, it was thought, the mind would vegetate—witness the "regressive" races that inhabited the place in modern times. The plains of central Asia, on the other hand, seemed just the sort of daunting habitat that would call out the best in an enterprising ape. In that environment, wrote the American paleontologist Henry Fairfield Osborn, "the struggle for existence was severe and evoked all the inventive and resourceful faculties of man . . . ; while the anthropoid apes were luxuriating in the forested lowlands of Asia and Europe, the Dawn Men were evolving in the invigorating atmosphere of the relatively dry uplands."

In hindsight, the contrasts made between dark and light, forest and plain, slovenly ape and resourceful man seem crudely moralistic. Higher evolution, one would think, was something reserved for the primate who had the guts and wits to go out there and grab it, as if the entrepreneurial spirit of the early twentieth century could be located in our species' very origins. But at the time the idea was highly influential. Among those impressed was a young anatomist in South

Africa named Raymond Dart. In 1925 Dart announced the discovery, near the town of Taung, of what he believed to be the skull of a juvenile "man-ape," which he called *Australopithecus africanus*. While Darwin had been correct in supposing Africa to be the home continent of our ancestors, it seemed that Osborn had been right about the creature's habitat: there are no forests around Taung, and scientists assumed there hadn't been any for millions of years. Forests might provide apes with "an easy and sluggish solution" to the problems of existence, wrote Dart, but "for the production of man a different apprenticeship was needed to sharpen the wits and quicken the higher manifestations of intellect—a more open veld country where competition was keener between swiftness and stealth, and where adroitness of thinking and movement played a preponderating role in the preservation of the species."

In the decades that followed Dart's discovery, more early hominids emerged from eastern and southern Africa, and most researchers concluded that they made their homes in the savanna as well. The question was less *whether* the savanna played a part in the origin of bipedalism—

that was obvious—than how. Dart originally proposed that *Australopithecus* had taken to two legs to avoid predators ("for sudden and swift bipedal movement, to elude capture"), but later he reversed this scenario and imagined his "killer ape" the eater rather than the eaten, forsaking the trees for "the more attractive fleshy foods that lay in the vast savannas of the southern plains."

Later studies suggested that the environments in eastern and southern Africa where early hominids lived were not the vast, unchanging plains Dart imagined. Instead they appeared to be variable, often characterized by seasonally semiarid terrain, a plain studded with scraggly trees and patches of denser woodland. But no matter: This "savanna mosaic" was still drier and more open than the thick forest that harbors the African apes today. It just made good sense, moreover, that our ancestors would have come down to the ground and assumed their bipedal stance in a habitat where there were not as many trees to climb around in. The satisfying darkness-into-light theme of early hominid development held up, albeit with a little less wattage.

For decades the popularity of the savanna hypothesis rested on the twin supports of its moral resonance and general plausibility: our origin should have happened this way, and it would make awfully good sense if it did. In East Africa, geography seemed to reinforce the sheer rightness of the hypothesis. Most of the earliest hominid fossils have come from the eastern branch of the great African Rift Valley; researchers believed that when these hominids were alive, the region was much like the dry open grasslands that dominate it today. The lusher, more forested western branch, meanwhile, is home to those lazy chimps and gorillas—but to no hominid fossils.

Still, despite such suggestive correspondence, until 20 years ago something was missing from the hypothesis: some hard data to link environment to human evolution. Then paleontologist Elisabeth Vrba of Yale began offering what was the strongest evidence that the drying up of African environments helped shape early human evolution. In studying the bones of antelope and other bovids from hominid sites in South Africa, Vrba noticed a dramatic change occurring between 2.5 and 2 million years ago. Many species that were adapted to wooded environments, she saw, suddenly disappeared from the fossil record, while those suited to grassy regions appeared and multiplied. This "turnover pulse" of extinctions and origins coincides with a sudden global cooling, which may have triggered the spread of savannas and the fragmentation of forests.

Other investigators, meanwhile, were documenting an earlier turnover pulse around 5 million years ago. For humans, both dates are full of significance. This earlier pulse corresponds to the date when our lineage is thought to have diverged from that of the apes and become bipedal. Vrba's second, later pulse marks the appearance of stone tools and the arrival on the scene of new hominid species, some with brains big enough

to merit inclusion in the genus *Homo*. The inference was clear: our early ancestors were savanna born and savanna bred.

"All the evidence, as I see it," Vrba wrote in 1993, "indicates that the lineage of upright primates known as australopithecines, the first hominids, was one of the founding groups of the great African savanna biota."

With empirical evidence drawn from two different sources, the turnover pulse is a great improvement on the traditional savanna hypothesis (which in retrospect looks not so much like a hypothesis as a really keen idea). Best of all, Vrba's hypothesis is testable. Let's say that global climate changes did indeed create open country in East Africa, which in turn triggered a turnover of species and pushed ahead the evolution of hominids. If so, then similar turnovers

in animal species should have appeared in the fossil record whenever global change occurred.

Over the last 15 years, Andrew Hill and John Kingston, both also at Yale, have been looking for signs of those dramatic shifts at some 400 sites in the Tugen Hills of Kenya. In the heart of the fossil-rich eastern branch of the Rift Valley, the Tugen Hills offer a look at a succession of geologic layers from 16 million years ago to a mere 200,000 years ago—studded with fragmentary remains of ancient apes and hominids. To gauge the past climate of the Tugen Hills, the researchers have looked at the signatures of the ancient soils preserved in rock. Different plants incorporate different ratios of isotopes of carbon in their tissues, and when those plants die and decompose, that distinctive ratio remains in the soil. Thus grasslands and

• **ARAMIS**
AGE: 4.4 million years old
SPECIES: *Ardipithecus ramidus*
BIPEDAL? Unknown
ENVIRONMENT: Dense woodlands

• **LAKE TURKANA**
AGE: 4.2 million years old
SPECIES: *Australopithecus anamensis*
BIPEDAL? Yes
ENVIRONMENT: Lakeside forests in an arid region

• **LAETOLI**
AGE: 3.5 million years old
SPECIES: *Australopithecus afarensis*
BIPEDAL? Yes
ENVIRONMENT: Primarily grasslands, with some forests

THE DAWN OF THE HOMINIDS

• **STERKFONTEIN**
AGE: 3 to 3.5 million years old
SPECIES: Probably *Australopithecus africanus*
BIPEDAL? Yes, but also still a tree climber
ENVIRONMENT: Forests

• **BAHR EL GHAZAL**
AGE: 3 to 3.5 million years old
SPECIES: Similar to *Australopithecus afarensis*
BIPEDAL? Probably
ENVIRONMENT: Gallery forests with grassy patches

• **HADAR**
AGE: 3.2 million years old
SPECIES: *Australopithecus afarensis* ("Lucy")
BIPEDAL? Yes
ENVIRONMENT: Forests and bushlands

Nenad Jakesevic

forests leave distinguishing isotopic marks. When Hill and Kingston looked at soils formed during Vrba's turnover pulses, however, they found nothing like the radical shifts to grasslands that she predicted. Instead of signs that the environment was opening up, they found that there was a little bit of grass all the time, with no dramatic changes, and no evidence that early hominids there ever encountered an open grassland.

"Elisabeth's turnover pulse hypothesis is very attractive," says Hill. "It would have been lovely if it had also been true."

Other research has also contradicted Vrba's hypothesis. Laura Bishop of Liverpool University in England, for instance, has been studying pig fossils from several East African sites. Some of those fossil animals, she has found, had limbs that were adapted not for open habitats but for heavy woods. Peter de Menocal of Columbia University's Lamont-Doherty Earth Observatory has been looking at long-term climate patterns in Africa by measuring the concentration of dust in ocean sediments. Over the past 5 million years, he has found, the African climate has cycled back and forth between dry and wet climates, but the pattern became dramatic only 2.8 million years ago, when Africa became particularly arid. Such a change could have played a role in the dawn of *Homo*, but it came over a million years too late to have had a hand in australopithecines' becoming bipedal.

WHAT MAY finally kill the savanna hypothesis—or save it—are the hominids themselves. More than anything else, walking on two feet is what makes a hominid a hominid. If those first bipedal footsteps were made on savanna, we should find fossils of the first hominids in open habitats. For almost 20 years, the earliest hominid known has been *Australopithecus afarensis*, exemplified by the 3.2-million-year-old skeleton called Lucy. Lucy had a chimp-size skull but an upright posture, which clinches the argument that hominids evolved bipedalism before big brains. But had Lucy completely let go of the trees? It's been a

matter of much debate: oddities such as her curved digits may be the anatomic underpinnings of a partially arboreal life-style or just baggage left over from her tree-climbing ancestry.

Nor did *afarensis* make clear a preference for one sort of habitat over another. Most of the fossils come from two sites: Hadar in Ethiopia, where Lucy was found, and Laetoli in Tanzania, where three hominids presumed to be *afarensis* left their footprints in a layer of newly erupted volcanic ash 3.5 million years ago. Laetoli has been considered one of the driest, barest habitats in the eastern rift and thus has given comfort to the savanna faithful. But at Hadar the *afarensis* fossils appear to have been laid down among woodlands along ancient rivers. Other ambiguous bones that may have belonged to *afarensis* and may have dated back as far as 4 million years ago have been found at nearby East African localities. Environments at these sites run the gamut from arid to lush, suggesting that Lucy and her kin may not have been confined to one particular habitat but rather lived in a broad range of them. So why give some special credit to the savanna for launching our lineage?

"I've always thought that there was scant evidence for the savanna hypothesis, based simply on the fact that hominids are extremely plastic behaviorally," says Bill Kimbel, director of science at the Institute for Human Origins in Berkeley, California.

At least *afarensis* had enough respect for conventional wisdom to stay on the right side of the Rift Valley. Or it did until last year. In November a team led by Michel Brunet of the University of Poitiers in France announced the discovery of a jawbone similar to that of *afarensis* and, at 3 to 3.5 million years old, well within the species' time range. The ecology where Brunet's hominid lived also has a familiar ring: "a vegetational mosaic of gallery forest and wooded savanna with open grassy patches." But in one important respect the fossil is out of left field—Brunet found it in Chad, in north central Africa, more than 1,500 miles from the eastern Rift Valley, where all the other *afarensis* specimens have been found.

This hominid's home is even farther west, in fact, than the dark, humid forests of the western rift, home to the great apes—clearly on the wrong side of the tracks.

In a normal year the Chad fossil would have been the biggest hominid news. But 1995 was anything but a normal year. In August, Meave Leakey of the National Museums of Kenya and her colleagues made public the discovery of a new hominid species, called *Australopithecus anamensis*, even older than *afarensis*. (The fossils were found at two sites near Lake Turkana in Kenya and derive their name from the Turkana word for "lake.") The previous spring, Tim White of the University of California at Berkeley and his associates had named a whole new genus, *Ardipithecus ramidus*, that was older still, represented by fossils found in Aramis, Ethiopia, over the previous three years. The character of *anamensis* and *ramidus* could well have decided the fate of the savanna hypothesis. If they were bipeds living in relatively open territory, they could breathe new life into a hypothesis that's struggling to survive. But if either showed that our ancestors were upright *before* leaving the forest, the idea that has dominated paleoanthropology for a century would be reduced to little more than a historical artifact.

The best hope for the savanna hypothesis rests with Leakey's new species. In its head and neck, *anamensis* shares a number of features with fossil apes, but Leakey's team also found a shinbone that is quite humanlike and emphatically bipedal—in spite of the deep antiquity of *anamensis*: the older of the two sites has been dated to 4.2 million years ago. And the region surrounding the sites was a dry, relatively open bushland.

This is good news for those, such as Peter Wheeler of Liverpool John Moores University in England, whose theories of bipedalism depend on an initial movement out of the closed-canopy forest. Wheeler maintains that standing upright exposes less body surface to the sun, making it possible for proto-hominids to keep cool enough out of the shade to exploit savanna resources. "It's pretty clear that by three and a half million years ago, australopithecines were living in a range of habitats," he says. "But if you look at the oldest evidence for bipedalism—Laetoli, and now the *anamensis* sites—these are actually more open habitats."

However, Alan Walker of Penn State, one of the codiscoverers of *anamensis*, disagrees. Though the regional climate may have been as hot and arid back then as it is now, he says, the local habitat of *anamensis* was probably quite different. Back then the lake was much bigger than it is today and would have supported a massive ring of vegetation. Animal fossils found at the *anamensis* sites—everything from little forest monkeys to grass-eating antelope—were lodged in deltalike sediments that must have been deposited by "monstrous great rivers," says Walker, with gallery forests as much as a mile or two wide on both banks.

Even Laetoli is proving to be a mixed blessing for savanna lovers. In the first studies, researchers focused their attention mainly on the abundance of fossils of arid-adapted antelope at the site. Based on these remains, they concluded that Laetoli was a grassland with scattered trees. But according to Kaye Reed of the Institute of Human Origins, these conclusions are debatable. For one thing, the antelope are gregarious herders, so one should expect to find more of their bones than those of more solitary species. Moreover, the original studies underplayed evidence for a more diverse community, which included woodland-dwelling antelope and an assortment of monkeys. In separate studies, Reed and Peter Andrews of the British Natural History Museum took a more thorough look at Laetoli, and both concluded that the original description was far too bleak. "Monkeys have to have trees to eat and sleep in," says Reed. "I don't want to give the impression that this was some kind of deep forest. But certainly Laetoli was more heavily wooded than we thought."

*Ardipithecus ramidus* poses a potentially more devastating blow to the savanna hypothesis. The 4.4-million-year-old species has a skull and teeth that are even more primitive and chimplike than *anamensis*. Other traits of its anatomy, how-

ever, align it with later hominids such as *afarensis*. It remains to be seen whether *ramidus* is an early cousin of our direct ancestors or is indeed at the very base of the hominid lineage (its name perhaps reveals the hope of its discoverers, deriving from the Afar word for "root"). What we do know is that the species lived in a densely wooded habitat along with forest-dwelling monkey species and the kudu, an antelope that prefers a bushy habitat.

"We interpret these initial results as evidence that the hominids lived and died in a wooded setting," says Tim White.

*A. ramidus* would be the final nail in the coffin of the savanna hypothesis, except for one crucial bit of missing information: none of its discoverers will yet say if it was bipedal. Researchers have unearthed a partial skeleton consisting of over 100 fragments of dozens of bones, including hand bones, foot bones, wrist bones—more than enough to determine whether the creature walked like a human or like a chimp. Unfortunately the fragile bones are encased in sediment that must be laboriously chipped away before a proper analysis can begin. Neither White nor any member of his team will comment on what the bones say about locomotion until a thorough study can be completed—which at this point won't be until 1998 at the earliest.

There are plenty of other puzzling bones to ponder in the meantime. Back in South Africa, where Dart found the first australopithecine, researchers have begun analyzing a horde of some 500 new and previously collected specimens from a site called Sterkfontein. Some of them may have a potent impact on the savanna hypothesis.

The most widely publicized is "Little Foot," a tantalizing string of four connected foot bones running from the ankle to the base of the big toe. Little Foot is between 3 and 3.5 million years old, hundreds of thousands of years younger than the *ramidus* and *anamensis* specimens. Yet according to Phillip Tobias and his Witwatersrand colleague Ronald Clarke, the fossil demonstrates that this early species of australopithecine—quite probably *A. africanus*—still spent time in the trees. While the anklebone, Tobias and

Clarke say, is built to take the weight of a bipedal stride, the foot is also surprisingly primitive. This is especially true of the big toe, which they contend splayed out to the side like a chimpanzee's, all the better to grasp tree branches when climbing.

ALTHOUGH not everyone agrees that Little Foot's foot is so apelike, a host of other fossils from Sterkfontein also speak of the trees. Lee Berger, also at Witwatersrand, has analyzed several shoulder girdles from the collection and found them even better suited to climbing and suspending behavior than those of *afarensis*. He and Tobias have analyzed a shinbone from the same site and concluded it was more chimplike than human. And in what is perhaps the most compelling finding so far, Berger and Henry McHenry of the University of California at Davis have analyzed the proportions of arms and legs of the Sterkfontein *africanus* specimens and found that they were closer to chimps than to humans.

The tree-climbing anatomy of *africanus* has prompted Tobias, long a savanna loyalist, to wonder why such an animal would be out on the South African veld, where today there aren't any trees big enough to climb around in. A possible answer came from recent reevaluations of the environments at several *africanus* sites. As in East Africa, the ancient fauna and pollen suggest that conditions there were warmer, wetter, and more wooded than previously thought. Tobias's colleague Marian Bamford has even recovered traces at Sterkfontein of liana vines, which grow primarily in dense forests. The climate at the site did become drier and more open 2.5 million years ago, but by then hominids had been walking on two legs for a least a million and a half years.

If they live up to their discovers' initial claims, the Sterkfontein fossils make hominid history more complicated than we thought. Lucy and her fellow *afarensis* were traipsing through Ethiopia at about the same time Little Foot and the other *africanus* hominids were in South Africa—and the two hominids were using different ways of moving around. While Lucy was more committed to life on the ground, Little Foot went for a mixed strategy, sometimes scuttling up trees. "What this suggests," says Berger, "is that bipedalism may have evolved not once but twice."

And in both cases, the South African researchers argue, bipedalism was not associated with the savanna. "The idea that bipedalism evolved as an adaptation to the savanna," declares Tobias, "can be thrown out the window."

If so, it shall be missed. For all its shortcomings—a shortage of evidence being the first among them—the savanna hypothesis provided a tidy, plausible explanation for a profound mystery: What set human beings apart from the rest of creation? If not the savanna, what did cause the first hominids to become bipedal? Why develop anatomy good only for walking on the ground when you are still living among the trees? For all the effort it has taken to bring down the savanna hypothesis, it will take much more to build up something else in its place.

"I don't really know why we became bipedal," says Andrew Hill. "It's such an unusual thing."

"We're back to square one," says Tobias.

"Square one" is not completely empty. Kevin Hunt of Indiana University, for instance, has recently revived the idea that bipedalism was initially an adaptation for woodland feeding rather than a new way of getting around. Chimps often stand while feeding in small trees and bushes, stabilizing themselves by hanging onto an overhanging branch. Hunt suggests that the earliest australopithecines made an anatomic commitment to this specialized way of obtaining food.

Nina Jablonski of the California Academy of Science in San Francisco sees the beginnings of our bipedalism mirrored instead in the upright threat displays of great apes. Perhaps our ancestors resorted to this behavior more than their ape cousins to maintain the social hierarchy. Originally Jablonski and her colleague George Chaplin of the University

of Western Australia linked the increase in bipedal threat displays to a move to the savanna, where there would be more competition for resources. But in light of the new evidence for wooded habitats, she now concedes that this "essentially primary cause" of bipedalism could have emerged in a forest.

There is a stubborn paradox in such models, based as they are on living primates: since chimps and gorillas have presumably been performing these behaviors for millennia without the evolution of bipedalism, how could the same behaviors have driven just such an evolution in hominids? In the early 1980's, Owen Lovejoy of Kent State in Ohio proposed an elegant explanation for bipedalism that bypassed this logical difficulty and had nothing to do with moving about on the savanna.

"Bipedality is a lousy form of locomotion," says Lovejoy. "It's slower and more awkward, and it puts the animal at greater risk of injury. The advantage must come from some other motivating selective force." To Lovejoy, the force is reproduction itself. In his view, what separated the protohominids from their ape contemporaries was a wholly new reproductive strategy, in which males provided food to females and their mutual offspring. With the males' assistance, the females could forage less and give birth more frequently than their ape counterparts because they could care for more than one child at a time. In return a male gained continual sexual access to a particular female, ensuring that the children he provisioned were most likely his own.

This monogamous arrangement would have provided an enormous evolutionary advantage, says Lovejoy, since it would directly affect the number of offspring an individual female could bear and raise to maturity. But the males would need the anatomic apparatus to carry food back to be shared in the first place. Bipedalism may have been a poor way of getting around, but by freeing the hands for carrying, it would have been an excellent way to bear more offspring.

And in evolution, of course, more offspring is the name of the game.

If the savanna hypothesis is barely kicking, it's worth remembering that it isn't dead. While scientists no longer believe in the classic portrait of protohominids loping about on a treeless gray plain, there's treeless, and then there's treeless. Despite the revisionism of recent years, the fact remains that Africa as a whole has gradually cooled and dried over the past 5 million years. Even if the trees did not disappear completely, early hominids may still have faced sparser forests than their ancestors. Bipedalism may still have been an important part of their adjustment to this new setting.

"We have to be careful about what we call savanna," says Peter Wheeler. "Most savanna is a range of habitats, including bushland and quite dense trees. My arguments for bipedalism being a thermoregulatory adaptation would still apply, unless there was continuous shade cover, as in a closed-canopy forest. Nobody is saying that about *anamensis*."

Unfortunately they *are* saying that about *anamensis's* older cousin, *Ardipithecus ramidus*, in its deep forest home. Which brings us full circle to the business of storytelling. Every reader knows that a good story depends on having strongly drawn characters, ones the author understands well. Rather suddenly, two new protagonists have been added to the opening chapters of human evolution. About *anamensis* we still know very little. But about *ramidus* we know next to nothing. Once upon a time, nearly four and a half million years ago, there was a hominid that lived in the middle of a dark forest. Did it walk on two legs or four? If it walked on two, why?

"The locomotor habit of *ramidus* is crucial," says Lovejoy, who is among those charged with the enviable task of analyzing its bones. "If it is bipedal, then the savanna hypothesis in all its mundane glory would be dead. But if it is quadrupedal, then the old idea, even though I think it is inherently illogical, would not be disproved."

# Early Hominid Fossils from Africa

*A new species of* Australopithecus, *the ancestor of* Homo, *pushes back the origins of bipedalism to some four million years ago*

## by Meave Leakey and Alan Walker

The year was 1965. Bryan Patterson, a paleoanthropologist from Harvard University, unearthed a fragment of a fossil arm bone at a site called Kanapoi in northern Kenya. He and his colleagues knew it would be hard to make a great deal of anatomic or evolutionary sense out of a small piece of elbow joint. Nevertheless, they did recognize some features reminiscent of a species of early hominid (a hominid is any upright-walking primate) known as *Australopithecus,* first discovered 40 years earlier in South Africa by Raymond Dart of the University of the Witwatersrand. In most details, however, Patterson and his team considered the fragment of arm bone to be more like those of modern humans than the one other *Australopithecus* humerus known at the time.

The age of the Kanapoi fossil proved somewhat surprising. Although the techniques for dating the rocks where the fossil was uncovered were still fairly rudimentary, the group working in Kenya was able to show that the bone was probably older than the various *Australopithecus* specimens previously found. Despite this unusual result, however, the significance of Patterson's discovery was not to be confirmed for another 30 years. In the interim, researchers identified the remains of so many important early hominids that the humerus from Kanapoi was rather forgotten.

Yet Patterson's fossil would eventually help establish the existence of a new species of *Australopithecus*—the oldest yet to be identified—and push back the origins of upright walking to more than four million years (Myr) ago. But to see how this happened, we need to trace the steps that paleoanthropologists have taken in constructing an outline for the story of hominid evolution.

### Evolving Story of Early Hominids

Scientists classify the immediate ancestors of the genus *Homo* (which includes our own species, *Homo sapiens*) in the genus *Australopithecus.* For several decades, it was believed that these ancient hominids first inhabited the earth at least three and a half million years ago. The specimens found in South Africa by Dart and others indicated that there were at least two types of *Australopithecus*—*A. africanus* and *A. robustus.* The leg bones of both species suggested that they had the striding, bipedal locomotion that is a hallmark of humans among living mammals. (The upright posture of these creatures was vividly confirmed in 1978 at the Laetoli site in Tanzania, where a team led by archaeologist Mary Leakey discovered a spectacular series of footprints made 3.6 Myr ago by three *Australopithecus* individuals as they walked across wet volcanic ash.) Both *A. africanus* and *A. robustus* were relatively small-brained and had canine teeth that differed from those of modern apes in that they hardly projected past the rest of the tooth row. The younger of the two species, *A. robustus,* had bizarre adaptations for chewing—huge molar and premolar teeth combined with bony crests on the skull where powerful chewing muscles would have been attached.

Paleoanthropologists identified more species of *Australopithecus* over the next several decades. In 1959 Mary Leakey unearthed a skull from yet another East African species closely related to *robustus*. Skulls of these species uncovered during the past 40 years in the northeastern part of Africa, in Ethiopia and Kenya, differed considerably from those found in South Africa; as a result, researchers think that two separate *robustus*-like species—a northern one and a southern one—existed.

In 1978 Donald C. Johanson, now at the Institute of Human Origins in Berkeley, Calif., along with his colleagues, identified still another species of *Australopithecus*. Johanson and his team had been studying a small number of hominid bones and teeth discovered at Laetoli, as well as a large and very important collection of specimens from the Hadar region of Ethiopia (including the famous "Lucy" skeleton). The group named the new species *afarensis*. Radiometric dating revealed that the species had lived between 3.6 and 2.9 Myr ago, making it the oldest *Australopithecus* known at the time.

This early species is probably the best studied of all the *Australopithecus* recognized so far, and it is certainly the one that has generated the most contro-versy over the past 20 years. The debates have ranged over many issues: whether the *afarensis* fossils were truly distinct from the *africanus* fossils from South Africa; whether there was one or several species at Hadar; whether the Tanzanian and Ethiopian fossils were of the same species; whether the fossils had been dated correctly.

But the most divisive debate concerns the issue of how extensively the bipedal *afarensis* climbed in trees. Fossils of *afarensis* include various bone and joint structures typical of tree climbers. Some scientists argue that such characteristics indicate that these hominids must have spent at least some time in the trees. But others view these features as simply evolutionary baggage, left over from arboreal ancestors. Underlying this discussion is the question of where *Australopithecus* lived—in forests or on the open savanna.

By the beginning of the 1990s, researchers knew a fair amount about the various species of *Australopithecus* and how each had adapted to its environmental niche. A description of any one of the species would mention that the creatures were bipedal and that they had ape-size brains and large, thickly enameled teeth in strong jaws, with nonprojecting canines. Males were typically larger than females, and individuals grew and matured rapidly. But the origins of *Australopithecus* were only hinted at, because the gap between the earliest well-known species in the group (*afarensis,* from about 3.6 Myr ago) and the postulated time of the last common ancestor of chimpanzees and humans (between 5 and 6 Myr ago) was still very great. Fossil hunters had unearthed only a few older fragments of bone, tooth and jaw from the intervening 1.5 million years to indicate the anatomy and course of evolution of the very earliest hominids.

## Filling the Gap

Discoveries in Kenya over the past several years have filled in some of the missing interval between 3.5 and 5 Myr ago. Beginning in 1982, expeditions run by the National Museums of Kenya to the Lake Turkana basin in northern Kenya began finding hominid fossils nearly 4 Myr old. But because these fossils were mainly isolated teeth—no jawbones or skulls were preserved—very little could be said about them except that they resembled the remains of *afarensis* from Laetoli. But our recent excavations at an unusual site, just inland from Allia Bay on the east side of Lake Turkana [*see maps*], yielded more complete fossils.

The site at Allia Bay is a bone bed, where millions of fragments of weathered tooth and bone from a wide variety of animals, including hominids, spill out of the hillside. Exposed at the top of the hill lies a layer of hardened volcanic ash called the Moiti Tuff, which has been dated radiometrically to just over 3.9 Myr old. The fossil fragments lie several meters below the tuff, indicating that the remains are older than the tuff. We do not yet understand fully why so many fossils are concentrated in this spot, but we can be certain that they were deposited by the precursor of the present-day Omo River.

Today the Omo drains the Ethiopian highlands located to the north, emptying into Lake Turkana, which has no outlet. But this has not always been so. Our colleagues Frank Brown of the Univer-

FAMILY TREE of the hominid species known as *Australopithecus* includes a number of species that lived between roughly 4 and 1.25 Myr ago. Just over 2 Myr ago a new genus, *Homo* (which includes our own species, *Homo sapiens*), evolved from one of the species of *Australopithecus*.

sity of Utah and Craig Feibel of Rutgers University have shown that the ancient Omo River dominated the Turkana area for much of the Pliocene (roughly 5.3 to 1.6 Myr ago) and the early Pleistocene (1.6 to 0.7 Myr ago). Only infrequently was a lake present in the area at all. Instead, for most of the past four million years, an extensive river system flowed across the broad floodplain, proceeding to the Indian Ocean without dumping its sediments into a lake.

The Allia Bay fossils are located in one of the channels of this ancient river system. Most of the fossils collected from Allia Bay are rolled and weathered bones and teeth of aquatic animals— fish, crocodiles, hippopotamuses and the like—that were damaged during transport down the river from some distance away. But some of the fossils are much better preserved; these come from the animals that lived on or near the riverbanks. Among these creatures are several different species of leaf-eating monkeys, related to modern colobus monkeys, as well as antelopes whose living relatives favor closely wooded areas. Reasonably well preserved hominid fossils can also be found here, suggesting that, at least occasionally, early hominids inhabited a riparian habitat.

Where do these *Australopithecus* fossils fit in the evolutionary history of hominids? The jaws and teeth from Allia Bay, as well as a nearly complete radius (the outside bone of the forearm) from the nearby sediments of Sibilot just to the north, show an interesting mixture of characteristics. Some of the traits are primitive ones—that is, they are ancestral features thought to be present before the split occurred between the chimpanzee and human lineages. Yet these bones also share characteristics seen in later hominids and are therefore said to have more advanced features. As our team continues to unearth more bones and teeth at Allia Bay, these new fossils add to our knowledge of the wide range of traits present in early hominids.

### Return to Kanapoi

Across Lake Turkana, some 145 kilometers (about 90 miles) south of Allia Bay, lies the site of Kanapoi,

where our story began. One of us (Leakey) has mounted expeditions from the National Museums of Kenya to explore the sediments located southwest of Lake Turkana and to document the faunas present during the earliest stages of the basin's history. Kanapoi, virtually unexplored since Patterson's day, has proved to be one of the most rewarding sites in the Turkana region.

A series of deep erosion gullies, known as badlands, has exposed the sediments at Kanapoi. Fossil hunting is difficult here, though, because of a carapace of lava pebbles and gravel that makes it hard to spot small bones and teeth. Studies of the layers of sediment, also carried out by Feibel, reveal that the fossils here have been preserved by deposits from a river ancestral to the present-day Kerio River, which once flowed into the Turkana basin and emptied into an ancient lake we call Lonyumun. This lake reached its maximum size about 4.1 Myr ago and thereafter shrank as it filled with sediments.

Excavations at Kanapoi have primarily yielded the remains of carnivore meals, so the fossils are rather fragmentary. But workers at the site have also recovered two nearly complete lower jaws, one complete upper jaw and lower face, the upper and lower thirds of a tibia (the larger bone of the lower leg), bits of skull and several sets of isolated teeth. After careful study of the fossils from both Allia Bay and Kanapoi—including Patterson's fragment of an arm bone—we felt that in details of anatomy, these specimens were different enough from previously known hominids to warrant designating a new species. So in 1995, in collaboration with both Feibel and Ian McDougall of the Australian National University, we named this new species *Australopithecus anamensis,* drawing on the Turkana word for lake (*anam*) to refer to both the present and ancient lakes.

To establish the age of these fossils, we relied on the extensive efforts of Brown, Feibel and McDougall, who have been investigating the paleogeographic history of the entire lake basin. If there study of the basin's development is correct, the *anamensis* fossils should be between 4.2 and 3.9 Myr

old. Currently McDougall is working to determine the age of the so-called Kanapoi Tuff—the layer of volcanic ash that covers most of the fossils at this site. We expect that once McDougall successfully ascertains the age of the tuff, we will be confident in both the age of the fossils and Brown's and Feibel's understanding of the history of the lake basin.

A major question in paleoanthropology today is how the anatomic mosaic of the early hominids evolved. By comparing the nearly contemporaneous Allia Bay and Kanapoi collections of *anamensis,* we can piece together a fairly accurate picture of certain aspects of the species, even though we have not yet uncovered a complete skull.

The jaws of *anamensis* are primitive—the sides sit close together and parallel to each other (as in modern apes), rather than widening at the back of the mouth (as in later hominids, including humans). In its lower jaw, *anamensis* is also chimp-like in terms of the shape of the region where the left and right sides of the jaw meet (technically known as the mandibular symphysis).

Teeth from *anamensis,* however, appear more advanced. The enamel is relatively thick, as it is in all other species of *Australopithecus;* in contrast, the tooth enamel of African great apes is much thinner. The thickened enamel suggests *anamensis* had already adapted to a changed diet—possibly much harder food—even though its jaws and some skull features were still very apelike. We also know that *anamensis* had only a tiny external ear canal. In this regard, it is more like chimpanzees and unlike all later hominids, including humans, which have large external ear canals. (The size of the external canal is unrelated to the size of the fleshy ear.)

The most informative bone of all the ones we have uncovered from this new hominid is the nearly complete tibia— the larger of the two bones in the lower leg. The tibia is revealing because of its important role in weight bearing: the tibia of a biped is distinctly different from the tibia of an animal that walks on all four legs. In size and practically all details of the knee and ankle joints, the tibia found at Kanapoi closely resembles the one from the fully bipedal

CHIMPANZEE          ANAMENSIS          HUMAN

MANDIBLE

The jawbones in *anamensis* and chimpanzees are U-shaped.

The human jaw widens at the back of the mouth.

TIBIA

The top of the tibia, near the knee, is somewhat T-shaped in chimpanzees.

In the tibias of *anamensis* and humans, the top of the bone is wider because of the extra spongy bone tissue present, which serves as a shock absorber in bipedal creatures.

HUMERUS

Primates such as chimpanzees that walk on their knuckles have a deep, oval hollow at the bottom of the humerus where the humerus and the ulna lock in place, making the elbow joint more stable.

Human and *anamensis* bones lack this feature, suggesting that, like humans, *anamensis* did not walk on its knuckles.

**FOSSILS** from *anamensis (center)* share features in common with both humans *(right)* and modern chimpanzees *(left)*. Scientists use the similarities and differences among these species to determine their interrelationships and thereby piece together the course of hominid evolution since the lineages of chimpanzees and humans split some five or six million years ago.

*afarensis* found at Hadar, even though the latter specimen is nearly a million years younger.

Fossils of other animals collected at Kanapoi point to a somewhat different paleoecological scenario from the setting across the lake at Allia Bay. The channels of the river that laid down the sediments at Kanapoi were probably lined with narrow stretches of forest that grew close to the riverbanks in other-

wise open country. Researchers have recovered the remains of the same spiral-horned antelope found at Allia Bay that very likely lived in dense thickets. But open-country antelopes and hartebeest appear to have lived at Kanapoi as well, suggesting that more open savanna prevailed away from the rivers. These results offer equivocal evidence regarding the preferred habitat of *anamensis:* we know that bushland was present at both

sites that have yielded fossils of the species, but there are clear signs of more diverse habitats at Kanapoi.

## An Even Older Hominid?

At about the same time that we were finding new hominids at Allia Bay and Kanapoi, a team led by our colleague Tim D. White of the University of California at Berkeley discovered fossil hominids in Ethiopia that are even older than *anamensis*. In 1992 and 1993 White led an expedition to the Middle Awash area of Ethiopia, where his team uncovered hominid fossils at a site known as Aramis. The group's finds include isolated teeth, a piece of baby's mandible (the lower jaw), fragments from an adult's skull and some arm bones, all of which have been dated to around 4.4 Myr ago. In 1994, together with his colleagues Berhane Asfaw of the Paleoanthropology Laboratory in Addis Ababa and Gen Suwa of the University of Tokyo, White gave these fossils a new name: *Australopithecus ramidus*. In 1995 the group renamed the fossils, moving them to a new genus, *Ardipithecus*. Other fossils buried near the hominids, such as seeds and the bones of forest monkeys and antelopes, strongly imply that these hominids, too, lived in a closed-canopy woodland.

This new species represents the most primitive hominid known—a link between the African apes and *Australopithecus*. Many of the *Ardipithecus ramidus* fossils display similarities to the anatomy of the modern African great apes, such as thin dental enamel and strongly built arm bones. In other features, though—such as the opening at the base of the skull, technically known as the foramen magnum, through which the spinal cord connects to the brain— the fossils resemble later hominids.

Describing early hominids as either primitive or more advanced is a complex issue. Scientists now have almost decisive molecular evidence that humans and chimpanzees once had a common ancestor and that this lineage had previously split from gorillas. This is why we often use the two living species of chimpanzee (*Pan troglodytes* and *P. paniscus*) to illustrate ancestral traits. But we must remember that since their last common ancestor with humans, chimpanzees have had exactly the same amount of time to evolve as humans have. Determining which features were present in the last common ancestor of humans and chimpanzees is not easy.

But *Ardipithecus,* with its numerous chimplike features, appears to have taken the human fossil record back close

to the time of the chimp-human split. More recently, White and his group have found parts of a single *Ardipithecus* skeleton in the Middle Awash region. As White and his team extract these exciting new fossils from the enclosing stone, reconstruct them and prepare them for study, the paleoanthropological community eagerly anticipates the publication of the group's analysis of these astonishing finds.

But even pending White's results, new *Australopithecus* fossil discoveries are offering other surprises, particularly about where these creatures lived. In 1995 a team led by Michel Brunet of the University of Poitiers announced the identification in Chad of *Australopithecus* fossils believed to be about 3.5 Myr old. The new fossils are very fragmentary—only the front part of a lower jaw and isolated tooth. In 1996, however, Brunet and his colleagues designated a new species for their specimen: *A. bahrelghazali*. Surprisingly, these fossils were recovered far from either eastern or southern Africa, the only areas where *Australopithecus* had been found until now. The site, in the Bahr el Ghazal region of Chad, lies 2,500 kilometers west of the western part of the Rift Valley, thus extending the range of *Australopithecus* well into the center of Africa.

The *bahrelghazali* fossils debunk a hypothesis about human evolution postulated in the pages of *Scientific American* by Yves Coppens of the College of France [see "East Side Story: The Origin of Humankind," May 1994]; ironically, Coppens is now a member of Brunet's team. Coppens's article proposed that the formation of Africa's Rift Valley subdivided a single ancient species, isolating the ancestors of hominids on the east side from the ancestors of modern apes on the west side. In general, scientists believe such geographical isolation can foster the development of new species by prohibiting continued interbreeding among the original populations. But the new Chad fossils show that early hominids did live west of the Rift Valley. The geographical separation of apes and hominids previously apparent in the fossil record may be more the result

of accidental circumstances of geology and discovery than the species' actual ranges.

The fossils of *anamensis* that we have identified should also provide some answers in the long-standing debate over whether early *Australopithecus* species lived in wooded areas or on the open savanna. The outcome of this discussion has important implications: for many years, paleoanthropologists have accepted that upright-walking behavior originated on the savanna, where it most likely provided benefits such as keeping the hot sun off the back or freeing hands for carrying food. Yet our evidence suggests that the earliest bipedal hominid known to date lived at least part of the time in wooded areas. The discoveries of the past several years represent a remarkable spurt in the sometimes painfully slow process of uncovering human evolutionary past. But clearly there is still much more to learn.

## The Authors

MEAVE LEAKEY and ALAN WALKER, together with Leakey's husband, Richard, have collaborated for many years on the discovery and analysis of early hominid fossils from Kenya. Leakey is head of the division of paleontology at the National Museums of Kenya in Nairobi. Walker is Distinguished Professor of anthropology and biology at Pennsylvania State University. He is a MacArthur Fellow and a member of the American Academy of Arts and Sciences.

## Further Reading

*AUSTRALOPITHECUS RAMIDUS*, A NEW SPECIES OF EARLY HOMINID FROM ARAMIS, ETHIOPIA. Tim D. White, Gen Suwa and Berhane Asfaw in *Nature,* Vol. 371, pages 306–312; September 22, 1994.
NEW FOUR-MILLION-YEAR-OLD HOMINID SPECIES FROM KANAPOI AND ALLIA BAY, KENYA. Meave G. Leakey, Craig S. Feibel, Ian McDougall and Alan Walker in *Nature,* Vol. 376, pages 565–571; August 17, 1995.
FROM LUCY TO LANGUAGE. Donald C. Johanson and Blake Edgar. Peter Nevraumont, Simon & Schuster, 1996.
RECONSTRUCTING HUMAN ORIGINS: A MODERN SYNTHESIS. Glenn C. Conroy. W. W. Norton, 1997.

# A New Human Ancestor?

*Ethiopian fossils reveal a new branch on the hominid family tree: a small-brained hominid that is a candidate for the ancestor of our lineage*

## Elizabeth Culotta

About two and half million years ago, on a grassy plain bordering a shallow lake in what is now eastern Ethiopia, a humanlike creature began dismembering an antelope carcass. Nothing remains of the hominid, but the antelope bones show that it wrenched a leg off the carcass, then used a stone tool to slice off the meat and smash the bone. After several tries, it managed to break off both ends of the bone and scrape out the juicy marrow inside.

At just about the same time, two other hominids died near the lake. One, perhaps 1.4 meters tall, had long legs and a human gait but long, apelike forearms. The other, a male, lay some distance away. His limb bones are gone, but the remains of his skull show he had a small brain, big teeth, and an apelike face.

These new fossils give different glimpses of each hominid, and no one can be sure all three belonged to the same species. But even if not, their details are starting to fill in a mysterious chapter of human prehistory. According to the international team that made all three discov-

eries, the big-toothed skull represents an unusual new species that is the best candidate for the ancestor of our own genus, *Homo*. Not everyone in the contentious field of paleoanthropology agrees, but the

Untangling the family tree. Fossil finds suggest an outline of our evolutionary history, but the ancestor of our genus remains in question.

SOURCE: ADAPTED FROM T. WHITE; PHOTOS: DAVID L. BRILL

new species, which Ethiopian anthropologist Berhane Asfaw and his colleagues have named *Australopithecus garhi* (*garhi* means "surprise" in the language spoken by the local Afar people), is certain to shake up views of the tran-

sition from the apelike australopithecines to humankind. And the scored bones from the first hominid's feast are the earliest recorded evidence of hominids butchering animals, bolstering the notion that meat eating was important in human evolution.

"They've put together a whole package here, so that you can say a fair amount about a time we don't know much about," says anthropologist F. Clark Howell of the University of California (UC), Berkeley. With its surprising mix of traits—primitive face and unusually big teeth—the new australopithecine doesn't match the profile many researchers expected for a human ancestor at this stage. "It's very exciting," says paleoanthropologist Alan Walker of Pennsylvania State University in University Park. "Until now it's all been just scraps of teeth and bits of mandible from this time. And this [morphology] is a surprise."

But this rare glimpse of a murky period in human evolution raises as many questions as it answers. *A. garhi* has few

CREDIT: DAVID L. BRILL

Treasure site. A garhi's skull was found on this Ethiopian desert slope.

traits that definitively link it to *Homo,* and like other hominids from the same period, it may simply be an evolutionary dead end that brings us only slightly closer to understanding our own ancestors, says paleoanthropologist Bernard Wood of George Washington University in Washington, D.C. The debate is complicated by the fact that paleoanthropologists are deeply divided over who the first humans, or members of *Homo,* were, and indeed what makes a human. "These are magnificent fossils," says Wood, but he's not ready to admit *A. garhi* into the gallery of our ancestors. "At this point it's impossible to tell what's ancestral to what," he says. "This won't be the last 'surprise.' "

Anthropologists have long been itching to know just what East African hominids were doing between 2 million and 3 million years ago, says one of the team's leaders, paleoanthropologist Tim White of UC Berkeley. Decades of fieldwork and analysis have allowed researchers to identify many characters in the human evolutionary story (see diagram), starting with apelike species such as the 4.2-million-year-old *A. anamensis.* Next in line, known from 3.7 million to 3.0 million years ago, is *A. afarensis,* best known for the famed "Lucy" skeleton: a meter-tall, small-brained, upright hominid that retained apelike limb proportions and a protruding lower face.

More than a million years separate Lucy from the first specimens usually considered to be part of our own genus,

which appear in East Africa around 2 million years ago and tend to have larger brains and a more human face, although they are highly variable. In the interim, the South African fossil record is diverse and confusing, and the East African record has been sparse. The period includes three species that fall into the "robust" australopithecine group— heavy-jawed hominids with skull crests and large back teeth, perhaps for eating hard roots and tubers—that are not part of our own lineage. More promising for those seeking a human ancestor is *A. africanus,* known from South Africa starting at around 2.8 million years ago, which has a more humanlike face than the Lucy species.

But the *A. africanus* fossils were found half a continent away from the East African cradle of *Homo,* and some anthropologists have been hoping for a stronger candidate for the root of our lineage. "After the split with the robust lineage, we have very little evidence," says Walker. That's why White and his team zeroed in on sediments in the desert of Ethiopia's Afar depression. They struck gold with three separate discoveries, all dated securely to 2.5 million years ago by radiometric techniques on an underlying volcanic rock layer.

One dramatic find came in 1997, when El Nio-driven rains washed away stones and dirt on steep slopes near the village of Bouri. Berkeley graduate student Yohannes Haile-Selassie spotted fragments of the skull—the color and thickness of a coconut shell—on the surface. A closer look revealed teeth poking out of the ground. Much of the rest of the skull had washed down the hill, so the team, which includes 40 members from 13 countries, took the slope apart. They dug tons of material from the hill, then sieved it and picked through it for bone—twice. "It was probably the most difficult fossil recovery we've ever

done," says White. "We spent 7 weeks on that slope." Although the delicate bones of the middle face were gone for good, the team found many more skull fragments.

After reconstructing the skull, the researchers were confronted with a face that is apelike in the lower part, with a protruding jaw resembling that of *A. afarensis.* The large size of the palate and teeth suggests that it is a male, with a small braincase of about 450 cubic centimeters. (A modern human brain is about 1400 cubic centimeters.) It is like no other hominid species and is clearly not a robust form. And in a few dental traits, such as the shape of the premolar and the size ratio of the canine teeth to the molars, *A. garhi* resembles specimens of early *Homo.* But its molars are huge—the second molar is 17.7 millimeters across, even larger than the *A. robustus* average. "Selection was driving bigger teeth in both lineages—that's a big surprise," says Walker.

The other dramatic skeletal find had come a year earlier: leg and arm bones of a single ancient hominid individual, found together. The new hominid femur or upper leg bone is relatively long, like that of modern humans. But the forearm is long too, a condition found in apes and other australopithecines but not in humans. The fossils show that human proportions evolved in steps, with the legs lengthening before the forearms shortened, says co-author Owen Lovejoy of Kent State University in Ohio.

The third major find, at the same stratigraphic level and only a meter away from the skeletal bones, preserves dramatic evidence of hominid behavior: bones of antelopes, horses, and other animals bearing cut marks, suggesting that butchery may be the oldest human profession. One antelope bone, described by a team including archaeologist J. Desmond Clark of UC Berkeley and White, records a failed hammerstone blow, which scratched the bone slightly and caused a bone flake to fly off; a second blow was struck from exactly the same angle. Both ends of the bone were broken off, presumably to get at the marrow.

Similarly, an antelope jawbone bears three successive curved marks, apparently made as a hominid sliced out the tongue. In cross section under the microscope, these marks show a parallel series of ragged V-shaped striations with rough inner walls—the telltale signature of a stone tool rather than a predator's teeth, says White. Marks on the leg bone of a three-toed horse show that hominids dismembered the animal and filleted the meat from the bone.

The Bouri sites yielded few of the stone tools the hominids must have used, perhaps because there is no local source of stone. The hominids "must have brought flakes and cobbles in from some distance, so that obviously shows quite a bit of forethought," says Clark. Tool use by this point is no surprise: At other sites, anthropologists have found tools dated to 2.6 million years ago. But there had been little hard evidence of what the oldest tools were used for. The new find shows that tools enabled hominids to get at "a whole new world of food"—bone marrow, says White.

Marrow is rich in fat, and few animals other than humans and hyenas can get at it. Anthropologists have theorized that just such a dietary breakthrough allowed the dramatic increase in brain size (*Science,* 29 May 1998, p. 1345), to perhaps 650 cc or larger, that took place in the *Homo* lineage by 2 million years ago. Two researchers recently proposed that cooked tubers were the crucial new food source (*Science,* 26 March, p. 2004), but most others have assumed it

was meat. The cut marks present convincing evidence that they were right, says Yale University anthropologist Andrew Hill.

Whether or not the three finds can be connected, *A. garhi,* as based on the new skull, is now a prime candidate as an ancestor of our genus. The species is in the right place—East Africa—and the right time—between the time of *A. afarensis* and that of early *Homo*—says White. But making the link to the human lineage isn't easy, in part because the nature of "early *Homo*" is itself something of a mystery. White notes that some of the early *Homo* specimens have large teeth, and that in the teeth "there's not much change at all from *A. garhi* to those specimens of early *Homo.*"

The link between *A. garhi* and *Homo* would be strengthened, of course, if researchers could show that the humanlike long bones come from *A. garhi* rather than from some other humanlike hominid. For now White is willing only to "make up a hypothesis to be tested": *A. garhi,* a small-brained, big-toothed hominid with humanlike leg proportions, began butchering animals by 2.5 million years ago. Thanks in part to the better diet, brain size rapidly increased to that seen in early *Homo,* and the trend toward large back teeth reversed— changes that quickly transformed other parts of the skull as well, such as flattening the protruding jaw.

But some other researchers don't buy that as a likely scenario. There's no reason to expect that every new branch on the hominid tree is our ancestor, says George Washington's Wood. He adds that he is not surprised by *A. garhi's* mix of humanlike and robust features, because, given that climate was changing, "we should expect a variety of creatures with mixtures of adaptations at this time." Other researchers note that the dental data linking the species to *Homo* are weak. "Nothing here aligns garhi closely with *Homo,*" says paleoanthropologist Fred Grine of the State University of New York, Stony Brook. "It's a possible candidate [for *Homo* ancestry], but no better than africanus."

Some anthropologists also say that there may not have been enough time for evolution to have transformed *A. garhi* into *Homo.* The oldest known specimen assigned to *Homo,* a 2.33-million-year-old palate from Hadar, Ethiopia, is more humanlike than *A. garhi,* with smaller teeth. That requires either a burst of evolution or some other explanation, such as sexual dimorphism, if *A. garhi* is to be considered part of our lineage, notes paleoanthropologist Juan Luis Arsuaga of the Universidad Complutense de Madrid in Spain. White says that only further discoveries and analysis will show just where the hominids of that long-vanished plain stand in relation to our own species: "*A. garhi* isn't the end; it's the first step."

# Scavenger Hunt

*As paleoanthropologists close in on their quarry, it may turn out
to be a different beast from what they imaged*

## Pat Shipman

*Pat Shipman is an assistant professor in
the Department of Cell Biology and
Anatomy at The Johns Hopkins University
School of Medicine.*

In both textbooks and films, ancestral
humans (hominids) have been portrayed
as hunters. Small-brained, big-browed,
upright, and usually mildly furry, early
hominid males gaze with keen eyes
across the gold savanna, searching for
prey. Skillfully wielding a few crude
stone tools, they kill and dismember
everything from small gazelles to elephants, while females care for young
and gather roots, tubers, and berries. The
food is shared by group members at
temporary camps. This familiar image
of Man the Hunter has been bolstered
by the finding of stone tools in association with fossil animal bones. But the
role of hunting in early hominid life
cannot be determined in the absence of
more direct evidence.

I discovered one means of testing the
hunting hypothesis almost by accident.
In 1978, I began documenting the microscopic damage produced on bones by
different events. I hoped to develop a diagnostic key for identifying the postmortem history of specific fossil bones,
useful for understanding how fossil assemblages were formed. Using a scanning
electron microscope (SEM) because of its
excellent resolution and superb depth of

field, I inspected high-fidelity replicas
of modern bones that had been subjected
to known events or conditions. (I had to
use replicas, rather than real bones, because specimens must fit into the SEM's
small vacuum chamber.) I soon established that such common events as
weathering, root etching, sedimentary
abrasion, and carnivore chewing produced
microscopically distinctive features.

In 1980, my SEM study took an un-
expected turn. Richard Potts (now of
Yale University), Henry Bunn (now of
the University of Wisconsin at Madison), and I almost simultaneously found
what appeared to be stone-tool cut
marks on fossils from Olduvai Gorge,
Tanzania, and Koobi Fora, Kenya. We
were working almost side by side at the
National Museums of Kenya, in Nairobi, where the fossils are stored. The
possibility of cut marks was exciting,
since both sites preserve some of the
oldest known archaeological materials.
Potts and I returned to the United States,
manufactured some stone tools, and
started "butchering" bones and joints
begged from our local butchers. Under
the SEM, replicas of these cut marks
looked very different from replicas of
carnivore tooth scratches, regardless of
the species of carnivore or the type of
tool involved. By comparing the marks
on the fossils with our hundreds of modern bones of known history, we were

able to demonstrate convincingly that
hominids using stone tools had processed carcasses of many different animals nearly two million years ago. For
the first time, there was a firm link between stone tools and at least some of
the early fossil animal bones.

This initial discovery persuaded some
paleoanthropologists that the hominid
hunter scenario was correct. Potts and I
were not so sure. Our study had shown
that many of the cut-marked fossils also
bore carnivore tooth marks and that some
of the cut marks were in places we hadn't
expected—on bones that bore little meat
in life. More work was needed.

In addition to more data about the
Olduvai cut marks and tooth marks, I
needed specific information about the
patterns of cut marks left by known
hunters performing typical activities associated with hunting. If similar patterns
occurred on the fossils, then the early
hominids probably behaved similarly to
more modern hunters; if the patterns
were different, then the behavior was
probably also different. Three activities
related to hunting occur often enough in
peoples around the world and leave
consistent enough traces to be used for
such a test.

First, human hunters systematically
disarticulate their kills, unless the animals are small enough to be eaten on
the spot. Disarticulation leaves cut marks

in a predictable pattern on the skeleton. Such marks cluster near the major joints of the limbs: shoulder, elbow, carpal joint (wrist), hip, knee, and hock (ankle). Taking a carcass apart at the joints is much easier than breaking or cutting through bones. Disarticulation enables hunters to carry food back to a central place or camp, so that they can share it with others or cook it or even store it by placing portions in trees, away from the reach of carnivores. If early hominids were hunters who transported and shared their kills, disarticulation marks would occur near joints in frequencies comparable to those produced by modern human hunters.

Second, human hunters often butcher carcasses, in the sense of removing meat from the bones. Butchery marks are usually found on the shafts of bones from the upper part of the front or hind limb, since this is where the big muscle masses lie. Butchery may be carried out at the kill site—especially if the animal is very large and its bones very heavy—or it may take place at the base camp, during the process of sharing food with others. Compared with disarticulation, butchery leaves relatively few marks. It is hard for a hunter to locate an animal's joints without leaving cut marks on the bone. In contrast, it is easier to cut the meat away from the midshaft of the bone without making such marks. If early hominids shared their food, however, there ought to be a number of cut marks located on the midshaft of some fossil bones.

Finally, human hunters often remove skin or tendons from carcasses, to be used for clothing, bags, thongs, and so on. Hide or tendon must be separated from the bones in many areas where there is little flesh, such as the lower limb bones of pigs, giraffes, antelopes, and zebras. In such cases, it is difficult to cut the skin without leaving a cut mark on the bone. Therefore, one expects to find many more cut marks on such bones than on the flesh-covered bones of the upper part of the limbs.

Unfortunately, although accounts of butchery and disarticulation by modern human hunters are remarkably consistent, quantitative studies are rare. Further, virtually all modern hunter-gatherers use metal tools, which leave more cut marks than stone tools. For these reasons I hesitated to compare the fossil evidence with data on modern hunters. Fortunately, Diane Gifford of the University of California, Santa Cruz, and her colleagues had recently completed a quantitative study of marks and damage on thousands of antelope bones processed by Neolithic (Stone Age) hunters in Kenya some 2,300 years ago. The data from Prolonged Drift, as the site is called, were perfect for comparison with the Olduvai material.

Assisted by my technician, Jennie Rose, I carefully inspected more than 2,500 antelope bones from Bed I at Olduvai Gorge, which is dated to between 1.9 and 1.7 million years ago. We made high-fidelity replicas of every mark that we thought might be either a cut mark or a carnivore tooth mark. Back in the United States, we used the SEM to make positive identifications of the marks. (The replication and SEM inspection was time consuming, but necessary: only about half of the marks were correctly identified by eye or by light microscope.) I then compared the patterns of cut mark and tooth mark distributions on Olduvai fossils with those made by Stone Age hunters at Prolonged Drift.

By their location, I identified marks caused either by disarticulation or meat removal and then compared their frequencies with those from Prolonged Drift. More than 90 percent of the Neolithic marks in these two categories were from disarticulation, but to my surprise, only about 45 percent of the corresponding Olduvai cut marks were from disarticulation. This difference is too great to have occurred by chance; the Olduvai bones did not show the predicted pattern. In fact, the Olduvai cut marks attributable to meat removal and disarticulation showed essentially the same pattern of distribution as the carnivore tooth marks. Apparently, the early hominids were not regularly disarticulating carcasses. This finding casts serious doubt on the idea that early hominids carried their kills back to camp to share with others, since both transport and sharing are difficult unless carcasses are cut up.

When I looked for cut marks attributable to skinning or tendon removal, a more modern pattern emerged. On both the Neolithic and Olduvai bones, nearly 75 percent of all cut marks occurred on bones that bore little meat; these cut marks probably came from skinning. Carnivore tooth marks were much less common on such bones. Hominids were using carcasses as a source of skin and tendon. This made it seem more surprising that they disarticulated carcasses so rarely.

A third line of evidence provided the most tantalizing clue. Occasionally, sets of overlapping marks occur on the Olduvai fossils. Sometimes, these sets include both cut marks and carnivore tooth marks. Still more rarely, I could see under the SEM which mark had been made first, because its features were overlaid by those of the later mark, in much the same way as old tire tracks on a dirt road are obscured by fresh ones. Although only thirteen such sets of marks were found, in eight cases the hominids made the cut marks after the carnivores made their tooth marks. This finding suggested a new hypothesis. Instead of hunting for prey and leaving the remains behind for carnivores to scavenge, perhaps hominids were scavenging from the carnivores. This might explain the hominids' apparently unsystematic use of carcasses: they took what they could get, be it skin, tendon, or meat.

Man the Scavenger is not nearly as attractive an image as Man the Hunter, but it is worth examining. Actually, although hunting and scavenging are different ecological strategies, many mammals do both. The only pure scavengers alive in Africa today are vultures; not one of the modern African mammalian carnivores is a pure scavenger. Even spotted hyenas, which have massive, bone-crushing teeth well adapted for eating the bones left behind by others, only scavenge about 33 percent of their food. Other carnivores that scavenge when there are enough carcasses around include lions, leopards, striped hyenas, and jackals. Long-term behavioral studies suggest that these carnivores scavenge when they can and kill when they must. There are only two nearly pure predators, or hunters—the cheetah and the wild dog—that rarely, if ever, scavenge.

What are the costs and benefits of scavenging compared with those of predation? First of all, the scavenger avoids the task of making sure its meal is dead: a predator has already endured the energetically costly business of chasing or stalking animal after animal until one is killed. But while scavenging may be cheap, it's risky. Predators rarely give up their prey to scavengers without defending it. In such disputes, the larger animal, whether a scavenger or a predator, usually wins, although smaller animals in a pack may defeat a lone, larger animal. Both predators and scavengers suffer the dangers inherent in fighting for possession of a carcass. Smaller scavengers such as jackals or striped hyenas avoid disputes to some extent by specializing in darting in and removing a piece of a carcass without trying to take possession of the whole thing. These two strategies can be characterized as that of the bully or that of the sneak: bullies need to be large to be successful, sneaks need to be small and quick.

Because carcasses are almost always much rarer than live prey, the major cost peculiar to scavenging is that scavengers must survey much larger areas than predators to find food. They can travel slowly, since their "prey" is already dead, but endurance is important. Many predators specialize in speed at the expense of endurance, while scavengers do the opposite.

The more committed predators among the East African carnivores (wild dogs and cheetahs) can achieve great top speeds when running, although not for long. Perhaps as a consequence, these "pure" hunters enjoy a much higher success rate in hunting (about three-fourths of their chases end in kills) than any of the scavenger-hunters do (less than half of their chases are successful). Wild dogs and cheetahs are efficient hunters, but they are neither big enough nor efficient enough in their locomotion to make good scavengers. In fact, the cheetah's teeth are so specialized for meat slicing that they probably cannot withstand the stresses of bone crunching and carcass dismembering carried out by scavengers. Other carnivores are less

successful at hunting, but have specializations of size, endurance, or (in the case of the hyenas) dentition that make successful scavenging possible. The small carnivores seem to have a somewhat higher hunting success rate than the large ones, which balances out their difficulties in asserting possession of carcasses.

In addition to endurance, scavengers need an efficient means of locating carcasses, which, unlike live animals, don't move or make noises. Vultures, for example, solve both problems by flying. The soaring, gliding flight of vultures expends much less energy than walking or cantering as performed by the part-time mammalian scavengers. Flight enables vultures to maintain a foraging radius two to three times larger than that of spotted hyenas, while providing a better vantage point. This explains why vultures can scavenge all of their food in the same habitat in which it is impossible for any mammal to be a pure scavenger. (In fact, many mammals learn where carcasses are located from the presence of vultures.)

Since mammals can't succeed as full-time scavengers, they must have another source of food to provide the bulk of their diet. The large carnivores rely on hunting large animals to obtain food when scavenging doesn't work. Their size enables them to defend a carcass against others. Since the small carnivores— jackals and striped hyenas—often can't defend carcasses successfully, most of their diet is composed of fruit and insects. When they do hunt, they usually prey on very small animals, such as rats or hares, that can be consumed in their entirety before the larger competitors arrive.

The ancient habitat associated with the fossils of Olduvai and Koobi Fora would have supported many herbivores and carnivores. Among the latter were two species of large saber-toothed cats, whose teeth show extreme adaptations for meat slicing. These were predators with primary access to carcasses. Since their teeth were unsuitable for bone crushing, the saber-toothed cats must have left behind many bones covered with scraps of meat, skin, and tendon.

Were early hominids among the scavengers that exploited such carcasses?

All three hominid species that were present in Bed I times (*Homo habilis, Australopithecus africanus, A. robustus*) were adapted for habitual, upright bipedalism. Many anatomists see evidence that these hominids were agile tree climbers as well. Although upright bipedalism is a notoriously peculiar mode of locomotion, the adaptive value of which has been argued for years (See Matt Cartmill's article, "Four Legs Good, Two Legs Bad," *Natural History,* November 1983), there are three general points of agreement.

First, bipedal running is nether fast nor efficient compared to quadrupedal gaits. However, at moderate speeds of 2.5 to 3.5 miles per hour, bipedal *walking* is more energetically efficient than quadrupedal walking. Thus, bipedal walking is an excellent means of covering large areas slowly, making it an unlikely adaptation for a hunter but an appropriate and useful adaptation for a scavenger. Second, bipedalism elevates the head, thus improving the hominid's ability to spot items on the ground—an advantage both to scavengers and to those trying to avoid becoming a carcass. Combining bipedalism with agile tree climbing improves the vantage point still further. Third, bipedalism frees the hands from locomotive duties, making it possible to carry items. What would early hominids have carried? Meat makes a nutritious, easy-to-carry package; the problem is that carrying meat attracts scavengers. Richard Potts suggests that carrying stone tools or unworked stones for toolmaking to caches would be a more efficient and less dangerous activity under many circumstances.

In short, bipedalism is compatible with a scavenging strategy. I am tempted to argue that bipedalism evolved because it provided a substantial advantage to scavenging hominids. But I doubt hominids could scavenge effectively without tools, and bipedalism predates the oldest known stone tools by more than a million years.

Is there evidence that, like modern mammalian scavengers, early hominids had an alternative food source, such as either hunting or eating fruits and insects? My husband, Alan Walker, has shown that the microscopic wear on an animal's teeth reflects its diet. Early hominid teeth wear more like that of chimpanzees and other modern fruit eaters than that of carnivores. Apparently, early hominids ate mostly fruit, as the smaller, modern scavengers do. This accords with the estimated body weight of early hominids, which was only about forty to eighty pounds—less than that of any of the modern carnivores that combine scavenging and hunting but comparable to the striped hyena, which eats fruits and insects as well as meat.

Would early hominids have been able to compete for carcasses with other carnivores? They were too small to use a bully strategy, but if they scavenged in groups, a combined bully-sneak strategy might have been possible. Perhaps they were able to drive off a primary predator long enough to grab some meat, skin, or marrow-filled bone before relinquishing the carcass. The effectiveness of this strategy would have been vastly improved by using tools to remove meat or parts of limbs, a task at which hominid teeth are poor. As agile climbers, early hominids may have retreated into the trees to eat their scavenged trophies, thus avoiding competition from large terrestrial carnivores.

In sum, the evidence on cut marks, tooth wear, and bipedalism, together with our knowledge of scavenger adaptation in general, is consistent with the hypothesis that two million years ago hominids were scavengers rather than accomplished hunters. Animal carcasses, which contributed relatively little to the hominid diet, were not systematically cut up and transported for sharing at base camps. Man the Hunter may not have appeared until 1.5 to 0.7 million years ago, when we do see a shift toward omnivory, with a greater proportion of meat in the diet. This more heroic ancestor may have been *Homo erectus*, equipped with Acheulean-style stone tools and, increasingly, fire. If we wish to look further back, we may have to become accustomed to a less flattering image of our heritage.

# Unit 5

## Unit Selections

25. ***Erectus Rising,*** James Shreeve
26. **Hard Times Among the Neanderthals,** Erik Trinkaus
27. **The Gift of Gab,** Matt Cartmill
28. **The Dating Game,** James Shreeve
29. **Who Were the Neandertals?** Kate Wong
30. **Fate of the Neandertals,** João Zilhão
31. **Archaeologists Rediscover Cannibals,** Ann Gibbons

## Key Points to Consider

❖ When, where, and why did *Homo erectus* evolve? Is it one species or two? Explain your reasoning.

❖ What evidence is there for hard times among the Neanderthals?

❖ When did language ability arise in our ancestry and why?

❖ How do we measure evolutionary time?

❖ Explain whether the Cro-Magnons were the first or the last modern humans to appear on Earth.

❖ Are Neanderthals part of our ancestry?

❖ How would you draw the late hominid family tree?

❖ How do you assess the evidence for cannibalism?

 **Links**
# www.dushkin.com/online/

25. **Archaeology Links (NC)**
 *http://www.arch.dcr.state.nc.us/links.htm#stuff*
26. **Human Prehistory**
 *http://users.hol.gr/~dilos/prehis.htm*

These sites are annotated on pages 4 and 5.

124

The most important aspect of human evolution is also the most difficult to decipher from the fossil evidence: our development as sentient, social beings, capable of communicating by means of language.

We detect hints of incipient humanity in the form of crudely chipped tools, the telltale signs of a home base, or the artistic achievements of ornaments and cave art. Yet none of these indicators of a distinctly hominid way of life can provide us with the nuances of the everyday lives of these creatures, their social relations, or their supernatural beliefs, if any. Most of what remains is the rubble of bones and stones from which we interpret what we can of their lifestyle, thought processes, and ability to communicate. Our ability to glean from the fossil record is not completely without hope, however. In fact, informed speculation is what makes possible such essays as "Hard Times Among the Neanderthals" by Erik Trinkaus and "The Gift of Gab" by Matt Cartmill. Each is a fine example of careful, systematic, and thought-provoking work that is based upon an increased understanding of hominid fossil sites as well as the more general environmental circumstances in which our predecessors lived.

Beyond the technological and anatomical adaptations, questions have arisen as to how our hominid forebears organized themselves socially and whether modern-day human behavior is inherited as a legacy of our evolutionary past or is a learned product of contemporary circumstances. Attempts to address these questions have given rise to the technique referred to as the "ethnographic analogy." This is a method whereby anthropologists use "ethnographies" or field studies of modern-day hunters and gatherers whose lives we take to be the best approximations we have to what life might have been like for our ancestors. Granted, these contemporary foragers have been living under conditions of environmental and social change just as industrial peoples have. Nevertheless, it seems that, at least in some aspects of their lives, they have not changed as much as we have. So, if we are to make any enlightened assessments of prehistoric behavior patterns, we are better off looking at them than at ourselves.

As if to show that controversial interpretations of the evidence are not limited to the earlier hominid period (see unit 2), in this unit we see how the question of cannibalism has arisen anew ("Archaeologists Rediscover Cannibals" by Ann Gibbons) and how long-held beliefs about *Homo erectus* are being threatened by new fossil evidence (see James Shreeve's essay "*Erectus* Rising"). We also consider new evidence bearing upon the fate of the Neanderthals in "Who Were the Neandertals?" and "Fate of the Neandertals." For some scientists, the new evidence fits in quite comfortably with previously held positions; for others it seems that reputations, as well as theories, are at stake.

# Late Hominid Evolution

# *Erectus* Rising

### *Oh No. Not This. The Hominids Are Acting Up Again . . .*

## James Shreeve

*James Shreeve is the coauthor, with anthropologist Donald Johanson, of* Lucy's Child: The Discovery of a Human Ancestor. *His book,* The Neandertal Enigma: Solving the Mystery of Modern Human Origins, *was published in 1995, and he is at work on a novel that a reliable source calls "a murder thriller about the species question."*

Just when it seemed that the recent monumental fuss over the origins of modern human beings was beginning to quiet down, an ancient ancestor is once more running wild. Trampling on theories. Appearing in odd places, way ahead of schedule. Demanding new explanations. And shamelessly flaunting its contempt for conventional wisdom in the public press.

The uppity ancestor this time is *Homo erectus*—alias Java man, alias Peking man, alias a mouthful of formal names known only to the paleontological cognoscenti. Whatever you call it, *erectus* has traditionally been a quiet, average sort of hominid: low of brow, thick of bone, endowed with a brain larger than that of previous hominids but smaller than those that followed, a face less apelike and projecting than that of its ancestors but decidedly more simian than its descendants'. In most scenarios of human evolution, *erectus*'s role was essentially to mark time—a million and a half years of it—between its obscure, presumed origins in East Africa just under 2 million years ago and its much more recent evolution into something deserving the name *sapiens*.

*Erectus* accomplished only two noteworthy deeds during its long tenure on Earth. First, some 1.5 million years ago, it developed what is known as the Acheulean stone tool culture, a technology exemplified by large, carefully crafted tear-shaped hand axes that were much more advanced than the bashed rocks that had passed for tools in the hands of earlier hominids. Then, half a million years later, and aided by those Acheulean tools, the species carved its way out of Africa and established a human presence in other parts of the Old World. But most of the time, *Homo erectus* merely existed, banging out the same stone tools millennium after millennium, over a time span that one archeologist has called "a period of unimaginable monotony."

Or so read the old script. These days, *erectus* has begun to ad-lib a more vigorous, controversial identity for itself. Research within the past year has revealed that rather than being 1 million years old, several *erectus* fossils from Southeast Asia are in fact almost 2 million years old. That is as old as the oldest African members of the species, and it would mean that *erectus* emerged from its home continent much earlier than has been thought—in fact, almost immediately after it first appeared. There's also a jawbone, found in 1991 near the Georgian city of Tbilisi, that resembles *erectus* fossils from Africa and may be as old as 1.8 million years, though that age is still in doubt. These new dates—and the debates they've engendered—have shaken *Homo erectus* out of its interpretive stupor, bringing into sharp relief just how little agreement there is on the rise and demise of the last human species on Earth, save one.

"Everything now is in flux," says Carl Swisher of the Berkeley Geochronology Center, one of the prime movers behind the redating of *erectus* outside Africa. "It's all a mess."

*Asian and African fossils were lumped into one farflung taxon, a creature not quite like us but human enough to be welcomed into our genus: Homo erectus.*

The focal point for the flux is the locale where the species was first found: Java. The rich but frustration-soaked history of paleoanthropology on that tropical island began just over 100 years ago, when a young Dutch anatomy professor named Eugène Dubois conceived the idée fixe that the "missing link" between ape and man was to be found in the jungled remoteness of the Dutch East Indies. Dubois had never left Holland, much less traveled to the Dutch East Indies, and his pick for the spot on Earth where humankind first arose owed as much to a large part of the Indonesian archipelago's being a Dutch colony as it did to any scientific evidence. He nevertheless found this missing link—the top of an oddly thick skull with massive browridges—in 1891 on the banks of the Solo River, near a community called Trinil in central Java. About a year later a thighbone that Dubois thought might belong to the same individual was found nearby; it looked so much like a modern human thighbone that Dubois assumed this ancient primate had walked upright. He christened the creature *Pithecanthropus erectus*—"erect ape-man"—and returned home in triumph.

Finding the fossil proved to be the easy part. Though Dubois won popular acclaim, neither he nor his "Java man" received the full approbation of the anatomists of the day, who considered his ape-man either merely an ape or merely a man. In an apparent pique, Dubois cloistered away the fossils for a quarter-century, refusing others the chance to view his prized possessions. Later, other similarly primitive human remains began to turn up in China and East Africa. All shared a collection of anatomical traits, including a long, low braincase with prominent browridges and a flattened forehead; a sharp angle to the back of the skull when viewed in profile; and a deep, robustly built jaw showing no hint of a chin. Though initially given separate regional names, the fossils were eventually lumped together into one far-flung taxon, a creature not quite like us but human enough to be welcomed into our genus: *Homo erectus*.

Over the decades the most generous source of new *erectus* fossils has been the sites on or near the Solo River in Java. The harvest continues: two more skulls, including one of the most complete *erectus* skulls yet known, were found at a famous fossil site called Sangiran just in the past year. Though the Javan yield of ancient humans has been rich, something has always been missing—the crucial element of time. Unless the age of a fossil can be determined, it hangs in limbo, its importance and place in the larger scheme of human evolution forever undercut with doubt. Until researchers can devise better methods for dating bone directly—right now there are no techniques that can reliably date fossilized, calcified bone more than 50,000 years old—a specimen's age has to be inferred from the geology that

surrounds it. Unfortunately, most of the discoveries made on the densely populated and cultivated island of Java have been made not by trained excavators but by sharp-eyed local farmers who spot the bones as they wash out with the annual rains and later sell them. As a result, the original location of many a prized specimen, and thus all hopes of knowing its age, are a matter of memory and word of mouth.

Despite the problems, scientists continue to try to pin down dates for Java's fossils. Most have come up with an upper limit of around 1 million years. Along with the dates for the Peking man skulls found in China and the Acheulean tools from Europe, the Javan evidence has come to be seen as confirmation that *erectus* first left Africa at about that time.

There are those, however, who have wondered about these dates for quite some time. Chief among them is Garniss Curtis, the founder of the Berkeley Geochronology Center. In 1971 Curtis, who was then at the University of California

---

*By the early 1970s most paleontologists were firmly wedded to the idea that Africa was the only human-inhabited part of the world until one million years ago.*

---

at Berkeley, attempted to determine the age of a child's skull from a site called Mojokerto, in eastern Java, by using the potassium-argon method to date volcanic minerals in the sediments from which the skull was purportedly removed. Potassium-argon dating had been in use since the 1950s, and Curtis had been enormously successful with it in dating ancient African hominids—including Louis Leakey's famous hominid finds at Olduvai Gorge in Tanzania. The method takes advantage of the fact that a radioactive isotope of potassium found in volcanic ash slowly and predictably decays over time into argon gas, which becomes trapped in the crystalline struc-

ture of the mineral. The amount of argon contained in a given sample, measured against the amount of the potassium isotope, serves as a kind of clock that tells how much time has passed since a volcano exploded and its ash fell to earth and buried the bone in question.

Applying the technique to the volcanic pumice associated with the skull from Mojokerto, Curtis got an extraordinary age of 1.9 million years. The wildly anomalous date was all too easy to dismiss, however. Unlike the ash deposits of East Africa, the volcanic pumices in Java are poor in potassium. Also, not unexpectedly, a heavy veil of uncertainty obscured the collector's memories of precisely where he had found the fossil some 35 years earlier. Besides, most paleontologists were by this time firmly wedded to the idea that Africa was the only human-inhabited part of the world until 1 million years ago. Curtis's date was thus deemed wrong for the most stubbornly cherished of reasons: because it couldn't possibly be right.

In 1992 Curtis—under the auspices of the Institute for Human Origins in Berkeley—returned to Java with his colleague Carl Swisher. This time he was backed up by far more sensitive equipment and a powerful refinement in the dating technique. In conventional potassium-argon dating, several grams' worth of volcanic crystals gleaned from a site are needed to run a single experiment. While the bulk of these crystals are probably from the eruption that covered the fossil, there's always the possibility that other materials, from volcanoes millions of years older, have gotten mixed in and will thus make the fossil appear to be much older than it actually is. The potassium-argon method also requires that the researcher divide the sample of crystals in two. One half is dissolved in acid and passed through a flame; the wavelengths of light emitted tell how much potassium is in the sample. The other half is used to measure the amount of argon gas that's released when the crystals are heated. This two-step process further increases the chance of error, simply by giving the experiment twice as much opportunity to go wrong.

The refined technique, called argon-argon dating, neatly sidesteps most of these difficulties. The volcanic crystals are first placed in a reactor and bombarded with neutrons; when one of these neutrons penetrates the potassium nucleus, it displaces a proton, converting the potassium into an isotope of argon that doesn't occur in nature. Then the artificially created argon and the naturally occurring argon are measured in a single experiment. Because the equipment used to measure the isotopes can look for both types of argon at the same time, there's no need to divide the sample, and so the argon-argon method can produce clear results from tiny amounts of material.

In some cases—when the volcanic material is fairly rich in potassium—all the atoms of argon from a single volcanic crystal can be quick-released by the heat from a laser beam and then counted. By doing a number of such single-crystal experiments, the researchers can easily pick out and discard any data from older, contaminant crystals. But even when the researchers are forced to sample more than one potassium-poor crystal to get any reading at all—as was the case at Mojokerto—the argon-argon method can still produce a highly reliable age. In this case, the researchers carefully heat a few crystals at a time to higher and higher temperatures, using a precisely controlled laser. If all the crystals in a sample are the same age, then the amount of argon released at each temperature will be the same. But if contaminants are mixed in, or if severe weathering has altered the crystal's chemical composition, the argon measurements will be erratic, and the researchers will know to throw out the results.

Curtis and Swisher knew that in the argon-argon step-heating method they had the technical means to date the potassium-poor deposits at Mojokerto accurately. But they had no way to prove that those deposits were the ones in which the skull had been buried: all they had was the word of the local man who had found it. Then, during a visit to the museum in the regional capital, where the fossil was being housed, Swisher noticed something odd. The hardened sediments that filled the inside of the fossil's

braincase looked black. But back at the site, the deposits of volcanic pumice that had supposedly sheltered the infant's skull were whitish in color. How could a skull come to be filled with black sediments if it had been buried in white ones? Was it possible that the site and the skull had nothing to do with each other after all? Swisher suspected something was wrong. He borrowed a pen-knife, picked up the precious skull, and nicked off a bit of the matrix inside.

"I almost got kicked out of the country at that point," he says. "These fossils in Java are like the crown jewels."

Luckily, his impulsiveness paid off. The knife's nick revealed white pumice under a thin skin of dark pigment: years earlier, someone had apparently painted the surface of the hardened sediments black. Since there were no other deposits within miles of the purported site that contained a white pumice visually or chemically resembling the matrix in the skull, its tie to the site was suddenly much stronger. Curtis and Swisher returned to Berkeley with pumice from that site and within a few weeks proclaimed the fossil to be 1.8 million years old, give or take some 40,000 years. At the same time, the geochronologists ran tests on pumice from the lower part of the Sangiran area, where *erectus* facial and cranial bone fragments had been found. The tests yielded an age of around 1.6 million years. Both numbers obviously shatter the 1-million-year barrier for *erectus* outside Africa, and they are a stunning vindication of Curtis's work at Mojokerto 20 years ago. "That was very rewarding," he says, "after having been told what a fool I was by my colleagues."

While no one takes Curtis or Swisher for a fool now, some of their colleagues won't be fully convinced by the new dates until the matrix inside the Mojokerto skull itself can be tested. Even then, the possibility will remain that the skull may have drifted down over the years into deposits containing older volcanic crystals that have nothing to do with its original burial site, or that it was carried by a river to another, older site. But Swisher contends that the chance of such an occurrence is remote: it would have to have happened at both Mojokerto and Sangiran for the

fossils' ages to be refuted. "I feel really good about the dates," he says. "But it has taken me a while to understand their implications."

The implications that can be spun out from the Javan dates depend on how one chooses to interpret the body of fossil evidence commonly embraced under the name *Homo erectus*. The earliest African fossils traditionally attributed to *erectus* are two nearly complete skulls from the site of Koobi Fora in Kenya, dated between 1.8 and 1.7 million years old. In the conventional view, these early specimens evolved from a more primitive, smaller-brained ancestor called *Homo habilis*, well represented by bones from Koobi Fora, Olduvai Gorge, and sites in South Africa.

If this conventional view is correct, then the new dates mean that *erectus* must have migrated out of Africa very soon after it evolved, quickly reaching deep into the farthest corner of Southeast Asia. This is certainly possible: at the time, Indonesia was connected to Asia by lower sea levels—thus providing an overland route from Africa—and Java is just 10,000 to 15,000 miles from Kenya, depending on the route. Even if *erectus* traveled just one mile a year, it would still take no more than 15,000 years to reach Java—a negligible amount of evolutionary time.

If *erectus* did indeed reach Asia almost a million years earlier than thought, then other, more controversial theories become much more plausible. Although many anthropologists believe that the African and Asian *erectus* fossils all represent a single species, other investigators have recently argued that the two groups are too different to be so casually lumped together. According to paleoanthropologist Ian Tattersall of the American Museum of Natural History in New York, the African skulls traditionally assigned to *erectus* often lack many of the specialized traits that were originally used to define the species in Asia, including the long, low cranial structure, thick skull bones, and robustly built faces. In his view, the African group deserves to be placed in a separate species, which he calls *Homo ergaster*.

# MEANWHILE, IN SIBERIA . . .

The presence of *Homo erectus* in Asia twice as long ago as previously thought has some people asking whether the human lineage might have originated in Asia instead of Africa. This long-dormant theory runs contrary to all current thinking about human evolution and lacks an important element: evidence. Although the new Javan dates do place the species in Asia at around the same time it evolved in Africa, all confirmed specimens of other, earlier hominids—the first members of the genus *Homo,* for instance, and the australopithecines, like Lucy—have been found exclusively in Africa. Given such an overwhelming argument, most investigators continue to believe that the hominid line began in Africa.

Most, but not all. Some have begun to cock an ear to the claims of Russian archeologist Yuri Mochanov. For over a decade Mochanov has been excavating a huge site on the Lena River in eastern Siberia—far from Africa, Java, or anywhere else on Earth an ancient hominid bone has ever turned up. Though he hasn't found any hominid fossils in Siberia, he stubbornly believes he's uncovered the next best thing: a trove of some 4,000 stone artifacts—crudely made flaked tools, but tools nonetheless—that he maintains are at least 2 million years old, and possibly 3 million. This, he says, would mean that the human lineage arose not in tropical Africa but in the cold northern latitudes of Asia.

"For evolutionary progress to occur, there had to be the appearance of new conditions: winter, snow, and, accompanying them, hunger," writes Mochanov. "[The ancestral primates] had to learn to walk on the ground, to change their carriage, and to become accustomed to meat—that is, to become 'clever animals of prey.'" And to become clever animals of prey, they'd need tools.

Although he is a well-respected investigator, Mochanov has been unable to convince either Western anthropologists or his Russian colleagues of the age of his site. Until recently the chipped rocks he was holding up as human artifacts were simply dismissed as stones broken by natural processes, or else his estimate of the age of the site was thought to be wincingly wrong. After all, no other signs of human occupation of Siberia appear until some 35,000 years ago.

But after a lecture swing through the United States earlier this year—in which he brought more data and a few prime examples of the tools for people to examine and pass around—many archeologists concede that it is difficult to explain the particular pattern of breakage of the rocks by any known natural process. "Everything I have heard or seen about the context of these things suggests that they are most likely tools," says anthropologist Rick Potts of the Smithsonian Institution, which was host to Mochanov last January.

They're even willing to concede that the site might be considerably older than they'd thought, though not nearly as old as Mochanov estimates. (To date the site, Mochanov compared the tools with artifacts found early in Africa; he also em-ployed an arcane dating technique little known outside Russia.) Preliminary results from an experimental dating technique performed on soil samples from the site by Michael Waters of Texas A&M and Steve Forman of Ohio State suggest that the layer of sediment bearing the artifacts is some 400,000 years old. That's a long way from 2 million, certainly, but it's still vastly older than anything else found in Siberia—and the site is 1,500 miles farther north than the famous Peking man site in China, previously considered the most northerly home of *erectus.*

"If this does turn out to be 400,000 years old, it's very exciting," says Waters. "If people were able to cope and survive in such a rigorous Arctic environment at such an early time, we would have to completely change our perception of the evolution of human adaptation."

"I have no problem with hominids being almost anywhere at that age—they were certainly traveling around," says Potts. "But the environment is the critical thing. If it was really cold up there"—temperatures in the region now often reach −50 degrees in deep winter—"we'd all have to scratch our heads over how these early hominids were making it in Siberia. There is no evidence that Neanderthals, who were better equipped for cold than anyone, were living in such climates. But who knows? Maybe a population got trapped up there, went extinct, and Mochanov managed to find it." He shrugs. "But that's just arm waving."

—*J. S.*

Most anthropologists believe that the only way to distinguish between species in the fossil record is to look at the similarities and differences between bones; the age of the fossil should not play a part. But age is often hard to ignore, and Tattersall believes that the new evidence for what he sees as two distinct populations living at the same time in widely separate parts of the Old World is highly suggestive. "The new dates help confirm that these were indeed two different species," he says. "In my view, *erectus* is a separate variant that evolved only in Asia."

Other investigators still contend that the differences between the African and Asian forms of *erectus* are too minimal to merit placing them in separate species. But if Tattersall is right, his theory raises the question of who the original emigrant out of Africa really was. *Homo ergaster* may have been the one to make the trek, evolving into *erectus* once it was established in Asia. Or perhaps a population of some even more primitive, as-yet-unidentified common ancestor ventured forth, giving rise to *erectus* in Asia while a sister population evolved into *ergaster* on the home continent.

Furthermore, no matter who left Africa first, there's the question of what precipitated the migration, a question made even more confounding by the new dates. The old explanation, that the primal human expansion across the hem of the Old World was triggered by the sophisticated Acheulean tools, is no longer tenable with these dates, simply because the tools had not yet been invented when the earliest populations would have moved out. In hindsight, that notion seems a bit shopworn anyway. Acheulean tools first appear in Africa around 1.5 million years ago, and soon after at a site in the nearby Middle East. But they've never been found in the Far East, in spite of the abundant fossil evidence for *Homo erectus* in the region.

Until now, that absence has best been explained by the "bamboo line." According to paleoanthropologist Geoffrey Pope of William Paterson College in New Jersey, *erectus* populations venturing from Africa into the Far East found the land rich in bamboo, a raw material more easily worked into cutting and butchering tools than recalcitrant stone.

Sensibly, they abandoned their less efficient stone industry for one based on the pliable plant, which leaves no trace of itself in the archeological record. This is still a viable theory, but the new dates from Java add an even simpler dimension to it: there are no Acheulean tools in the Far East because the first wave of *erectus* to leave Africa didn't have any to bring with them.

So what *did* fuel the quick-step migration out of Africa? Some researchers say the crucial development was not cultural but physical. Earlier hominids like *Homo habilis* were small-bodied creatures with more apelike limb proportions, notes paleoanthropologist Bernard Wood of the University of Liverpool, while African *erectus* was built along more modern lines. Tall, relatively slender, with long legs better able to range over distance and a body better able to dissipate heat, the species was endowed with the physiology needed to free it from the tropical shaded woodlands of Africa that sheltered earlier hominids. In fact, the larger-bodied *erectus* would have required a bigger feeding range to sustain itself, so it makes perfect sense that the expansion out of Africa should begin soon after the species appeared. "Until now, one was always having to account for what kept *erectus* in Africa so long after it evolved," says Wood. "So rather than raising a problem, in some ways the new dates in Java solve one."

Of course, if those dates are right, the accepted time frame for human evolution outside the home continent is nearly doubled, and that has implications for the ongoing debate over the origins of modern human beings. There are two opposing theories. The "out of Africa" hypothesis says that *Homo sapiens* evolved from *erectus* in Africa, and then—sometime in the last 100,000 years—spread out and replaced the more archaic residents of Eurasia. The "multiregional continuity" hypothesis says that modern humans evolved from *erectus* stock in various parts of the Old World, more or less simultaneously and independently. According to this scenario, living peoples outside Africa should look for their most recent ancestors not in African fossils but in the anatomy of ancient fossils within their own region of origin.

As it happens, the multiregionalists have long claimed that the best evidence for their theory lies in Australia, which is generally thought to have become inhabited around 50,000 years ago, by humans crossing over from Indonesia. There are certain facial and cranial characteristics in modern Australian aborigines, the multiregionalists say, that can be traced all the way back to the earliest specimens of *erectus* at Sangiran—characteristics that differ from and precede those of any more recent, *Homo sapiens* arrival from Africa. But if the new Javan dates are right, then these unique characteristics, and thus the aborigines' Asian *erectus* ancestors, must have been evolving separately from the rest of humankind for almost 2 million years. Many anthropologists, already skeptical of the multiregionalists' potential 1-million-year-long isolation for Asian *erectus*, find a 2-million-year-long isolation exceedingly difficult to swallow. "Can anyone seriously propose that the lineage of Australian aborigines could go back that far?" wonders paleoanthropologist Chris Stringer of the Natural History Museum in London, a leading advocate of the out-of-Africa theory.

The multiregionalists counter that they've never argued for *complete* isolation—that there's always been some flow of genes between populations, enough interbreeding to ensure that clearly beneficial *sapiens* characteristics would quickly be conferred on peoples throughout the Old World. "Just as genes flow now from Johannesburg to Beijing and from Melbourne to Paris, they have been flowing that way ever since humanity evolved," says Alan Thorne of the Australian National University in Canberra, an outspoken multiregionalist.

Stanford archeologist Richard Klein, another out-of-Africa supporter, believes the evidence actually *does* point to just such a long, deep isolation of Asian populations from African ones. The fossil record, he says, shows that while archaic forms of *Homo sapiens* were developing in Africa, *erectus* was remaining much the same in Asia. In fact, if some *erectus* fossils from a site called Ngandong in Java turn out to be as young as 100,000 years, as some researchers believe, then *erectus* was still alive on Java at the same time that fully modern human beings were living in Africa and the Middle East. Even more important, Klein says, is the cultural evidence. That Acheulean tools never reached East Asia, even after their invention in Africa, could mean the inventors never reached East Asia either. "You could argue that the new dates show that until very recently there was a long biological and cultural division between Asia on one hand, and Africa and Europe on the other," says Klein. In other words, there must have been two separate lineages of *erectus,* and since there aren't two separate lineages of modern humans, one of those must have gone extinct: presumably the Asian lineage, hastened into oblivion by the arrival of the more culturally adept, tool-laden *Homo sapiens.*

Naturally this argument is anathema to the multiregionalists. But this tenacious debate is unlikely to be resolved without basketfuls of new fossils, new ways of interpreting old ones—and new dates. In Berkeley, Curtis and Swisher are already busy applying the argon-argon method to the Ngandong fossils, which could represent some of the last surviving *Homo erectus* populations on Earth. They also hope to work their radiometric magic on a key *erectus* skull from Olduvai Gorge. In the meantime, at least one thing has become clear: *Homo erectus,* for so long the humdrum hominid, is just as fascinating, contentious, and elusive a character as any other in the human evolutionary story.

## FURTHER READING

*Eugène Dubois & the Ape-Man from Java.* Bert Theunissen. Kluwer Academic, 1989. When a Dutch army surgeon, determined to prove Darwin right, traveled to Java in search of the missing link between apes and humans, he inadvertently opened a paleontological Pandora's box. This is Dubois's story, the story of the discovery of *Homo erectus.*

# Hard Times Among the Neanderthals

*Although life was difficult, these prehistoric people may not have been as exclusively brutish as usually supposed*

## Erik Trinkaus

Throughout the century that followed the discovery in 1856 of the first recognized human fossil remains in the Neander Valley (*Neanderthal* in German) near Düsseldorf, Germany, the field of human paleontology has been beset with controversies. This has been especially true of interpretations of the Neanderthals, those frequently maligned people who occupied Europe and the Near East from about 100,000 years ago until the appearance of anatomically modern humans about 35,000 years ago.

During the last two decades, however, a number of fossil discoveries, new analyses of previously known remains, and more sophisticated models for interpreting subtle anatomical differences have led to a reevaluation of the Neanderthals and their place in human evolution.

This recent work has shown that the often quoted reconstruction of the Neanderthals as semierect, lumbering caricatures of humanity is inaccurate. It was based on faulty anatomical interpretations that were reinforced by the intellectual biases of the turn of the century. Detailed comparisons of Neanderthal skeletal remains with those of modern humans have shown that there is nothing in Neanderthal anatomy that conclusively indicates locomotor, manipulative, intellectual, or linguistic abilities

inferior to those of modern humans. Neanderthals have therefore been added to the same species as ourselves—*Homo sapiens*—although they are usually placed in their own subspecies, *Homo sapiens neanderthalensis.*

Despite these revisions, it is apparent that there are significant anatomical differences between the Neanderthals and present-day humans. If we are to understand the Neanderthals, we must formulate hypotheses as to why they evolved from earlier humans about 100,000 years ago in Europe and the Near East, and why they were suddenly replaced about 35,000 years ago by peoples largely indistinguishable from ourselves. We must determine, therefore, the behavioral significance of the anatomical differences between the Neanderthals and other human groups, since it is patterns of successful behavior that dictate the direction of natural selection for a species.

In the past, behavioral reconstructions of the Neanderthals and other prehistoric humans have been based largely on archeological data. Research has now reached the stage at which behavioral interpretations from the archeological record can be significantly supplemented by analyses of the fossils themselves. These analyses promise to tell us

a considerable amount about the ways of the Neanderthals and may eventually help us to determine their evolutionary fate.

One of the most characteristic features of the Neanderthals is the exaggerated massiveness of their trunk and limb bones. All of the preserved bones suggest a strength seldom attained by modern humans. Furthermore, not only is this robustness present among the adult males, as one might expect, but it is also evident in the adult females, adolescents, and even children. The bones themselves reflect this hardiness in several ways.

First, the muscle and ligament attachment areas are consistently enlarged and strongly marked. This implies large, highly developed muscles and ligaments capable of generating and sustaining great mechanical stress. Secondly, since the skeleton must be capable of supporting these levels of stress, which are frequently several times as great as body weight, the enlarged attachments for muscles and ligaments are associated with arm and leg bone shafts that have been reinforced. The shafts of all of the arm and leg bones are modified tubular structures that have to absorb stress from bending and twisting without fracturing. When the habitual load on a bone

Photographs by Erik Trinkaus

*Diagonal lines on these two arm bones from Shanidar 1 are healed fractures. The bone on the right is normal. That on the left is atrophied and has a pathological tip, caused by either amputation or an improperly healed elbow fracture.*

the force per unit area of cartilage is reduced, decreasing the pressure on the cartilage.

Most of the robustness of Neanderthal arm bones is seen in muscle and ligament attachments. All of the muscles that go from the trunk or the shoulder blade to the upper end of the arm show massive development. This applies in particular to the muscles responsible for powerful downward movements of the arm and, to a lesser extent, to muscles that stabilize the shoulder during vigorous movements.

Virtually every major muscle or ligament attachment on the hand bones is clearly marked by a large roughened area or a crest, especially the muscles used in grasping objects. In fact, Neanderthal hand bones frequently have clear bony crests, where on modern human ones it is barely possible to discern the attachment of the muscle on the dried bone.

In addition, the flattened areas on the ends of the fingers, which provide support for the nail and the pulp of the finger tip, are enormous among the Neanderthals. These areas on the thumb and the index and middle fingers are usually two to three times as large as those of similarly sized modern human hands. The overall impression is one of arms to rival those of the mightiest blacksmith.

Neanderthal legs are equally massive; their strength is best illustrated in the development of the shafts of the leg bones. Modern human thigh and shin bones possess characteristic shaft shapes adapted to the habitual levels and directions of the stresses acting upon them. The shaft shapes of the Neanderthals are similar to those in modern humans, but the cross-sectional areas of the shafts are much greater. This implies significantly higher levels of stress.

Further evidence of the massiveness of Neanderthal lower limbs is provided by the dimensions of their knee and ankle joints. All of these are larger than in modern humans, especially with respect to the overall lengths of the bones.

The development of their limb bones suggests that the Neanderthals frequently generated high levels of mechanical stress in their limbs. Since most mechanical stress in the body is pro-

increases, the bone responds by laying down more bone in those areas under the greatest stress.

In addition, musculature and body momentum generate large forces across the joints. The cartilage, which covers joint surfaces, can be relatively easily overworked to the point where it degenerates, as is indicated by the prevalence of arthritis in joints subjected to significant wear and tear over the years. When the surface area of a joint is increased, duced by body momentum and muscular contraction, it appears that the Neanderthals led extremely active lives. It is hard to conceive of what could have required such exertion, especially since the maintenance of vigorous muscular activity would have required considerable expenditure of energy. That level of energy expenditure would undoubtedly have been maladaptive had it not been necessary for survival.

The available evidence from the archeological material associated with the Neanderthals is equivocal on this matter. Most of the archeological evidence at Middle Paleolithic sites concerns stone

tool technology and hunting activities. After relatively little change in technology during the Middle Paleolithic (from about 100,000 years to 35,000 years before the present), the advent of the Upper Paleolithic appears to have brought significant technological advances. This transition about 35,000 years ago is approximately coincident with the replacement of the Neanderthals by the earliest anatomically modern humans. However, the evidence for a significant change in hunting patterns is not evident in the animal remains left behind. Yet even if a correlation between the robustness of body build and the level of hunting ef-

ficiency could be demonstrated, it would only explain the ruggedness of the Neanderthal males. Since hunting is exclusively or at least predominantly a male activity among humans, and since Neanderthal females were in all respects as strongly built as the males, an alternative explanation is required for the females.

Some insight into why the Neanderthals consistently possessed such massiveness is provided by a series of partial skeletons of Neanderthals from the Shanidar Cave in northern Iraq. These fossils were excavated between 1953 and 1960 by anthropologist Ralph Solecki of Columbia University and have been studied principally by T. Dale Stewart, an anthropologist at the Smithsonian Institution, and myself. The most remarkable aspect of these skeletons is the number of healed injuries they contain. Four of the six reasonably complete adult skeletons show evidence of trauma during life.

The identification of traumatic injury in human fossil remains has plagued paleontologists for years. There has been a tendency to consider any form of damage to a fossil as conclusive evidence of prehistoric violence between humans if it resembles the breakage patterns caused by a direct blow with a heavy object. Hence a jaw with the teeth pushed in or a skull with a depressed fracture of the vault would be construed to indicate blows to the head.

The central problem with these interpretations is that they ignore the possibility of damage after death. Bone is relatively fragile, especially as compared with the rock and other sediment in which it is buried during fossilization. Therefore when several feet of sediment caused compression around fossil remains, the fossils will almost always break. In fact, among the innumerable cases of suggested violence between humans cited over the years, there are only a few exceptional examples that cannot be readily explained as the result of natural geologic forces acting after the death and burial of the individual.

One of these examples is the trauma of the left ninth rib of the skeleton of Shanidar 3, a partially healed wound inflicted by a sharp object. The implement

*The ankle and big toe of Shanidar 1's right foot show evidence of arthritis, which suggests an injury to those parts. The left foot is normal though incomplete.*

*The scar on the left ninth rib of Shanidar 3 is a partially healed wound inflicted by a sharp object. This wound is one of the few examples of trauma caused by violence.*

cut obliquely across the top of the ninth rib and probably pierced the underlying lung. Shanidar 3 almost certainly suffered a collapsed left lung and died several days or weeks later, probably as a result of secondary complications. This is deduced from the presence of bony spurs and increased density of the bone around the cut.

The position of the wound on the rib, the angle of the incision, and the cleanness of the cut make it highly unlikely that the injury was accidentally inflicted. In fact, the incision is almost exactly what would have resulted if Shanidar 3 had been stabbed in the side by a right-handed adversary in face-to-face conflict. This would therefore provide conclusive evidence of violence between humans, the *only* evidence so far found of such violence among the Neanderthals.

In most cases, however, it is impossible to determine from fossilized re-

mains the cause of an individual's death. The instances that can be positively identified as prehistoric traumatic injury are those in which the injury was inflicted prior to death and some healing took place. Shortly after an injury to bone, whether a cut or a fracture, the damaged bone tissue is resorbed by the body and new bone tissue is laid down around the injured area. As long as irritation persists, new bone is deposited, creating a bulge or spurs of irregular bone extending into the soft tissue. If the irritation ceases, the bone will slowly re-form so as to approximate its previous, normal condition. However, except for superficial injuries or those sustained during early childhood, some trace of damage persists for the life of the individual.

In terms of trauma, the most impressive of the Shanidar Neanderthals is the first adult discovered, known as Shanidar 1. This individual suffered a number of injuries, some of which may be related. On the right forehead there are scars from minor surface injuries, probably superficial scalp cuts. The outside of the left eye socket sustained a major blow that partially collapsed that part of the bony cavity, giving it a flat rather than a rounded contour. This injury possibly caused loss of sight in the left eye and pathological alterations of the right side of the body.

Shanidar 1's left arm is largely preserved and fully normal. The right arm, however, consists of a highly atrophied but otherwise normal collarbone and shoulder blade and a highly abnormal upper arm bone shaft. That shaft is atrophied to a fraction of the diameter of the left one but retains most of its original length. Furthermore, the lower end of the right arm bone has a healed fracture of the atrophied shaft and an irregular, pathological tip. The arm was apparently either intentionally amputated just above the elbow or fractured at the elbow and never healed.

This abnormal condition of the right arm does not appear to be a congenital malformation, since the length of the bone is close to the estimated length of the normal left upper arm bone. If, however, the injury to the left eye socket also affected the left side of the brain,

directly or indirectly, by disrupting the blood supply to part of the brain, the result could have been partial paralysis of the right side. Motor and sensory control areas for the right side are located on the left side of the brain, slightly behind the left eye socket. This would explain the atrophy of the whole right arm since loss of nervous stimulation will rapidly lead to atrophy of the affected muscles and bone.

The abnormality of the right arm of Shanidar 1 is paralleled to a lesser extent in the right foot. The right ankle joint shows extensive arthritic degeneration, and one of the major joints of the inner arch of the right foot has been completely reworked by arthritis. The left foot, however, is totally free of pathology. Arthritis from normal stress usually affects both lower limbs equally; this degeneration therefore suggests that the arthritis in the right foot is a secondary result of an injury, perhaps a sprain, that would not otherwise be evident on skeletal remains. This conclusion is supported by a healed fracture of the right fifth instep bone, which makes up a major portion of the outer arch of the foot. These foot pathologies may be tied into the damage to the left side of the skull; partial paralysis of the right side would certainly weaken the leg and make it more susceptible to injury.

The trauma evident on the other Shanidar Neanderthals is relatively minor by comparison. Shanidar 3, the individual who died of the rib wound, suffered debilitating arthritis of the right ankle and neighboring foot joints, but lacks any evidence of pathology on the left foot; this suggests a superficial injury similar to the one sustained by Shanidar 1. Shanidar 4 had a healed broken rib. Shanidar 5 received a transverse blow across the left forehead that left a large scar on the bone but does not appear to have affected the brain.

None of these injuries necessarily provides evidence of deliberate violence among the Neanderthals; all of them could have been accidentally self-inflicted or accidentally caused by another individual. In either case, the impression gained of the Shanidar Neanderthals is of a group of invalids. The crucial variable, however, appears to be age. All four of these individuals died at relatively advanced ages, probably between 40 and 60 years (estimating the age at death for Neanderthals beyond the age of 25 is extremely difficult); they therefore had considerable time to accumulate the scars of past injuries. Shanidar 2 and 6, the other reasonably complete Shanidar adults, lack evidence of trauma, but they both died young, probably before reaching 30.

Other Neanderthal remains, all from Europe, exhibit the same pattern. Every fairly complete skeleton of an elderly adult shows evidence of traumatic injuries. The original male skeleton from the Neander Valley had a fracture just below the elbow of the left arm, which probably limited movement of that arm for life. The "old man" from La Chapelle-aux-Saints, France, on whom most traditional reconstructions of the Neanderthals have been based, suffered a broken rib. La Ferrassi 1, the old adult male from La Ferrassie, France, sustained a severe injury to the right hip, which may have impaired his mobility.

In addition, several younger specimens and ones of uncertain age show traces of trauma. La Quina 5, the young adult female from La Quina, France, was wounded on her right upper arm. A young adult from Sala, Czechoslovakia, was superficially wounded on the right forehead just above the brow. And an individual of unknown age and sex from the site of Krapina, Yugoslavia, suffered a broken forearm, in which the bones never reunited after the fracture.

The evidence suggests several things. First, life for the Neanderthals was rigorous. If they lived through childhood and early adulthood, they did so bearing the scars of a harsh and dangerous life. Furthermore, this incident of trauma correlates with the massiveness of the Neanderthals; a life style that so consistently involved injury would have required considerable strength and fortitude for survival.

There is, however, another, more optimistic side to this. The presence of so many injuries in a prehistoric human group, many of which were debilitating

The right hand of Shanidar 4 demonstrates the enlarged finger tips and strong muscle markings characteristic of Neanderthal hands.

and sustained years before death, shows that individuals were taken care of long after their economic usefulness to the social group had ceased. It is perhaps no accident that among the Neanderthals, for the first time in human history, people lived to a comparatively old age. We also find among the Neanderthals the first intentional burials of the dead, some of which involved offerings. Despite the hardships of their life style, the Neanderthals apparently had a deep-seated respect and concern for each other.

Taken together, these different pieces of information paint a picture of life among the Neanderthals that, while harsh and dangerous, was not without personal security. Certainly the hardships the Neanderthals endured were beyond those commonly experienced in the prehistoric record of human caring and respect as well as of violence between individuals. Perhaps for these reasons, despite their physical appearance, the Neanderthals should be considered the first modern humans.

# The Gift *of* Gab

*Grooves and holes in fossil skulls may reveal when our ancestors began to speak. The big question, though, is what drove them to it?*

## By Matt Cartmill

*MATT CARTMILL is a professor at Duke, where he teaches anatomy and anthropology and studies animal locomotion. Cartmill is also the author of numerous articles and books on the evolution of people and other animals, including an award-winning book on hunting,* A View to a Death in the Morning. *He is the president of the American Association of Physical Anthropologists.*

People can talk. Other animals can't. They can all communicate in one way or another—to lure mates, at the very least—but their whinnies and wiggles don't do the jobs that language does. The birds and beasts can use their signals to attract, threaten, or alert each other, but they can't ask questions, strike bargains, tell stories, or lay out a plan of action.

Those skills make *Homo sapiens* a uniquely successful, powerful, and dangerous mammal. Other creatures' signals carry only a few limited kinds of information about what's happening at the moment, but language lets us tell each other in limitless detail about what used to be or will be or might be. Language lets us get vast numbers of big, smart fellow primates all working together on a single task—building the Great Wall of China or fighting World War II or flying to the moon. It lets us construct and communicate the gorgeous fantasies of literature and the profound fables of myth. It lets us cheat death by pouring out our knowledge, dreams, and memories into younger people's minds. And it does powerful things for us inside our own minds because we do a lot of our thinking by talking silently to ourselves. Without language, we would be only a sort of upright chimpanzee with funny feet and clever hands. With it, we are the self-possessed masters of the planet.

How did such a marvelous adaptation get started? And if it's so marvelous, why hasn't any other species come up with anything similar? These may be the most important questions we face in studying human evolution. They are also the least understood. But in the past few years, linguists and anthropologists have been making some breakthroughs, and we are now beginning to have a glimmering of some answers.

*COULD NEANDERTHALS talk? They seem to have had nimble tongues, but some scientists think the geometry of their throats prevented them from making many clear vowel sounds.*

We can reasonably assume that by at least 30,000 years ago people were talking—at any rate, they were producing carvings, rock paintings, and jewelry, as well as ceremonial graves containing various goods. These tokens of art and religion are high-level forms of symbolic behavior, and they imply that the everyday symbol-handling machinery of human language must have been in place then as well.

Language surely goes back further than that, but archeologists don't agree on just how far. Some think that earlier, more basic human behaviors—hunting in groups, tending fires, making tools—also demanded language. Others think these activities are possible without speech. Chimpanzees, after all, hunt communally, and with human guidance they can learn to tend fires and chip flint.

Paleontologists have pored over the fossil bones of our ancient relatives in search of evidence for speech abilities. Because the most crucial organ for language is the brain, they have looked for signs in the impressions left by the brain on the inner surfaces of fossil skulls, particularly impressions made by parts of the brain called speech areas because damage to them can impair a person's ability to talk or understand language. Unfortunately, it turns out that you can't tell whether a fossil hominid was able to talk simply by looking at brain impressions on the inside of its skull. For one thing, the fit between the brain and the bony braincase is loose in people and other large mammals, and so the impressions we derive from fossil skulls are disappointingly fuzzy. Moreover, we now know that language functions are not tightly localized but spread across many parts of the brain.

Faced with these obstacles, researchers have turned from the brain to other organs used in speech, such as the throat and tongue. Some have measured the fossil skulls and jaws of early hominids, tried to reconstruct the shape of their vocal tracts, and then applied the laws of acoustics to them to see whether they might have been capable of producing human speech.

All mammals produce their vocal noises by contracting muscles that compress the rib cage. The air in the lungs is driven out through the windpipe to the larynx, where it flows between the vocal cords. More like flaps than cords, these structures vibrate in the breeze, producing a buzzing sound that becomes the voice. The human difference lies in what happens to the air after it gets past the vocal cords.

In people, the larynx lies well below the back of the tongue, and most of the air goes out through the mouth when we talk. We make only a few sounds by exhaling through the nose—for instance, nasal consonants like *m* or *n,* or the so-called nasal vowels in words like the French *bon* and *vin.* But in most mammals, including apes, the larynx sticks farther up behind the tongue, into the back of the nose, and most of the exhaled air passes out through the nostrils. Nonhuman mammals make mostly nasal sounds as a result.

At some point in human evolution the larynx must have descended from its previous heights, and this change had some serious drawbacks. It put the opening of the windpipe squarely in the path of descending food, making it dangerously easy for us to choke to death if a chunk of meat goes down the wrong way—something that rarely happens to a dog or a cat. Why has evolution exposed us to this danger?

Some scientists think that the benefits outweighed the risks, because lowering the larynx improved the quality of our vowels and made speech easier to understand. The differences between vowels are produced mainly by changing the size and shape of the airway between the tongue and the roof of the mouth. When the front of the tongue almost touches the palate, you get the *ee* sound

**IN CHIMPANZEES** the larynx sits high in the throat.

**IN HUMANS** its lower position permits complex sounds.

Illustrations by Dugald Stermer

in *beet;* when the tongue is humped up high in the back (and the lips are rounded), you get the *oo* sound in *boot,* and so on. We are actually born with a somewhat apelike throat, including a flat tongue and a larynx lying high up in the neck, and this arrangement makes a child's vowels sound less clearly separated from each other than an adult's.

Philip Lieberman of Brown University thinks that an ape-like throat persisted for some time in our hominid ancestors. His studies of fossil jaws and skulls persuade him that a more modern throat didn't evolve until some 500,000 years ago, and that some evolutionary lines in the genus *Homo* never did ac-

quire modern vocal organs. Lieberman concludes that the Neanderthals, who lived in Europe until perhaps 25,000 years ago, belonged to a dead-end lineage that never developed our range of vowels, and that their speech—if they had any at all—would have been harder to understand than ours. Apparently, being easily understood wasn't terribly important to them—not important enough, at any rate, to outweigh the risk of inhaling a chunk of steak into a lowered larynx. This suggests that vocal communication wasn't as central to their lives as it is to ours.

Many paleoanthropologists, especially those who like to see Neanderthals as a separate species, accept this story. Others have their doubts. But the study of other parts of the skeleton in fossil hominids supports some of Lieberman's conclusions. During the 1980s a nearly complete skeleton of a young *Homo* male was recovered from 1.5-million-year-old deposits in northern Kenya. Examining the vertebrae attached to the boy's rib cage, the English anatomist Ann MacLarnon discovered that his spinal cord was proportionately thinner in this region than it is in people today. Since that part of the cord controls most of the muscles that drive air in and out of the lungs, MacLarnon concluded that the youth may not have had the kind of precise neural control over breathing movements that is needed for speech.

This year my colleague Richard Kay, his student Michelle Balow, and I were able to offer some insights from yet another part of the hominid body. The tongue's movements are controlled almost solely by a nerve called the hypoglossal. In its course from the brain to the tongue, this nerve passes through a hole in the skull, and Kay, Balow, and I found that this bony canal is relatively big in modern humans—about twice as big in cross section as that of a like-size chimpanzee. Our larger canal presumably reflects a bigger hypoglossal nerve, giving us the precise control over tongue movements that we need for speech.

We also measured this hole in the skulls of a number of fossil hominids.

Australopithecines have small canals like those of apes, suggesting that they couldn't talk. But later *Homo* skulls, beginning with a 400,000-year-old skull from Zambia, all have big, humanlike hypoglossal canals. These are also the skulls that were the first to house brains as big as our own. On these counts our work supports Lieberman's ideas. We disagree only on the matter of Neanderthals. While he claims their throats couldn't have produced human speech, we find that their skulls also had human-size canals for the hypoglossal nerve, suggesting that they could indeed talk.

---

*THE VERDICT IS STILL out on the language abilities of Neanderthals. I tend to think they must have had fully human language. After all, they had brains larger than those of most humans.*

---

In short, several lines of evidence suggest that neither the australopithecines nor the early, small-brained species of *Homo* could talk. Only around half a million years ago did the first big-brained *Homo* evolve language. The verdict is still out on the language abilities of Neanderthals. I tend to think that they must have had fully human language. After all, they had brains larger than those of most modern humans, made elegant stone tools, and knew how to use fire. But if Lieberman and his friends are right about those vowels, Neanderthals may have sounded something like the Swedish chef on *The Muppet Show*.

We are beginning to get some idea of when human language originated, but the fossils can't tell us how it got started, or what the intermediate stages between animal calls and human language might have been like. When trying to understand the origin of a trait that doesn't fossilize, it's sometimes useful to look for similar but simpler versions of it in other creatures living today. With luck, you can find a series of forms that suggest how simple primitive makeshifts could have evolved into more complex and elegant versions. This is how Darwin attacked the problem of the evolution of the eye. Earlier biologists had pointed to the human eye as an example of a marvelously perfect organ that must have been specially created all at once in its final form by God. But Darwin pointed out that animal eyes exist in all stages of complexity, from simple skin cells that can detect only the difference between light and darkness, to pits lined with such cells, and so on all the way to the eyes of people and other vertebrates. This series, he argued, shows how the human eye could have evolved from simpler precursors by gradual stages.

Can we look to other animals to find simpler precursors of language? It seems unlikely. Scientists have sought experimental evidence of language in dolphins and chimpanzees, thus far without success. But even if we had no experimental studies, common sense would tell us that the other animals can't have languages like ours. If they had, we would be in big trouble because they would organize against us. They don't. Outside of Gary Larson's *Far Side* cartoons and George Orwell's *Animal Farm*, farmers don't have to watch their backs when they visit the cowshed. There are no conspiracies among cows, or even among dolphins and chimpanzees. Unlike human slaves or prisoners, they never plot rebellions against their oppressors.

Even if language as a whole has no parallels in animal communication, might some of its peculiar properties be foreshadowed among the beasts around us? If so, that might tell us something about how and in what order these properties were acquired. One such property is reference. Most of the units of human languages refer to things—to individuals (like *Fido*), or to types of objects (*dog*), actions (*sit*), or properties (*furry*). Animal signals don't have this kind of referential meaning. Instead, they have what is called instrumental meaning: this is, they act as stimuli that trigger desired responses from others. A frog's mating croak doesn't *refer* to sex. Its purpose is to get some, not to talk about it. People, too, have signals of this purely animal sort—for example, weeping, laughing, and screaming—but these stand outside language. They have powerful meanings for us but not the kind of meaning that words have.

---

*AUSTRALOPITHECUS africanus and other early hominids couldn't speak.*

---

Some animal signals have a focused meaning that looks a bit like reference. For example, vervet monkeys give different warning calls for different predators. When they hear the "leopard" call, vervets climb trees and anxiously look down; when they hear the "eagle" call, they hide in low bushes or look up. But although the vervets' leopard call is in some sense about leopards, it isn't a word for leopard. Like a frog's croak or human weeping, its meaning is strictly instrumental; it's a stimulus that elicits an automatic response. All a vervet can "say" with it is *Eeek! A leopard!*—not "I really hate leopard!" or "No leopards here, thank goodness" or "A leopard ate Alice yesterday."

In these English sentences, such referential words as *leopard* work their magic through an accompanying framework of nonreferential, grammatical words, which set up an empty web of meaning that the referential symbols fill in. When Lewis Carroll tells us in "Jabberwocky" that "the slithy toves did gyre and gimble in the wabe," we have no idea what he is talking about, but we do know certain things—for instance, that all this happened in the past and that there was more than one tove but only one wabe. We know these things because of the grammatical structure of the sentence, a structure that linguists call syntax. Again, there's nothing much like it in any animal signals.

But if there aren't any intermediate stages between animal calls and human speech, then how could language evolve? What was there for it to evolve from? Until recently, linguists have shrugged off these questions—or else concluded that language didn't evolve at all, but just sprang into existence by accident, through some glorious random mutation. This theory drives Darwinians crazy, but the linguists have been content with it because it fits neatly into some key ideas in modern linguistics.

Forty years ago most linguists thought that people learn to talk through the same sort of behavior reinforcement used in training an animal to do tricks: when children use a word correctly or produce a grammatical sentence, they are rewarded. This picture was swept away in the late 1950s by the revolutionary ideas of Noam Chomsky. Chomsky argued that the structures of syntax lie in unconscious linguistic patterns—so-called deep structures—that are very different from the surface strings of words that come out of our mouths. Two sentences that look different on the surface (for instance, "A leopard ate Alice" and "Alice was eaten by a leopard") can mean the same thing because they derive from a single deep structure. Conversely, two sentences with different deep structures and different meanings can look exactly the same on the surface (for example, "Fleeing leopards can be dangerous"). Any models of language learning based strictly on the observable behaviors of language, Chomsky insisted, can't account for these deep-lying patterns of meaning.

Chomsky concluded that the deepest structures of language are innate, not learned. We are all born with the same fundamental grammar hard-wired into our brains, and we are preprogrammed to pick up the additional rules of the lo-

cal language, just as baby ducks are hard-wired to follow the first big animal they see when they hatch. Chomsky could see no evidence of other animals' possessing this innate syntax machinery. He concluded that we can't learn anything about the origins of language by studying other animals and they can't

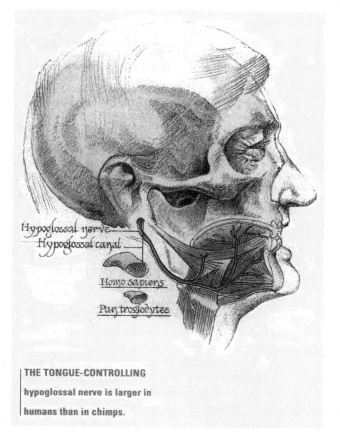

**THE TONGUE-CONTROLLING**

hypoglossal nerve is larger in

humans than in chimps.

Hypoglossal nerve
Hypoglossal canal

*Homo sapiens*

*Pan troglodytes*

learn language from us. If language learning were just a matter of proper training, Chomsky reasoned, we ought to be able to teach English to lab rats, or at least to apes.

As we have seen, apes aren't built to talk. But they can be trained to use sign language or to point to word-symbols on a keyboard. Starting in the 1960s, several experimenters trained chimpanzees and other great apes to use such signs to ask for things and answer questions to get rewards. Linguists, however, were unimpressed. They said that the apes' signs had a purely instrumental meaning: the animals were just doing tricks to get a treat. And there was no trace of syntax in the random-looking jumble of signs the apes produced; an ape that

signed "You give me cookie please" one minute might sign "Me cookie please you cookie eat give" the next.

Duane Rumbaugh and Sue Savage-Rumbaugh set to work with chimpanzees at the Yerkes Regional Primate Research Center in Atlanta to try to answer the linguists' criticisms. After many years of mixed results, Sue made a surprising break- through with a young bonobo (or pygmy chimp) named Kanzi. Kanzi had watched his mother, Matata, try to learn signs with little success. When Sue gave up on her and started with Kanzi, she was astonished to discover that he already knew the meaning of 12 of the keyboard symbols. Apparently, he had learned them without any training or rewards. In the years that followed, he learned new symbols quickly and used them referentially, both to answer questions and to "talk" about things that he intended to do or had already done. Still more amazingly, he had a considerable understanding of spoken English—including its syntax. He grasped such grammatical niceties as case structures ("Can you throw a potato to the turtle?") and if-then implication ("You can have some cereal if you give Austin your monster mash to play with"). Upon hearing such sentences, Kanzi behaved appropriately 72 percent of the time—more than a 30-month-old human child given the same tests.

Kanzi is a primatologist's dream and a linguist's nightmare. His language-learning abilities seem inexplicable. He didn't need any rewards to learn language, as the old behaviorists would have predicted; but he also defies the Chomskyan model, which can't explain why a speechless ape would have an innate tendency to learn English. It looks as though some animals can develop linguistic abilities for reasons unrelated to language itself.

Neuroscientist William Calvin of the University of Washington and linguist Derek Bickerton of the University of Hawaii have a suggestion as to what those reasons might be. In their forthcoming book, *Lingua ex Machina,* they argue that the ability to create symbols—signs that refer to things—is potentially present in any animal that can learn to interpret natural signs, such as a trail of footprints. Syntax, meanwhile,

---

*BRAIN ENLARGEMENT in hominids may have been the result of evolutionary pressures that favored intelligence. As a side effect, human evolution crossed a threshold at which language became possible.*

---

emerges from the abstract thought required for a social life. In apes and some other mammals with complex and subtle social relationships, individuals make alliances and act altruistically towards others, with the implicit understanding that their favors will be returned. To succeed in such societies, animals need to choose trustworthy allies and to detect and punish cheaters who take but never give anything in return. This demands fitting a shifting constellation of indi-

viduals into an abstract mental model of social roles (debtors, creditors, allies, and so on) connected by social expectations ("If you scratch my back, I'll scratch yours"). Calvin and Bickerton believe that such abstract models of social obligation furnished the basic pattern for the deep structures of syntax.

These foreshadowings of symbols and syntax, they propose, laid the groundwork for language in a lot of social animals but didn't create language itself. That had to wait until our ancestors evolved brains big enough to handle the large-scale operations needed to generate and process complex strings of signs. Calvin and Bickerton suggest that brain enlargement in our ancestry was the result of evolutionary pressures that favored intelligence and motor coordination for making tools and throwing weapons. As a side effect of these selection pressures, which had nothing to do with communication, human evolution crossed a threshold at which language became possible. Big-brained, nonhuman animals like Kanzi remain just on the verge of language.

This story reconciles natural selection with the linguists' insistence that you can't evolve language out of an animal communication system. It is also consistent with what we know about language from the fossil record. The earliest hominids with modern-size brains also seem to be the first ones with modern-size hypoglossal canals. Lieberman thinks that these are also the first hominids with modern vocal tracts. It may be no coincidence that all three of these changes seem to show up together around half a million years ago. If

Calvin and Bickerton are right, the enlargement of the brain may have abruptly brought language into being at this time, which would have placed new selection pressures on the evolving throat and tongue.

---

*FOSSILS HINT that language dawned 500,000 years ago.*

---

This account may be wrong in some of its details, but the story in its broad outlines solves so many puzzles and ties up so many loose ends that something like it must surely be correct. It also promises to resolve our conflicting views of the boundary between people and animals. To some people, it seems obvious that human beings are utterly different from any beasts. To others, it's just as obvious that many other animals are essentially like us, only with fewer smarts and more fur. Each party finds the other's view of humanity alien and threatening. The story of language origins sketched above suggests that both parties are right: the human difference is real and profound, but it is rooted in aspects of psychology and biology that we share with our close animal relatives. If the growing consensus on the origins of language can join these disparate truths together, it will be a big step forward in the study of human evolution.

# The Dating Game

*By tracking changes in ancient atoms, archeologists are establishing
the astonishing antiquity of modern humanity.*

## James Shreeve

*James Shreeve wrote fiction before turning to science writing. He is the coauthor (with anthropologist Donald Johanson) of* Lucy's Child: The Discovery of a Human Ancestor *and the author of* Nature: The Other Earthlings.

Four years ago archeologists Alison Brooks and John Yellen discovered what might be the earliest traces of modern human culture in the world. The only trouble is, nobody believes them. Sometimes they can't quite believe it themselves.

Their discovery came on a sun-soaked hillside called Katanda, in a remote corner of Zaire near the Ugandan border. Thirty yards below, the Semliki River runs so clear and cool the submerged hippos look like giant lumps of jade. But in the excavation itself, the heat is enough to make anyone doubt his eyes.

Katanda is a long way from the plains of Ice Age Europe, which archeologists have long believed to be the setting for the first appearance of truly modern culture: the flourish of new tool technologies, art, and body ornamentation known as the Upper Paleolithic, which began about 40,000 years ago. For several years Brooks, an archeologist at George Washington University had been pursuing the heretical hypothesis that humans in Africa had invented sophisticated technologies even earlier, while their European counterparts were still getting by with the same sorts of tools they'd been using for hundreds of thousands of years. If conclusive evidence hadn't turned up, it was only because nobody had really bothered to look for it.

"In France alone there must be three hundred well-excavated sites dating from the period we call the Middle Paleolithic," Brooks says. "In Africa there are barely two dozen on the whole continent."

One of those two dozen is Katanda. On an afternoon in 1988 John Yellen—archeology program director at the National Science Foundation and Brooks's husband—was digging in a densely packed litter of giant catfish bones, river stones, and Middle Paleolithic stone tools. From the rubble he extricated a beautifully crafted, fossilized bone harpoon point. Eventually two more whole points and fragments of five others turned up, all of them elaborately barbed and polished. A few feet away, the scientists uncovered pieces of an equally well crafted daggerlike tool. In design and workmanship the harpoons were not unlike those at the very end of the Upper Paleolithic, some 14,000 years ago. But there was one important difference. Brooks and Yellen believe the deposits John was standing in were at least five times that old. To put this in perspective, imagine discovering a prototypical Pontiac in Leonardo da Vinci's attic.

"If the site is as old as we think it is," says Brooks, "it could clinch the argument that modern humans evolved in Africa."

Ever since the discovery the couple have devoted themselves to chopping away at that stubborn little word *if*. In the face of the entrenched skepticism of their colleagues, it is an uphill task. But they do have some leverage. In those same four years since the first harpoon was found at Katanda, a breakthrough has revived the question of modern human origins. The breakthrough is not some new skeleton pulled out of the ground. Nor is it the highly publicized Eve hypothesis, put forth by geneticists, suggesting that all humans on Earth today share a common female ancestor who lived in Africa 200,000 years ago. The real advance, abiding quietly in the shadows while Eve draws the limelight, is simply a new way of telling time.

To be precise, it is a whole smorgasbord of new ways of telling time. Lately they have all converged on the same exhilarating, mortifying revelation: what little we thought we knew about the origins of our own species was hopelessly wrong. From Africa to the Middle East to Australia, the new dating methods are overturning conventional wisdom with insolent abandon, leaving the anthropological community dazed amid a rubble of collapsed certitudes. It is in this shell-shocked climate that Alison Brooks's Pontiac in Leonardo's attic might actually find a hearing.

"Ten years ago I would have said it was impossible for harpoons like these to be so old," says archeologist Michael Mehlman of the Smithsonian's National Museum of Natural History. "Now I'm reserving judgment. Anything can happen."

An archeologist with a freshly uncovered skull, stone tool, or bone Pontiac in hand can take two general approaches to determine its age. The first is called relative dating. Essentially the archeologist places the find in the context of the surrounding geological deposits. If the new discovery is found in a brown sediment lying beneath a yellowish layer of sand, then, all things being equal, it is older than the yellow sand layer or any other deposit higher up. The fossilized remains of extinct animals found near the object also provide a "biostratigraphic" record that can offer clues to a new find's relative age. (If a stone tool is found alongside an extinct species of horse, then it's a fair bet the tool was made while that kind of horse was still running around.) Sometimes the tools themselves can be used as a guide, if they match up in character and style with tools from other, better-known sites. Relative dating methods like these can tell you whether a find is older or younger than something else, but they cannot pin an age on the object in calendar years.

The most celebrated *absolute* method of telling archeological time, radiocarbon dating, came along in the 1940s. Plants take in carbon from the atmosphere to build tissues, and other organisms take in plants, so carbon ends up in everything from wood to woodchucks. Most carbon exists in the stable form of carbon 12. But some is made up of the unstable, radioactive form carbon 14. When an organism dies, it contains about the same ratio of carbon 12 to carbon 14 that exists in the atmosphere. After death the radioactive carbon 14 atoms begin to decay, changing into stable atoms of nitrogen. The amount of carbon 12, however, stays the same. Scientists can look at the amount of carbon 12 and—based on the ratio—deduce how much carbon 14 was originally present. Since the decay rate of carbon 14 is constant and steady (half of it disappears every 5,730 years), the difference between the amount of carbon 14 originally in a charred bit of wood or bone

and the amount present now can be used as a clock to determine the age of the object.

Conventional radiocarbon dates are extremely accurate up to about 40,000 years. This is far and away the best method to date a find—as long as it is younger than this cutoff point. (In older materials, the amount of carbon 14 still left undecayed is so small that even the slightest amount of contamination in the experimental process leads to highly inaccurate results.) Another dating technique, relying on the decay of radioactive potassium rather than carbon, is available to date volcanic deposits *older* than half a million years. When it was discovered in the late 1950s, radiopotassium dating threw open a window on the emergence of the first members of the human family—the australopithecines, like the famous Lucy, and her more advanced descendants, *Homo habilis* and *Homo erectus*. Until now, however, the period between half a million and 40,000 years—a stretch of time that just happens to embrace the origin of *Homo sapiens*—was practically unknowable by absolute dating techniques. It was as if a geochronological curtain were drawn across the mystery of our species' birth. Behind that curtain the hominid lineage underwent an astonishing metamorphosis, entering the dateless, dark centuries a somewhat precocious bipedal ape and emerging into the range of radiocarbon dating as the culturally resplendent, silver-tongued piece of work we call a modern human being.

Fifteen years ago there was some general agreement about how this change took place. First, what is thought of as an *anatomically* modern human being—with the rounded cranium, vertical forehead, and lightly built skeleton of people today—made its presence known in Europe about 35,000 years ago. Second, along with those first modern-looking people, popularly known as the Cro-Magnons, came the first signs of complex human *behavior,* including tools made of bone and antler as well as of stone, and art, symbolism, social status, ethnic identity, and probably true human language too. Finally, in any one region there was no overlap in time be-

tween the appearance of modern humans and the disappearance of "archaic" humans such as the classic Neanderthals, supporting the idea that one group had evolved from the other.

"Thanks to the efforts of the new dating methods," says Fred Smith, an anthropologist at Northern Illinois University, "we now know that each of these ideas was wrong."

The technique doing the most damage to conventional wisdom is called thermoluminescence, TL for short. (Reader take heed: the terrain of geochronology is full of terms long enough to tie between two trees and trip over, so acronyms are a must.) Unlike radiocarbon dating, which works on organic matter, TL pulls time out of stone.

If you were to pick an ordinary rock up off the ground and try to describe its essential rockness, phrases like "frenetically animated" would probably not leap to mind. But in fact minerals are in a state of constant inner turmoil. Minute amounts of radioactive elements, both within the rock itself and in the surrounding soil and atmosphere, are constantly bombarding its atoms, knocking electrons out of their normal orbits. All this is perfectly normal rock behavior, and after gallivanting around for a hundredth of a second or two, most electrons dutifully return to their normal positions. A few, however, become trapped en route—physically captured within crystal impurities or electronic aberrations in the mineral structure itself. These tiny prisons hold on to their electrons until the mineral is heated, whereupon the traps spring open and the electrons return to their more stable position. As they escape, they release energy in the form of light—a photon for every homeward-bound electron.

Thermoluminescence was observed way back in 1663 by the great English physicist Robert Boyle. One night Boyle took a borrowed diamond to bed with him, for reasons that remain obscure. Resting the diamond "upon a warm part of my Naked Body," Boyle noticed that it soon emitted a warm glow. So taken was he with the responsive gem that the next day he delivered a paper on the subject at the Royal Society, noting his surprise at the glow since his "constitution," he felt, was "not of the hottest."

Three hundred years later another Englishman, Martin Aitken of Oxford University, developed the methods to turn thermoluminescence into a geophysical timepiece. The clock works because the radioactivity bombarding a mineral is fairly constant, so electrons become trapped in those crystalline prisons at a steady rate through time. If you crush the mineral you want to date and heat a few grains to a high enough temperature—about 900 degrees, which is more body heat than Robert Boyle's constitution could ever have produced—all the electron traps will release their captive electrons at once, creating a brilliant puff of light. In a laboratory the intensity of that burst of luminescence can easily be measured with a device called a photomultiplier. The higher the spike of light, the more trapped electrons have accumulated in the sample, and thus the more time has elapsed since it was last exposed to heat. Once a mineral is heated and all the electrons have returned "home," the clock is set back to zero.

Now, our lineage has been making flint tools for hundreds of thousands of years, and somewhere in that long stretch of prehistory we began to use fire as well. Inevitably, some of our less careful ancestors kicked discarded tools into burning hearths, setting their electron clocks back to zero and opening up a ripe opportunity for TL timekeepers in the present. After the fire went out, those flints lay in the ground, pummeled by radioactivity, and each trapped electron was another tick of the clock. Released by laboratory heat, the electrons flash out photons that reveal time gone by.

In the late 1980s Hélène Valladas, an archeologist at the Center for Low-Level Radioactivity of the French Atomic Energy Commission near Paris, along with her father, physicist Georges Valladas, stunned the anthropological community with some TL dates on burned flints taken from two archeological sites in Israel. The first was a cave called Kebara, which had already yielded an astonishingly complete Neanderthal skeleton. Valladas dated flints from the Neanderthal's level at 60,000 years before the present.

In itself this was no surprise, since the date falls well within the known range of the Neanderthals' time on Earth. The shock came a year later, when she used the same technique to pin a date on flints from a nearby cave called Qafzeh, which contained the buried remains of early modern human beings. This time, the spikes of luminescence translated into an age of around 92,000 years. In other words, the more "advanced" human types were a full 30,000 years *older* than the Neanderthals they were supposed to have descended from.

If Valladas's TL dates are accurate, they completely confound the notion that modern humans evolved from Neanderthals in any neat and tidy way. Instead, these two kinds of human, equally endowed culturally but distinctly different in appearance, might have shared the same little nook of the Middle East for tens of thousands of years. To some, this simply does not make sense.

"If these dates are correct, what does this do to what else we know, to the stratigraphy, to fossil man, to the archeology?" worries Anthony Marks, an archeologist at Southern Methodist University. "It's all a mess. Not that the dates are necessarily wrong. But you want to know more about them."

Marks's skepticism is not entirely unfounded. While simple in theory, in practice TL has to overcome some devilish complications. ("If these new techniques were easy, we would have thought of them a long time ago," says geochronologist Gifford Miller of the University of Colorado.) To convert into calendar years the burst of luminescence when a flint is heated, one has to know both the sensitivity of that particular flint to radiation and the dose of radioactive rays it has received each year since it was "zeroed" by fire. The sensitivity of the sample can be determined by assaulting it with artificial radiation in the lab. And the annual dose of radiation received from *within* the sample itself can be calculated fairly easily by measuring how much uranium or other radioactive elements the sample contains. But determining the annual dose

from the environment *around* the sample—the radioactivity in the surrounding soil, and cosmic rays from the atmosphere itself—is an iffier proposition. At some sites fluctuations in this environmental dose through the millennia can turn the "absolute" date derived from TL into an absolute nightmare.

Fortunately for Valladas and her colleagues, most of the radiation dose for the Qafzeh flints came from within the flints themselves. The date there of 92,000 years for the modern human skeletons is thus not only the most sensational number so far produced by TL, it is also one of the surest.

"The strong date at Qafzeh was just good luck," says Valladas. "It was just by chance that the internal dose was high and the environmental dose was low."

More recently Valladas and her colleague Norbert Mercier turned their TL techniques to the French site of Saint-Césaire. Last summer they confirmed that a Neanderthal found at Saint-Césaire was only 36,000 years old. This new date, combined with a fresh radiocarbon date of about 40,000 years tagged on some Cro-Magnon sites in northern Spain, strongly suggests that the two types of humans shared the same corner of Europe for several thousand years as the glaciers advanced from the north.

While Valladas has been busy in Europe and the Middle East, other TL timekeepers have produced some astonishing new dates for the first human occupation of Australia. As recently as the 1950s, it was widely believed that Australia had been colonized only some five thousand years ago. The reasoning was typically Eurocentric: since the Australian aborigines were still using stone tools when the first white settlers arrived, they must have just recently developed the capacity to make the difficult sea crossing from Indonesia in the first place. A decade later archeologists grudgingly conceded that the date of first entry might have been closer to the beginning of the Holocene period, 10,000 years ago. In the 1970s radiocarbon dates on human occupation sites pushed the date back again, as far as 32,000 years ago. And now TL studies at two sites in northern Australia drop that first human footstep on the continent—and the sea voyage that preceded it—all the way back to 60,000 years before the present. If these dates stand up, then the once-maligned ancestors of modern aborigines were building ocean-worthy craft some 20,000 years *before* the first signs of sophisticated culture appeared in Europe.

"Luminescence has revolutionized the whole period I work in," says Australian National University archeologist Rhys Jones, a member of the team responsible for the new TL dates. "In effect, we have at our disposal a new machine—a new time machine."

With so much at stake, however, nobody looks to TL—or to any of the other new "time machines"—as a geochronological panacea. Reputations have been too badly singed in the past by dating methods that claimed more than they could deliver. In the 1970s a flush of excitement over a technique called amino acid racemization led many workers to believe that another continent—North America—had been occupied by humans fully 70,000 years ago. Further testing at the same American sites proved that the magical new method was off by one complete goose egg. The real age of the sites was closer to 7,000 years.

"To work with wrong dates is a luxury we cannot afford," British archeologist Paul Mellars intoned ominously earlier this year, at the beginning of a London meeting of the Royal Society to showcase the new dating technologies. "A wrong date does not simply inhibit research. It could conceivably throw it into reverse."

Fear of just such a catastrophe—not to mention the risk that her own reputation could go up in a puff of light—is what keeps Alison Brooks from declaring outright that she has found exquisitely crafted bone harpoons in Zaire that are more than 40,000 years older than such creations are supposed to be. So far the main support for her argument has been her redating of another site, called Ishango, four miles down the Semliki River from the Katanda site. In the 1950s the Belgian geologist Jean de Heinzelin excavated a harpoon-rich "aquatic civilization" at Ishango that he thought was 8,000 years old. Brooks's radiocarbon dating of the site in the mid-1980s pushed the age back to 25,000. By tracing the layers of sediment shared between Ishango and Katanda, Brooks and her colleagues are convinced that Katanda is much farther down in the stratigraphy—twice as old as Ishango, or perhaps even more. But even though Brooks and Yellen talk freely about their harpoons at meetings, they have yet to utter such unbelievable numbers in the unforgiving forum of an academic journal.

"It is precisely because no one believes us that we want to make our case airtight before we publish," says Brooks. "We want dates confirming dates confirming dates."

Soon after the harpoons were discovered, the team went to work with thermoluminescence. Unfortunately, no burned flints have been found at the site. Nevertheless, while TL works best on materials that have been completely zeroed by such extreme heat as a campfire, even a strong dose of sunlight can spring some of the electron traps. Thus even ordinary sediments surrounding an archeological find might harbor a readable clock: bleached out by sunlight when they were on the surface, their TL timers started ticking as soon as they were buried by natural processes. Brooks and Yellen have taken soil samples from Katanda for TL, and so far the results are tantalizing—but that's all.

"At this point we think the site is quite old," says geophysicist Allen Franklin of the University of Maryland, who with his Maryland colleague Bill Hornyak is conducting the work. "But we don't want to put a number on it."

As Franklin explains, the problem with dating sediments with TL is that while some of the electron traps might be quickly bleached out by sunlight, others hold on to their electrons more stubbornly. When the sample is then heated in a conventional TL apparatus, these stubborn traps release electrons that were captured perhaps millions of years before the sediments were last exposed to sunlight-teasing date-hungry archeologists with a deceptively old age for the sample.

Brooks does have other irons in the dating fire. The most promising is called electron spin resonance—or ESR, among friends. Like TL, electron spin resonance fashions a clock out of the steadily accumulating electrons caught in traps. But whereas TL measures that accumulation by the strength of the light given off when the traps open, ESR literally counts the captive electrons themselves while they still rest undisturbed in their prisons.

All electrons "spin" in one of two opposite directions—physicists call them up and down. (Metaphors are a must here because the nature of this "spinning" is quantum mechanical and can be accurately described only in huge mathematical equations.) The spin of each electron creates a tiny magnetic force pointing in one direction, something like a compass needle. Under normal circumstances, the electrons are paired so that their opposing spins and magnetic forces cancel each other out. But trapped electrons are unpaired. By manipulating an external magnetic field placed around the sample to be dated, the captive electrons can be induced to "resonate"—that is, to flip around and spin the other way. When they flip, each electron absorbs a finite amount of energy from a microwave field that is also applied to the sample. This loss of microwave energy can be measured with a detector, and it is a direct count of the number of electrons caught in the traps.

ESR works particularly well on tooth enamel, with an effective range from a thousand to 2 million years. Luckily for Brooks and Yellen, some nice fat hippo teeth have been recovered from Katanda in the layer that also held the harpoons. To date the teeth, they have called in Henry Schwarcz of McMaster University in Ontario, a ubiquitous, veteran geochronologist. In the last ten years Schwarcz has journeyed to some 50 sites throughout Europe, Africa, and western Asia, wherever his precious and arcane services are demanded.

Schwarcz also turned up at the Royal Society meeting, where he explained both the power and the problems of the ESR method. On the plus side is that teeth are hardy remains, found at nearly every archeological site in the world, and that ESR can test a tiny sample again and again—with the luminescence techniques, it's a one-shot deal. ESR can also home in on certain kinds of electron traps, offering some refinement over TL, which lumps them all together.

On the minus side, ESR is subject to the same uncertainties as TL concerning the annual soaking of radiation a sample has received from the environment. What's more, even the radiation from *within* a tooth cannot be relied on to be constant through time. Tooth enamel has the annoying habit of sucking up uranium from its surroundings while it sits in the ground. The more uranium the tooth contains, the more electrons are being bombarded out of their normal positions, and the faster the electron traps will fill up. Remember: you cannot know how old something is by counting filled traps unless you know the rate at which the traps were filled, year by year. If the tooth had a small amount of internal uranium for 50,000 years but took in a big gulp of the hot stuff 10,000 years ago, calculations based on the tooth's current high uranium level would indicate the electron traps were filled at a much faster rate than they really were. "The big question is, When did the uranium get there?" Schwarcz says. "Did the tooth slurp it all up in three days, or did the uranium accumulate gradually through time?"

One factor muddying the "big question" is the amount of moisture present around the sample during its centuries of burial: a wetter tooth will absorb uranium faster. For this reason, the best ESR sites are those where conditions are driest. Middle Eastern and African deserts are good bets. As far as modern human origins go, the technique has already tagged a date of about 100,000 years on some human fossils from an Israeli cave called Skhul, neatly supporting the TL date of 92,000 from Qafzeh, a few miles

away. If a new ESR date from a Neanderthal cave just around the corner from Skhul is right, then Neanderthals were also in the Middle East at about the same time. Meanwhile, in South Africa, a human jawbone from the site of Border Cave—"so modern it boggles the mind," as one researcher puts it—has now been dated with ESR at 60,000 years, nearly twice as old as any fossil like it in Europe.

But what of the cultural change to modern human behavior—such as the sophisticated technological development expressed by the Katanda harpoons? Schwarcz's dating job at Katanda is not yet finished, and given how much is at stake, he too is understandably reluctant to discuss it. "The site has good potential for ESR," he says guardedly. "Let's put it this way: if the initial results had indicated that the harpoons were not very old after all, we would have said 'So what?' to them and backed off. Well, we haven't backed off."

There are other dating techniques being developed that may, in the future, add more certainty to claims of African modernity. One of them, called uranium-series dating, measures the steady decay of uranium into various daughter elements inside anything formed from carbonates (limestone and cave stalactites, for instance). The principle is very similar to radiocarbon dating—the amount of daughter elements in a stalactite, for example, indicates how long that stalactite has been around—with the advantage that uranium-series dates can stretch back half a million years. Even amino acid racemization, scorned for the last 15 years, is making a comeback, thanks to the discovery that the technique, unreliable when applied to porous bone, is quite accurate when used on hard ostrich eggshells.

In the best of all possible worlds, an archeological site will offer an opportu-

nity for two or more of these dating techniques to be called in so they can be tested against each other. When asked to describe the ideal site, Schwarcz gets a dreamy look on his face. "I see a beautiful human skull sandwiched between two layers of very pure flow-stone," he says, imagining uranium-series dating turning those cave limestones into time brackets. "A couple of big, chunky hippo teeth are lying next to it, and a little ways off, a bunch of burned flints."

Even without Schwarcz's dream site, the dating methods used separately are pointing to a common theme: the alarming antiquity of modern human events where they are not supposed to be happening in the first place. Brooks sees suggestive traces of complexity not just at Katanda but scattered all over the African continent, as early as 100,000 years before the present. A classic stone tool type called the blade, long considered a trademark of the European Upper Paleolithic, appears in abundance in some South African sites 40,000 to 50,000 years before the Upper Paleolithic begins. The continent may even harbor the earliest hints of art and a symbolic side to human society: tools designed with stylistic meaning; colorful, incandescent minerals, valueless but for their beauty, found hundreds of miles away from their source. More and more, the Cro-Magnons of Europe are beginning to look like the last modern humans to show themselves and start acting "human" rather than the first.

That's not an easy notion for anthropologists and archeologists to swallow. "It just doesn't fit the pattern that those harpoons of Alison's should be so old," says Richard Klein, a paleoanthropologist at the University of Chicago. Then he shrugs. "Of course, if she's right, she has made a remarkable discovery indeed."

Only time will tell.

# Who Were the NEANDERTALS?

*Controversial evidence indicates that these hominids interbred with anatomically modern humans and sometimes behaved in surprisingly modern ways*

## by Kate Wong, *staff writer*

It was such a neat and tidy story. No match for the anatomically modern humans who swept in with a sophisticated culture and technology, the Neandertals—a separate species—were quickly driven to extinction by the invading moderns. But neat and tidy stories about the past have a way of unraveling, and the saga of the Neandertals, it appears, is no exception. For more than 200,000 years, these large-brained hominids occupied Europe and western Asia, battling the bitter cold of glacial maximums and the daily perils of prehistoric life. Today they no longer exist. Beyond these two facts, however, researchers fiercely debate who the Neandertals were, how they lived and exactly what happened to them.

The steadfast effort to resolve these elusive issues stems from a larger dispute over how modern humans evolved. Some researchers posit that our species arose recently (around 200,000 years ago) in Africa and subsequently replaced archaic hominids around the world, whereas others propose that these ancient populations contributed to the early modern human gene pool. As the best known of these archaic groups,

Neandertals are critical to the origins controversy. Yet this is more than an academic argument over certain events of our primeval past, for in probing Neandertal biology and behavior, researchers must wrestle with the very notion of what it means to be fully human and determine what, if anything, makes us moderns unique. Indeed, spurred by recent discoveries, paleoanthropologists and archaeologists are increasingly asking, How much like us were they?

Comparisons of Neandertals and modern humans first captured the attention of researchers when a partial Neandertal skeleton turned up in Germany's Neander Valley in 1856. Those remains—a heavily built skull with the signature arched browridge and massive limb bones—were clearly different, and Neandertals were assigned to their own species, *Homo neanderthalensis* (although even then there was disagreement: several German scientists argued that these were the remains of a crippled Cossack horseman). But it was the French discovery of the famous "Old Man" of La Chapelle-aux-Saints some 50 years later that led to the characterization of Neandertals as primitive

protohumans. Reconstructions showed them as stooped, lumbering, apelike brutes, in stark contrast to upright, graceful *Homo sapiens*. The Neandertal, it seemed, represented the ultimate "other," a dim-witted ogre lurking behind the evolutionary threshold of humanity.

Decades later reevaluation of the La Chapelle individual revealed that certain anatomical features had been misinterpreted. In fact, Neandertal posture and movement would have been the same as ours. Since then, paleoanthropologists have struggled to determine whether the morphological features that do characterize Neandertals as a group—such as the robustness of their skeletons, their short limbs and barrel chests, prominent browridges and low, sloping foreheads, protruding midfaces and chinless jaws—warrant designating them as a separate species. Researchers agree that some of these characteristics represent environment adaptations. The Neandertals' stocky body proportions, for example, would have allowed them to retain heat more effectively in the extremely cold weather brought on by glacial cycles. But other traits, such as the form of the

Neandertal

- LARGER OCCIPITAL BUN
- RECEDING FOREHEAD
- STRONG BROWRIDGE
- PROJECTING MIDFACE
- RETROMOLAR GAP
- NO CHIN

Early Modern European

- SMALLER OCCIPITAL BUN
- STEEP FOREHEAD
- DELICATE BROWRIDGE
- VERTICAL MIDFACE
- NO RETROMOLAR GAP; LAST LOWER MOLAR MISSING ON THIS SPECIMEN
- CHIN

ERIK TRINKAUS/MUSÉE DE L'HOMME *(top)*; ARCHEOLOGICKY ÚSTAV AV CR *(bottom)*

**CHARACTERISTIC DIFFERENCES** are shown between a Neandertal, represented by a French specimen, La Ferrassie 1, and an early modern, Dolní Vestonice 16, from the Czech Republic. Each aspect can be found in both groups, varying in degree and frequency, but they tend to appear as suites of features.

Neandertal browridge, lack any clear functional significance and seem to reflect the genetic drift typical of isolated populations.

For those scholars who subscribe to the replacement model of modern human origins, the distinctive Neandertal morphology clearly resulted from following an evolutionary trajectory separate from that of moderns. But for years, another faction of researchers has challenged this interpretation, arguing that many of the features that characterize Neandertals are also seen in the early

modern Europeans that followed them. "They clearly have a suite of features that are, overall, different, but it's a frequency difference, not an absolute difference," contends David W. Frayer, a paleoanthropologist at the University of Kansas. "Virtually everything you can find in Neandertals you can find elsewhere."

He points to one of the earliest-known modern Europeans, a fossil from a site in southwestern Germany called Vogelherd, which combines the skull shape of moderns with features that are

typically Neandertal, such as the distinct space between the last molar and the ascending part of the lower jaw known as a retromolar gap, and the form of the mandibular foramen—a nerve canal in the lower jaw. Additional evidence, according to Frayer and Milford H. Wolpoff of the University of Michigan, comes from a group of early moderns discovered in Moravia (Czech Republic) at a site called Mladec. The Mladec people, they say, exhibit characteristics on their skulls that other scientists have described as uniquely Neandertal traits.

Although such evidence was once used to argue that Neandertals could have independently evolved into modern Europeans, this view has shifted somewhat. "It's quite clear that people entered Europe as well, so the people that are there later in time are a mix of Neandertals and those populations coming into Europe," says Wolpoff, who believes the two groups differed only as much as living Europeans and aboriginal Australians do. Evidence for mixing also appears in later Neandertal fossils, according to Fred H. Smith, a paleoanthropologist at Northern Illinois University. Neandertal remains from Vindija cave in northwestern Croatia reflect "the assimilation of some early modern features," he says, referring to their more modern-shaped browridges and the slight presence of a chin on their mandibles.

Those who view Neandertals as a separate species, however, maintain that the Vindija fossils are too fragmentary to be diagnostic and that any similarities that do exist can be attributed to convergent evolution. These researchers likewise dismiss the mixing argument for the early moderns from Mladec. "When I look at the morphology of these people, I see robustness, I don't see Neandertal," counters Christopher B. Stringer of the Natural History Museum in London.

Another reason to doubt these claims for interbreeding, some scientists say, is that they contradict the conclusions reached by Svante Pääbo, then at the University of Munich, and his colleagues, who in July 1997 announced that they had retrieved and analyzed mitochondrial DNA (mtDNA) from a Neandertal fossil. The cover of the journal *Cell*, which contained their report,

# GUIDE TO TERMINOLOGY

**Neandertal** can also be spelled Neanderthal. Around 1900 German orthography changed, and the silent "h" in certain words, such as "thal" (meaning "valley"), was dropped. The designation *Homo neanderthalensis* remains the same, but the common name can be spelled either way.

**Paleolithic,** or Old Stone Age, is the period ranging from the beginning of culture to the end of the last glaciation. It is subdivided into Lower, Middle and Upper stages.

**Mousterian** is a Middle Paleolithic, stone tool–based cultural tradition associated with Neandertals and with early moderns in the Near East.

**Aurignacian** is an Upper Paleolithic cultural tradition associated with moderns that includes advanced tools and art objects.

**Châtelperronian** is an Upper Paleolithic cultural tradition associated with Neandertals. It resembles both the Mousterian and the Aurignacian.

said it all: "Neandertals Were Not Our Ancestors." From the short stretch of mtDNA they sequenced, the researchers determined that the difference between the Neandertal mtDNA and living moderns' mtDNA was considerably greater than the differences found among living human populations. But though it seemed on the surface that the species question had been answered, undercurrents of doubt have persisted [see "Ancestral Quandary," by Kate Wong, News and Analysis, January 1998].

New fossil evidence from western Europe has intensified interest in whether Neandertals and moderns mixed. In January 1999 researchers announced the discovery in central Portugal's Lapedo Valley of a largely complete skeleton from a four-year-old child buried 24,500 years ago in the Gravettian style known from other early modern Europeans. According to Erik Trinkaus of Washington University, Cidália Duarte of the Portuguese Institute of Archaeology in Lisbon and their colleagues, the specimen, known as Lagar Velho 1, bears a combination of Neandertal and modern human traits that could only have resulted from extensive interbreeding between the two populations [see box "The Hybrid Child from Portugal"].

If the mixed ancestry interpretation for Lagar Velho 1 holds up after further scrutiny, the notion of Neandertals as a variant of our species will gain new strength. Advocates of the replacement model do allow for isolated instances of interbreeding between moderns and the

archaic species, because some other closely related mammal species interbreed on occasion. But unlike central and eastern European specimens that are said to show a combination of features, the Portuguese child dates to a time when Neandertals are no longer thought to have existed. For Neandertal features to have persisted thousands of years after those people disappeared, Trinkaus and Duarte say, coexisting populations of Neandertals and moderns must have mixed significantly.

Their interpretation has not gone unchallenged. In a commentary accompanying the team's report in the *Proceedings of the National Academy of Sciences USA* last June, paleoanthropologists Ian Tattersall of the American Museum of Natural History in New York City and Jeffrey H. Schwartz of the University of Pittsburgh argued that Lagar Velho 1 is instead most likely "a chunky Gravettian child." The robust body proportions that Trinkaus and his colleagues view as evidence for Neandertal ancestry, Stringer says, might instead reflect adaptation to Portugal's then cold climate. But this interpretation is problematic, according to Jean-Jacques Hublin of France's CNRS, who points out that although some cold-adapted moderns exhibit such proportions, none are known from that period in Europe. Rather Hublin is troubled that Lagar Velho 1 represents a child, noting that "we do not know anything about the variation in children of a given age in this range of time."

## SURVIVAL SKILLS

Taxonomic issues aside, much research has focused on Neandertal behavior, which remained largely misunderstood until relatively recently. Neandertals were often portrayed as incapable of hunting or planning ahead, recalls archaeologist John J. Shea of the State University of New York at Stony Brook. "We've got reconstructions of Neandertals as people who couldn't survive a single winter, let alone a quarter of a million years in the worst environments in which humans ever lived," he observes. Analysis of animal remains from the Croatian site of Krapina, however, indicates that Neandertals were skilled hunters capable of killing even large animals such as rhinoceroses, according to University of Cambridge archaeologist Preston T. Miracle. And Shea's studies suggest that some Neandertals employed sophisticated stone-tipped spears to conquer their quarry—a finding supported last year when researches reported the discovery in Syria of a Neandertal-made stone point lodged in a neckbone of a prehistoric wild ass. Moreover, additional research conducted by Shea and investigations carried out by University of Arizona archaeologists Mary C. Stiner and Steven L. Kuhn have shown that Neandertal subsistence strategies varied widely with the environment and the changing seasons.

Such demonstrations refute the notion that Neandertals perished because they could not adapt. But it may be that moderns were better at it. One popular theory posits that modern humans held some cognitive advantage over Neandertals, perhaps a capacity for the most human trait of all: symbolic thought, including language. Explanations such as this one arose from observations that after 40,000 years ago, whereas Neandertal culture remained relatively static, that of modern Europeans boasted a bevy of new features, many of them symbolic. It appeared that only moderns performed elaborate burials, expressed themselves through body ornaments, figurines and cave paintings, and crafted complex bone and antler tools—an in-

# THE HYBRID CHILD FROM PORTUGAL

by Erik Trinkaus and Cidália Duarte

On a chilly afternoon in late November 1998, while inspecting the Abrigo do Lagar Velho rock-shelter in central Portugal's Lapedo Valley, two archaeology scouts spotted loose sediment in a rodent hole along the shelter's back wall. Knowing that burrowing animals often bring deeper materials to the surface, one of the scouts reached in to see what might have been unearthed. When he withdrew his hand, he held in it something extraordinary: bones of a human child buried nearly 25,000 years ago.

Subsequent excavation of the burial, led by one of us (Duarte), revealed that the four-year-old had been ceremonially interred—covered with red ocher and laid on a bed of burnt vegetation, along with pierced deer teeth and a marine shell—in the Gravettian style known from modern humans of that time across Europe. Based on the abrupt cultural transition seen in archaeological remains from the Iberian Peninsula, it seemed likely that when moderns moved into the area after 30,000 years ago, they rapidly replaced the native Neandertals. So it stood to reason that this specimen, called Lagar Velho 1, represented an early modern child. In fact, it didn't occur to us at first that it could be anything else.

This wonderfully complete skeleton does have a suite of features that align it predominantly with early modern Europeans. These include a prominent chin and certain other details of the mandible (lower jaw), small front teeth, characteristic proportions and muscle markings on the thumb, the narrowness of the front of the pelvis, and several aspects of the shoulder blade and forearm bones. Yet intriguingly, a number of features also suggest Neandertal affinities—specifically the front of the mandible (which slopes backward despite the chin), details of the incisor teeth, the pectoral muscle markings, the knee proportions and the short, strong lower-leg bones. Thus, the Lagar Velho child appears to exhibit a complex mosaic of Neandertal and early modern human features.

This anatomical amalgam is not the result of any abnormalities. Taking normal human growth patterns into consideration, our analysis indicates that except for a bruised forearm, a couple of lines on the bones indicating times when growth was trivially arrested (by sickness or lack of food) and the fact that it died as a child, Lagar Velho 1 developed normally. The combination can only have resulted from a mixed ancestry—something that had not been previously documented for western Europe. We therefore conclude that Lagar Velho 1 resulted from interbreeding between indigenous Iberian Neandertals and early modern humans dispersing throughout Iberia sometime after 30,000 years ago. Because the child lived several millennia after Neandertals are thought to have disappeared, its anatomy probably reflects a true mixing of these populations during the period when they coexisted and not a rare chance mating between a Neandertal and an early modern human.

Fieldwork conducted last summer yielded major portions of the skull and most of the remaining teeth, along with more archaeological material. And in an effort to fully understand this remarkable specimen, we have organized a team of specialists to examine the skeleton

JOSÉ PAULO B. RUAS/PORTUGUESE INSTITUTE OF ARCHAEOLOGY

**MORPHOLOGICAL MOSAIC** found on this 24,500-year-old skeleton from Portugal indicates that Neandertals and modern humans are members of the same species who interbred freely. The child—Lagar Velho 1—is modern overall but bears some Neandertal traits, such as short lower-limb bones and a backward-sloping mandible.

further. Among the projects planned are CT scan analyses of the skull and limb bones and computer-based virtual reconstruction of the damaged skull. Rigorous study is necessary because the discovery of an individual with such a mosaic of features has profound implications. First, it rejects the extreme Out of Africa model of modern human emergence, which proposes that early moderns originating in Africa subsequently displaced all archaic humans in other regions. Instead the Lagar Velho child's anatomy supports a scenario that combines a dispersal of anatomically modern humans out of Africa with mixing between that population and the archaic populations it encountered. (The African ancestry of early modern Europeans is reflected in their relatively long lower-leg bones, a tropical adaptation. Lagar Velho 1, however, has the short shins of the cold-adapted Neandertals.)

Lagar Velho 1 also provides insights into the behavioral similarities of Neandertals and early modern humans. Despite the paleontological evidence indicating anatomical differences between these two groups, their overall adaptive patterns, social behaviors and means of communication (including language) cannot have contrasted greatly. To their contemporaries, the Neandertals were just another group of Pleistocene hunter-gatherers, fully as human as themselves.

*ERIK TRINKAUS is a paleoanthropologist at Washington University.*

*CIDÁLIA DUARTE is completing her Ph.D. in physical anthropology at the University of Alberta in Canada and is the human osteologist at the Portuguese Institute of Archaeology in Lisbon.*

dustry broadly referred to as Upper Paleolithic. Neandertal assemblages, in contrast, contained only Middle Paleolithic stone tools made in the Mousterian style.

Yet hints that Neandertals thought symbolically had popped up. Neandertal burials, for example, are well known across Europe, and several, it has been argued, contain grave goods. (Other researchers maintain that for Neandertals, interment merely constituted a way of concealing the decomposing body, which might have attracted unwelcome predators. They view the purported grave goods as miscellaneous objects that happened to be swept into the grave.) Evidence for art, in the form of isolated pierced teeth and engraved bone fragments, and red and yellow ocher, has been reported from a few sites, too, but given their relative rarity, researchers tend to assign alternative explanations to these items.

The possibility that Neandertals might have engaged in modern practices was taken more seriously in 1980, when researchers reported a Neandertal from the Saint-Césaire rock-shelter in Charente-Maritime, France, found in association with stone tools manufactured according to a cultural tradition known as the Châtelperronian, which was assumed to have been the handiwork of moderns. Then, in 1996, Hublin and his colleagues made an announcement that catapulted the Châtelperronian into the archaeological limelight. Excavations that began in the late 1940s at a site called the Grotte du Renne at Arcy-sur-Cure near Auxerre, France, had yielded numerous blades, body ornaments and

bone tools and revealed evidence of huts and hearths—all hallmarks of the Upper Paleolithic. The scant human remains found amid the artifacts were impossible to identify initially, but using computer tomography to examine the hidden inner-ear region preserved inside an otherwise uninformative skull fragment, Hublin's team identified the specimen as Neandertal.

In response, a number of scientists suggested that Neandertals had acquired the modern-looking items either by stealing them, collecting artifacts discarded by moderns or perhaps trading for them. But this view has come under fire, most recently from archaeologists Francesco d'Errico of the University of Bordeaux and João Zilhão of the Portuguese Institute of Archaeology, who argue that the Châtelperronian artifacts at the Grotte du Renne and elsewhere, though superficially similar to those from the Aurignacian, reflect an older, different method of manufacture [see box "A Case for Neandertal Culture"].

Most researchers are now convinced that Neandertals manufactured the Châtelperronian tools and ornaments, but what prompted this change after hundreds of thousands of years is unclear. Cast in this light, "it's more economical to see that as a result of imitation or acculturation from modern humans than to assume that Neandertals invented it for themselves," reasons Cambridge archaeologist Paul A. Mellars. "It would be an extraordinary coincidence if they invented all these things shortly before the modern humans doing the same things arrived." Furthermore, Mellars disagrees with

d'Errico and Zilhão's proposed order of events. "The dating evidence proves to me that [Neandertals] only started to do these things after the modern humans had arrived in western Europe or at least in northern Spain," he asserts. (Unfortunately, because scientists have been unable to date these sites with sufficient precision, researchers can interpret the data differently.)

From his own work on the Grotte du Renne body ornaments, New York University archaeologist Randall White argues that these artifacts reflect manufacturing methods known—albeit at lower frequencies—from Aurignacian ornaments. Given the complicated stratigraphy of the Grotte due Renne site, the modern-looking items might have come from overlying Aurignacian levels. But more important, according to White, the Châtelperronian does not exist outside of France, Belgium, Italy and northern Spain. Once you look at the Upper Paleolithic from a pan-European perspective, he says, "the Châtelperronian becomes post-Aurignacian by a long shot."

Still, post-Aurignacian does not necessarily mean after contact with moderns. The earliest Aurignacian sites do not include any human remains. Researchers have assumed that they belonged to moderns because moderns are known from younger Aurignacian sites. But "who the Aurignacians were biologically between 40,000 and 35,000 years ago remains very much an unanswered question," White notes.

He adds that if you look at the Near East around 90,000 years ago, anatomically modern humans and Neandertals

# A CASE FOR NEANDERTAL CULTURE

by João Zilhão and Francesco d'Errico

Ever since the discovery nearly 150 years ago of the specimen that defined the Neandertals, researchers have tended to deny Neandertals the behavioral capabilities of modern humans, such as the use of symbols or of complex techniques for tool manufacture. Instead Neandertals were characterized as subhuman, stuck in primitive technical traditions impervious to innovation. And when sophisticated cultural remains were linked to late Neandertals at several sites in western Europe, the evidence was explained away. The most spectacular of these sites, a cave in north-central France named Grotte du Renne (one in a string of sites collectively known as the Arcy-sur-Cure caves), yielded a wealth of complex bone and stone tools, body ornaments and decorated objects, found in association with Neandertal remains. Other sites in France and along the Cantabrian and Pyrenean mountain ranges bore similar artifacts made in this tradition, called the Châtelperronian.

Because early modern Europeans had a comparable industry known as Aurignacian—which often appears at the same sites that contain Châtelperronian materials—some researchers have suggested that the archaeological layers were disrupted,

mixing Aurignacian artifacts into the Neandertal-associated levels. Other scholars have interpreted this to mean that Neandertals picked up these ideas from moderns, either collecting or trading for items manufactured by moderns or imitating the newcomers' practices without really grasping the underlying symbolic nature of some of the objects.

Our reassessment of the evidence from the Grotte du Renne shows that the Neandertal-associated personal ornaments and tools found there did not result from a mixing of the archaeological strata, as demonstrated by the presence of finished objects and the by-products of their manufacture in the same stratigraphic level. Moreover, the Châtelperronian artifacts recovered at the Grotte du Renne and other sites, such as Quinçay, in the Poitou-Charentes region of France, were created using techniques different from those favored by Aurignacians. With regard, for example, to the pendants—modified bear, wolf and deer teeth, among others—Neandertals carved a furrow around the tooth root so that a string of some sort could be tied around it for suspension, whereas Aurignacians pierced their pendants. As archaeologist François Lévêque and a colleague

have described, even when, as they did on occasion, Neandertals put a hole through a tooth, they took an unusual approach, puncturing the tooth. Moderns, on the other hand, preferred to scrape the tooth thin and then pierce it.

Similarly, the new knapping techniques and tool types that appear among late Neandertals at other sites in France, Italy and Spain fail to show any influence from the Aurignacian. Instead they maintain affinities with the preceding local traditions, of which they seem to represent an autonomous development.

If the Neandertals' Châtelperronian culture was an outcome of contact with moderns, then the Aurignacian should predate the Châtelperronian. Yet our reanalysis of the radiometric dates for the archaeological sequences reveals that apart from a few debatable instances of mixture, wherever both cultures are represented at the same site, the Châtelperronian always underlies the Aurignacian, suggesting its priority. Furthermore, consideration of the hundreds of datings available from this period in Europe and the Near East shows that wherever the context of the dated samples is well known, the earliest occurrences of the Aurignacian are apparently

COURTESY OF DOMINIQUE BAFFIER *(left and right panels),* FROM "LES DERNIERS NÉANDERTALIENS." LA MAISON DES ROCHES, 1999; FRANCESCO D'ERRICO *(center panel)*

**PENDANTS, BONE TOOLS AND KNIVES** from the Grotte du Renne site seem to be the handiwork of Neandertals. That the advanced items underlie early modern human cultural remains from the same site and are manufactured according to methods different from those favored by the moderns suggests that some Neandertals independently developed a modern culture.

from no earlier than around 36,500 years ago. The same radiometric data, however, indicate that by then Neandertals were already moving toward modernity on their own. In other words, the Châtelperronian and other late Neandertal cultures, such as the Uluzzian of Italy, emerged in Europe around 40,000 years ago, long before any moderns established themselves in those areas.

That this autonomous development included the manufacture and use of symbolic objects created for visual display on the body, as are often observed in traditional societies, reflects various social roles within Neandertal cultures. Thus,

"modern" behavior seems to have emerged in different regions and among different groups of humans, as would happen later in history with the invention of agriculture, writing and state society.

An alternative explanation, taking into account the broadly simultaneous appearance of personal ornaments in many parts of the Old World, is that contacts between modern and archaic humans challenged each group's personal, social and biological identities, igniting an explosion of production of symbolic objects by all those involved. On the strength of the available data, however, we favor the hypothesis of independent invention.

Regardless of which is eventually proved correct, the behavioral barrier that seemed to separate moderns from Neandertals and gave us the impression of being a unique and particularly gifted human type—the ability to produce symbolic cultures—has definitively collapsed.

*JOÃO ZILHÃO is director of the Portuguese Institute of Archaeology, Ministry of Culture, in Lisbon.*

*FRANCISCO D'ERRICO is a CNRS researcher at the Institute of Prehistory and Quaternary Geology, University of Bordeaux, in France.*

were both making Mousterian stone tools, which, though arguably less elaborate than Aurignacian tools, actually require a considerable amount of know-how. "I cannot imagine that Neandertals were producing these kinds of technologically complex tools and passing that on from generation to generation without talking about it," White declares. "I've seen a lot of people do this stuff, and I can't stand over somebody's shoulder and learn how to do it without a lot of verbal hints." Thus, White and others do not buy the argument that moderns were somehow cognitively superior, especially if Neandertals' inferiority meant that they lacked language. Instead it seems that moderns invented a culture that relied more heavily on material symbols.

Researchers have also looked to Neandertal brain morphology for clues to their cognitive ability. According to Ralph L. Holloway of Columbia University, all the brain asymmetries that characterize modern humans are found in Neandertals. "To be able to discriminate between the two," he remarks, "is, at the moment, impossible." As to whether Neandertal anatomy would have permitted speech, studies of the base of the skull conducted by Jeffrey T. Laitman of the Mount Sinai School of Medicine suggest that if they talked, Neandertals had a somewhat limited vocal repertoire. The significance of such physical constraints, however, is unclear.

## FADING AWAY

If Neandertals possessed basically the same cognitive ability as moderns, it makes their disappearance additionally puzzling. But the recent redating of Neandertal remains from Vindija cave in Croatia emphasizes that this did not happen overnight. Smith and his colleagues have demonstrated that Neandertals still lived in central Europe 28,000 years ago, thousands of years after moderns had moved in [see box "The Fate of the Neandertals"]. Taking this into consideration, Stringer imagines that moderns, whom he views as a new species, replaced Neandertals in a long, slow process. "Gradually the Neandertals lost out because moderns were a bit more innovative, a bit better able to cope with rapid environmental change quickly, and they probably had bigger social networks," he supposes.

On the other hand, if Neandertals were an equally capable variant of our own species, as Smith and Wolpoff believe, long-term overlap of Neandertals and the new population moving into Europe would have left plenty of time for mingling, hence the mixed morphology that these scholars see in late Neandertals and early moderns in Europe. And if these groups were exchanging genes, they were probably exchanging cultural ideas, which might account for some of the similarity between, say, the Châtelperronian and the Aurignacian.

Neandertals as entities disappeared, Wolpoff says, because they were outnumbered by the newcomers. Thousands of years of interbreeding between the small Neandertal population and the larger modern human population, he surmises, diluted the distinctive Neandertal features, which ultimately faded away.

"If we look at Australians a thousand years from now, we will see that the European features have predominated [over those of native Australians] by virtue of many more Europeans," Wolpoff asserts. "Not by virtue of better adaptation, not by virtue of different culture, not by virtue of anything except many more Europeans. And I really think that's what describes what we see in Europe—we see the predominance of more people."

From the morass of opinions in this notoriously contentious field, one consensus emerges: researchers have retired the old vision of the shuffling, cultureless Neandertal. Beyond that, whether these ancient hominids were among the ancestors of living people or a very closely related species that competed formidably with our own for the Eurasian territory and eventually lost remains to be seen. In either case, the details will most likely be extraordinarily complicated. "The more we learn, the more questions arise, the knottier it gets," muses archaeologist Lawrence G. Straus of the University of New Mexico. "That's why simple explanations just don't cut it."

# THE FATE OF THE NEANDERTALS

by Fred H. Smith

Strong evidence has accumulated in recent years that the emergence of modern humans in Europe resulted largely from the immigration of peoples into the continent, probably from the Near East, starting sometime between 40,000 and 30,000 years ago. Most researchers envision these early modern populations as having moved into Anatolia and the Balkans, then up through the plains and valleys of central Europe, and finally into northern and western Europe. Meanwhile the indigenous Neandertals, it was thought, were systematically pushed into more peripheral and undesirable parts of the landscape by these expanding populations of moderns. The Neandertals' last bastion appeared to be the Iberian Peninsula, where fossils from a Spanish site called Zafarraya have been dated to 32,000 years ago and tools attributed to Neandertals have been dated to around 28,000 years ago. Many scholars argued that after

this time no traces of Neandertals remained in Europe and that Neandertals did not make any biological contributions to early modern humans. It seemed that Neandertals were sent into complete extinction by a superior human species—us.

Now new evidence from an important site in northwestern Croatia calls aspects of this conventional wisdom into question. By performing accelerator mass spectrometry dating directly on two Neandertal specimens from Vindija cave, my colleagues and I have demonstrated that Neandertals were living in some of the most desirable real estate in central Europe as late as 28,000 years ago. These dates, the most recent known for Neandertal fossils, show that these humans were not quickly relegated to the periphery; they competed quite well with intruding modern populations for a long time.

This overlap of Neandertal and early modern peoples for several millennia in

the heart of Europe allowed considerable opportunity for various interactions, and Vindija may reflect some of them. Work by my Croatian colleagues Ivor Karavanic of the University of Zagreb and Jakov Radovcic of the Croatian Natural History museum has revealed a combination of Mousterian and Aurignacian tools in the same stratigraphic level as the dated Neandertal fossils, suggesting that Neandertals either made advanced implements or traded with moderns for them. Morphologically, the Vindija Neandertals look more modern than do most other Neandertals, which suggests that their ancestors interbred with early moderns.

The likelihood of gene flow between the groups is also supported by evidence that Neandertals left their mark on early modern Europeans. Fossils representing early modern adults from central European sites such as Vogelherd in southwestern Germany and Mladec in Moravia (Czech

SUSAN CARLSON

**MOVEMENT OF MODERNS** into Europe did not displace the Neandertals, who were still living in central and western Europe 28,000 years ago. A number of the early modern European specimens bear some Neandertal features, which suggests that during the long period of overlap the two populations mixed.

Republic) have features that are difficult to explain unless they have some Neandertal contribution to their ancestry. For example, Neandertals and early modern Europeans virtually all exhibit a projection of the back of the skull called an occipital bun (aspects of the shape and position of the buns differ between them because the overall skull shapes are not the same). Yet fossils from the Near Eastern sites of Skhul and Qafzeh, which presumably represent the ancestors of early modern Europeans, do not have this morphology. It is hard to explain how the growth phenomenon responsible for this bunning could reappear independently and could reappear independently and ubiquitously in early modern Europeans. Instead it is far more logical to recognize this morphology as a link to the Neandertals. The Portuguese child discovered recently offers more intriguing clues [see box "The Hybrid Child from Portugal"].

I believe the evidence shows that the behavioral and biological interactions between Neandertal and early modern human populations were very complex—too complex for the origins of modern humans in Europe to have involved a simple, complete biological replacement of the Neandertals. Neandertals as organisms no longer exist, and Neandertal genes may not have persisted to the present day, but those genes were there in the beginnings of modern European biological history.

*FRED H. SMITH is chairman of the department of anthropology at Northern Illinois University.*

# Fate of the Neandertals

*Our robust cousins interbred with modern humans, a preeminent European archaeologist argues.*

## by JOÃO ZILHÃO

The bones of a four-year-old child, buried for millennia in the rear of a rock-shelter in the Lapedo Valley 85 miles north of Lisbon, Portugal, comprised the first complete Palaeolithic skeleton ever dug in Iberia. Our November 28, 1998, find made national news, but an even greater surprise was in store when my colleague, Washington University anthropologist Erik Trinkaus, who measured the bones weeks after the discovery, reported that the child's anatomy could only have resulted from a mixed Neandertal-early modern human ancestry. Here, finally, was proof that Neandertals did not simply disappear from Europe 28,000 years ago. Instead, they interbred with modern humans and became part of our family.

The discovery was made by João Maurício and Pedro Souto, archaeology field assistants and members of a local archaeology group, who visited the valley at my request to check on reports that a student from a nearby village had found some prehistoric paintings. The reports turned out to be genuine. The student showed them a few small, red anthropomorphic figures in a style characteristic of the Copper Age (fourth and third millennia B.C.) painted on the back wall of a shallow rock-shelter on the north side of the valley.

While they were there, João and Pedro decided to inspect a larger shelter they saw on the opposite side of the valley. When they go there, the first thing they noticed was that archaeological deposits in the shelter had recently been destroyed; we later learned that in 1992 the landowner had bulldozed the upper six to nine feet of the shelter's fill to widen a rural trail used to reach property located farther up the valley. All that was left was a foot-and-a-half remnant of the original deposit in a fissure running along most of the length of the shelter's back wall. This remnant corresponds to a section of the original stratigraphic sequence lying between two and three feet below the former ground surface.

The remnant was extremely rich in charcoal, stone tools, and animal remains, including fossilized horse teeth, all suggesting an Upper Palaeolithic age (between 30,000 and 10,000 years ago) for the site. While collecting surface material that had fallen from the remnant, João and Pedro inspected a recess in the back wall. In the loose sediments they recovered several small bones stained with red ochre they thought could be human. Recognizing the potential signifi-

João Zilhão © Instituto Português Arqueologia

**The Lagar Velho child must have been wrapped in a shroud of red ochre-painted animal skin, whose decay caused the transfer of mineral pigment to the skeleton and sediment.**

Reprinted with the permission of *Archaeology* magazine, Vol. 53, No. 4, July/August 2000, pp. 24-31. © 2000 by the Archaeological Institute of America.

cance of the discovery, they stopped investigating and reported their finds to me.

The following weekend, on December 6, I went to the site with my colleagues Cristina Araújo, a fellow archaeologist, and Cidália Duarte, a bioarchaeologist specializing in burial taphonomy (how bodies are buried and preserved). João and Pedro presented their finds and two things almost immediately became clear. First, the bones they thought could be human were indeed the left forearm and hand bones of a young child. Second, stone tools found in the fissure dated the deposit to the Middle Solutrean and the Proto-Solutrean, that is, the period between 20,000 and 22,000 years ago. Since the juvenile human bones that lay some nine feet below this remnant belonged to a single individual and were very well preserved, the implication was obvious: a child had

been buried at the site either in late Middle Palaeolithic or in early Upper Palaeolithic times, between 40,000 and 25,000 years ago. The ochre staining of the bones (a feature of all burials from the Gravettian period between 25,000 and 27,000 years ago) and rough estimates of the rate of sedimentation at the site led us to believe that a date closer to 25,000 years ago was more likely.

This conclusion prompted me to start a salvage excavation of the site, which we called the Lagar Velho rock-shelter after the ruin of an ancient olive-oil press at its entrance. The excavation began on December 12, 1998, continuing without interruption through Christmas and the New Year until January 7, 1999. Subsequently, in July and August, deep testing of the preserved deposits under the burial and in

the central part of the shelter further documented the site's stratigraphy. The surface of the site was also excavated and extensively screened, enabling the recovery of many of the child's missing teeth and skull fragments. We realized the bulldozer had come within an inch or two of the skeleton, leaving it miraculously intact except for the skull, which had been crushed into more than 100 pieces. The presence of ancient fractures in the cranial fragments suggests that natural processes had collapsed it inward not long after burial, but fresh breaks show that further fragmentation occurred when the site was bulldozed, scattering skull fragments east of the burial.

The broken left side of the child's lower jaw, including the chin region, had been recovered at the outset in a very thin layer of disturbed deposits overlying the burial. The chin featured the characteristic "snowplow" shape found in Cro-Magnon people, the first anatomically modern humans, whose appearance on the European continent coincides with the disappearance of Neandertals. The day after that lower jaw was recovered, discovery of a pierced marine shell of the species *Littorina obtusata*, the most common ornament in the Upper Palaeolithic of Portugal, reinforced the hypothesis that this was an early Upper Palaeolithic burial. The shell was found near the neck vertebrae, suggesting that the dead child was wearing it as a pendant when he was buried. As the excavation continued, we were able to uncover a nearly complete, *in situ* skeleton (minus an intact skull), and establish that the body had been laid on its back, left side parallel to the cliff base, head to the east, feet crossed. Four red deer (*Cervus elaphus*) canines pierced through the root were found with the cranial remains. They suggest that the child was buried with some kind of decorated head wear. Pierced red deer canines

Courtesy João Zilhão

**View of the Lagar Velho rock-shelter. Right, archaeologists Cidália Duarte and Cristina Araújo excavated the child's skeleton.**

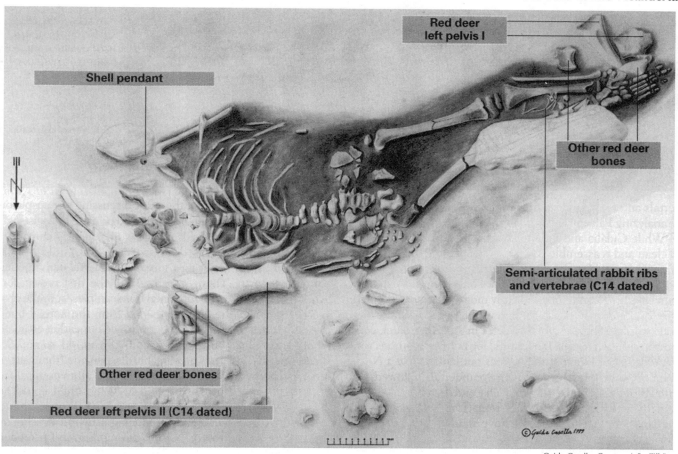

Drawing of the Lagar Velho child's grave shows the skeleton and location of offerings.

Guida Casella: Courtesy João Zilhão

have also been found on the skulls of Gravettian period people buried in Italy and Moravia.

*The chin featured the characteristic "snow-plow" shape found in Cro-Magnon people, the first anatomically modern humans, whose appearance on the European continent coincides with the disappearance of Neandertals.*

The skeleton, especially the skull pieces, were heavily stained with red ochre as was the sediment in which the bones lay. This, and the fact that both the upper and the lower surfaces of the bones were stained, indicates that the body must have been wrapped in a shroud of ochre-painted skin, whose subsequent decay caused the transfer of the mineral pigment to the skeleton and sediment. The presence of a semi-rigid durable wrap around the body would also have provided the space for the post-mortem collapse of the child's ankle ligaments, evident in the position of the feet. At the base of the pit, immediately below and in contact with the child's legs, there was a think black lens of charcoal, which belonged to a single branch of Scots pine. This suggests that a ritual fire was lit before the deposition of the body; the adjacent deposits contained no traces of charcoal.

Red deer bones found in association with the burial pit are distinct from those found in the surrounding and immediately underlying sediments. The latter present eroded surfaces, have a shine suggesting they were chewed and digested by carnivores, often display actual teeth punctures, and are associated with coprolites. In contrast, the deer bones found by the head and feet of the child's skeleton are well preserved, show no evidence of being mauled by carnivores, were in direct contact with the body, and provided a C14 date showing contemporaneity with the burial. Furthermore, no artifacts or other evidence of habitation were recovered at this level in this part of the shelter. The simplest explanation is that these bones belonged to parts of deer carcasses deposited in the grave as food offerings. The same may be true of the rabbit bones that overlay the child's right leg (three vertebrae, four ribs, and one sacrum fragment). They were also stained red, and two of the ribs were complete, suggesting that they were originally joined to the vertebrae.

Throughout the 1998–1999 salvage work we were able to count on the invaluable advice of Erik Trinkaus, to whom I e-mailed digital pictures of the

This pierced shell was found near the child's neck vertebrae, suggesting that it had been worn as a pendant. The four red deer canines, possibly head-wear decorations, were found nearly ten feet from the burial with fragments of the child's skull.
José Paulo Ruas © Instituto Portugués Arqueologia

excavation daily. Realizing the potential significance of the burial, Cidália Duarte and I invited him to the site to study the skeleton. An authority on Neandertals and early modern humans, Erik was already involved in analyzing Palaeolithic human material from Portugal.

While Cidália and I completed the fieldwork, Erik began to clean and reassemble the skeleton and work toward a preliminary anatomical description. After returning to the United States, he was able to compare the bones with his extensive data base on Neandertals and early modern humans. On January 25, I got a message from him which began with the ominous words: "The end of last week I made some quick comparisons of the Lagar Velho [child's] leg bone proportions with some data that I have, and it comes out looking like a Neandertal!" Other resemblances with Neandertals followed, but throughout this initial stage Cidália and I kept in mind Erik's cautionary remark in that first message: "unless I have made some silly mistake."

We decided to check and double check all the measurements ourselves, and eventually concluded that Erik had made no mistake—the child did present a mosaic of Neandertal and modern human features. Most prominent among the former, the arctic body proportions (with short limbs, especially the lower parts of the arms and legs), the robusticity of the limb bones and the angle at which the jaw bones meet at the chin; among the latter, the characteristic "snow-plow" chin and the size of the dentition. Body proportions are particularly important in this regard because the study of present-day populations has proved that they are genetically inher-

ited and that the basic patterns of body shape are already established in the fetal state of development. This makes it possible to compare the bones of the Lagar Velho child not only with those of other children but also with available adult skeletons from the same time period. Among the two possible ancestral populations of the group to which this child belonged, it is well-established that all Neandertals had arctic body proportions.

---

*We all grew increasingly convinced: the child possessed an anatomy that could only be explained as the result of a mixed Neandertal-early modern human ancestry.*

---

On the contrary, all European early modern humans had tropical body proportions (long limbs), betraying their recent (in evolutionary time) African origin, in spite of the fact that they had been living for many millennia in the very cold steppe-tundra environments then present throughout the unglaciated parts of the continent located north of the Pyrenees.

In the following months, after discussing our suspicions with human palaeontologists and primate biologists who study natural hybrids, we grew increasingly convinced; the child possessed an anatomy that could only be explained as the result of a mixed Neandertal-early modern human ances-

try. Then, in early April, the first radiocarbon results started to arrive. Obtained from samples from the charcoal lens under the child's legs and from the animal bones associated with the grave, they confirmed our earlier estimates that the age of the burial was ca. 25,000 years old, some 3,000 years after Neandertals presumably disappeared from western Iberia. This made it clear that the mosaic of anatomical features in the Lagar Velho child could not have been the result of a rare, chance encounter producing a hybrid descendant from a Neandertal mother and a modern human father (or vice versa). On the contrary, it had to represent a mixture of populations. Put another way, Neandertals had not simply disappeared without descendants, they had been absorbed, through extensive interbreeding, into the modern human groups that had started to take over Iberia ca. 30,000 years ago. They had contributed to the gene pool of subsequent early Upper Palaeolithic populations of the peninsula and, therefore, had to be counted among our ancestors: they were family.

This conclusion contrasts with the prevailing view of the Neandertals as an evolutionary dead end, a side branch of the human tree, that has become so popular in the wake of the Eve hypothesis based on mitochondrial DNA (mtDNA). First proposed in 1987, this hypothesis states that Europeans descended entirely from anatomically modern human populations that gradually evolved in Africa from an ancestral *Homo erectus* stock after 250,000 years ago. Having begun to spread from there to the rest of the world some 50,000 years ago, these anatomically modern groups eventually replaced, without admixture, all indigenous anatomically archaic human forms of Eurasia. Thus, Neandertals became extinct with no descendants.

This view received strong support from the publication, in 1997, by Svante Pääbo of the University of Munich and his colleagues, of a comparison between mtDNA extracted from the original Feldhofer Cave Neandertal type specimen found in 1856 and that of present-day human populations. It inferred that the difference was so significant as to put Neandertals outside the range of modern humanity, suggesting that they had belonged to an altogether different biological species and that interbreeding, although conceivable, could not have been significant. Possible support for this view comes from the mtDNA analysis of the rib of a 29,000-year-old fetal or neo-natal skeleton from Mezmaiskaya Cave, in the northern Caucasus, recently published in the journal *Nature*. The significance of the latter, however, remains to be seen. It is reported as a Neandertal infant, but its classification is in fact uncertain.

Analysis of the Lagar Velho child's mtDNA would certainly help to test our interpretation. Unfortunately, this is likely to be impossible, due to the chemical weathering undergone by the child's fragile bones. However, as we prepared the preliminary publication of the burial and of our interpretation of the child's anatomy, the journal to which we had submitted it (*Proceedings of the National Academy of Sciences USA*) published a major paper on the variability of the DNA of African apes, our closest living relatives. This work showed that contemporary interbreeding populations of chimpanzees are genetically more diverse than modern humans and our Late Pleistocene fossil ancestors, including the one Neandertal specimen Pääbo analyzed. By primate standards, therefore, the results obtained by Pääbo's team indicated that present-day humans ought to be considered abnormally homogeneous. This low DNA variability is consistent with a single recent origin for modern humans (the Out-of-Africa model), but does not imply that Neandertals were a different

Courtesy Francesco d'Errico

Bone tube of a swan's left wing, left interior, manufactured by Neandertals at the Grotte due Renne in Burgundy, France, provide unequivocal evidence for local production of the bone tools—not traded with or scavenged from modern humans. Decorated bird-bond tubes (far left) and bone awls (top) indicate that symbolism was not imported but permeated all aspects of life in late Neandertal society. In most late Neandertal ornaments a furrow was carved around tooth roots, below, which were punctured then smoothed and the perforation enlarged. The earliest European modern humans, on the other hand, always pierced their teeth pendants by first scraping them thin.

species. It simply confirms, from genetic data, what palaeontologists have established for about a century on the basis of fossil bones: that Neandertals, as a separate, well-defined geographic variant of humanity that became differentiated during the Middle Pleistocene, are now extinct. That does not mean that they did not contribute to the gene pool of subsequent populations. The Lagar Velho child's anatomical mosaic suggests that they did, even if such a contribution eventually became so diluted as to become unrecognizable today.

Recent developments in the archaeology of the last Neandertals and the earliest modern humans in Europe point to a similar conclusion. Ever since the original Neander Valley fossil was discovered, most researchers have doubted that the Neandertals were capable of using symbols or manufacturing complex bone and ivory objects. While modern humans are thought to have created cave art and delicate carvings and to have engaged in specialized hunting, Neandertals have been viewed as scavengers or opportunistic hunters. When cultural remains found in late Neandertal sites suggested otherwise, the evidence was dismissed.

The earliest modern humans in Europe are associated with characteristic stone and bone tool-kits, called Aurignacian, whose first appearance in the archaeological record has been assumed for the last decade to date to ca. 40,000 years ago. In France and northern Spain, local Neandertals were thought to have copied some of the stone and bone tools of their new neighbors, the Aurignacian moderns, as well as their personal ornaments, giving rise to a new Neandertal cultural entity, the Châtelperronian. It was argued, however, that such an imitation would have been carried out with no real understanding of the underlying symbolic meaning of the objects.

Other kinds of explanations postulated post-depositional disturbance of sites to deny Neandertals any role in the

A warming period between 50,000 and 30,000 years ago hastened the migration of modern humans into Europe from Africa and the Near East. Modern humans prevailed over scattered populations of Neandertals possibly because of higher rates of fertility. By 30,000 years ago, Neandertals were reduced to small pockets of Europe. Aurignacian refers to a tool-kit developed by early modern humans ca. 36,000 years ago, Châtelperronian to a kit used by late Neandertals. The terms Middle and Upper Palaeolithic on these maps refer to stages of cultural development.

manufacture of those items. Scholars such as Yvette Taborin of the University of Paris I and Randall White of New York University, for instance, suggested that the presence of personal ornaments and bone tools at the key site of Grotte du Renne, in Burgandy, France, would have been the result of a mixing of archaeological strata. Others, such as

Jean-Jacques Hublin of Paris' Musée de l'Homme and Paul Mellars of Cambridge University suggested as an alternative explanation that such a presence might be due to Neandertals having collected or traded for objects manufactured by neighboring moderns.

The reassessment of the evidence from Grotte du Renne by Francesco d'Errico of the University of Bordeaux I, myself, and other colleagues showed that Châtelperronian Neandertals were indeed the makers of the personal ornaments and bone tools found there. Moreover, the grooved or perforated teeth of fox, wolf, bear, hyena, red deer, horse, marmot, bear, and reindeer recovered at the Grotte du Renne and other sites (such as Quinçay, in the Charente, France) were made with techniques different from those used by Aurignacian modern humans. The same is true of the different knapping techniques and tool types that appear among late Neandertals in various regions of Europe. These innovations everywhere fail to show any influence from the Aurignacian, while maintaining affinities with preceding Neandertal traditions.

D'Errico and I have also closely examined the archaeological record to verify whether the arrival of early modern humans in western Europe did indeed predate these Neandertal innovations, as had to be the case if the emergence of the innovations had been triggered by contact with the newcomers. We found, however, that wherever archaeological layers of both cultures are represented at the same sites, the Châtelperronian always underlies the Aurignacian. Similarly, research on hundreds of radiometric datings available for this period in Europe and the Near East shows that, wherever the context of the dated samples is well established, the first Aurignacian ones date to no earlier than ca. 36,500 years ago. The radiometric data, however, indicate that, by then, Neandertals had already accomplished their own transition to behavioral modernity. In other words, there is no doubt that the Châtelperronian and other late Neandertal cultures emerged in Europe well before any modern humans established themselves in neighboring areas.

This autonomous development included the manufacture and use of symbolic objects created for visual display on the body that reflected, as often observed in present-day traditional societies, different social roles. It is also at about 40,000 years ago that the earliest evidence for personal ornaments appears in the anatomically modern human populations of eastern and southern Af-

rica. Thus, "modern" behavior seems to have appeared independently in different regions and among different groups of humans, much as would happen later in history with the invention of agriculture, writing, and social organization. On the strength of available data, our hypothesis that late Neandertal groups invented their own tools and ornaments is firmly supported. The notion that we were the only human type capable of developing a symbolic culture has collapsed.

---

*Even if we can't see it in today's Europeans, the Lagar Velho child's anatomy suggests that Neandertals did contribute to the gene pool of the continent's earliest modern humans.*

---

If the two groups did not represent biologically different species and had attained a similar level of cultural achievement, why then did modern humans prevail? Why was it that the immigrants absorbed the locals and not the other way around? These are the really interesting questions for archaeologists and geneticists to ask. Biogeographic and demographic explanations may provide the answers. In the Pleistocene period, under climatic conditions much colder than today's, most of Eurasia was uninhabitable. The northernmost areas were covered by ice sheets and barren tundras, and population densities in the settled areas must have been much lower than in Africa. Erik Trinkaus' palaeodemographic analysis of Neandertal remains reveals those populations were highly unstable. Therefore, it is quite likely that between 100,000 and 40,000 years ago a large majority of all the planet's human beings lived in Africa, where the modern morphological form evolved.

If these African groups also had a higher fertility, as is commonly the case with warm climate populations of the

same species when compared with those from colder climates, we can plausibly explain what happened. Africans started to disperse into the neighboring regions, a process that must have been hastened by a warming period between ca. 50,000 and ca. 30,000 years ago, during which the savannas of eastern Africa, and their faunas, spread into the Middle East. Given enough time, even a very small difference in fertility would put the much smaller and more scattered populations of Neandertals at a demographic disadvantage, especially if interbreeding were common.

Once modern humans became established throughout most of the European continent, their absorption of remnant Neandertal populations was just a matter of time. Radiometric data suggest that isolated Neandertal communities existed until quite late, not only in Iberia, where the evidence is the strongest, but also in Croatia and Crimea. In the case of southwestern Europe, the Ebro River in northern Spain seems to have represented some sort of biocultural "frontier" separating Aurignacian modern humans established north of the Cantabrian-Pyrenean mountains since ca. 36,500 years ago from Neandertals surviving south of them until ca. 28,000 years ago. That Neandertals held on for so long shows just how well-adapted they must have been. No wonder that, when modern humans started to cross that "frontier," they saw them as fellow human beings and interbred, as demonstrated by the Lagar Velho child.

If, for our anatomically modern ancestors, Neandertals were just people—perhaps a little funny-looking, but people nonetheless—why should we believe otherwise and persist, against all available biological and cultural evidence, in trying to put them in an entirely different category?

---

JOÃO ZILHÃO is director-general of the Instituto Português de Arqueologia, the department of the Ministry of Culture that supervises all archaeological activity in Portugal.

# Archaeologists Rediscover Cannibals

*At digs around the world, researchers have unearthed strong new evidence that people ate their own kind from the early days of human evolution through recent prehistory*

When Arizona State University bioarchaeologist Christy G. Turner II first looked at the jumbled heap of bones from 30 humans in Arizona in 1967, he was convinced that he was looking at the remains of a feast. The bones of these ancient American Indians had cut marks and burns, just like animal bones that had been roasted and stripped of their flesh. "It just struck me that here was a pile of food refuse," says Turner, who proposed in *American Antiquity* in 1970 that these people from Polacca Wash, Arizona, had been the victims of cannibalism.

But his paper was met with "total disbelief," says Turner. "In the 1960s, the new paradigm about Indians was that they were all peaceful and happy. So, to find something like this was the antithesis of the new way we were supposed to be thinking about Indians"—particularly the Anasazi, thought to be the ancestors of living Pueblo Indians. Not only did Turner's proposal fly in the face of conventional wisdom about the Anasazi culture, but it was also at odds with an emerging consensus that earlier claims of cannibalism in the fossil record rested on shaky evidence. Where earlier generations of archaeologists had seen the remains of cannibalistic feasts, current researchers saw bones scarred by ancient burial practices, war, weathering, or scavenging animals.

To Turner, however, the bones from Polacca Wash told a more disturbing tale, and so he set about studying every prehistoric skeleton he could find in the Southwest and Mexico to see if it was an isolated event. Now, 30 years and 15,000 skeletons later, Turner is putting the final touches on a 1500-page book to be published next year by the University of Utah press in which he says, "Cannibalism was practiced intensively for almost four centuries" in the Four Corners region. The evidence is so strong that Turner says "I would bet a year of my salary on it."

He isn't the only one now betting on cannibalism in prehistory. In the past decade, Turner and other bioarchaeologists have put together a set of clear-cut criteria for distinguishing the marks of

PHOTOS BY: C. TURNER/BERKELEY

**Cannibals' house?** The Peñasco Blanco great house at Chaco Canyon, New Mexico, where some bones bear cut marks (*upper left*); others were smashed, perhaps to extract marrow.

cannibalism from other kinds of scars. "The analytical rigor has increased across the board," says paleoanthropologist Tim D. White of the University of California, Berkeley. Armed with the new criteria, archaeologists are finding what they say are strong signs of cannibalism throughout the fossil record. This summer, archaeologists are excavating several sites in Europe where the practice may have occurred among our ancestors, perhaps as early as 800,000 years ago. More recently, our brawny cousins, the Neandertals, may have eaten each other. And this behavior wasn't limited to the distant past—strong new evidence suggests that in addition to the Anasazi, the Aztecs of Mexico and the people of Fiji also ate their own kind in the past 2500 years.

These claims imply a disturbing new view of human history, say Turner and others. Although cannibalism is still relatively rare in the fossil record, it is frequent enough to imply that extreme hunger was not the only driving force. Instead of being an aberration, practiced only by a few prehistoric Donner Parties, killing people for food may have been standard human behavior—a means of social control, Turner suspects, or a mob response to stress, or a form of infanticide to thin the ranks of neighboring populations.

Not surprisingly, some find these claims hard to stomach: "These people haven't explored all the alternatives," says archaeologist Paul Bahn, author of the *Cambridge Encyclopedia* entry on cannibalism. "There's no question, for example, that all kinds of weird stuff is done to human remains in mortuary practice"—and in warfare. But even the most prominent skeptic of earlier claims of cannibalism, cultural anthropologist William Arens of the State University of New York, Stony Brook, now admits the case is stronger: "I think the procedures are sounder, and there is more evidence for cannibalism than before."

White learned how weak most earlier scholarship on cannibalism was in 1981, when he first came across what he thought might be a relic of the practice—a massive skull of an early human ancestor from a site called Bodo in Ethiopia. When he got his first look at this 600,000-year-old skull

on a museum table, White noticed that it had a series of fine, deep cuts marks on its cheekbone and inside its eye socket, as if it had been defleshed. To confirm his suspicions, White wanted to compare the marks with a "type collection" for cannibalism—a carefully studied assemblage of bones showing how the signature of cannibalism differs from damage by animal gnawing, trampling, or excavation.

T. D. WHITE/BERKELEY
**Unkind cuts. A Neandertal bone from Vindija Cave, Croatia.**

"We were naïve at the time," says White, who was working with archaeologist Nicholas Toth of Indiana University in Bloomington. They learned that although the anthropological literature was full of fantastic tales of cannibalistic feasts among early humans at Zhoukoudian in China, Krapina cave in Croatia, and elsewhere, the evidence was weak—or lost.

Indeed, the weakness of the evidence had already opened the way to a backlash, which was led by Arens. He had deconstructed the fossil and historical record for cannibalism in a book called *The Man-Eating Myth: Anthropology and Anthropophagy* (Oxford, 1979). Except for extremely rare cases of starvation or insanity, Arens said, none of the accounts of cannibalism stood up to scrutiny—not even claims that it took place among living tribes in Papua New Guinea (including the Fore, where cannibalism is thought to explain the spread of the degenerative brain disease kuru). There were no reliable eye witnesses for claims of cannibalism, and the archae-

ological evidence was circumstantial. "I didn't deny the existence of cannibalism," he now says, "but I found that there was no good evidence for it. It was bad science."

Physical anthropologists contributed to the backlash when they raised doubts about what little archaeological evidence there was (*Science,* 20 June 1986, p. 1479). Mary Russell, then at Case Western Reserve University in Cleveland, argued, for example, that cut marks on the bones of 20 Neandertals at Krapina Cave could have been left by Neandertal morticians who were cleaning the bones for secondary burial, and the bones would have been smashed when the roof caved in, for example. In his 1992 review in the *Cambridge Encyclopedia,* Bahn concluded that cannibalism's "very existence in prehistory is hard to swallow."

## Rising from the ashes

But even as some anthropologists have the ax to Krapina and other notorious cases, a new, more rigorous case for cannibalism in prehistory was emerging, starting in the American Southwest. Turner and his late wife, Jacqueline Turner, had been systematically studying tray after tray of prehistoric bones in museums and private collections in the United States and Mexico. They had identified a pattern of bone processing in several hundred specimens that showed little respect for the dead. "There's no known mortuary practice in the Southwest where the body is dismembered, the head is roasted and dumped into a pit unceremoniously, and other pieces get left all over the floor," says Turner, describing part of the pattern.

White, meanwhile, was identifying other telltale signs. To fill the gap he discovered when he looked for specimens to compare with the Bodo skull, he decided to study in depth one of the bone assemblages the Turners and others had cited. He chose Mancos, a small Anasazi pueblo on the Colorado Plateau from A.D. 1150, where archaeologists had recovered the scattered and broken remains of at least 29 individuals. The project evolved into a landmark book,

*Prehistoric Cannibalism at Mancos* (Princeton, 1992). While White still doesn't know why the Bodo skull was defleshed—"it's a black box," he says—he extended the blueprint for identifying cannibalism.

In his book, White describes how he painstakingly sifted through 2106 bone fragments, often using an electron microscope to identify cut marks, burn traces, percussion and anvil damage, disarticulations, and breakages. He reviewed how to distinguish marks left by butchering from those left by animal gnawing, trampling, or other wear and tear. He also proposed a new category of bone damage, which he called "pot

T. D. WHITE/BERKELEY

**Close shave.** Was flesh stripped from the 600,000-year-old Bodo skull in an act of cannibalism?

polish"—shiny abrasions on bone tips that come from being stirred in pots (an idea he tested by stirring deer bones in a replica of an Anasazi pot). And he outlined how to compare the remains of suspected victims with those of ordinary game animals at other sites to see if they were processed the same way.

When he applied these criteria to the Mancos remains, he concluded that they were the leavings of a feast in which 17 adults and 12 children had their heads cut off, roasted, and broken open on rock anvils. Their long bones were broken—he believes for marrow—and their vertebral bodies were missing, perhaps crushed and boiled for oil. Finally, their bones were dumped, like animal bones.

In their forthcoming book, the Turners describe a remarkably similar pattern of bone processing in 300 individuals from 40 different bone assemblages in the Four Corners area of the Southwest, dating from A.D. 900 to A.D. 1700. The strongest case, he says, comes from bones unearthed at the Peñasco Blanco great house at Chaco Canyon in New Mexico, which was the highest center of the Anasazi culture and, he argues, the home of cannibals who terrorized victims within 100 miles of Chaco Canyon, where most of the traumatized bones have been excavated. "Whatever drove the Anasazi to eat people, it happened at Chaco," says Turner.

The case for cannibalism among the Anasazi that Turner and White have put together hasn't swayed all the critics. "These folks have a nice package, but I don't think it proves cannibalism," says Museum of New Mexico archaeologist Peter Bullock. "It's still just a theory."

But even critics like Bullock acknowledge that Turner and White's studies, along with work by the University of Colorado, Boulder's, Paolo Villa and colleagues at another recent site, Fontbrégoua Cave in southeastern France (*Science,* 25 July 1986, p. 431), have raised the standards for how to investigate a case of cannibalism. In fact, White's book has become the unofficial guidebook for the field, says physical anthropologist Carmen Pijoan at the Museum of Anthropology in Mexico City, who has done a systematic review of sites in Mexico where human bones were defleshed. In a forthcoming book chapter, she singles out three sites where she applied diagnostic criteria outlined by Turner, White, and Villa to bones from Aztec and other early cultures and concludes that all "three sites, spread over 2000 years of Mexican prehistory, show a pattern of violence, cannibalism, and sacrifice through time."

White's book "is my bible," agrees paleontologist Yolanda Fernandez-Jalvo of the Museum of Natural History in Madrid, who is analyzing bones that may be the oldest example of cannibalism in the fossil record—the remains of at least six individuals who died 800,000 years ago in an ancient cave at Atapuerca in northern Spain.

## Age-old practices

The Spanish fossils have caused considerable excitement because they may represent a new species of human ancestor (*Science,* 30 May, pp. 1331 and 1392). But they also show a pattern familiar from the more recent sites: The bones are highly fragmented and are scored with cut marks, which Fernandez-Jalvo thinks were made when the bodies were decapitated and the bones defleshed. A large femur was also smashed open, perhaps for marrow, says Fernandez-Jalvo, and the whole assemblage had been dumped, like garbage. The treatment was no different from that accorded animal bones at the site. The pattern, says Peter Andrews, a paleoanthropologist at The Natural History Museum, London, is "pretty strong evidence for cannibalism, as opposed to ritual defleshing." He and others note, however, that the small number of individuals at the site and the absence of other sites of similar antiquity to which the bones could be compared leave room for doubt.

A stronger case is emerging at Neandertal sites in Europe, 45,000 to more than 130,000 years old. The new criteria for recognizing cannibalism have not completely vindicated the earlier claims about Krapina Cave, partly because few animal bones are left from the excavation of the site in 1899 to compare with the Neandertal remains. But nearby Vindija Cave, excavated in the 1970s, did yield both animal and human remains. When White and Toth examined the bones recently, they found that both sets showed cut marks, breakage, and disarticulation, and had been dumped on the cave floor. It's the same pattern seen at Krapina, and remarkably similar to that at Mancos, says White, who will publish his conclusions in a forthcoming book with Toth. Marseilles prehistorian Alban DeFleur is finding that Neandertals may also have feasted on their kind in the Moula-Guercy Cave in the Ardeche region of France, where animal and Neandertal bones show similar processing. Taken together, says White, "the evidence from Krapina, Vindija, and Moula is strong."

Not everyone is convinced, however. "White does terrific analysis, but he hasn't proved this is cannibalism," says Bahn. "Frankly, I don't see how he can unless you find a piece of human gut [with human bone or tissue in it]." No matter how close the resemblance to butchered animals, he says, the cut marks and other bone processing could still be the result of mortuary practices. Bullock adds that warfare, not cannibalism, could explain the damage to the bones.

White, however, says such criticism resembles President Clinton's famous claim about marijuana: "Some [although not all] of the Anasazi and Neandertals processed their colleagues. They skinned them, roasted them, cut their muscles off, severed their joints, broke their long bones on anvils with hammerstones, crushed their spongy bones, and put the pieces into pots." Borrowing a line from a review of his book, White says: "To say they didn't eat them is the archaeological equivalent of saying Clinton lit up and didn't inhale."

White's graduate student David DeGusta adds that he has compared human bones at burial sites in Fiji and at a nearby trash midden from the last 2000 years. The intentionally buried bones were less fragmentary and had no bite marks, burns, percussion pits, or other signs of food processing. The human bones in the trash midden, however, were processed like those of pigs. "This site really challenges the claim that these assemblages of bones are the result of mortuary ritual," says DeGusta.

After 30 years of research, Turner says it is a modern bias to insist that cannibalism isn't part of human nature. Many other species eat their own, and our ancestors may have had their own "good" reasons—whether to terrorize subject peoples, limit their neighbors' offspring, or for religious or medicinal purposes. "Today, the only people who eat other people outside of starving are the crazies," says Turner. "We're dealing with a world view that says this is bad and always has been bad. . . . But in the past, that view wasn't necessarily the group view. Cannibalism could have been an adaptive strategy. It has to be entertained."

—Ann Gibbons

# Unit 6

## Unit Selections

32. **The Lost Man,** Douglas Preston
33. **Black, White, Other,** Jonathan Marks
34. **Racial Odyssey,** Boyce Rensberger
35. **Culture, Not Race, Explains Human Diversity,** Mark Nathan Cohen
36. **The Tall and the Short of It,** Barry Bogin

## Key Points to Consider

❖ Discuss whether the human species can be subdivided into racial categories. Support your position.

❖ How and why did the concept of race develop?

❖ Would you allow archaeologists to study the remains of Kennewick Man, or would you immediately repatriate the bones to Native Americans? Why?

❖ Why is it culture, not race, that best explains human differences in behavior?

❖ To what extent is height a barometer of the health of a society, and why?

 **Links** **www.dushkin.com/online/**

27. **Cult Archaeology Topics**
   *http://www.usd.edu/anth/cultarch/culttopics.html*
28. **Hominid Evolution Survey**
   *http://www.geocities.com/SoHo/Atrium/1381/index.html*
29. **Human Genome Project Information**
   *http://www.ornl.gov/TechResources/Human_Genome/home.html*
30. **OMIM Home Page-Online Mendelian Inheritance in Man**
   *http://www3.ncbi.nlm.nih.gov/omim/*
31. **Patterns of Human Variability: The Concept of Race**
   *http://www.as.ua.edu/ant/bindon/ant101/syllabus/race/race1.htm*

These sites are annotated on pages 4 and 5.

The field of biological anthropology has come a long way since the days when one of its primary concerns was the classification of human beings according to racial type. Although human diversity is still a matter of major interest in terms of how and why we differ from one another, most anthropologists have concluded that human beings cannot be sorted into sharply distinct entities. Without denying the fact of human variation throughout the world, the prevailing view today is that the differences between us exist along geographical gradients, as differences in degree, rather than in terms of the separate and discrete reproductive entities perceived in the past.

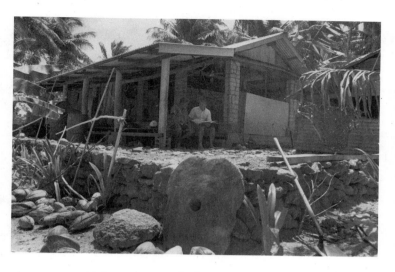

One of the old ways of looking at human "races" was that each such group was a subspecies of human that, if left reproductively isolated long enough, would eventually evolve into separate species. While this concept of subspecies, or racial varieties within a species, would seem to apply to some living creatures (such as the dog and wolf or the horse and zebra) and might even be relevant to hominid diversification in the past, the current consensus is that it is not happening today, at least within the human species.

A more recent attempt to salvage the idea of human races has been to perceive them not so much as reproductively isolated entities but as so many clusters of gene frequencies, separable only by the fact that the proportions of traits (such as skin color, hair form, etc.) differ in each artificially constructed group. But, if such "groups" exist only because we say they do and do not have an objective reality of their own, what is to be learned from the exercise? What is its practical value?

It would seem to be more productive to study human traits in terms of their particular adaptiveness (as in "Racial Odyssey" by Boyce Rensberger and "The Tall and the Short of It" by Barry Bogin) or how they help us reconstruct human prehistory (as in "The Lost Man" by Douglas Preston).

Lest anyone think that anthropologists are "in denial" regarding the existence of human races and that the viewpoint expressed here is merely an expression of contemporary political correctness, it should be remembered that serious, scholarly attempts to classify people according to race have been going on now for 200 years and, so far, nothing of value has come of them.

Complicating the matter, as Jonathan Marks elucidates in "Black, White, Other," is that there actually are two concepts of race: the strictly biological one, which was originally set forth by Linnaeus in the 1700s, and the one of popular culture, which has been around since time immemorial. These "two constantly intersecting ways of thinking about the divisions between us," says Marks, have resulted not only in fuzzy thinking about racial biology, but they have also infected the way we think about people and, therefore, the way we treat each other in the social sense.

What we should recognize, claim most anthropologists, is that, despite the superficial physical and biological differences between us, when it comes to intelligence, all human beings are basically the same (as discussed by Mark Nathan Cohen in "Culture, Not Race, Explains Human Diversity"). The degrees of variation within our species may be accounted for by the subtle and changing selective forces experienced as one moves from one geographical area to another. However, no matter what the environmental pressures have been, the same intellectual demands have been made upon us all. This is not to say, of course, that we do not vary from each other as individuals. Rather, what is being said is that when we look at these artificially created groups of people called "races," we find the same range of intellectual skills within each group. Indeed, even when we look at traits other than intelligence, we find much greater variation within each group than we find between groups.

It is time, therefore, to put the idea of human races to rest, at least as far as science is concerned. If such notions remain in the realm of social discourse, then so be it. That is where the problems associated with notions of race have to be solved anyway. At least, says Marks, in speaking for the anthropological community: "You may group humans into a small number of races if you want to, but you are denied biology as a support for it."

## A REPORTER AT LARGE

# The Lost Man

*Is it possible that the first Americans weren't who we think they were? And why is the government withholding Kennewick Man, who might turn out to be the most significant archeological find of the decade?*

## DOUGLAS PRESTON

ON Sunday, July 28, 1996, in the middle of the afternoon, two college students who were watching a hydroplane race on the Columbia River in Kennewick, Washington, decided to take a shortcut along the river's edge. While wading through the shallows, one of them stubbed his toe on a human skull partly buried in the sand. The students picked it up and, thinking it might be that of a murder victim, hid it in some bushes and called the police.

Floyd Johnson, the Benton County coroner, was called in, and the police gave him the skull in a plastic bucket. Late in the afternoon, Johnson called James Chatters, a forensic anthropologist and the owner of a local consulting firm called Applied Paleoscience. "Hey, buddy, I got a skull for you to look at," Johnson said. Chatters had often helped the police identify skeletons and distinguish between those of murder victims and those found in Indian burial sites. He is a small, determined, physically powerful man of forty-eight who used to be a gymnast and a wrestler. His work occasionally involves him in grisly or spectacular murders, where the victims

are difficult to identify, such as burnings and dismemberments.

"When I looked down at the skull," Chatters told me, "right off the bat I saw it had a very large number of Caucasoid features"—in particular, a long, narrow braincase, a narrow face, and a slightly projecting upper jaw. But when Chatters took it out of the bucket and laid it on his worktable he began to see some unusual traits. The crowns of the teeth were worn flat, a common characteristic of prehistoric Indian skulls, and the color of the bone indicated that it was fairly old. The skull sutures had fused, indicating that the individual was past middle age. And, for a prehistoric Indian of what was then an advanced age, he or she was in exceptional health; the skull had, for example, all its teeth and no cavities.

As dusk fell, Chatters and Johnson went out to the site to see if they could find the rest of the skeleton. There, working in the dying light, they found more bones, lying around on sand and mud in about two feet of water. The remains were remarkably complete: only the sternum, a few rib fragments, and

some tiny hand, wrist, and foot bones were missing. The bones had evidently fallen out of a bank during recent flooding of the Columbia River.

The following day, Chatters and Johnson spread the bones out in Chatters's laboratory. In forensic anthropology, the first order of business is to determine sex, age, and race. Determining race was particularly important, because if the skeleton turned out to be Native American it fell under a federal law called the Native American Graves Protection and Repatriation Act, or NAGPRA. Passed in 1990, NAGPRA requires the government—in this case, the Army Corps of Engineers, which controls the stretch of the Columbia River where the bones were found—to ascertain if human remains found on federal lands are Native American and, if they are, to "repatriate" them to the appropriate Indian tribe.

Chatters determined that the skeleton was male, Caucasoid, from an individual between forty and fifty-five years old, and about five feet nine inches tall—much taller than most prehistoric Native Americans in the Northwest. In physical anthropology, the term "Caucasoid" does not necessarily mean "white" or "European"; it is a descriptive term applied to certain biological features of a diverse category that includes, for example, some south-Asian groups as well as Europeans. (In contrast, the term "Caucasian" is a culturally defined racial category.) "I thought maybe we had an early pioneer or fur trapper," he said. As he was cleaning the pelvis, he noticed a gray object embedded in the bone, which had partly healed and fused around it. He took the bone to be X-rayed, but the object did not show up, meaning that it was not made of metal. So he requested a CAT scan. To his surprise, the scan revealed the object to be part of a willow-leaf-shaped spear point, which had been thrust into the bone and broken off. It strongly resembled a Cascade projectile point—an Archaic Indian style in wide use from around nine thousand to forty-five hundred years ago.

The Army Corps of Engineers asked Chatters to get a second opinion. He put the skeleton into his car and drove it a hundred miles to Ellensburg, Washington, where an anthropologist named Catherine J. Mac Millan ran a forensic consulting business called the Bone-Apart Agency. "He didn't say anything," Mac Millan told me. "I examined the bones, and I said 'Male, Caucasian.' He said 'Are you sure?' and I said 'Yeah.' And then he handed me the pelvis and showed me the ancient point embedded in it, and he said, 'What do you think now?' And I said, 'That's extremely interesting, but it still looks Caucasian to me.'" "In her report to the Benton County coroner's office she wrote that in her opinion the skeleton was "Caucasian male."

Toward the end of the week, Chatters told Floyd Johnson and the Army Corps of Engineers that he thought they needed to get a radiocarbon date on Kennewick Man. The two parties agreed, so Chatters sent the left fifth metacarpal bone—a tiny bone in the hand—to the University of California at Riverside.

On Friday, August 23rd, Jim Chatters received a telephone call from the radiocarbon lab. The bone was between ninety-three hundred and ninety-six hundred years old. He was astounded. "It was just a phone call," he said. "I thought, Maybe there's been a mistake.

I had to see the report with my own eyes." The report came on Monday, in the form of a fax. "I got very nervous then," Chatters said. He knew that, because of their age, the bones on his worktable had to be one of the most important archeological finds of the decade. "It was just a tremendous responsibility." The following Tuesday, the coroner's office issued a press release on the find, and it was reported in the Seattle Times, and other local papers.

Chatters called in a third physical anthropologist, Grover S. Krantz, a professor at Washington State University. Krantz looked at the bones on Friday, August 30th. His report noted some characteristics common to both Europeans and Plains Indians but concluded that "this skeleton cannot be racially or culturally associated with any existing American Indian group." He also wrote, "The Native Repatriation Act has no more applicability to this skeleton than it would if an early Chinese expedition had left one of its members there."

Fifteen minutes after Krantz finished looking at the bones, Chatters received a call from Johnson. Apologetically, the coroner said, "I'm going to have to come over and get the bones." The Army Corps of Engineers had demanded that all study of the bones cease, and had required him to put the skeleton in the county sheriff's evidence locker. On the basis of the carbon date, the Corps had evidently decided that the skeleton was Native American and that it fell under NAGPRA.

"When I heard this, I panicked," Chatters said. "I was the only one who'd recorded any information on it. There were all these things I should have done. I didn't even have photographs of the postcranial skeleton. I thought, Am I going to be the last scientist to see these bones?"

On September 9th, the Umatilla Indians, leading a coalition of five tribes and bands of the Columbia River basin, formally claimed the skeleton under NAGPRA, and the Corps quickly made a preliminary decision to "repatriate" it. The Umatilla Indian Reservation lies just over the border, in northeastern Oregon, and the other tribes live in Washington and Idaho; all consider the Kennewick area part of their traditional

territories. The Umatillas announced that they were going to bury the skeleton in a secret site, where it would never again be available to science.

Three weeks later, the New York Times picked up the story, and from there it went to Time and on around the world. Television crews from as far away as France and Korea descended on Kennewick. The Corps received more than a dozen other claims for the skeleton, including one from a group known as the Asatru Folk Assembly, the California-based followers of an Old Norse religion, who wanted the bones for their own religious purposes.

On September 2nd, the Corps had directed that the bones be placed in a secure vault at the Pacific Northwest National Laboratory, in Richland, Washington. Nobody outside of the Corps has seen them since. They are now at the center of a legal controversy that will likely determine the course of American archeology.

WHAT was a Caucasoid man doing in the New World more than ninety-three centuries ago? In the reams of press reports last fall, that question never seemed to be dealt with. I called up Douglas Owsley, who is the Division Head for Physical Anthropology at the National Museum of Natural History, Smithsonian Institution, in Washington, D.C., and an expert on Paleo-American remains. I asked him how many well-preserved skeletons that old had been found in North America.

He replied, "Including Kennewick, about seven."

Then I asked if any others had Caucasoid features, and there was a silence that gave me the sense that I was venturing onto controversial ground.

He guardedly replied, "Yes."

"How many?"

"Well," he said, "in varying degrees, all of them."

Kennewick Man's bones are part of a growing quantity of evidence that the earliest inhabitants of the New World may have been a Caucasoid people. Other, tentative evidence suggests that these people may have originally come from Europe. The new evidence is fragmentary, contradictory, and controversial. Critical research remains to be done, and many studies are still unpublished. At the least, the new evidence calls into question the standard Beringian Walk theory, which holds that the first human beings to reach the New World were Asians of Mongoloid stock, who crossed from Siberia to Alaska over a land bridge. The new evidence involves three basic questions. Who were the original Americans? Where did they come from? And what happened to them?

"You're dealing with such a black hole," Owsley told me. "It's hard to draw any firm conclusions from such a small sample of skeletons, and there is more than one group represented. That's why Kennewick is so important."

KENNEWICK MAN made his appearance at the dawn of a new age in physical anthropology. Scientists are now able to extract traces of organic material from a person's bone and perform a succession of powerful biochemical assays which can reveal an astonishing amount of information about the person. In March, for example, scientists at Oxford University announced that they had compared DNA extracted from the molar cavity of a nine-thousand-year-old skeleton known as Cheddar Man to DNA collected from fifteen pupils and five adults from old families in the village of Cheddar, in Somersetshire. They had established a blood tie between Cheddar Man and a schoolteacher who lived just half a mile from the cave where the bones were found.

In the few weeks that Kennewick Man was in the hands of scientists, they discovered a great deal about him. Isotopic-carbon studies of the bones indicate that he had a diet high in marine food—that he may have been a fisherman who ate a lot of salmon. He seems to have been a tall, good-looking man, slender and well proportioned. (Studies have shown that "handsomeness" is largely the result of symmetrical features and good health, both of which Kennewick Man had.) Archeological finds of similar age in the area suggest that he was part of a small band of people who moved about, hunting, fishing, and gathering wild plants. He may have

lived in a simple sewn tent or mat hut that could be disassembled and carried. Some nearby sites contain large numbers of fine bone needles, indicating that a lot of delicate sewing was going on: Kennewick Man may have worn tailored clothing. For a person at that time to live so long in relatively good health indicates that he was clever or lucky, or both, or had family and close friends around him.

He appears to have perished from recurring infections caused by the stone point in his hip. Because of the way his bones were found, and the layer of soil from which they presumably emerged, it may be that he was not deliberately buried but died near the river and was swept away and covered up in a flood. He may have perished alone on a fishing trip, far from his family.

Chatters made a cast of the skull before the skeleton was taken from his office. In the months since, he has been examining it to figure out how Kennewick Man may have looked. He plans to work with physical anthropologists and a forensic sculptor to make a facial reconstruction. "On the physical characteristics alone, he could fit on the streets of Stockholm without causing any kind of notice," Chatters told me. "Or on the streets of Jerusalem or New Delhi, for that matter. I've been looking around for someone who matches this Kennewick gentleman, looking for weeks and weeks at people on the street, thinking, This one's got a little bit here, that one a little bit there. And then, one evening, I turned on the TV, and there was Patrick Stewart"—Captain Picard, of "Star Trek"—"and I said, 'My God, there he is! Kennewick Man!'"

IN September, following the requirements of NAGPRA, the Corps advertised in a local paper its intention of repatriating the skeleton secreted in the laboratory vault. The law mandated a thirty-day waiting period after the advertisements before the Corps could give a skeleton to a tribe.

Physical anthropologists and archeologists around the country were horrified by the seizure of the skeleton. They protested that it was not possible to demonstrate a relationship between

nine-thousand-year-old remains and any modern tribe of the area. "Those tribes are relatively new," says Dennis Stanford, the chairman of the Department of Anthropology at the Smithsonian's National Museum of Natural History. "They pushed out other tribes that were there." Both Owsley and Richard L. Jantz, a biological anthropologist at the University of Tennessee, wrote letters to the Army Corps of Engineers in late September saying that the loss to science would be incalculable if Kennewick Man were to be reburied before being studied. They received no response. Robson Bonnichsen, the director of the Center for the Study of the First Americans, at Oregon State University, also wrote to the Corps and received no reply. Three representatives and a United States senator from the state of Washington got in touch with the Corps, pleading that it allow the skeleton to be studied before reburial, or, at least, refrain from repatriating the skeleton until Congress could take up the issue. The Corps rebuffed them.

The Umatillas themselves issued a statement, which was written by Armand Minthorn, a tribal religious leader. Minthorn, a small, well-spoken young man with long braids, is a member of a new generation of Native American activists, who see religious fundamentalism—in this case, the Washat religion—as a road back to Native American traditions and values:

> Our elders have taught us that once a body goes into the ground, it is meant to stay there until the end of time. . . . If this individual is truly over 9,000 years old, that only substantiates our belief that he is Native American. From our oral histories, we know that our people have been part of this land since the beginning of time. We do not believe that our people migrated here from another continent, as the scientists do. . . . Scientists believe that because the individual's head measurement does not match ours, he is not Native American. Our elders have told us that Indian people did not always look the way we look today. Some scientists say that if this individual is not studied further, we, as Indians, will be destroying evidence of our history. We already know our history. It is passed on to us through

our elders and through our religious practices.

Despite the mounting protests, the Corps refused to reconsider its decision to ban scientific study of the Kennewick skeleton. As the thirty-day waiting period came to a close, anthropologists around the country panicked. Just a week before it ended, on October 23rd, a group of eight anthropologists filed suit against the Corps. The plaintiffs included Douglas Owsley, Robson Bonnichsen, and also Dennis Stanford. Stanford, one of the country's top Paleo-Indian experts, is a formidable opponent. While attending graduate school in New Mexico, he roped in local rodeos, and helped support his family by leasing an alfalfa farm. There's still a kind of laconic, frontier toughness about him. "Kennewick Man has the potential to change the way we view the entire peopling of the Americas," he said to me. "We had to act. Otherwise, I might as well retire."

The eight are pursuing the suit as individuals. Their academic institutions are reluctant to get involved in a lawsuit as controversial as this, particularly at a time when most of them are negotiating with tribes over their own collections.

In the suit, the scientists have argued that Kennewick Man may not meet the NAGPRA definition of "Native American" as being "of, or relating to, a tribe, people, or culture that is indigenous to the United States." The judge trying the case has asked both sides to be prepared to define the word "indigenous" as it is used in NAGPRA. This will be an interesting exercise, since no human beings are indigenous to the New World: we are all immigrants.

The scientists have also argued that the Corps had had no evidence to support its claim that the skeleton had a connection to the Umatillas. Alan Schneider, the scientists' attorney, says, "Our analysis of NAGPRA is that first you have to make a determination if the human remains are Native American. And then you get to the question of cultural affiliation. The Army Corps assumed that anyone who died in the continental United States prior to a certain date is automatically Native American."

The NAGPRA law appears to support the scientists' point of view. It says that when there are no known lineal descendants "cultural affiliation" should be determined using "geographical, kinship, biological, archeological, anthropological, linguistic, folkloric, oral traditional, historical," or other "relevant information or expert opinion" before human remains are repatriated. In other words, human remains must often be studied before anyone can say whom they are related to.

The Corps, represented by the Justice Department, has refused to comment on most aspects of the case. "It's really as if the government didn't want to know the truth about Kennewick Man," Alan Schneider told me in late April. "It seems clear that the government will *never* allow this skeleton to be studied, for any reason, unless it is forced to by the courts."

Preliminary oral arguments in the case were heard on June 2nd in the United States District Court for the District of Oregon. The scientists asked for immediate access to study the bones, and the Corps asked for summary judgment. Judge John Jelderks denied both motions, and said that he would have a list of questions for the Corps that it is to answer within a reasonable time. With the likelihood of appeals, the case could last a couple of years longer, and could ultimately go to the Supreme Court.

Schneider was not surprised that the Corps had sided with the Indians. "It constantly has a variety of issues it has to negotiate with Native American tribes," he told me, and he specified, among others, land issues, water rights, dams, salmon fishing, hydroelectric projects, and toxic-waste dumps. The Corps apparently decided, Schneider speculated, that in this case its political interests would be better served by supporting the tribes than by supporting a disgruntled group of anthropologists with no institutional backing, no money, and no political power. There are large constituencies for the Indians' point of view: fundamentalist Christians and liberal supporters of Indian rights. Fundamentalists of all varieties tend to object to scientific research into the origins of humankind, because the results usually contradict their various creation myths. A novel coalition of conservative Chris-

tians and liberal activists was important in getting NAGPRA through Congress.

KENNEWICK MAN, early as he is, was not one of the first Americans. But he could be their descendant. There is evidence that those mysterious first Americans were a Caucasoid people. They may have come from Europe and may be connected to the Clovis people of America. Kennewick may provide evidence of a connection between the Old World and the New.

The Clovis mammoth hunters were the earliest widespread culture that we know of in the Americas. They appeared abruptly, seemingly out of nowhere, all over North and South America about eleven thousand five hundred years ago—two thousand years before Kennewick. (They were called Clovis after a town in New Mexico near an early site—a campground beside an ancient spring which is littered with projectile points, tools, and the remains of fires.) We have only a few fragments of human bone from the Clovis people and their immediate descendants, the Folsom, and these remains are so damaged that nothing can be learned from them at present.

The oldest bones that scientists have been able to study are the less than a dozen human remains that are contemporaneous with Kennewick. They date from between eight thousand and nearly eleven thousand years ago—the transition period between the Paleo-Indian and the Archaic Indian traditions. Most of the skeletons have been uncovered accidentally in recent years, primarily because of the building boom in the West. (Bones do not survive well in the East: the soil is too wet and acidic.) Some other ancient skeletons, though, have been discovered gathering dust in museum drawers. Among these oldest remains are the Spirit Cave mummy and Wizard's Beach Willie, both from Nevada; the Hourglass Cave and Gordon's Creek skeletons, from Colorado; the Buhl Burial, from Idaho; and remains from Texas, California, and Minnesota.

Douglas Owsley and Richard Jantz made a special study of several of these ancient remains. The best-preserved specimen they looked at was a partial mummy from Spirit Cave, Nevada, which is more than nine thousand years old. Owsley and Jantz compared the Spirit Cave skull with thirty-four population samples from around the world, including ten Native American groups. In an as yet unpublished letter to the Nevada State Museum, they concluded that the Spirit Cave skull was "very different" from any historic-period Native American groups. They wrote, "In terms of its closest classification, it does have a 'European' or 'Archaic Caucasoid' look, because morphometrically it is most similar to the Ainu from Japan and a Medieval period Norse population." Additional early skeletons that they and others have looked at also show Caucasoid-like traits that, in varying degrees, resemble Kennewick Man's. Among these early skeletons, there are no close resemblances to modern Native Americans.

But, even though the skeletons do look Caucasoid, other evidence indicates that the concept of "race" may not be applicable to human beings of ten or fifteen thousand years ago. Recent studies have discovered that all Eurasians may have looked Caucasoid-like in varying degrees. In addition, some researchers believe that the Caucasoid type first emerged in Western Asia or the Middle East, rather than in Europe. The racial differences we see today may be a late (and trivial) development in human evolution. If this is the case, then Kennewick may indeed be a direct ancestor of today's Native Americans—an idea that some preliminary DNA and dental studies seem to support.

BIOLOGY, however, isn't the whole story. There is some archeological evidence that the Clovis people of America—Kennewick Man's predecessors—came from Europe, which could account for his Caucasoid features. When the Clovis people appeared in the New World, they possessed an advanced stone and bone technology, and employed it in hunting big game. (It is no small feat to kill a mammoth or a mastodon with a hand-held spear or an atlatl.) If the Clovis people—or their precursors—had migrated to North America from Asia, one would expect to find early forms of their distinctive

tools, of the right age, in Alaska or eastern Siberia. We don't. But we do find such artifacts in Europe and parts of Russia.

Bruce Bradley is the country's leading expert on Paleo-Indian flaked-stone technology. In 1970, as a recent college graduate, Bradley spent time in Europe studying paleolithic artifacts, including those of the Solutrean people, who lived in southwestern France and Spain between twenty thousand and sixteen thousand years ago. During his stay in Europe, Bradley learned how to flake out a decent Solutrean point. Then he came back to America and started studying stone tools made by the Clovis people. He noticed not only striking visual similarities between the Old World Solutrean and the New World Clovis artifacts, as many researchers had before, but also a strikingly similar use of flaking technology.

"The artifacts don't just look identical," Bradley told me. "They are *made* the same way." Both the European Solutrean and the American Clovis stone tools are fashioned using the same complex flaking techniques. He went on, "As far as I know, overshot flaking is unique to Solutrean and Clovis, and the only diving flaking that is more than eleven thousand years old is that of Solutrean and Clovis."

To argue his case, he drove from Cortez, Colorado, where he lives, to see me, in Santa Fe, bringing with him a trunkful of Solutrean artifacts, casts of Clovis bone and stone tools, and detailed illustrations of artifacts, along with a two-pound chunk of gray Texas flint and some flaking tools.

Silently, he laid a piece of felt on my desk and put on it a cast of a Clovis knife from Blackwater Draw, New Mexico. On top of that, he put a broken Solutrean knife from Laugerie-Haute, in France. They matched perfectly—in size, shape, thickness, and pattern of flaking. As we went through the collection, the similarities could be seen again and again. "It isn't just the flaking as you see it on the finished piece that is the same," Bradley explained. "Both cultures had a very specific way of preparing the edge before striking it to get a very specific type of flake. I call these

deep technologies. These are not mere resemblances—they are deep, complex, abstract concepts applied to the stone."

I remarked that according to other archeologists I had talked to the resemblances were coincidental, the result of two cultures—one Old World, the other New World—confronting the same problems and solving them in the same way. "Maybe," Bradley said. "But a lot of older archeologists were not trained with technology in mind. They see convergence of form or look, but they don't see the technology that goes into it. I'm not saying this is the final answer. But there is so much similarity that we cannot say, 'This is just coincidence,' and ignore it."

To show me what he meant, he brought out the piece of gray flint, and we went into the back yard. "This isn't just knocking away at a stone," he said, hefting the piece of flint and examining it from various angles with narrowed eyes. "After the initial flaking of a spear point, there comes a stage where you have almost limitless choices on how to continue." He squatted down and began to work on the flint with hammer stones and antler billets, his hands deftly turning and shaping the material—knapping, chipping, scraping, pressing, flaking. The pile of razor-sharp flakes grew bigger, and the chunk of flint began to take on a definite shape. Over the next ninety minutes, Bradley reduced the nodule to a five-inch-long Clovis spear point.

It was a revelation to see that making a Clovis point was primarily an intellectual process. Sometimes ten minutes would pass while Bradley examined the stone and mapped out the next flaking sequence. "After thirty years of intense practice, I'm still at the level of a mediocre Clovis craftsman," he said, wiping his bloodied hands and reviving himself with a cup of cocoa. "This is as difficult and complex as a game of chess."

Those are not the only similarities between the Old World Solutrean and the New World Clovis cultures. As we went through Bradley's casts of Clovis artifacts, he compared them with pictures of similar Solutrean artifacts. The Clovis people, for example, produced enigmatic bone rods that were bevelled on both ends and crosshatched; so did the Solutrean. The Clovis people fashioned distinctive spear points out of mammoth ivory; so did the Solutrean. Clovis and Solutrean shaft wrenches (tools thought to have been used for straightening spears) look almost identical. At the same time, there are significant differences between the Clovis and the Solutrean tool kits; the Clovis people fluted their spear points, for instance, while the Solutrean did not.

"To get to the kind of complexity you find in Clovis tools, I see a long technological development," Bradley said. "It isn't one person in one place inventing something. But there is no evolution in Clovis technology. It just appears, full blown, all over the New World, around eleven thousand five hundred years ago. Where's the evolution? *Where did that advanced Clovis technology come from?*"

When I mentioned the idea of a possible Old World Solutrean origin for the New World Clovis to Lawrence Straus, a Solutrean expert at the University of New Mexico, he said, "There are two gigantic problems with it—thousands of years of separation and thousands of miles of ocean." Pointing out that the Solutrean technology itself appeared relatively abruptly in the South of France, he added, "I think this is a fairly clear case of mankind's ability to reinvent things."

But Bradley and other archeologists have pointed out that these objections may not be quite so insurmountable. Recently, in southern Virginia, archeologists discovered a layer of non-Clovis artifacts beneath a Clovis site. The layer dates from fifteen thousand years ago—much closer to the late Solutrean period, sixteen thousand five hundred years ago. Only a few rough tools have been found, but if more emerge they might provide evidence for the independent development of Clovis—or provide a link to the Solutrean. The as yet unnamed culture may be precisely the precursor to Clovis which archeologists have been looking for since the nineteen-thirties. The gap between Solutrean and Clovis may be narrowing.

The other problem is how the Solutrean people—if they are indeed the ancestors of the Clovis—might have reached America in the first place. Although most of them lived along riverbanks and on the seacoast of France and Spain, there is no evidence that they had boats. No Paleo-Indian boats have been found on the American side, either, but there is circumstantial evidence that the Paleo-Indians used boats. The ancestors of the Australian aborigines got to Australia in boats from the Indonesian archipelago at least fifty thousand years ago.

But the Solutrean people may not have needed boats at all: sixteen thousand years ago, the North Atlantic was frozen from Norway to Newfoundland. Seasonal pack ice probably extended as far south as Britain and Nova Scotia. William Fitzhugh, the director of the Arctic Studies Center, at the Smithsonian, points out that if human beings had started in France, crossed the English Channel, then hopped along the archipelago from Scotland to the Faeroes to Iceland to Greenland to Newfoundland, and, finally, Nova Scotia, the biggest distance between landfalls would have been about five hundred miles, which Fitzhugh says could have been done on foot over ice. It would still have been a stupendous journey, but perhaps not much more difficult than the Beringian Walk, across thousands of miles of tundra, muskeg, snow, and ice.

"For a long time, most archeologists have been afraid to challenge the Beringian Walk paradigm," Bradley said. "I don't want to try to convince anybody. But I do want to shake the bushes. You could put all the archeological evidence for the Asian-Clovis connection in an envelope and mail it for thirty-two cents. The evidence for a European-Clovis connection you'd have to send in a U.P.S. box, at least."

Robson Bonnichsen, the director of the Center for the Study of the First Americans, at Oregon State University, is another archeologist whose research is challenging the established theories. "There is a presumption, written into almost every textbook on prehistory, that Paleo-Americans such as Clovis are the direct ancestors of today's Native Americans," he told me. "But now we have a very limited number of skeletons from that early time, and it's not clear that that's true. We're getting some hints from people working with genetic data

that these earliest populations might have some shared genetic characteristics with latter-day European populations. A lot more research is needed to sort all this out. Now, for the first time, we have the technology to do this research, especially in molecular biology. Which is why we *must* study Kennewick."

This summer, Bonnichsen hopes to go to France and recover human hair from Solutrean and other Upper Paleolithic sites. He will compare DNA from that hair with DNA taken from naturally shed Paleo-American hair recovered from the United States to see if there is a genetic link. Human hair can survive thousands of years in the ground, and, using new techniques, Bonnichsen and his research team have been finding hair in the places where people worked and camped.

BONNICHSEN and most other archeologists tend to favor the view that if the ancestors of Clovis once lived in Europe they came to America via Asia—the Beringian Walk theory with somewhat different people doing the walking. C. Vance Haynes, Jr., the country's top Paleo-Indian geochronologist, who is a professor of anthropology at the University of Arizona, and is a plaintiff in the lawsuit, said to me, "When I look at Clovis and ask myself where in the world the culture was derived from, I would say Europe." In an article on the origins of Clovis, Haynes noted that there were extraordinary resemblances between New World Clovis and groups that lived in Czechoslovakia and Ukraine twenty thousand years ago. He noted at least nine "common traits" shared by Clovis and certain Eastern European cultures: large blades, end scrapers, burins, shaft wrenches, cylindrical bone points, knapped bone, unifacial flake tools, red ochre, and circumferentially chopped mammoth tusks. He also pointed out that an eighteen-thousand-year-old burial site of two children near Lake Baikal, in Central Asia, exhibits remarkable similarities to what appears to be a Clovis burial site of two cremated children in Montana. The similarities extend beyond tools and points buried with the remains: red ochre, a kind of iron oxide, was placed in both graves. This suggests a migratory group carrying its technology from Europe across Asia. "If you want to speculate, I see a band moving eastward from Europe through Siberia, and meeting people there, and having cultural differences," Haynes said to me. "Any time there's conflict, it drives people, and maybe it just drove them right across the Bering land bridge. And exploration could have been as powerful a driving force thirteen thousand years ago as it was in 1492."

ONCE the Clovis people or their predecessors reached the New World, what happened to them? This is the second—and equally controversial—half of the theory: that the Clovis people or their immediate successors, the Folsom people, may have been supplanted by the ancestors of today's Native Americans. In this scenario, Kennewick Man may have been part of a remnant Caucasoid population related to Clovis and Folsom. Dennis Stanford, of the Smithsonian, said to me, "For a long time, I've held the theory that the Clovis and the Folsom were overwhelmed by a migration of Asians over the Bering land bridge. It may not just have been a genetic swamping or a pushing aside. The north Asians may have been carrying diseases that the Folsom and the Clovis had no resistance to"—just as European diseases wiped out a large percentage of the Native American population after the arrival of Columbus. Stanford explained that at several sites the Paleo-Indian tradition of Clovis and Folsom was abruptly replaced by Archaic Indian traditions, which had advanced but very different lithic technologies. The abruptness of the transition and the sharp change in technology, Stanford feels, suggest a rapid replacement of Folsom by the Archaic cultural complex, rather than an evolution from one into the other. The Archaic spear point embedded in Kennewick Man's hip could even be evidence of an ancient conflict: the Archaic Indian tradition was just beginning to appear in the Pacific Northwest at the time of Kennewick Man's death.

OWSLEY and other physical anthropologists who have studied the skulls of the earliest Americans say that the living population they most closely match is the mysterious Ainu, the aboriginal inhabitants of the Japanese islands. Called the Hairy People by the Japanese, the Ainu are considered by some researchers to be a Causasoid group who, before mixing with the Japanese, in the late nineteenth and twentieth centuries, had European faces, wavy hair, thick beards, and a European-type distribution of body hair. Early travellers reported that some also had blue eyes. Linguists have not been able to connect the Ainu language with any other on earth. The American Museum of Natural History, in New York, has a collection of nineteenth-century photographs of pure-blood Ainu, which I have examined: they stare from the glass plates like fierce, black-bearded Norwegians.

Historically, the Ainu have been the "Indians" of Japan. After the ancestors of the Japanese migrated from the mainland a couple of thousand years ago, they fought the Ainu and pushed them into the northernmost islands of the Japanese archipelago. The Japanese later discriminated against the Ainu, forcing their children to attend Japanese schools, and suppressing their religion and their language. Today, most Ainu have lost their language and many of their distinct physical characteristics, although there has recently been a movement among them to recapture their traditions, their religion, their language, and their songs. Like the American Indians, the Ainu suffer high rates of alcoholism. The final irony is that the Ainu, like the American Indians for Americans, have become a popular Japanese tourist attraction. Many Ainu now make a living doing traditional dances and selling handicrafts to Japanese tourists. The Japanese are as fascinated by the Ainu as we are by the Indians. The stories are mirror images of each other, with only the races changed.

If the Ainu are a remnant population of those people who crossed into America thirteen or more millennia ago, then they are right where one might expect to find them, in the extreme eastern part

of Asia. Stanford says, "That racial type goes all the way to Europe, and I suspect that originally they were the same racial group at both ends. At that point in time, this racial diversification hadn't developed. They could have come into the New World from two directions at once, east and west."

THERE is a suspicion among anthropologists that some of the people behind the effort to rebury Kennewick and other ancient skeletons are afraid that the bones could show that the earliest Americans were Caucasoid. I asked Armand Minthorn about this. "We're not afraid of the truth," he said calmly. "We already know our truth. We're not telling the scientists what *their* truth is."

The Umatillas were infuriated by the research that Chatters did on the skeleton before it was seized by the Corps. "Scientists have dug up and studied Native Americans for decades," Minthorn wrote. "We view this practice as desecration of the body and a violation of our most deeply-held religious beliefs." Chatters told me that he had received "vitriolic" and "abusive" telephone calls from tribe members, accusing him of illegalities and racism. (The latter was an odd charge, since Chatters's wife is of Native American descent.) A client of his, he said, received an unsigned letter from one of the tribes, telling the client not to work with Chatters anymore. "They're going to ruin my livelihood," the forensic consultant said.

In a larger sense, the anger of the Umatillas and other Native American tribes is understandable, and even justified. If you look into the acquisition records of most large, old natural-history museums, you will see a history of unethical, and even grisly, collecting practices. Fresh graves were dug up and looted, sometimes in the dead of night. "It is most unpleasant to steal bones from a grave," the eminent anthropologist Franz Boas wrote in his diary just around the turn of the century, "but what is the use, someone has to do it." Indian skulls were bought and sold among collectors like arrowheads and pots. Skeletons were exhibited with no regard for

# ANTHROPOLOGY

## Anthropologists 1, Army Corps 0

American anthropologists won a round in an important legal battle last week, when a U.S. District Court in Portland, Oregon, ordered the Army Corps of Engineers to reopen the case of 9300-year-old human skeleton found on federal land in Washington state. The corps, which has jurisdiction over the skeleton—one of the oldest in the Americas—had planned to turn it over to American Indian tribes for reburial last October under the 1990 Native American Graves Protection and Repatriation Act (NAGPRA). But scientists sued to prevent the handover until they had studied the bones.

Now, although the court stopped short of allowing study of the skeleton, it opened the door for future research by recognizing that the scientists have a legitimate claim that must be considered. "It's a landmark ruling," exulted Alan Schneider, the Portland attorney for the scientists. "This is the first case where a court has held that a third party like a scientist has standing to challenge a government agency's overenforcement of NAGPRA."

The male skeleton, known as "Kennewick Man" for the town where it was discovered in the bank of the Columbia River last summer, is a rare representative of the earliest people to inhabit the Americas. It also had a projectile point embedded in its pelvis and facial features that may be Caucasoid-like, offering clues about early Americans (*Science,* 11 October 1996, p. 172).

As soon as the skeleton was discovered, Smithsonian Institution skeletal biologist Douglas Owsley sought permission to study it, and a team at the University of California, Davis, extracted ancient DNA from a bit of its finger bone for analysis. Owsley and others say that without scientific study it's impossible to know whether the skeleton has a biological or cultural tie to any living people—knowledge needed to determine which tribe, if any, should receive it.

But Owsley says he was told by the corps "flat-out that there would be no scientific study." The corps ordered a halt to the DNA work as soon as it learned of it in October, and announced that it would hand over the skeleton to the Confederated Tribes of the Umatilla Indian Reservation under the auspices of NAGPRA, which requires remains or cultural objects to be given to a culturally affiliated tribe. It later rescinded that order but has kept the skeleton locked away and unavailable for study. Court documents suggest that corps officials were concerned about alienating the Indians. In an 18 September 1996 e-mail message, a corps official wrote: "All risk to us seems to be associated with not repatriating the remains."

In the new decision, U.S. District Court Magistrate John Jelderks invalidated all the corps' orders in the case and criticized the "flawed" procedures used by the agency, which he said "acted before it had all the evidence or fully appreciated the scope of the problem." Jelderks also asked the corps to report back to him with its decision on the case and to answer several questions, including whether repatriation under NAGPRA required a biological or cultural link between bones and living tribes, and how such a link would be determined.

Corps attorney Daria Zane declined to comment for the record. As for the scientists, although they still can't study the skeleton, they're pleased. "Hopefully, the Army Corps will come to its senses," says Owsley. "They are using government lawyers and taxpayers' dollars to argue against academic freedom."

—Ann Gibbons

From *Science,* Vol. 277, July 11, 1997, p. 173. © 1997 by The American Association for the Advancement of Science. Reprinted by permission

---

tribal sensitivities. During the Indian wars, warriors who had been killed on the battlefield were sometimes decapitated by Army doctors so that scientists back in the East could study their heads. The American Museum of Natural History "collected" six live Inuits in Greenland and brought them to New York to study; four of them died of respiratory diseases, whereupon the museum macerated their corpses and installed the bones in its collection. When I worked at the museum, in the nineteen-eighties, entire hallways were lined with glass cases containing Indian bones and mummified body parts—a small fraction of the museum's collection, which includes an estimated twenty thousand or more human remains, of all races. Before NAGPRA, the Smithsonian had some thirty-five thousand sets of human remains in storage; around eighteen thousand of them were Native American.

Now angry Native Americans, armed with NAGPRA and various state reburial laws, are emptying such museums of bones and grave goods. Although most anthropologists agree that burials identified with particular tribes should be returned, many have been horrified to discover that some tribes are trying to get everything—even skeletons and priceless funerary objects that are thousands of years old.

An amendment that was introduced in Congress last January would tighten NAGPRA further. The amended law could have the effect of hindering much archeology in the United States involving human remains, and add to the cost of construction projects that inadvertently uncover human bones. (Or perhaps the law would merely guarantee that such remains would be quietly destroyed.)

Native Americans have already claimed and reburied two of the earliest skeletons, the Buhl Burial and the Hourglass Cave skeleton, both of which apparently had some Caucasoid characteristics. The loss of the Buhl Burial was particularly significant to anthropologists, because it was more than ten thousand years old—a thousand years older than Kennewick Man—and had been found buried with its grave goods. The skeleton, of a woman between eighteen and twenty years old, received, in the opinion of some anthropologists, inadequate study before it was turned over to the Shoshone-Bannock tribe. The Northern

Paiute have asked that the Spirit Cave mummy be reburied. If these early skeletons are all put back in the ground, anthropologists say, much of the history of the peopling of the Americas will be lost.

WHEN Darwin proposed his theory of natural selection, it was seized upon and distorted by economists, social engineers, and politicians, particularly in England: they used it to justify all sorts of vicious social and economic policies. The scientific argument about the original peopling of the Americas threatens to be distorted in a similar way. Some tabloids and radio talk shows have referred to Kennewick as a "white man" and have suggested that his discovery changes everything with respect to the rights of Native Americans in this country. James

Chatters said to me, "There are some less racially enlightened folks in the neighborhood who are saying, 'Hey, our ancestors were here first, so we don't owe the Indians anything.'"

This is clearly racist nonsense: these new theories cannot erase or negate the existing history of genocide, broken treaties, and repression. But it does raise an interesting question: If the original inhabitants of the New World were Europeans who were pushed out by Indians, would it change the Indians' position in the great moral landscape?

"No," Stanford said in reply to this question. "Whose ancestors are the people who were pushed out? And who did the pushing? The answer is that we're all the descendants of those folks. If you go back far enough, eventually we all have a common ancestor—*we're all the same*. When the story is finally written, the peopling of the Americas will turn out to be far more complicated than anyone imagined. There have been a lot of people who came here, at many different times. Some stayed and some left, some made it and some didn't, some got pushed out and some did the pushing. It's the history of humankind: the tough guy gets the ground."

Chatters put it another way. "We didn't go digging for this man. He fell out—he was actually a volunteer. I think it would be wrong to stick him back in the ground without waiting to hear the story he has to tell. We need to look at things as human beings, not as one race or another. The message this man brings to us is one of unification: there may be some commonality in our past that will bring us together."

# Black, White, Other

*Racial categories are cultural constructs masquerading as biology*

## Jonathan Marks

*New York-born Jonathan Marks earned an undergraduate degree in natural science at Johns Hopkins. After getting his Ph.D. in anthropology, Marks did a post-doc in genetics at the University of California at Davis and is now an associate professor of anthropology at Yale University. He is the coauthor, with Edward Staski, of the introductory textbook* Evolutionary Anthropology *(San Diego: Harcourt, Brace Jovanovich, 1992). His new book,* Human Biodiversity: Genes, Race, and History *is published (1995) by Aldine de Gruyter.*

While reading the Sunday edition of the *New York Times* one morning last February, my attention was drawn by an editorial inconsistency. The article I was reading was written by attorney Lani Guinier. (Guinier, you may remember, had been President Clinton's nominee to head the civil rights division at the Department of Justice in 1993. Her name was hastily withdrawn amid a blast of criticism over her views on political representation of minorities.) What had distracted me from the main point of the story was a photo caption that described Guinier as being "half-black." In the text of the article, Guinier had described herself simply as "black."

How can a person be black and half black at the same time? In algebraic terms, this would seem to describe a situation where $x = \frac{1}{2}x$, to which the only solution is $x = 0$.

The inconsistency in the *Times* was trivial, but revealing. It encapsulated a longstanding problem in our use of racial categories—namely, a confusion between biological and cultural heredity. When Guinier is described as "half-black," that is a statement of biological ancestry, for one of her two parents is black. And when Guinier describes herself as black, she is using a cultural category, according to which one can either be black or white, but not both.

Race—as the term is commonly used—is inherited, although not in a strictly biological fashion. It is passed down according to a system of folk heredity, an all-or-nothing system that is different from the quantifiable heredity of biology. But the incompatibility of the two notions of race is sometimes starkly evident—as when the state decides that racial differences are so important that interracial marriages must be regulated or outlawed entirely. Miscegenation laws in this country (which stayed on the books in many states through the 1960s) obliged the legal system to define who belonged in what category. The resulting formula stated that anyone with one-eighth or more black ancestry was a "negro." (A similar formula, defining Jews, was promulgated by the Germans in the Nuremberg Laws of the 1930s.)

Applying such formulas led to the biological absurdity that having one black great-grandparent was sufficient to define a person as black, but having seven white great grandparents was insufficient to define a person as white.

Here, race and biology are demonstrably at odds. And the problem is not semantic but conceptual, for race is presented as a category of nature.

Human beings come in a wide variety of sizes, shapes, colors, and forms—or, because we are visually oriented primates, it certainly seems that way. We also come in larger packages called populations; and we are said to belong to even larger and more confusing units, which have long been known as races. The history of the study of human variation is to a large extent the pursuit of those human races—the attempt to identify the small number of fundamentally distinct kinds of people on earth.

This scientific goal stretches back two centuries, to Linnaeus, the father of biological systematics, who radically established *Homo sapiens* as one species within a group of animals he called Primates. Linnaeus's system of naming groups within groups logically implied further breakdown. He consequently sought to establish a number of subspecies within *Homo sapiens*. He identified five: four geographical species (from Europe, Asia, Africa, and America) and one grab-bag subspecies called *monstrosus*. This category was dropped by subsequent researchers (as was Linnaeus's use of criteria such as personality and dress to define his subspecies).

While Linnaeus was not the first to divide humans on the basis of the continents on which they lived, he had given the division a scientific stamp. But in attempting to determine the proper number of subspecies, the heirs of Linnaeus always seemed to find different answers, depending upon the criteria they applied. By the mid-twentieth century, scores of anthropologists—led by Harvard's Earnest Hooton—had expended enormous energy on the problem. But these scholars could not convince one another about the precise nature of the fundamental divisions of our species.

Part of the problem—as with the *Times's* identification of Lani Guinier—was that we humans have two constantly intersecting ways of thinking about the divisions among us. On the one hand, we like to think of "race"—as Linnaeus did—as an objective, biological category. In this sense, being a member of a race is supposed to be the equivalent of being a member of a species or of a phylum—except that race, on the analogy of subspecies, is an even narrower (and presumably more exclusive and precise) biological category.

The other kind of category into which we humans allocate ourselves—when we say "Serb" or "Hutu" or "Jew" or "Chicano" or "Republican" or "Red Sox fan"—is cultural. The label refers to little or nothing in the natural attributes of its members. These members may not live in the same region and may not even know many others like themselves. What they share is neither strictly nature nor strictly community. The groupings are constructions of human social history.

Membership in these *un*biological groupings may mean the difference between life and death, for they are the categories that allow us to be identified (and accepted or vilified) socially. While membership in (or allegiance to) these categories may be assigned or adopted from birth, the differentia that mark members from nonmembers are symbolic and abstract; they serve to distinguish people who cannot be readily distinguished by nature. So important are these symbolic distinctions that some of the strongest animosities are often expressed between very similar-looking peoples. Obvious examples are Bosnian Serbs and Muslims, Irish and English, Huron and Iroquois.

Obvious natural variation is rarely so important as cultural difference. One simply does not hear of a slaughter of the short people at the hands of the tall, the glabrous at the hands of the hairy, the red-haired at the hands of the brown-haired. When we do encounter genocidal violence between different looking peoples, the two groups are invariably socially or culturally distinct as well. Indeed, the tragic frequency of hatred and genocidal violence between biologically indistinguishable peoples implies that biological differences such as skin color are not motivations but, rather, excuses. They allow nature to be invoked to reinforce group identities and antagonisms that would exist without these physical distinctions. But are there any truly "racial" biological distinctions to be found in our species?

Obviously, if you compare two people from different parts of the world (or whose ancestors came from different parts of the world), they will differ physically, but one cannot therefore define three or four or five basically different kinds of people, as a biological notion of race would imply. The anatomical properties that distinguish people—such as pigmentation, eye form, body build—are not clumped in discrete groups, but distributed along geographical gradients, as are nearly all the genetically determined variants detectable in the human gene pool.

These gradients are produced by three forces. Natural selection adapts populations to local circumstances (like climate) and thereby differentiates them from other populations. Genetic drift (random fluctuations in a gene pool) also differentiates populations from one another, but in non-adaptive ways. And gene flow (via intermarriage and other child-producing unions) acts to homogenize neighboring populations.

In practice, the operations of these forces are difficult to discern. A few features, such as body build and the graduated distribution of the sickle cell anemia gene in populations from western Africa, southern Asia, and the Mediterranean can be plausibly related to the effects of selection. Others, such as the graduated distribution of a small deletion in the mitochondrial DNA of some

East Asian, Oceanic, and Native American peoples, or the degree of flatness of the face, seem unlikely to be the result of selection and are probably the results of random biohistorical factors. The cause of the distribution of most features, from nose breadth to blood group, is simply unclear.

The overall result of these forces is evident, however. As Johann Friedrich Blumenbach noted in 1775, "you see that all do so run into one another, and that one variety of mankind does so sensibly pass into the other, that you cannot mark out the limits between them." (Posturing as an heir to Linnaeus, he nonetheless attempted to do so.) But from humanity's gradations in appearance, no defined groupings resembling races readily emerge. The racial categories with which we have become so familiar are the result of our imposing arbitrary cultural boundaries in order to partition gradual biological variation.

Unlike graduated biological distinctions, culturally constructed categories are ultrasharp. One can be French or German, but not both; Tutsi or Hutu, but not both; Jew or Catholic, but not both; Bosnian Muslim or Serb, but not both; black or white, but not both. Traditionally, people of "mixed race" have been obliged to choose one and thereby identify themselves unambiguously to census takers and administrative bookkeepers—a practice that is now being widely called into question.

A scientific definition of race would require considerable homogeneity within each group, and reasonably discrete differences between groups, but three kinds of data militate against this view: First, the groups traditionally described as races are not at all homogeneous. Africans and Europeans, for instance, are each a collection of biologically diverse populations. Anthropologists of the 1920s widely recognized *three* European races: Nordic, Alpine, and Mediterranean. This implied that races could exist within races. American anthropologist Carleton Coon identified *ten* European races in 1939. With such protean use, the term race came to have little value in describing actual biological entities within *Homo sapiens*. The scholars were not only grappling with a broad north-south gradient in human appearance across Europe, they were trying to bring the data into line with their belief in profound and fundamental constitutional differences between groups of people.

But there simply isn't one European race to contrast with an African race, nor three, nor ten: the question (as scientists long posed it) fails to recognize the actual patterning of diversity in the human species. Fieldwork revealed, and genetics later quantified, the existence of far more biological diversity within any group than between groups. Fatter and thinner people exist everywhere, as do people with type O and type A blood. What generally varies from one population to the next is the *proportion* of people in these groups expressing the trait or gene. Hair color varies strikingly among Europeans and native Australians, but little among other peoples. To focus on discovering differences between presumptive races, when the vast majority of detectable variants do not help differentiate them, was thus to define a very narrow—if not largely illusory—problem in human biology. (The fact that Africans are biologically more diverse than Europeans, but have rarely been split into so many races, attests to the cultural basis of these categorizations.)

Second, differences between human groups are only evident when contrasting geographical extremes. Noting these extremes, biologists of an earlier era sought to identify representatives of "pure," primordial races presumably located in Norway, Senegal, and Thailand. At no time, however, was our species composed of a few populations within which everyone looked pretty much the same. Ever since some of our ancestors left Africa to spread out through the Old World, we humans have always lived in the "in-between" places. And

human populations have also always been in genetic contact with one another. Indeed, for tens of thousands of years, humans have had trade networks; and where goods flow, so do genes. Consequently, we have no basis for considering *extreme* human forms the most pure, or most representative, of some ancient primordial populations. Instead, they represent populations adapted to the most disparate environments.

And third, between each presumptive "major" race are unclassifiable populations and people. Some populations of India, for example, are darkly pigmented (or "black"), have Europeanlike ("Caucasoid") facial features, but inhabit the continent of Asia (which should make them "Asian"). Americans might tend to ignore these "exceptions" to the racial categories, since immigrants to the United States from West Africa, Southeast Asia, and northwest Europe far outnumber those from India. The very existence of unclassifiable peoples undermines the idea that there are just three human biological groups in the Old World. Yet acknowledging the biological distinctiveness of such groups leads to a rapid proliferation of categories. What about Australians? Polynesians? The Ainu of Japan?

Categorizing people is important to any society. It is, at some basic psychological level, probably necessary to have group identity about who and what you are, in contrast to who and what you are not. The concept of race, however, specifically involves the recruitment of biology to validate those categories of self-identity.

Mice don't have to worry about that the way humans do. Consequently, classifying them into subspecies entails less of a responsibility for a scientist than classifying humans into sub-species

does. And by the 1960s, most anthropologists realized they could not defend any classification of *Homo sapiens* into biological subspecies or races that could be considered reasonably objective. They therefore stopped doing it, and stopped identifying the endeavor as a central goal of the field. It was a biologically intractable problem—the old square-peg-in-a-round-hole enterprise; and people's lives, or welfares, could well depend on the ostensibly scientific pronouncement. Reflecting on the social history of the twentieth century, that was a burden anthropologists would no longer bear.

This conceptual divorce in anthropology—of cultural from biological phenomena was one of the most fundamental scientific revolutions of our time. And since it affected assumptions so rooted in our everyday experience, and resulted in conclusions so counterintuitive—like the idea that the earth goes around the sun, and not vice-versa—it has been widely underappreciated.

Kurt Vonnegut, in *Slaughterhouse Five*, describes what he remembered being taught about human variation: "At that time, they were teaching that there was absolutely no difference between anybody. They may be teaching that still." Of course there are biological differences between people, and between populations. The question is: How are those differences patterned? And the answer seems to be: Not racially. Populations are the only readily identifiable units of humans, and even they are fairly fluid, biologically similar to populations nearby, and biologically different from populations far away.

In other words, the message of contemporary anthropology is: You may group humans into a small number of races if you want to, but you are denied biology as a support for it.

# Racial Odyssey

## Boyce Rensberger

The human species comes in an artist's palette of colors: sandy yellows, reddish tans, deep browns, light tans, creamy whites, pale pinks. It is a rare person who is not curious about the skin colors, hair textures, bodily structures and facial features associated with racial background. Why do some Africans have dark brown skin, while that of most Europeans is pale pink? Why do the eyes of most "white" people and "black" people look pretty much alike but differ so from the eyes of Orientals? Did one race evolve before the others? If so, is it more primitive or more advanced as a result? Can it be possible, as modern research suggests, that there is no such thing as a pure race? These are all honest, scientifically worthy questions. And they are central to current research on the evolution of our species on the planet Earth.

Broadly speaking, research on racial differences has led most scientists to three major conclusions. The first is that there are many more differences among people than skin color, hair texture and facial features. Dozens of other variations have been found, ranging from the shapes of bones to the consistency of ear wax to subtle variations in body chemistry.

The second conclusions is that the overwhelming evolutionary success of the human species is largely due to its great genetic variability. When migrating bands of our early ancestors reached a new environment, at least a few already had physical traits that gave them an edge in surviving there. If the coming centuries bring significant environmental changes, as many believe they will, our chances of surviving them will be immeasurably enhanced by our diversity as a species.

There is a third conclusion about race that is often misunderstood. Despite our wealth of variation and despite our constant, everyday references to race, no one has ever discovered a reliable way of distinguishing one race from another. While it is possible to classify a great many people on the basis of certain physical features, there are no known feature or groups of features that will do the job in all cases.

Skin color won't work. Yes, most Africans from south of the Sahara and their descendants around the world have skin that is darker than that of most Europeans. But there are millions of people in India, classified by some anthropologists as members of the Caucasoid, or "white," race who have darker skins than most Americans who call themselves black. And there are many Africans living in sub-Sahara Africa today whose skins are no darker than the skins of many Spaniards, Italians, Greeks or Lebanese.

What about stature as a racial trait? Because they are quite short, on the average, African Pygmies have been considered racially distinct from other dark-skinned Africans. If stature, then, is a racial criterion, would one include in the same race the tall African Watusi and the Scandinavians of similar stature?

The little web of skin that distinguishes Oriental eyes is said to be a particular feature of the Mongoloid race. How, then, can it be argued that the American Indian, who lacks this epicanthic fold, is Mongoloid?

Even more hopeless as racial markers are hair color, eye color, hair form, the shapes of noses and lips or any of the other traits put forth as typical of one race or another.

## NO NORMS

Among the tall people of the world there are many black, many white and many in between. Among black people of the world there are many with kinky hair, many with straight or wavy hair, and many in between. Among the broad-nosed, full-lipped people of the world there are many with dark skins, many with light skins and many in between.

How did our modern perceptions of race arise? One of the first to attempt a scientific classification of peoples was Carl von Linné, better known as Linnaeus. In 1735, he published a classification that remains the standard today. As Linnaeus saw it there were four races, classifiable geographically and by skin color. The names Linnaeus gave them were *Homo sapiens Africanus nigrus* (black African human being), *H. sapiens Americanus rubescens* (red American human being), *H. sapiens Asiaticus fuscusens* (brownish Asian human being), and *H. sapiens Europaeus albescens* (white European human being). All, Linnaeus recognized, were members of a single human species.

A species includes all individuals that are biologically capable of interbreeding and producing fertile offspring. Most matings between species are fruitless, and even when they succeed, as when a horse and a donkey interbreed and produce a mule, the progeny are sterile. When a poodle mates with a collie, however, the offspring are fertile, showing that both dogs are members of the same species.

Even though Linnaeus's system of nomenclature survives, his classifications were discarded, especially after voyages of discovery revealed that there were many more kinds of people than could be pigeonholed into four categories. All over the world there are small populations that don't fit. Among the better known are:

- The so-called Bushmen of southern Africa, who look as much Mongoloid as Negroid.
- The Negritos of the South Pacific, who do look Negroid but are very far from Africa and have no known links to that continent.
- The Ainu of Japan, a hairy aboriginal people who look more Caucasoid than anything else.
- The Lapps of Scandinavia, who look as much like Eskimos as like Europeans.

- The aborigines of Australia, who often look Negroid but many of whom have straight or wavy hair and are often blond as children.
- The Polynesians, who seem to be a blend of many races, the proportions differing from island to island.

To accommodate such diversity, many different systems of classification have been proposed. Some set up two or three dozen races. None has ever satisfied all experts.

## CLASSIFICATION SYSTEM

Perhaps the most sweeping effort to impose a classification upon all the peoples of the world was made by the American anthropologist Carleton Coon. He concluded there are five basic races, two of which have major subdivisions: Caucasoids; Mongoloids; full-size Australoids (Australian aborigines); dwarf Australoids (Negritos—Andaman Islanders and similar peoples); full-size Congoids (African Negroids); dwarf Congoids (African Pygmies); and Capoids (the so-called Bushmen and Hottentots).

In his 1965 classic, *The Living Races of Man,* Coon hypothesized that before A.D. 1500 there were five pure races—five centers of human population that were so isolated that there was almost no mixing.

Each of these races evolved independently, Coon believed, diverging from a pre-*Homo sapiens* stock that was essentially the same everywhere. He speculated that the common ancestor evolved into *Homo sapiens* in five separate regions at five different times, beginning about 35,000 years ago. The populations that have been *Homo sapiens* for the shortest periods of time, Coon said, are the world's "less civilized" races.

The five pure races remained distinct until A.D. 1500; then Europeans started sailing the world, leaving their genes—as sailors always have—in every port and planting distant colonies. At about the same time, thousands of Africans were captured and forcibly settled in many parts of the New World.

That meant the end of the five pure races. But Coon and other experts held that this did not necessarily rule out the idea of distinct races. In this view, there *are* such things as races; people just don't fit into them very well anymore.

The truth is that there is really no hard evidence to suggest that five or any particular number of races evolved independently. The preponderance of evidence today suggests that as traits typical of fully modern people arose in any one place, they spread quickly to all human populations. Advances in intelligence were almost certainly the fastest to spread. Most anthropologists and geneticists now believe that human beings have always been subject to migrating and mixing. In other words, there probably never were any such things as pure races.

Race mixing has not only been a fact of human history but is, in this day of unprecedented global mobility, taking place at a more rapid rate than ever. It is not farfetched to envision the day when, generations hence, the entire "complexion" of major population centers will be different. Meanwhile, we can see such changes taking place before our eyes, for they are a part of everyday reality.

## HYBRID VIGOR

Oddly, those who assert scientific validity for their notions of pure and distinct races seem oblivious of a basic genetic principle that plant and animal breeders know well: too much inbreeding can lead to proliferation of inferior traits. Cross-breeding with different strains often produces superior combinations and "hybrid vigor."

The striking differences among people may very well be a result of constant genetic mixing. And as geneticists and ecologists know, in diversity lies strength and resilience.

To understand the origin and proliferation of human differences, one must first know how Darwinian evolution works.

Evolution is a two-step process. Step one is mutation: somehow a gene in the ovary or testes of an individual is altered, changing the molecular configu-

# DISEASE ORIGINS

The gene for sickle cell anemia, a disease found primarily among black people, appears to have evolved because its presence can render its bearer resistant to malaria. Such a trait would have obvious value in tropical Africa.

A person who has sickle cell anemia must have inherited genes for the disease from both parents. If a child inherits only one sickle cell gene, he or she will be resistant to malaria but will not have the anemia. Paradoxically, inheriting genes from both parents does not seem to affect resistance to malaria.

In the United States, where malaria is practically nonexistent, the sickle cell gene confers no survival advantage and is disappearing. Today only about 1 out of every 10 American blacks carries the gene.

Many other inherited diseases are found only in people from a particular area. Tay-Sachs disease, which often kills before the age of two, is almost entirely confined to Jews from parts of Eastern Europe and their descendants elsewhere. Paget's disease, a bone disorder, is found most often among those of English descent. Impacted wisdom teeth are a common problem among Asians and Europeans but not among Africans. Children of all races are able to digest milk because their bodies make lactase, the enzyme that breaks down lactose, or milk sugar. But the ability to digest lactose in adulthood is a racially distributed trait.

About 90 percent of Orientals and blacks lose this ability by the time they reach adulthood and become quite sick when they drink milk.

Even African and Asian herders who keep cattle or goats rarely drink fresh milk. Instead, they first treat the milk with fermentation bacteria that break down lactose, in a sense predigesting it. They can then ingest the milk in the form of yogurt or cheese without any problem.

About 90 percent of Europeans and their American descendants, on the other hand, continue to produce the enzyme throughout their lives and can drink milk with no ill effects.

---

ration that stores instructions for forming a new individual. The children who inherit that gene will be different in some way from their ancestors.

Step two is selection: for a racial difference, or any other evolutionary change to arise, it must survive and be passed through several generations. If the mutation confers some disadvantage, the individual dies, often during embryonic development. But if the change is beneficial in some way, the individual should have a better chance of thriving than relatives lacking the advantage.

## NATURAL SELECTION

If a new trait is beneficial, it will bring reproductive success to its bearer. After several generations of multiplication, bearers of the new trait may begin to outnumber nonbearers. Darwin called this natural selection to distinguish it from the artificial selection exercised by animal breeders.

Skin color is the human racial trait most generally thought to confer an evolutionary advantage of this sort. It has long been obvious in the Old World that the farther south one goes, the darker the skin color. Southern Europeans are usually somewhat darker than northern Europeans. In North Africa, skin colors are darker still, and, as one travels south, coloration reaches its maximum at the Equator. The same progressions holds in Asia, with the lightest skins to the north. Again, as one moves south, skin color darkens, reaching in southern India a "blackness" equal to that of equatorial Africans.

This north-south spectrum of skin color derives from varying intensities of the same dark brown pigment called melanin. Skin cells simply have more or less melanin granules to be seen against a background that is pinkish because of the underlying blood vessels. All races can increase their melanin concentration by exposure to the sun.

What is it about northerly latitudes in the Northern Hemisphere that favors less pigmentation and about southerly latitudes that favors more? Exposure to intense sunlight is not the only reason why people living in southerly latitudes are dark. A person's susceptibility to rickets and skin cancer, his ability to withstand cold and to see in the dark may also be related to skin color.

The best-known explanation says the body can tolerate only a narrow range of intensities of sunlight. Too much causes sunburn and cancer, while too little deprives the body of vitamin D, which is synthesized in the skin under the influence of sunlight. A dark complexion protects the skin from the harmful effects of intense sunlight. Thus, albinos born in equatorial regions have a high rate of skin cancer. On the other hand, dark skin in northerly latitudes screens out sunlight needed for the synthesis of vitamin D. Thus, dark-skinned children living in northern latitudes had high rates of rickets—a bone-deforming disease caused by a lack of vitamin D—before their milk was routinely fortified. In the sunny tropics, dark skin admits enough light to produce the vitamin.

Recently, there has been some evidence that skin colors are linked to differences in the ability to avoid injury from the cold. Army researchers found that during the Korean War blacks were more susceptible to frostbite than were whites. Even among Norwegian soldiers in World War II, brunettes had a slightly higher incidence of frostbite than did blonds.

## EYE PIGMENTATION

A third link between color and latitude involves the sensitivity of the eye to various wavelengths of light. It is known that dark-skinned people have more pigmentation in the iris of the eye and at the back of the eye where the image falls. It has been found that the less pigmented the eye, the more sensitive it is to colors at the red end of the spectrum. In situations illuminated with reddish light, the northern European can see more than a dark African sees.

It has been suggested that Europeans developed lighter eyes to adapt to the longer twilights of the North and their greater reliance on firelight to illuminate caves.

Although the skin cancer-vitamin D hypothesis enjoys wide acceptance, it may well be that resistance to cold, possession of good night vision and other yet unknown factors all played roles in the evolution of skin colors.

Most anthropologists agree that the original human skin color was dark brown, since it is fairly well established that human beings evolved in the tropics of Africa. This does not, however, mean that the first people were Negroids, whose descendants, as they moved north, evolved into light-skinned Caucasoids. It is more likely that the skin color of various populations changed several times from dark to light and back as people moved from one region to another.

Consider, for example, that long before modern people evolved, *Homo erectus* had spread throughout Africa, Europe and Asia. The immediate ancestor of *Homo sapiens, Homo erectus,* was living in Africa 1.5 million years ago and in Eurasia 750,000 years ago. The earliest known forms of *Homo sapiens* do not make their appearance until somewhere between 250,000 and 500,000 years ago. Although there is no evidence of the skin color of any hominid fossil, it is probable that the *Homo erectus* population in Africa had dark skin. As subgroups spread into northern latitudes, mutations that reduced pigmentation conferred survival advantages on them and lighter skins came to predominate. In other words, there were probably black *Homo erectus* peoples in Africa and white ones in Europe and Asia.

Did the black *Homo erectus* populations evolve into today's Negroids and the white ones in Europe into today's Caucasoids? By all the best evidence, nothing like this happened. More likely,

wherever *Homo sapiens* arose it proved so superior to the *Homo erectus* populations that it eventually replaced them everywhere.

If the first *Homo sapiens* evolved in Africa, they were probably dark-skinned; those who migrated northward into Eurasia lost their pigmentation. But it is just as possible that the first *Homo sapiens* appeared in northern climes, descendants of white-skinned *Homo erectus.* These could have migrated southward toward Africa, evolving darker skins. All modern races, incidentally, arose long after the brain had reached its present size in all parts of the world.

North-south variations in pigmentation are quite common among mammals and birds. The tropical races tend to be darker in fur and feather, the desert races tend to be brown, and those near the Arctic Circle are lighter colored.

There are exceptions among humans. The Indians of the Americas, from the Arctic to the southern regions of South America, do not conform to the north-south scheme of coloration. Though most think of Indians as being reddish-brown, most Indians tend to be relatively light skinned, much like their presumed Mongoloid ancestors in Asia. The ruddy complexion that lives in so many stereotypes of Indians is merely what years of heavy tanning can produce in almost any light-skinned person. Anthropologists explain the color consistency as a consequence of the relatively recent entry of people into the Americas—probably between 12,000 and 35,000 years ago. Perhaps they have not yet had time to change.

Only a few external physical differences other than color appear to have adaptive significance. The strongest cases can be made for nose shape and stature.

## WHAT'S IN A NOSE

People native to colder or drier climates tend to have longer, more beak-shaped noses than those living in hot and humid regions. The nose's job is to warm and humidify air before it reaches sensitive lung tissues. The colder or drier the air is, the more surface area is needed in-

side the nose to get it to the right temperature or humidity. Whites tend to have longer and beakier noses than blacks or Orientals. Nevertheless, there is great variation within races. Africans in the highlands of East Africa have longer noses than Africans from the hot, humid lowlands, for example.

Stature differences are reflected in the tendency for most northern peoples to have shorter arms, legs and torsos and to be stockier than people from the tropics. Again, this is an adaptation to heat or cold. One way of reducing heat loss is to have less body surface, in relation to weight or volume, from which heat can escape. To avoid overheating, the most desirable body is long limbed and lean. As a result, most Africans tend to be lankier than northern Europeans. Arctic peoples are the shortest limbed of all.

Hair forms may also have a practical role to play, but the evidence is weak. It has been suggested that the more tightly curled hair of Africans insulates the top of the head better than does straight or wavy hair. Contrary to expectation, black hair serves better in this role than white hair. Sunlight is absorbed and converted to heat at the outer surface of the hair blanket; it radiates directly into the air. White fur, common on Arctic animals that need to absorb solar heat, is actually transparent and transmits light into the hair blanket, allowing the heat to form within the insulating layer, where it is retained for warmth.

Aside from these examples, there is little evidence that any of the other visible differences among the world's people provide any advantage. Nobody knows, for example, why Orientals have epicanthic eye folds or flatter facial profiles. The thin lips of Caucasoids and most Mongoloids have no known advantages over the Negroid's full lips. Why should middle-aged and older Caucasoid men go bald so much more frequently than the men of other races? Why does the skin of Bushmen wrinkle so heavily in the middle and later years? Or why does the skin of Negroids resist wrinkling so well? Why do the Indian men in one part of South America have blue penises? Why do Hottentot women have such unusually large buttocks?

There are possible evolutionary explanations for why such apparently useless differences arise.

One is a phenomenon known as sexual selection. Environmentally adaptive traits arise, Darwin thought, through natural selection—the environment itself chooses who will thrive or decline. In sexual selection, which Darwin also suggested, the choice belongs to the prospective mate.

In simple terms, ugly individuals will be less likely to find mates and reproduce their genes than beautiful specimens will. Take the blue penis as an example. Women might find it unusually attractive or perhaps believe it to be endowed with special powers. If so, a man born with a blue penis will find many more opportunities to reproduce his genes than his ordinary brothers.

Sexual selection can also operate when males compete for females. The moose with the larger antlers or the lion with the more imposing mane will stand a better chance of discouraging less well-endowed males and gaining access to females. It is possible that such a process operated among Caucasoid males, causing them to become markedly hairy, especially around the face.

## ATTRACTIVE TRAITS

Anthropologists consider it probable that traits such as the epicanthic fold or the many regional differences in facial features were selected this way.

Yet another method by which a trait can establish itself involves accidental selection. It results from what biologists call genetic drift.

Suppose that in a small nomadic band a person is born with perfectly parallel fingerprints instead of the usual loops, whorls or arches. That person's children would inherit parallel fingerprints, but they would confer no survival advantages. But if our family decides to strike out on its own, it will become the founder of a new band consisting of its own descendants, all with parallel fingerprints.

Events such as this, geneticists and anthropologists believe, must have occurred many times in the past to produce the great variety within the human species. Among the apparently neutral traits that differ among populations are:

### Ear Wax

There are two types of ear wax. One is dry and crumbly and the other is wet and sticky. Both types can be found in every major population, but the frequencies differ. Among northern Chinese, for example, 98 percent have dry ear wax. Among American whites, only 16 percent have dry ear wax. Among American blacks the figure is 7 percent.

### Scent Glands

As any bloodhound knows, every person has his or her own distinctive scent. People vary in the mixture of odoriferous compounds exuded through the skin—most of it coming from specialized glands called apocrine glands. Among whites, these are concentrated in the armpits and near the genitals and anus. Among blacks, they may also be found on the chest and abdomen. Orientals have hardly any apocrine glands at all. In the words of the Oxford biologist John R. Baker, "The Europids and Negrids are smelly, the Mongoloids scarcely or not at all." Smelliest of all are northern European, or so-called Nordic, whites. Body odor is rare in Japan. It was once thought to indicate a European in the ancestry and to be a disease requiring hospitalization.

### Blood Groups

Some populations have a high percentage of members with a particular blood group. American Indians are overwhelmingly group O—100 percent in some regions. Group A is most common among Australian aborigines and the Indians in western Canada. Group B is frequent in northern India, other parts of Asia and western Africa.

Advocates of the pure-race theory once seized upon blood groups as possibly unique to the original pure races. The proportions of groups found today, they thought, would indicate the degree of mixing. It was subsequently found that chimpanzees, our closest living relatives, have the same blood groups as humans.

### Taste

PTC (phenylthiocarbamide) is a synthetic compound that some people can taste and others cannot. The ability to taste it has no known survival value, but it is clearly an inherited trait. The proportion of persons who can taste PTC varies in different populations: 50 to 70 percent of Australian aborigines can taste it, as can 60 to 80 percent of all Europeans. Among East Asians, the percentage is 83 to 100 percent, and among Africans, 90 to 97 percent.

### Urine

Another indicator of differences in body chemistry is the excretion of a compound known as BAIB (beta-amino-isobutyric acid) in urine. Europeans seldom excrete large quantities, but high levels of excretion are common among Asians and American Indians. It had been shown that the differences are not due to diet.

No major population has remained isolated long enough to prevent any unique genes from eventually mixing with those of neighboring groups. Indeed, a map showing the distribution of so-called traits would have no sharp boundaries, except for coastlines. The intensity of a trait such as skin color, which is controlled by six pairs of genes and can therefore exist in many shades, varies gradually from one population to another. With only a few exceptions, every known genetic possibility possessed by the species can be found to some degree in every sizable population.

## EVER-CHANGING SPECIES

One can establish a system of racial classification simply by listing the features of populations at any given moment. Such a concept of race is, however, inappropriate to a highly mobile and ever-changing species such as *Homo sapiens*. In the short view, races may seem distinguishable, but in biology's long haul, races come and go. New ones arise and blend into neighboring groups to create new and racially stable populations. In time, genes from these groups flow into other neighbors, continuing the production of new permutations.

Some anthropologists contend that at the moment American blacks should be considered a race distinct from African blacks. They argue that American blacks are a hybrid of African blacks and European whites. Indeed, the degree of mixture can be calculated on the basis of a blood component known as the Duffy factor.

In West Africa, where most of the New World's slaves came from, the Duffy factor is virtually absent. It is present in 43 percent of American whites. From the number of American blacks who are now "Duffy positive" it can be calculated that whites contributed 21 percent of the genes in the American

black population. The figure is higher for blacks in northern and western states and lower in the South. By the same token, there are whites who have black ancestors. The number is smaller because of the tendency to identify a person as black even if only a minor fraction of his ancestors were originally from Africa.

The unwieldiness of race designations is also evident in places such as Mexico where most of the people are, in effect, hybrids of Indians (Mongoloid by some classifications) and Spaniards (Caucasoid). Many South American populations are tri-hybrids—mixtures of Mongoloid, Caucasoid and Negroid. Brazil is a country where the mixture has been around long enough to constitute a racially stable population. Thus,

in one sense, new races have been created in the United States, Mexico and Brazil. But in the long run, those races will again change.

Sherwood Washburn, a noted anthropologist, questions the usefulness of racial classification: "Since races are open systems which are intergrading, the number of races will depend on the purpose of the classification. I think we should require people who propose a classification of races to state in the first place why they wish to divide the human species."

The very notion of a pure race, then, makes no sense. But, as evolutionists know full well, a rich genetic diversity within the human species most assuredly *does*.

# Culture, Not Race, Explains Human Diversity

## By Mark Nathan Cohen

WE ARE NOT LIKELY to convince students that racist views are wrong if we teach them only about biology and ignore culture. The basic facts about the broad patterns of human biological variation and "race" are fairly clear and well established: Individual human beings undeniably differ in myriad ways, and each specific difference may be important. Variation in skin color, for example, affects susceptibility to sunburn, skin cancer, and rickets. Variations in body build affect the ability to keep warm or cool; variations in the shape of the nose affect its ability in warm and moisten the air inhaled. Unseen genetic variations protect some people from (and predispose other people to) diseases ranging from malaria and smallpox to diabetes and cancer.

However, "races" as imagined by the public do not actually exist. Any definition of "race" that we attempt produces more exceptions than sound classifications. No matter what system we use, most people don't fit.

As almost every introductory textbook in physical anthropology explains, the distinctions among human populations are generally graded, not abrupt. In other words, skin color comes in a spectrum from dark to light, not just in black or white; noses come in a range of shapes, not just broad or narrow. Furthermore, the various physical traits such as skin color and nose shape (plus the enormous number of invisible traits) come in an infinite number of combinations; one cannot predict other traits by knowing one trait that a person possesses. A person with dark skin can have any blood type and can have a broad nose (a combination common in West Africa), a narrow nose (as many East Africans do), or even blond hair (a combination seen in Australia and New Guinea).

Of the 50,000 to 100,000 pairs of genes needed to make a human being, perhaps 35,000 to 75,000 are the same in all people, and 15,000 to 25,000 may take different forms in different people, thus accounting for human variation. But only a tiny number of these genes

> # We ... have to stop teaching or accepting the idea that humans are divided into three races— Caucasian, Negroid, and Mongoloid—an idea that is at least 50 years out of date.

 From the *Chronicle of Higher Education*, April 17, 1998, pp. B4-B5. © 1998 by Mark Nathan Cohen. Reprinted by permission.

# Many scholars of colonialism have described how members of oppressed minorities create a sense of community by choosing to ignore their colonizers' culture.

affect what many people might consider to be racial traits. For example, geneticists believe that skin color is based on no more than 4 to 10 pairs of genes. The genes of black and white Americans probably are 99.9 per cent alike.

In addition, studies of the human family tree based on detailed genetic analysis suggest that traits such as skin color are not even good indicators of who is related to whom, because the traits occur independently in several branches of the human family. When we consider the pairs of genes that may differ among humans, we see that, beyond the genes determining skin color, black people from Africa, Australia, and the south of India are not particularly closely related to each other genetically.

All of this means that variations among "races" cannot possibly explain the differences in behavior or intelligence that people think they see. Although black Americans on average receive lower scores on standardized tests than do white Americans, neither "race" is actually a biological group. Skin color alone cannot account for the differences in group averages. Although we know a great deal about the role of many of our genes—for instance, which ones cause sickle-cell anemia—no genes are known to control differences in specific behavior or in intelligence among human groups. Even if someone discovered such genes, we have no reason to assume that they would correlate with skin color any more than most other genes do.

Anthropologists and other academics must do a better job of communicating these facts to our students and to the public at large. But even if we make sure that everyone understands these facts, racism will persist—unless we convince people that a different explanation for variations in behavior makes

more sense. The alternative that we need to emphasize is the concept of culture—but a concept of culture far deeper and more sophisticated than that taught by many multiculturalists.

The anthropological concept of culture can be explained best by an analogy with language. Just as language is more than vocabulary, culture is more than, say, art and music. Language has rules of grammer and sound that limit and give structure to communication, usually without conscious thought. In English, for example, we use word order to convey the relationship among the words in a sentence. Latin uses suffixes to show relationships; Swahili uses prefixes. Even languages as similar as French, Spanish, and Italian use different subsets of the many sounds the human mouth can make.

Equally, culture structures our behavior, thoughts, perceptions, values, goals, morals, and cognitive processes—also usually without conscious thought. Just as each language is a set of arbitrary conventions shared by those who speak the language, so each culture is made up of its own arbitrary conventions. Many languages work perfectly well; many cultures do, too.

Just as familiarity with the language of one's childhood makes it harder to learn the sounds and grammer of another language, so one's culture tends to blind one to alternatives. All of us—Americans as well as members of remote Amazonian tribes—are governed by culture. Our choices in life are circumscribed largely by arbitrary rules, and we have a hard time seeing the value of other people's choices and the shortcomings of our own. For example, many societies exchange goods not for profit, but to foster social relationships, as most Americans do within their own families. Some peoples prefer to main-

tain their surrounding environment rather than to seek "progress." Other groups have a very different sense than we do of the balance between individual freedom and responsibility to one's community.

Besides teaching our students about the importance of culture, we need to revive the anthropological concept of cultural relativism—perhaps the most important concept that liberal education can teach. The enemies of relativism have claimed that the concept means that everything is equal—that no moral judgments are possible, that Americans must accept whatever other people do. But this is not what relativism means.

What it does mean is that we must look carefully at what other people are doing and try to understand their behavior in context before we judge it. It means that other people may not share our desires or our perceptions. It also means that we have to recognize the arbitrary nature of our own choices and be willing to reexamine them by learning about the choices that other people have made. In medicine, for example, many cultures have long tried to treat the whole patient, mind and body together, which some of our doctors are just beginning to focus on, having been trained instead to concentrate on treating a particular disease.

THE KEY POINT is that what we see as "racial" differences in behavior may reflect the fact that people have different values, make different choices, operate within different cultural "grammars," and categorize things (and therefore think) in different ways. Over the years, we have learned that culture shapes many things we once thought were determined by biology, including sexuality, aggression, perception, and susceptibility to disease. But many people still confuse the effects of biology and those of culture.

For example, we still use analogy problems to test students' skill in logic, which we then define as innate, genetically driven intelligence, which, some argue, differs by "race." But solving the problems depends on putting items into categories, and the categories we use are cultural, not universal. Giving the correct answer depends less on inherent intelligence than it does on knowing the classification rules used by those who created the test. Most U.S. students would flunk analogy problems put to them by Mesoamerican peasants, who divide things into "hot" and "cold"—

In addition, psychologists, in particular, must stop assuming that only one pattern exists for human cognition, perception, formation of categories, and so forth. All too many psychologists believe that standardized I.Q. tests are equally valid for assessing individuals from different cultural backgrounds. Operating from that mistaken assumption, they teach a narrow view of "correct" human behavior, which promotes racism.

We must realize that students from some minority groups are likely to do badly on I.Q. tests for a variety of reasons beyond the poor health, nutrition, and education that many of them have

even noticing what someone from another group would consider crucial. A student who did not grow up in the middle class might well believe that to appear smart, one should give a slow, thoughtful answer—not a snap answer or sound bite. Such a student will probably be put off by the idea of competitiveness and individual ranking, and thus by the whole experience of the I.Q. test.

ANTHROPOLOGISTS must do a better job of communicating these and other important facts about human biological and cultural variation to their students and to the public at

---

# Cultural relativism is the only road to tolerance and real freedom of thought, because it lets us get outside the blinders imposed by our own culture.

---

categories that, in their usage, go far beyond physical temperature.

To communicate the importance of culture to students, we have to make some adjustments in our teaching. First, we have to stop teaching world and American history in ways that deny the contributions of others and prevent thoughtful analysis of our own actions. Teaching along these lines has improved, but it can be better yet. For instance, how many students are taught that George Washington and Benjamin Franklin were speculators who wanted to enrich themselves with land on the Western frontier—land the British had intended to reserve for Native American use?

We also have to stop teaching or accepting the idea that humans are divided into three races—Caucasian, Negroid, and Mongoloid—an idea that is at least 50 years out of date. I constantly face students who have been taught the concept of three races in the 1990s by high-school and college teachers in other social sciences.

experienced because of poverty. The content of the tests is biased toward students in the mainstream, both in terms of the subject matter of the questions and in more-subtle ways, such as expectations about what is important in a problem.

And some minority students see no reason to try to do well on I.Q. tests. They may not expect to go to college. Their sense of self-worth may depend on their lack of interest in the mainstream culture, which they feel has rejected them. Many scholars of colonialism have described how members of oppressed minorities create a sense of community by choosing to ignore their colonizers' culture. John Ogbu, an anthropologist at the University of California at Berkeley, has shown that the same phenomenon occurs in U.S. schools.

Thus, scores on I.Q. tests depend not only on how "smart" one is, but also on familiarity with middleclass, white American culture. Different cultural groups are likely to pay more attention to different parts of test questions, not

large. Rather than revel in the details of obscure populations, our courses in cultural anthropology should focus on interpretations of significant contemporary events. We have to demonstrate to students that not all events outside—and even within—the United States can be understood from the single cultural perspective that other social sciences tend to teach.

We can be more outspoken in the media about alternative perspectives on international events, seeking opportunities to explain cultural practices and conventions in other countries that may lead to their different decisions or priorities. Indeed, anthropologists have to be more confident about the significance of their discipline and more willing to assert the importance of their knowledge. We need to find ways to work both with faculty members in other disciplines and with policy makers to convey our awareness that, in virtually every contemporary problem, different participants not only speak differently but also think differently.

For example, we could attempt to understand the behavior of Iranians in the United States' 20-year-old confrontation with Iran by looking objectively at their culture and history, and at ours. One of the most obvious points is that traditional Iranian leadership involves a blend of religious and secular power that is foreign to Americans. The result is that leaders of the two countries have very different agendas. And many Iranians have a different sense of the proper balance among business, profit, family, community, and spirituality.

We must show our students that they, just as much as our adversaries or "primitive peoples" in isolated cultures, are bound by the arbitrary rules of their own culture. If we don't teach these points, we are failing to show that racist assumptions about why people behave as they do are not legitimate.

We also have to stop focusing on details of the human fossil record in our introductory physical-anthropology courses. Basic courses should deal instead with human variation in a variety of populations, by looking at such issues as fertility, mortality, growth, nutrition, adaptation to the environment, and disease. It would be productive to teach, for example, that hypertension and diabetes are not simply natural results of individual genetic endowment or the aging process but, in fact, rarely occur among people whose food does not go through the commercial processing that is customary in the West.

Finally, administrators and professors across the disciplines need to recognize that it is crucial for all students to understand the concepts of culture and cultural relativism—not the inaccurate caricatures of these concepts that have been bandied about in the culture wars, but the sophisticated, carefully defined and nuanced versions that anthropologists have evolved over decades of work. Cultural relativism is the only road to tolerance and real freedom of thought, because it lets us get outside the blinders imposed by our own culture. It must be built into courses taught in core curricula—not taught only as an elective frill if a student happens to sign up for an anthropology course.

---

*Mark Nathan Cohen is a professor of anthropology at the State University of New York College at Plattsburgh and the author of* Culture of Intolerance: Chauvinism, Class, and Racism in the United States *(Yale University Press, 1998).*

COMMENTARY

# The Tall and the Short of It

## BY BARRY BOGIN

*BARRY BOGIN is a professor of anthropology at the University of Michigan in Dearborn and the author of* Patterns of Human Growth.

BAFFLED BY YOUR FUTURE PROSPECTS? As a biological anthropologist, I have just one word of advice for you: plasticity. *Plasticity* refers to the ability of many organisms, including humans, to alter themselves—their behavior or even their biology—in response to changes in the environment. We tend to think that our bodies get locked into their final form by our genes, but in fact we alter our bodies as the conditions surrounding us shift, particularly as we grow during childhood. Plasticity is as much a product of evolution's fine-tuning as any particular gene, and it makes just as much evolutionary good sense. Rather than being able to adapt to a single environment, we can, thanks to plasticity, change our bodies to cope with a wide range of environments. Combined with the genes we inherit from our parents, plasticity accounts for what we are and what we can become.

Anthropologists began to think about human plasticity around the turn of the century, but the concept was first clearly defined in 1969 by Gabriel Lasker, a biological anthropologist at Wayne State University in Detroit. At that time scientists tended to consider only those adaptations that were built into the genetic makeup of a person and passed on automatically to the next generation. A classic example of this is the ability of adults in some human societies to drink milk. As children, we all produce an enzyme called lactase, which we need to break down the sugar lactose in our mother's milk. In many of us, however, the lactase gene slows down dramatically as we approach adolescence—probably as the result of another gene that regulates its activity. When that regulating gene turns down the production of lactase, we can no longer digest milk.

Lactose intolerance—which causes intestinal gas and diarrhea—affects between 70 and 90 percent of African Americans, Native Americans, Asians, and people who come from around the Mediterranean. But others, such as people of central and western European descent and the Fulani of West Africa, typically have no problem drinking milk as adults. That's because they are descended from societies with long histories of raising goats and cattle. Among these people there was a clear benefit to being able to drink milk, so natural selection gradually changed the regulation of their lactase gene, keeping it functioning throughout life.

That kind of adaptation takes many centuries to become established, but Lasker pointed out that there are two other kinds of adaptation in humans that need far less time to kick in. If people have to face a cold winter with little or no heat, for example, their metabolic rates rise over the course of a few weeks and they produce more body heat. When summer returns, the rates sink again.

Lasker's other mode of adaptation concerned the irreversible, lifelong modification of people as they develop—that is, their plasticity. Because we humans take so many years to grow to adulthood, and because we live in so many different environments, from forests to cities and from deserts to the Arctic, we are among the world's most variable species in our physical form and behavior. Indeed, we are one of the most plastic of all species.

One of the most obvious manifestations of human malleability is our great range of height, and it is a subject I've made a special study of for the last 25 years. Consider these statistics: in 1850 Americans were the tallest people in the world, with American men averaging

5'6". Almost 150 years later, American men now average 5'8", but we have fallen in the standings and are now only the third tallest people in the world. In first place are the Dutch. Back in 1850 they averaged only 5'4"—the shortest men in Europe—but today they are a towering 5'10". (In these two groups, and just about everywhere else, women average about five inches less than men at all times.)

---

*In an age when DNA is king, it's worth considering why Americans are no longer the world's tallest people, and some Guatemalans no longer pygmies.*

---

So what happened? Did all the short Dutch sail over to the United States? Did the Dutch back in Europe get an infusion of "tall genes"? Neither. In both America and the Netherlands life got better, but more so for the Dutch, and height increased as a result. We know this is true thanks in part to studies on how height is determined. It's the product of plasticity in our childhood and in our mothers' childhood as well. If a girl is undernourished and suffers poor health, the growth of her body, including her reproductive system, is usually reduced. With a shortage of raw materials, she can't build more cells to construct a bigger body; at the same time, she has to invest what materials she can get into repairing already existing cells and tissues from the damage caused by disease. Her shorter stature as an adult is the result of a compromise her body makes while growing up.

Such a woman can pass on her short stature to her child, but genes have nothing to do with it for either of them. If she becomes pregnant, her small reproductive system probably won't be able to supply a normal level of nutrients and oxygen to her fetus. This harsh environment reprograms the fetus to grow more slowly than it would if the woman was healthier, so she is more likely to give birth to a smaller baby. Low-birth-weight babies (weighing less than 5.5 pounds) tend to continue their prenatal program of slow growth through childhood. By the time they are teenagers, they are usually significantly shorter than people of normal birth weight. Some particularly striking evidence of this reprogramming comes from studies on monozygotic twins, which develop from a single fertilized egg cell and are therefore identical genetically. But in certain cases, monozygotic twins end up being nourished by unequal portions of the placenta. The twin with the smaller fraction of the placenta is often born with low birth weight, while the other one is normal. Follow-up studies show that this difference between the twins can last throughout their lives.

As such research suggests, we can use the average height of any group of people as a barometer of the health of their society. After the turn of the century both the United States and the Netherlands began to protect the health of their citizens by purifying drinking water, installing sewer systems, regulating the safety of food, and, most important, providing better health care and diets to children. The children responded to their changed environment by growing taller. But the differences in Dutch and American societies determined their differing heights today. The Dutch decided to provide public health benefits to all the public, including the poor. In the United States, meanwhile, improved health is enjoyed most by those who can afford it. The poor often lack adequate housing, sanitation, and health care. The difference in our two societies can be seen at birth: in 1990 only 4 percent of Dutch babies were born at low birth weight, compared with 7 percent in the United States. For white Americans the rate was 5.7 percent, and for black Americans the rate was a whopping 13.3 percent. The disparity between rich and poor in the United States carries through to adulthood: poor Americans are shorter than the better-off by about one inch. Thus, despite great affluence in the United States, our average height has fallen to third place.

People are often surprised when I tell them the Dutch are the tallest people in the world. Aren't they shrimps compared with the famously tall Tutsi (or "Watusi," as you probably first encountered them) of Central Africa? Actually, the supposed great height of the Tutsi is one of the most durable myths from the age of European exploration. Careful investigation reveals that today's Tutsi men average 5'7" and that they have maintained that average for more than 100 years. That means that back in the 1800s, when puny European men first met the Tutsi, the Europeans suffered strained necks from looking up all the time. The two-to-three-inch difference in average height back then could easily have turned into fantastic stories of African giants by European adventures and writers.

The Tutsi could be as tall or taller than the Dutch if equally good health care and diets were available in Rwanda and Burundi, where the Tutsi live. But poverty rules the lives of most African people, punctuated by warfare, which makes the conditions for growth during childhood even worse. And indeed, it turns out that the Tutsi and other Africans who migrate to Western Europe or North America at young ages end up taller than Africans remaining in Africa.

At the other end of the height spectrum, Pygmies tell a similar story. The shortest people in the world today are the Mbuti, the Efe, and other Pygmy peoples of Central Africa. Their average stature is almost 4'9" for adult men and 4'6" for women. Part of the reason Pygmies are short is indeed genetic: some evidently lack the genes for producing the growth-promoting hormones that course through other people's bodies, while others are genetically incapable of using these hormones to trigger the cascade of reactions that lead to growth. But another important reason for their small size is environmental. Pygmies living as hunter-gatherers in the forests of Central African countries appear to be undernourished, which further limits their growth. Pygmies who live on farms and ranches outside the forest are better fed than their hunter-gatherer relatives and are taller as well. Both genes and nutrition thus account for the size of Pygmies.

Peoples in other parts of the world have also been labeled pygmies, such as some groups in Southeast Asia and the Maya of Guatemala. Well-meaning explorers and scientists have often claimed that they are genetically short, but here we encounter another myth of height. A group of extremely short people in New Guinea, for example, turned out to eat a diet deficient in iodine and other essential nutrients. When they were supplied with cheap mineral and vitamin supplements, their supposedly genetic short stature vanished in their children, who grew to a more normal height.

ANOTHER WAY FOR THESE SO-CALLED pygmies to stop being pygmies is to immigrate to the United States. In my own research, I study the growth of two groups of Mayan children. One group lives in their homeland of Guatemala, and the other is a group of refugees living in the United States. The Maya in Guatemala live in the village of San Pedro, which has no safe source of drinking water. Most of the water is contaminated with fertilizers and pesticides used on nearby agricultural fields. Until recently, when a deep well was dug, the townspeople depended on an unreliable supply of water from rain-swollen streams. Most homes still lack running water and have only pit toilets. The parents of the Mayan children work mostly at clothing factories and are paid only a few dollars a day.

I began working with the school-children in this village in 1979, and my research shows that most of them eat only 80 percent of the food they need. Other research shows that almost 30 percent of the girls and 20 percent of the boys are deficient in iodine, that most of the children suffer from intestinal parasites, and that many have persistent ear and eye infections. As a consequence, their health is poor and their height reflects it: they average about three inches shorter than better-fed Guatemalan children.

The Mayan refugees I work with in the United States live in Los Angeles and in the rural agricultural community of Indiantown in central Florida. Although the adults work mostly in minimum-wage jobs, the children in these communities are generally better off than their counterparts in Guatemala. Most Maya arrived in the 1980s as refugees escaping a civil war as well as a political system that threatened them and their children. In the United States they found security and started new lives, and before long their children began growing faster and bigger. My data show that the average increase in height among the first generation of these immigrants was 2.2 inches, which means that these so-called pygmies have undergone one of the largest single-generation increases in height ever recorded. When people such as my own grandparents migrated from the poverty of rural life in Eastern Europe to the cities of the United States just after World War I, the increase in height of the next generation was only about one inch.

One reason for the rapid increase in stature is that in the United States the Maya have access to treated drinking water and to a reliable supply of food. Especially critical are school breakfast and lunch programs for children from low-income families, as well as public assistance programs such as the federal Woman, Infants, and Children (WIC) program and food stamps. That these programs improve health and growth is no secret. What is surprising is how fast they work. Mayan mothers in the United States tell me that even their babies are bigger and healthier than the babies they raised in Guatemala, and hospital statistics bear them out. These women must be enjoying a level of health so improved from that of their lives in Guatemala that their babies are growing faster in the womb. Of course, plasticity means that such changes are dependent on external conditions, and unfortunately the rising height—and health—of the Maya is in danger from political forces that are attempting to cut funding for food stamps and the WIC program. If that funding is cut, the negative impact on the lives of poor Americans, including the Mayan

refugees, will be as dramatic as were the former positive effects.

Height is only the most obvious example of plasticity's power; there are others to be found everywhere you look. The Andes-dwelling Quechua people of Peru are well-adapted to their high-altitude homes. Their large, barrel-shaped chests house big lungs that inspire huge amounts of air with each breath, and they manage to survive on the lower pressure of oxygen they breathe with an unusually high level of red blood cells. Yet these secrets of mountain living are

*One way for the so-called pygmies of Guatemala to stop being pygmies is to immigrate to the United States.*

not hereditary. Instead the bodies of young Quechua adapt as they grow in their particular environment, just as those of European children do when they live at high altitudes.

Plasticity may also have a hand in determining our risks for developing a number of diseases. For example, scientists have long been searching for a cause for Parkinson's disease. Because Parkinson's tends to run in families, it is natural to think there is a genetic cause. But while a genetic mutation linked to some types of Parkinson's disease was reported in mid-1997, the gene accounts for only a fraction of people with the disease. Many more people with Parkinson's do not have the gene, and not all people with the mutated gene develop the disease.

Ralph Garruto, a medical researcher and biological anthropologist at the National Institutes of Health, is investigating the role of the environment and human plasticity not only in Parkinson's but in Lou Gehrig's disease as well. Garruto and his team traveled to the islands of Guam and New Guinea, where rates of both diseases are 50 to 100 times higher than in the United States. Among the native Chamorro people of Guam these diseases kill one person out of every five over the age of 25. The scientists found that both diseases are linked to a shortage of calcium in the diet. This shortage sets off a cascade of events that result in the digestive system's absorbing too much of the aluminum present in the diet. The aluminum wreaks havoc on various parts of the body, including the brain, where it destroys neurons and eventually causes paralysis and death.

The most amazing discovery made by Garruto's team is that up to 70 percent of the people they studied in Guam had some brain damage, but only 20 percent progressed all the way to Parkinson's or Lou Gehrig's disease. Genes and plasticity seem to be working hand in hand to produce these lower-than-expected rates of disease. There is a certain amount of genetic variation in the ability that all people have in coping with calcium shortages—some can function better than others. But thanks to plasticity, it's also possible for people's bodies to gradually develop ways to protect themselves against aluminum poisoning. Some people develop biochemical barriers to the aluminum they eat, while others develop ways to prevent the aluminum from reaching the brain.

An appreciation of plasticity may temper some of our fears about these diseases and even offer some hope. For if Parkinson's and Lou Gehrig's diseases can be prevented among the Chamorro by plasticity, then maybe medical researchers can figure out a way to produce the same sort of plastic changes in you and me. Maybe Lou Gehrig's disease and Parkinson's disease—as well as many other, including some cancers—aren't our genetic doom but a product of our development, just like variations in human height. And maybe their danger will in time prove as illusory as the notion that the Tutsi are giants, or the Maya pygmies—or Americans still the tallest of the tall.

# Unit 7

## Key Points to Consider

❖ What is "forensic anthropology"? How can it be applied to modern life?

❖ Will the human demographic explosion amount to a death sentence for primates? Defend your answer.

❖ Is there any way to prevent epidemics in the human species? How?

❖ What is the evolutionary significance of art?

❖ Should we attempt to take control of our genetic future? Why or why not?

❖ What social policy issues are involved in the nature versus nurture debate?

❖ What relevance does the concept of natural selection have to the treatment of disease?

❖ Is there any necessary conflict between science and religion with respect to explaining how we humans came to be as we are?

 **Links**      **www.dushkin.com/online/**

These sites are annotated on pages 4 and 5.

Anthropology continues to evolve as a discipline, not only in the tools and techniques of the trade, but also in the application of whatever knowledge we stand to gain about ourselves. It is in this context that Patrick Huyghe, in "Profile of an Anthropologist: No Bone Unturned," describes "forensic anthropology," a whole new field involving the use of physical similarities and differences between people in order to identify human remains. Sometimes an awareness of our biological and behavioral past may help us to better understand the present. In "The Natural History of Art" by Richard Coniff, we learn that even one's personal taste in art may be influenced by ancestral adaptations to certain types of ecological settings. In showing how our evolutionary past may make a difference in bodily health, Lori Oliwenstein (in "Dr. Darwin") talks about how the symptoms of disease must first be interpreted as to whether they represent part of the aggressive strategy of microbes or the defensive mechanisms of the patient before treatment can be applied.

One theme that ties the articles of this section together, then, is that they have as much to do with the present as they have to do with the past. According to Edward J. Larson and Larry Witham ("Scientists and Religion in America"), those who apply the scientific method to understanding our place in the universe are less inclined to opt for a religious explanation.

As we reflect upon where we have been and how we came to be as we are in the evolutionary sense, the inevitable question arises as to what will happen next. This is the most difficult issue of all, since our biological future depends so much on long-range ecological trends that no one seems to be able to predict. There is no better example of this problem than the recent explosion of new diseases, as described in "The Viral Superhighway" by George Armelagos. Some wonder if we will even survive long enough as a species to experience any significant biological changes. Perhaps our capacity for knowledge is outstripping

the wisdom to use it wisely, and the consequent destruction of our earthly environments and wildlife (as recounted in "Gorilla Warfare" by Craig Stanford) is placing us in ever greater danger of creating the circumstances of our own extinction.

Counterbalancing this pessimism is the view that because it has been our conscious decision making (and not the genetically predetermined behavior that characterizes some species) that has gotten us into this mess, then it will be the conscious will of our generation and future generations that will get us out. But, can we wait much longer for humanity to collectively come to its senses? Or is it already too late?

# Living With the Past

## Profile of an Anthropologist

# No Bone Unturned

## Patrick Huyghe

The research of some physical anthropologists and archaeologists involves the discovery and analysis of old bones (as well as artifacts and other remains). Most often these bones represent only part of a skeleton or maybe the mixture of parts of several skeletons. Often these remains are smashed, burned, or partially destroyed. Over the years, physical anthropologists have developed a remarkable repertoire of skills and techniques for teasing the greatest possible amount of information out of sparse material remains.

Although originally developed for basic research, the methods of physical anthropology can be directly applied to contemporary human problems.... In this profile, we look briefly at the career of Clyde C. Snow, a physical anthropologist who has put these skills to work in a number of different settings....

As you read this selection, ask yourself the following questions:

- Given what you know of physical anthropology, what sort of work would a physical anthropologist do for the Federal Aviation Administration?
- What is anthropometry? *How might anthropometric surveys of pilots and passengers help in the design of aircraft equipment?*
- What is forensic anthropology? *How can a biological anthropologist be an expert witness in legal proceedings?*

Clyde Snow is never in a hurry. He knows he's late. He's always late. For Snow, being late is part of the job. In fact, he doesn't usually begin to work until death has stripped some poor individual to the bone, and no one—neither the local homicide detectives nor the pathologists—can figure out who once gave identity to the skeletonized remains. No one, that is, except a shrewd, laconic, 60-year-old forensic anthropologist.

Snow strolls into the Cook County Medical Examiner's Office in Chicago on this brisk October morning wearing a pair of Lucchese cowboy boots and a three-piece pin-striped suit. Waiting for him in autopsy room 160 are a bunch of naked skeletons found in Illinois, Wisconsin, and Minnesota since his last visit. Snow, a native Texan who now lives in rural Oklahoma, makes the trip up to Chicago some six times a year. The first case on his agenda is a pale brown skull found in the garbage of an abandoned building once occupied by a Chicago cosmetics company.

Snow turns the skull over slowly in his hands, a cigarette dangling from his fingers. One often does. Snow does not seem overly concerned about mortality, though its tragedy surrounds him daily.

"There's some trauma here," he says, examining a rough edge at the lower back of the skull. He points out the area to Jim Elliott, a homicide detective with the Chicago police. "This looks like a chopping blow by a heavy bladed instrument. Almost like a decapitation." In a place where the whining of bone saws drifts through hallways and the sweet-sour smell of death hangs in the air, the word surprises no one.

Snow begins thinking aloud. "I think what we're looking at here is a female, or maybe a small male, about thirty to forty years old. Probably Asian." He turns the skull upside down, pointing out the degree of wear on the teeth. "This was somebody who lived on a really rough diet. We don't normally find this kind of dental wear in a modern Western population."

"How long has it been around?" Elliott asks.

Snow raises the skull up to his nose. "It doesn't have any decompositional odors," he says. He pokes a finger in the skull's nooks and crannies. "There's no soft tissue left. It's good and dry. And it doesn't show signs of having been buried. I would say that this has been lying around in an attic or a box for years. It feels like a souvenir skull," says Snow.

Souvenir skulls, usually those of Japanese soldiers, were popular with U.S. troops serving in the Pacific during World War II; there was also a trade in skulls during the Vietnam War years. On closer inspection, though, Snow begins to wonder about the skull's Asian origins—the broad nasal aperture and the jutting forth of the upper-tooth-bearing part of the face suggest Melanesian features. Sifting through the objects found in the abandoned building with the skull, he finds several loose-leaf albums of 35-millimeter transparencies documenting life among the highland tribes of New Guinea. The slides, shot by an anthropologist, include graphic scenes of ritual warfare. The skull, Snow con-

Reprinted with permission from *Discover* magazine, December 1988, pp. 51–56. © 1988 by The Walt Disney Company.

cludes, is more likely to be a trophy from one of these tribal battles than the result of a local Chicago homicide.

"So you'd treat it like found property?" Elliott asks finally. "Like somebody's garage-sale property?"

"Exactly," says Snow.

Clyde Snow is perhaps the world's most sought-after forensic anthropologist. People have been calling upon him to identify skeletons for more than a quarter of a century. Every year he's involved in some 75 cases of identification, most of them without fanfare. "He's an old scudder who doesn't have to blow his own whistle," says Walter Birkby, a forensic anthropologist at the University of Arizona. "He know's he's good."

Yet over the years Snow's work has turned him into something of an unlikely celebrity. He has been called upon to identify the remains of the Nazi war criminal Josef Mengele, reconstruct the face of the Egyptian boy-king Tutankhamen, confirm the authenticity of the body autopsied as that of President John F. Kennedy, and examine the skeletal remains of General Custer's men at the battlefield of the Little Bighorn. He has also been involved in the grim task of identifying the bodies in some of the United States' worst airline accidents.

Such is his legend that cases are sometimes attributed to him in which he played no part. He did not, as the *New York Times* reported, identify the remains of the crew of the *Challenger* disaster. But the man is often the equal of his myth. For the past four years, setting his personal safety aside, Snow has spent much of his time in Argentina, searching for the graves and identities of some of the thousands who "disappeared" between 1976 and 1983, during Argentina's military regime.

Snow did not set out to rescue the dead from oblivion. For almost two decades, until 1979, he was a physical anthropologist at the Civil Aeromedical Institute, part of the Federal Aviation Administration in Oklahoma City. Snow's job was to help engineers improve aircraft design and safety features by providing them with data on the human frame.

One study, he recalls, was initiated in response to complaints from a flight attendants' organization. An analysis of accident patterns had revealed that inadequate restraints on flight attendants' jump seats were leading to deaths and injuries and that aircraft doors weighing several hundred pounds were impeding evacuation efforts. Snow points out that ensuring the survival of passengers in emergencies is largely the flight attendants' responsibility. "If they are injured or killed in a crash, you're going to find a lot of dead passengers."

Reasoning that equipment might be improved if engineers had more data on the size and strength of those who use it, Snow undertook a study that required meticulous measurement. When his report was issued in 1975, Senator William Proxmire was outraged that $57,800 of the taxpayers' money had been spent to caliper 423 airline strewardesses from head to toe. Yet the study, which received one of the senator's dubious Golden Fleece Awards, was firmly supported by both the FAA and the Association of Flight Attendants. "I can't imagine," says Snow with obvious delight, "how much coffee Proxmire got spilled on him in the next few months."

It was during his tenure at the FAA that he developed an interest in forensic work. Over the years the Oklahoma police frequently consulted the physical anthropologist for help in identifying crime victims. "The FAA figured it was a kind of community service to let me work on these cases," he says.

The experience also helped to prepare him for the grim task of identifying the victims of air disasters. In December 1972, when a United Airlines plane crashed outside Chicago, killing 43 of the 61 people aboard (including the wife of Watergate conspirator Howard Hunt, who was found with $10,000 in her purse), Snow was brought in to help examine the bodies. That same year, with Snow's help, forensic anthropology was recognized as a specialty by the American Academy of Forensic Sciences. "It got a lot of anthropologists interested in forensics," he says, "and it made a lot of pathologists out there aware that there were anthropologists who could help them."

Each nameless skeleton poses a unique mystery for Snow. But some, like the second case awaiting him back in the autopsy room at the Cook County morgue, are more challenging than others. This one is a real chiller. In a large cardboard box lies a jumble of bones along with a tattered leg from a pair of blue jeans, a sock shrunk tightly around the bones of a foot, a pair of Nike running shoes without shoelaces, and, inside the hood of a blue windbreaker, a mass of stringy, blood-caked hair. The remains were discovered frozen in ice about 20 miles outside Milwaukee. A rusted bicycle was found lying close by. Paul Hibbard, chief deputy medical examiner for Waukesha County, who brought the skeleton to Chicago, says no one has been reported missing.

Snow lifts the bones out of the box and begins reconstructing the skeleton on an autopsy table. "There are two hundred six bones and thirty-two teeth in the human body," he says, "and each has a story to tell." Because bone is dynamic, living tissue, many of life's significant events—injuries, illness, childbearing—leave their mark on the body's internal framework. Put together the stories told by these bones, he says, and what you have is a person's "osteobiography."

Snow begins by determining the sex of the skeleton, which is not always obvious. He tells the story of a skeleton that was brought to his FAA office in the late 1970s. It had been found along with some women's clothes and a purse in a local back lot, and the police had assumed that it was female. But when Snow examined the bones, he realized that "at six foot three, she would have probably have been the tallest female in Oklahoma."

Then Snow recalled that six months earlier the custodian in his building had suddenly not shown up for work. The man's supervisor later mentioned to Snow, "You know, one of these days when they find Ronnie, he's going to be dressed as a woman." Ronnie, it turned out, was a weekend transvestite. A copy of his dental records later confirmed that the skeleton in women's clothing was indeed Snow's janitor.

The Wisconsin bike rider is also male. Snow picks out two large bones that look something like twisted oysters—the innominates, or hipbones, which along with the sacrum, or lower backbone, form the pelvis. This pelvis is narrow and steep-walled like a male's, not broad and shallow like a female's. And the sciatic notch (the V-shaped space where the sciatic nerve passes through the hipbone) is narrow, as is normal in a male. Snow can also determine a skeleton's sex by checking the size of the mastoid processes (the bony knobs at the base of the skull) and the prominence of the brow ridge, or by measuring the head of an available limb bone, which is typically broader in males.

From an examination of the skull he concludes that the bike rider is "predominantly Caucasoid." A score of bony traits help the forensic anthropologist assign a skeleton to one of the three major racial groups: Negroid, Caucasoid, or Mongoloid. Snow notes that the ridge of the boy's nose is high and salient, as it is in whites. In Negroids and Mongoloids (which include American Indians as well as most Asians) the nose tends to be broad in relation to its height. However, the boy's nasal margins are somewhat smoothed down, usually a Mongoloid feature. "Possibly a bit of American Indian admixture," says Snow. "Do you have Indians in your area?" Hibbard nods.

Age is next. Snow takes the skull and turns it upside down, pointing out the basilar joint, the junction between the two major bones that form the underside of the skull. In a child the joint would still be open to allow room for growth, but here the joint has fused—something that usually happens in the late teen years. On the other hand, he says, pointing to the zigzagging lines on the dome of the skull, the cranial sutures are open. The cranial sutures, which join the bones of the braincase, begin to fuse and disappear in the mid-twenties.

Next Snow picks up a femur and looks for signs of growth at the point where the shaft meets the knobbed end. The thin plates of cartilage—areas of incomplete calcification—that are visible at this point suggest that the boy hadn't yet attained his full height. Snow double-checks with an examination of the pubic symphysis, the joint where the

two hipbones meet. The ridges in this area, which fill in and smooth over in adulthood, are still clearly marked. He concludes that the skeleton is that of a boy between 15 and 20 years old.

"One of the things you learn is to be pretty conservative," says Snow. "It's very impressive when you tell the police, 'This person is eighteen years old,' and he turns out to be eighteen. The problem is, if the person is fifteen you've blown it—you probably won't find him. Looking for a missing person is like trying to catch fish. Better get a big net and do your own sorting."

Snow then picks up a leg bone, measures it with a set of calipers, and enters the data into a portable computer. Using the known correlation between the height and length of the long limb bones, he quickly estimates the boy's height. "He's five foot six and a half to five foot eleven," says Snow. "Medium build, not excessively muscular, judging from the muscle attachments that we see." He points to the grainy ridges that appear where muscle attaches itself to the bone. The most prominent attachments show up on the teenager's right arm bone, indicating right-handedness.

Then Snow examines the ribs one by one for signs of injury. He finds no stab wounds, cuts, or bullet holes, here or elsewhere on the skeleton. He picks up the hyoid bone from the boy's throat and looks for the tell-tale fracture signs that would suggest the boy was strangled. But, to Snow's frustration, he can find no obvious cause of death. In hopes of identifying the missing teenager, he suggests sending the skull, hair, and boy's description to Betty Pat Gatliff, a medical illustrator and sculptor in Oklahoma who does facial reconstructions.

Six weeks later photographs of the boy's likeness appear in the *Milwaukee Sentinel*. "If you persist long enough," says Snow, "eighty-five to ninety percent of the cases eventually get positively identified, but it can take anywhere from a few weeks to a few years."

Snow and Gatliff have collaborated many times, but never with more glitz than in 1983, when Snow was commissioned by Patrick Barry, a Miami orthopedic surgeon and amateur Egyptologist,

to reconstruct the face of the Egyptian boy-king Tutankhamen. Normally a facial reconstruction begins with a skull, but since Tutankhamen's 3,000-year-old remains were in Egypt, Snow had to make do with the skull measurements from a 1925 postmortem and X-rays taken in 1975. A plaster model of the skull was made, and on the basis on Snow's report—"his skull is Caucasoid with some Negroid admixtures"—Gatliff put a face on it. What did Tutankhamen look like? Very much like the gold mask on his sarcophagus, says Snow, confirming that it was, indeed, his portrait.

Many cite Snow's use of facial reconstructions as one of his most important contributions to the field. Snow, typically self-effacing, says that Gatliff "does all the work." The identification of skeletal remains, he stresses, is often a collaboration between pathologists, odontologists, radiologists, and medical artists using a variety of forensic techniques.

One of Snow's last tasks at the FAA was to help identify the dead from the worst airline accident in U.S. history. On May 25, 1979, a DC-10 crashed shortly after takeoff from Chicago's O'Hare Airport, killing 273 people. The task facing Snow and more than a dozen forensic specialists was horrific. "No one ever sat down and counted," says Snow, "but we estimated ten thousand to twelve thousand pieces or parts of bodies." Nearly 80 percent of the victims were identified on the basis of dental evidence and fingerprints. Snow and forensic radiologist John Fitzpatrick later managed to identify two dozen others by comparing postmortem X-rays with X-rays taken during the victim's lifetime.

Next to dental records, such X-ray comparisons are the most common way of obtaining positive identifications. In 1978, when a congressional committee reviewed the evidence on John F. Kennedy's assassination, Snow used X-rays to show that the body autopsied at Bethesda Naval Hospital was indeed that of the late president and had not—as some conspiracy theorists believed—been switched.

The issue was resolved on the evidence of Kennedy's "sinus print," the scalloplike pattern on the upper margins of the sinuses that is visible in X-rays of the forehead. So characteristic is a person's sinus print that courts throughout the world accept the matching of antemortem and postmortem X-rays of the sinuses as positive identification.

Yet another technique in the forensic specialist's repertoire is photo superposition. Snow used it in 1977 to help identify the mummy of a famous Oklahoma outlaw named Elmer J. McCurdy, who was killed by a posse after holding up a train in 1911. For years the mummy had been exhibited as a "dummy" in a California funhouse—until it was found to have a real human skeleton inside it. Ownership of the mummy was eventually traced back to a funeral parlor in Oklahoma, where McCurdy had been embalmed and exhibited as "the bandit who wouldn't give up."

Using two video cameras and an image processor, Snow superposed the mummy's profile on a photograph of McCurdy that was taken shortly after his death. When displayed on a single monitor, the two coincided to a remarkable degree. Convinced by the evidence, Thomas Noguchi, then Los Angeles County corner, signed McCurdy's death certificate ("Last known occupation: Train robber") and allowed the outlaw's bones to be returned to Oklahoma for a decent burial.

It was this technique that also allowed forensic scientists to identify the remains of the Nazi "Angel of Death," Josef Mengele, in the summer of 1985. A team of investigators, including Snow and West German forensic anthropologist Richard Helmer, flew to Brazil after an Austrian couple claimed that Mengele lay buried in a grave on a São Paulo hillside. Tests revealed that the stature, age, and hair color of the unearthed skeleton were consistent with information in Mengele's SS files; yet without X-rays or dental records, the scientists still lacked conclusive evidence. When an image of the reconstructed skull was superposed on 1930s photographs of Mengele, however, the match was eerily compelling. All doubts were removed a few months later when Mengele's dental X-rays were tracked down.

In 1979 Snow retired from the FAA to the rolling hills of Norman, Oklahoma, where he and his wife, Jerry, live in a sprawling, early-1960s ranch house. Unlike his 50 or so fellow forensic anthropologists, most of whom are tied to academic positions, Snow is free to pursue his consultancy work full-time. Judging from the number of miles that he logs in the average month, Snow is clearly not ready to retire for good.

His recent projects include a reexamination of the skeletal remains found at the site of the Battle of the Little Bighorn, where more than a century ago Custer and his 210 men were killed by Sioux and Cheyenne warriors. Although most of the enlisted men's remains were moved to a mass grave in 1881, an excavation of the battlefield in the past few years uncovered an additional 375 bones and 36 teeth. Snow, teaming up again with Fitzpatrick, determined that these remains belonged to 34 individuals.

The historical accounts of Custer's desperate last stand are vividly confirmed by their findings. Snow identified one skeleton as that of a soldier between the ages of 19 and 23 who weighed around 150 pounds and stood about five foot eight. He'd sustained gunshot wounds to his chest and left forearm. Heavy blows to his head had fractured his skull and sheared off his teeth. Gashed thigh bones indicated that his body was later dismembered with an ax or hatchet.

Given the condition and number of the bodies, Snow seriously questions the accuracy of the identifications made by the original nineteenth-century burial crews. He doubts, for example, that the skeleton buried at West Point is General Custer's.

For the last four years Snow has devoted much of his time to helping two countries come to terms with the horrors of a much more recent past. As part of a group sponsored by the American Association for the Advancement of Science, he has been helping the Argentinian National Commission on Disappeared Persons to determine the fate of some of those who vanished during their country's harsh military rule: between 1976 and 1983 at least 10,000 people were systematically swept off the streets by roving

death squads to be tortured, killed, and buried in unmarked graves. In December 1986, at the invitation of the Aquino government's Human Rights Commission, Snow also spent several weeks training Philippine scientists to investigate the disappearances that occurred under the Marcos regime.

But it is in Argentina where Snow has done the bulk of his human-rights work. He has spent more than 27 months in and around Buenos Aires, first training a small group of local medical and anthropology students in the techniques of forensic investigation, and later helping them carefully exhume and examine scores of the *desaparecidos,* or disappeared ones.

Only 25 victims have so far been positively identified. But the evidence has helped conflict seven junta members and other high-ranking military and police officers. The idea is not necessarily to identify all 10,000 of the missing, says Snow. "If you have a colonel who ran a detention center where maybe five hundred people were killed, you don't have to nail them with five hundred deaths. Just one or two should be sufficient to get him convicted." Forensic evidence from Snow's team may be used to prosecute several other military officers, including General Suarez Mason. Mason is the former commander of the I Army Corps in Buenos Aires and is believed to be responsible for thousands of disappearances. He was recently extradited from San Francisco back to Argentina, where he is expected to stand trial this winter [1988].

The investigations have been hampered by a frustrating lack of ante mortem information. In 1984, when commission lawyers took depositions from relatives and friends of the disappeared, they often failed to obtain such basic information as the victim's height, weight, or hair color. Nor did they ask for the missing person's X-rays (which in Argentina are given to the patient) or the address of the victim's dentist. The problem was compounded by the inexperience of those who carried out the first mass exhumations prior to Snow's arrival. Many of the skeletons were inadvertently destroyed by bulldozers as they were brought up.

Every unearthed skeleton that shows signs of gunfire, however, helps to erode the claim once made by many in the Argentinian military that most of the *desaparecidos* are alive and well and living in Mexico City, Madrid, or Paris. Snow recalls the case of a 17-year-old boy named Gabriel Dunayavich, who disappeared in the summer of 1976. He was walking home from a movie with his girlfriend when a Ford Falcon with no license plates snatched him off the street. The police later found his body and that of another boy and girl dumped by the roadside on the outskirts of Buenos Aires. The police went through the motions of an investigation, taking photographs and doing an autopsy, then buried the three teenagers in an unmarked grave.

A decade later Snow, with the help of the boy's family, traced the autopsy reports, the police photographs, and the grave of the three youngsters. Each of them had four or five closely spaced bullet wounds in the upper chest—the signature, says Snow, of an automatic weapon. Two also had wounds on their arms from bullets that had entered behind the elbow and exited from the forearm.

"That means they were conscious when they were shot," says Snow. "When a gun was pointed at them, they naturally raised their arm." It's details like these that help to authenticate the last moments of the victims and bring a dimension of reality to the judges and jury.

Each time Snow returns from Argentina he says that this will be the last time. A few months later he is back in Buenos Aires. "There's always more work to do," he says. It is, he admits quietly, "terrible work."

"These were such brutal, cold-blooded crimes," he says. "The people who committed them not only murdered; they had a system to eliminate all trace that their victims even existed."

Snow will not let them obliterate their crimes so conveniently. "There are human-rights violations going on all around the world," he says. "But to me murder is murder, regardless of the motive. I hope that we are sending a message to governments who murder in the name of politics that they can be held to account."

# Gorilla Warfare

### *The fate of Africa's rarest apes hinges on battles over their territory as well as their taxonomy*

## By Craig B. Stanford

Hᴵɢʜ ᴀᴍᴏɴɢ ᴛʜᴇ Vɪʀᴜɴɢᴀ Vᴏʟᴄᴀ-noes, along the eastern edge of the Democratic Republic of Congo (DRC), there lives a group of gorillas with little interest in international politics. Day by day and week by week they wander through meadows of bracken fern, eating bamboo and nettles, mating in polygynous groups and fastidiously grooming one another. Although there are only around 600 mountain gorillas left in the world—half of them here and half in Uganda's aptly named Bwindi-Impenetrable National Park—the gorillas themselves seem unconcerned about that fact. Their most aggressive, most territorial act toward people is to bite a farmer on the behind now and again.

But if the forest, to a gorilla's eye, seems peaceful and unbroken, from a human perspective it is riven by disputes, crosshatched by historical, political and biological borders. The volcanoes themselves may be dormant, but they straddle three of the most incendiary places on earth: the southwestern tip of Uganda, the easternmost edge of Congo (formerly Zaïre and officially known as the DRC) and the northernmost lip of Rwanda. The first has a history of violent dictatorship; the other two are still shuddering with brutal conflicts. On any given day, therefore, the visitor cannot be sure whether he will run into gorillas or guerrillas on the trail.

The gorillas don't care: every year they walk across the spine of the volcanoes, spend several months in Uganda, then walk back home to Congo. But the camera-laden Westerners who have hiked for hours to watch them have no such lux-ury. Political instability put an end to gorilla viewing in Congo as well as in Rwanda. Tourists are still free to watch the Bwindi gorillas, but when the Virunga gorillas reach the Congo border the tourists have to stop and watch them disappear into the trees. Then the tourists turn and head back to camp.

This past March 1st, however, that peaceful pattern was suddenly threatened. That morning a group of guerrillas plunged across the Congo border and into Uganda, in violation of international law, in search of unsuspecting ecotourists. Known as the Interahamwe, the guerrillas were Hutus from Rwanda who for years had fought the Tutsi minority that ruled their country. When war erupted in Rwanda in 1994, after a plane carrying the Rwandan president was shot down, the Interahamwe began a brutal campaign of genocide against the Tutsi. In the ensuing slaughter, carried out by both sides, often with machetes, between 10,000 and 20,000 Interahamwe were chased into eastern Congo, where dense forest and political chaos afforded them the best possible cover. There they regrouped and licked their wounds, stealing radios and other supplies to maintain their ragtag revolutionary army.

With Ugandan soldiers patrolling nearby, the Ugandan army did not suspect that the rebels would risk an attack, especially on Western tourists. But the Interahamwe were furious not only with the Rwandan government, they were also incensed with the Ugandan and Western governments, which had supported Rwanda. And so, on that March dawn, more than a hundred rebels charged into Bwindi-Impenetrable park, armed with assault rifles, and headed toward the ecotourism center at Buhoma. Soon a warden was dead and fourteen Western tourists had been seized and taken hostage in the forest. Among them was Mitchell A. Keiver, a Canadian research assistant who worked with me at a nearby camp where I study gorillas and chimpanzees.

Uɴᴛɪʟ ʀᴇᴄᴇɴᴛʟʏ, ᴍᴏᴜɴᴛᴀɪɴ ɢᴏʀɪʟʟᴀs had good reason not to fear the region's bloody politics: they were worth far too much alive. Before neighboring Rwanda slid into genocidal chaos, gorilla tourism among the Virunga volcanoes was that nation's second-largest source of revenue, after

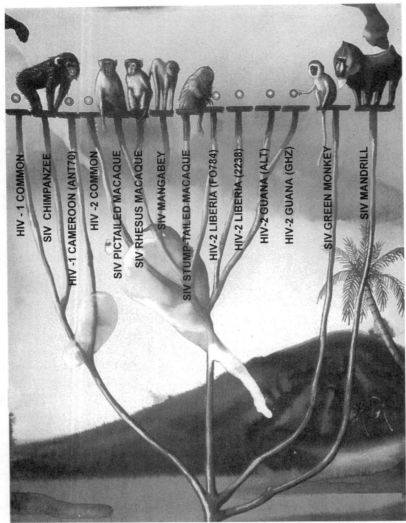

*Alexis Rockman,* HIV's Extended Family (Primates), *1993*

coffee. As many as a million Rwandans were killed during the massacres, and two million more were forced to flee, but only five gorillas were killed by the military. No matter who ended up controlling Rwanda, both sides must have reasoned, the gorillas had to remain safe and sound.

Mountain gorillas owe much of their fame, and thus their value as tourist attractions, to the pioneering field research of the primatologist Dian Fossey and the dramatization of her life in the 1988 film *Gorillas in the Mist.* Fossey's work reversed the popular image of gorillas, born of countless Tarzan and King Kong movies. Rather than bloodthirsty, chest-thumping behemoths—testosterone in black leather—gorillas were depicted as the easygoing animals they are, threatened by people rather than threat-

ening to them. They are herbivores, after all, and exceedingly shy ones at that. A 400-pound male, unaccustomed to tourists, will bolt into the forest, trailing a stream of diarrhea, at the mere sight of a person.

Fossey's work, and the movie about her, sparked an international effort to protect the gorillas. But that effort, in some ways, depends on borders and classifications as arbitrary and disputed as the invisible line that separates Uganda from Congo. Like most animal and plant species, gorillas have traditionally been broken into subspecies, or races, by taxonomists. According to the current classification, there are three kinds of gorilla in Africa (though that number may soon rise), each with a different look, lifestyle and habitat, and a dramatically different population status.

The mountain gorillas of Bwindi and the Virungas, officially known as *Gorilla gorilla beringei,* are a relict population that long ago migrated from the west and evolved in isolation. Much farther west are the western lowland gorillas, which make up a second subspecies, and, compared with their montane cousins, there are lots of them. The western lowland gorilla was the first to be named and therefore carries the doubly redundant moniker *Gorilla gorilla gorilla.* Estimates of its population vary greatly, but a conservative count would put it between 100,000 and 150,000.

The rest of African gorilladom is represented by *Gorilla gorilla graueri,* the eastern lowland gorilla, with traits somewhere between those of the lowlanders to the west and the highlanders to the east. According to a recent survey carried out by the Wildlife Conservation Society, about 7,000 eastern lowland gorillas are left, all in war-torn Congo.

LOWLAND GORILLAS ARE SMALLER, grayer and shorter-haired than gorillas in the mountains. Unlike their more sedentary cousins, lowland gorillas may travel miles each day in search of fruit. The lowland social system, in turn, seems to reflect that mobility: it would be unusual indeed to find mountain gorillas wandering far from the core of their group, whereas lowlanders disperse on a daily basis.

All three gorilla subspecies are in trouble, but G. *g. beringei* is clearly in the direst straits. In the past several hundred years, hunters, farmers and loggers have painted the gorillas into a mountaintop corner. The villages and farms that surround them are among the most densely populated on the continent, leaving few resources for the gorillas; logging has reduced their habitat to a few small patches of forest, and poachers have sold the babies to zoos and chopped up the adults to sell as tourist trinkets. The 600 that remain would be a paltry number for any species, but for gorillas, which reproduce once every four years, it could be disastrously small.

Logging and hunting are closely linked in western and central Africa. Every year, nearly 16,000 square miles of forest are felled on the continent. And as logging roads reach into the great forest tracts, they give hunters with rifles access to apes that once had only tribes with spears to fear. The logging companies themselves encourage hunting, which feeds their workers in forest camps, and gorillas and chimpanzees are sold as table items to wealthy and middle-class Africans, who see bush meat as a status symbol. "People don't want beef or chicken anymore—they call it 'white man's meat,'" one conservationist told *The New York Times*. As a result, the bush-meat trade kills some 3,000 lowland gorillas every year. Even western lowland gorillas, with their population of 100,000, will not withstand such pressures for long.

The one point of light in this bleak vista is ecotourism. In recent years Uganda has recovered from its years of political chaos to become something of a model African country for wildlife conservation. The Ugandan Wildlife Authority has built a thriving industry around the viewing of mountain gorillas. In Bwindi the country boasts a UNESCO World Heritage site, as well as one of the most beautiful forest landscapes on the African continent. In Buhoma, the site of the now-infamous kidnappings, several camps were set up for gorilla-watching. The fanciest of them, run by the world-renowned safari organization Abercrombie and Kent, took visitors back in time to the Africa of Ernest Hemingway. Great green tents sheltered tourists from the frequent rain, local cooks prepared exotic feasts, and waiters in white shirts and bow ties served mixed drinks on hot

afternoons. The only concession to modernity was that no animal was killed there. Tourists, as they say, shot only with their cameras, not with guns.

IT IS A SCENE TO PROVOKE A SNEER, PERHAPS, from some conservationists. But the fact is, in Bwindi, eco-tourism *works*. Poaching is under control and the remaining gorilla habitat is protected in national parks and reserves. So comfortable have the gorillas grown around people in recent years that they have taken to foraging in farmers' fields (hence the occasional butt bite), and they allow people to sit by them. That approachability, combined with the animals' rarity, their fame and their relatively sedentary ways (compared to the lifestyle of their wide-ranging lowland cousins), have made the mountain gorillas into ideal tourist attractions.

Indeed, gorilla-watching has become the centerpiece of the modern tourist's African safari. People pay as much as $3,130 for package tours in which they slog through rugged, wet terrain in order to spend an hour a day sitting with a group of habituated gorillas. Multiply that by several groups of gorillas, each visited by six high-rolling tourists a day, and the tourist income adds up quickly. Every year the farmers who live around Bwindi and the Virungas, scratching out a living from the steep volcanic slopes, get 20 percent of the revenue collected from gorilla-tracking permits. And gorilla tourism heavily subsidizes the Ugandan Wildlife Authority's budget as well. The fate of the mountain gorillas,

in other words, is inseparable from the fate of the people who live around them.

Thanks to ecotourism, mountain gorillas are among the best-protected primates in the world. But a double-edged sword hangs over the area, one edge political, the other taxonomic. Deprive the gorillas of their safeguarded wildlife preserves, and loggers and poachers will soon drive them to extinction. Change their biological classification, and their conservation status could be put in jeopardy. Both lines of protection, unfortunately, are in danger of being cut.

IN 1996 THE PRIMATOLOGISTS ESTEBAN E. Sarmiento of the American Museum of Natural History in New York City, and Thomas M. Butynski and Jan Kalina of Zoo Atlanta proposed a new classification scheme for mountain gorillas. The Bwindi gorillas, they argued, should be recognized as a new and separate subspecies from the Virunga gorillas. The suggestion made a certain sense. The Bwindi and Virunga gorillas already live in distinct groups, about twenty-five miles apart. Five hundred years ago, before subsistence farmers finished clearing the land between the two mountain ranges, the two gorilla habitats were one. Since the separation, however, the populations no longer mingle or interbreed, and their differing habitats—or, perhaps, the random accumulation of genetic mutations in both groups—have, over the centuries, wrought differences in the two groups' looks and behavior.

Because my research project began just after Sarmiento, Butynski and Kalina published their paper, I was in a

## FAMILY PORTRAIT

GENES DO NOT ALWAYS A SPECIES MAKE. ACCORDING TO A PAPER published in the April issue of the *Proceedings of the National Academy of Sciences* (PNAS), the breadth of genetic variation across the various primate species is anything but consistent. Indeed, a single band of fifty-five West African chimpanzees has more genetic variation than all of humanity.

Far to one side of the phylogenetic tree, like a branch badly in need of pruning, sit the orangutans. Although Sumatran and Bornean orangutans ostensibly belong to one species, DNA from the two groups is as distinct as chimpanzee DNA is from bonobo DNA. Gorillas are almost as motley a group. Although mountain and eastern lowland gorillas share much of the same DNA, western lowland gorillas have genes so varied that the animals could easily be split into three or more subspecies. Over on the other half of

the primate tree, the genes within any given chimpanzee subspecies are relatively uniform compared to those within gorilla and orangutan subspecies. Yet compared to those of their close cousins, human beings, they are a veritable genetic menagerie. The reason for the shrunken human gene pool, the authors of the PNAS paper suggest, is that our ancestors once nearly went extinct—though exactly when and how is still unclear.

If genes alone determined species, in other words, taxonomists would have their work cut out for them. In addition to coming up with a new name for one group of orangutans and a few new names for gorillas, they would have to fend off Christian fundamentalists: The fact that humanity is just a hairless species of chimpanzee would be a hard sell in any era.

—BURKHARD BILGER

perfect position to observe those differences. From our camp— a collection of mud-and-thatch huts clinging to the steep side of a mountain—gorillas and chimpanzees can be heard in the forest below around the clock. And we spend most of our waking hours collecting information on the animals' habits. The Bwindi gorillas, we have found, tend to eat more fruit than the Virunga gorillas, and so they travel farther each day. Whereas the Virunga gorillas almost always sleep on the ground, the Bwindi gorillas sometimes sleep in trees. Most obviously, the Virunga gorillas have shaggier coats and a slightly larger build.

Are such differences enough to redefine the two populations as separate subspecies? That depends on your definition of the term. In 1942 the biologist Ernst Mayr defined a subspecies as a population of animals that has adapted genetically to a unique environmental niche and that reproduces in isolation from others of the species. Two populations of squirrels that live on opposite sides of the Grand Canyon might fit that definition, and so would the Bwindi and Virunga gorillas. But over the years the concept of subspecies has undergone an evolution of its own. Some biologists now define it genetically; others focus on social structure or the mechanisms of mate recognition; still others proceed mathematically, by grouping physical traits through cladistic analysis. In general, the various factions can be grouped into two larger camps—the "lumpers" and the "splitters"—but even members of the same camp agree on few specifics. Mayr himself, in 1982, recanted his earlier view, describing subspecies as merely convenient pigeonholing devices for taxonomists.

To most laypeople, genetic differences seem the most plausible way to divide up species. The longer two populations live and breed apart, the more distinctive mutations accumulate in their genes. What could be clearer and simpler? Yet speciation and evolutionary distance are not intimately connected. Two animal populations can look quite different from each other—Great Danes and Chihuahuas,

for instance—yet remain closely related genetically. Or they can look very much alike—the orangutans from Borneo and those from Sumatra are a good example—even though they diverged from the same ancestral stocks many thousands or even millions of years ago [see "Family Portrait"].

FACED WITH SO MANY VARIABLES, AND so little agreement about how to weigh them, biologists have little choice but to use a scorecard approach. And that substantially complicates the classification question for mountain gorillas. In 1996 Karen J. Garner and Oliver A. Ryder, two geneticists at the Zoological Society of San Diego in California, compared the mitochondrial DNA of all the gorilla populations. Whereas mountain-gorilla DNA is quite different from lowland-gorilla DNA, they found, the DNA of the Bwindi and Virunga populations is virtually indistinguishable. How, then, should those groups be classified? Should they be put in separate subspecies, on the basis of their looks, behavior and biogeography, or should they be kept together, on the basis of their genes?

In this case, I believe one must side with the lumpers. Genetic evidence may be no trump card in matters of speciation, but among mountain gorillas the physical and behavioral differences are even less definitive. Gorillas in the Virungas live more than 10,000 feet above sea level, in cold, misty meadows rich in herbs and ground cover but poor in fruit. Bwindi gorillas live in lower and warmer mountains, and so they have access to more fruit trees. Hence the physical circumstances alone can explain why Bwindi gorillas eat more fruit and travel farther to find it, whereas Virunga gorillas make do with foliage. Gorillas are smart, flexible primates, and they have simply adapted their behavior to local conditions.

The physical differences between the groups are just as easy to explain. When my cat and I moved from Michigan to southern California some years ago, she stopped putting on a layer of fat and thick fur every winter. That is because cats, like many animals, have an inherent ability to respond to low nighttime

temperatures, decreasing daylight hours and other signs of approaching cold. Gorillas can no doubt respond to their environment in a similar way.

As abstract and academic as the speciation debate seems, it could become a matter of life or death for mountain gorillas. If the Bwindi gorillas are biologically split from the Virunga gorillas, the world has effectively "lost" half its mountain gorillas, and gained another critically endangered gorilla population. Some would argue that the new status might draw even more attention to the gorillas' plight, enhancing their protection. But what if one subspecies thrives while the other declines? If the bloodlines must be kept separate, gorillas from one group could not be recruited into the other, and the weak group might well become extinct. Taxonomists, it seems, could end up killing the mountain gorilla as effectively as poachers do.

At the same time, political instability is a rising threat to the tourist business. For years, Rwandan rebels have occasionally shot at gorilla-watchers in Congo, and in 1994, when genocidal war broke out in Rwanda, most gorilla research and ecotourism in that country and Congo were shut down. Tourists and investigators still felt relatively insulated from the trouble. But as early as last August there were clear signs that they were not. That month a band of Interahamwe rebels kidnapped a group of eight Western tourists who were following gorillas in Congo. Four of those hostages—two New Zealanders and two Swedes—were never heard from again.

Only six months later, the incident at Buhoma brought the danger across the border to Uganda.

WHEN I FIRST HEARD ABOUT THE rebel attack I was in Pasadena, California, with my wife and three children, only three days after returning from Africa. I had originally planned to bring the family to my field station, as I had done when working in Tanzania. But the logistical hassles finally convinced my wife and me against it.

In the middle of the night, therefore, when an E-mail message arrived from a colleague in Rwanda, saying "ATTACK ON BUHOMA. MORE DETAILS LATER," I felt a faint trace of relief mixed with my concern. Unfortunately, the details that followed soon dashed that small comfort.

---

**FOURTEEN HOSTAGES**
*were rounded up, ordered to take off their shoes and pushed into the forest barefoot. Later eight of them were murdered.*

---

Although the park rangers managed to wound at least four of the attackers, they were quickly overwhelmed. In the next hour the tourism center and several vehicles were set on fire, and the deputy warden, Paul Ross Wagaba, was killed. When the fourteen hostages, nearly all of them tourists, had been rounded up, they were divided into two groups, ordered to take off their shoes, and pushed into the forest barefoot on a forced march back to Congo.

At first I didn't believe that Mitch could be among them. He and I had parted only a few days before in Kampala, the Ugandan capital, and the itinerary he described to me then would not have put him in Buhoma on the morning of the attack. When I called to reassure his parents, however, at their farm in Three Hills, Alberta, Mitch's mother told me that he had called her after I left Uganda. He had changed his plans slightly, she said, and had been in the ecotourism center on that morning after all. There were thirteen tourists in the group, a Canadian official had told her, and one investigator.

A hike through the Ugandan forest can be exhausting even for someone in great shape; for those hostages it must have been excruciating. Mitch's group of six hostages climbed for several hours, up steep forest trails. When they reached the border between Uganda and Congo, they convinced the rebels to express their grievances in a two-page note, composed in French on the spot. "This is a punishment for the Anglo-Saxons who sold us out," the note read, in part. "You are protecting the minority and oppressing the majority." Then Mitch and the others were released. They later learned that the eight hostages in the second group had been brutally murdered.

A WEEK AFTER HIS ORDEAL Mitch flew home to Three Hills. But he is already back in Uganda, working for the International Gorilla Conservation Programme in Kabale. Although I canceled my next research trip, my Ugandan field assistants continue to collect data every day at my camp, and the national park was reopened to tourism only a month after the attack had shut it down. Three tourists a day, on average, have visited the gorillas since, but that is down from twelve or more before the attack. If poaching patrols and basic operations are to continue, the shortfall in income will have to be made up by nongovernmental organizations; regardless, gorilla conservation efforts are likely to suffer.

There is still cause for hope. Two years ago representatives from Congo, Rwanda and Uganda met for the first time to define shared goals for gorilla conservation. Although their political troubles run deep, their economic incentives for protecting the gorillas run even deeper. Nevertheless, as effective as ecotourism can be in Bwindi, the attack was a lesson in its limitations. Tourist dollars may give local villagers a reason to share in the ethic of protecting gorillas. But money alone can't put out the political fires that so recently spread to Buhoma.

In the past two centuries the people of Africa have suffered under the same forces that have decimated gorilla populations and destroyed much of the animals' habitat. Myriad governments have been born and died, their countries carved and recarved at the whims of colonial powers and dictators, their people pushed together or shoved apart with no regard for their own ancient ethnic rivalries. Uganda was a British colony; Congo was a Belgian colony; Rwanda was part of German East Africa and then forced into the Belgian League of Nations. All three countries are inherently flammable, and Western aid and Western tourists, in some ways, only add fuel to the blaze.

WHEREAS MY COLLEAGUES AND I were understandably preoccupied with the Western victims, many Ugandans reacted differently. The deaths of a few tourists at the rebels' hands, they pointed out, provoked nearly as much sympathy and outrage from Westerners as the deaths of a million Rwandans in 1994. Once again Westerners were demonstrating their neocolonial myopia, showing more concern for white people who happen to be living or traveling in Africa than for the Africans themselves.

The mountain gorillas, for their part, know too little to care: their travels mock the very idea of political nation states. As long as they remain pawns in the battle zone that is east-central Africa, however, they are in mortal danger, and even the most dedicated conservationists are helpless to protect them. Through science we may try to fix what people have botched through politics and economics. We may declare some species endangered and others healthy, drawing new borders between species or erasing them altogether. But in Africa, the divisions that matter the most are the ones between people, not between animals, and they cut deeper than any border on a map. Only by healing those rifts can we ever hope to save the mountain gorillas.

---

*CRAIG B. STANFORD is an associate professor of anthropology at the University of Southern California in Los Angeles. He is the author of* CHIMPANZEE AND RED BOLOBUS, *published last year by Harvard University Press, and* THE HUNTING APES, *published this year by Princeton University Press.*

# The Viral Superhighway

*Environmental disruptions and international travel have brought on
a new era in human illness, one marked by diabolical new diseases*

## By George J. Armelagos

*So the Lord sent a pestilence upon Is-
rael from the morning until the ap-
pointed time; and there died of the
people from Dan to Beer-sheba seventy thousand men.*
—2 Sam. 24:15

SWARMS OF CROP-DESTROYING LOCUSTS,
rivers fouled with blood, lion-
headed horses breathing fire and
sulfur: the Bible presents a lurid assortment of plagues, described as acts of retribution by a vengeful God. Indeed,
real-life epidemics—such as the influenza
outbreak of 1918, which killed 21 million
people in a matter of months—can be so
sudden and deadly that it is easy, even for
nonbelievers, to view them as angry messages from the beyond.

How reassuring it was, then, when
the march of technology began to give
people some control over the scourges
of the past. In the 1950s the Salk vaccine, and later, the Sabin vaccine, dramatically reduced the incidence of polio.
And by 1980 a determined effort by
health workers worldwide eradicated
smallpox, a disease that had afflicted humankind since earliest times with blindness, disfigurement and death, killing
nearly 300 million people in the twentieth century alone.

But those optimistic years in the second half of our century now seem, with
hindsight, to have been an era of inflated
expectations, even arrogance. In 1967
the surgeon general of the United States,
William H. Stewart, announced that vic-

tory over infectious diseases was immi-
nent—a victory that would close the
book on modern plagues. Sadly, we now
know differently. Not only have deadly
and previously unimagined new illnesses such as AIDS and Legionnaires'
disease emerged in recent years, but historical diseases that just a few decades
ago seemed to have been tamed are returning in virulent, drug-resistant varieties.
Tuberculosis, the ancient lung disease
that haunted nineteenth-century Europe,
afflicting, among others, Chopin, Dosto-
yevski and Keats, is aggressively mutating into strains that defy the standard
medicines; as a result, modern TB victims
must undergo a daily drug regimen so
elaborate that health-department workers often have to personally monitor patients to make sure they comply [see "A
Plague Returns," by Mark Earnest and
John A. Sbarbaro, September/October
1993]. Meanwhile, bacteria and viruses
in foods from chicken to strawberries to
alfalfa sprouts are sickening as many as
80 million Americans each year.

And those are only symptoms of a
much more general threat. Deaths from
infectious diseases in the United States
rose 58 percent between 1980 and 1992.
Twenty-nine new diseases have been reported in the past twenty-five years, a
few of them so bloodcurdling and bizarre that descriptions of them bring to
mind tacky horror movies. Ebola virus,
for instance, can in just a few days reduce a healthy person to a bag of teem-

ing flesh spilling blood and organ parts
from every orifice. Creutzfeldt-Jakob
disease, which killed the choreographer
George Balanchine in 1983, eats away
at its victims' brains until they resemble
wet sponges. Never slow to fan mass
hysteria, Hollywood has capitalized on
the phenomenon with films such as *Outbreak,* in which a monkey carrying a
deadly new virus from central Africa in-
fects unwitting Californians and starts
an epidemic that threatens to annihilate
the human race.

The reality about infectious disease is
less sensational but alarming nonetheless.
Gruesome new pathogens such as Ebola
are unlikely to cause a widespread epidemic because they sicken and kill so
quickly that victims can be easily identified and isolated; on the other hand, the
seemingly innocuous practice of overpre-
scribing antibiotics for bad colds could ultimately lead to untold deaths, as familiar
germs evolve to become untreatable. We
are living in the twilight of the antibiotic
era: within our lifetimes, scraped knees
and cut fingers may return to the realm of
fatal conditions.

Through international travel, global
commerce and the accelerating destruction of ecosystems worldwide, people
are inadvertently exposing themselves to
a Pandora's box of emerging microbial
threats. And the recent rumblings of biological terrorism from Iraq highlight the
appalling potential of disease organisms
for being manipulated to vile ends. But

This article is reprinted by permission of *The Sciences* and is from the January/February 1998 issue, pp. 24-29. Individual subscriptions are $28 per year. Write to: The Sciences, 2 East 63rd Street, New York, NY 10021.

although it may appear that the apocalypse has arrived, the truth is that people today are not facing a unique predicament. Emerging diseases have long loomed like a shadow over the human race.

PEOPLE AND PATHOGENS HAVE A LONG history together. Infections have been detected in the bones of human ancestors more than a million years old, and evidence from the mummy of the Egyptian pharaoh Ramses V suggests that he may have died from smallpox more than 3,000 years ago. Widespread outbreaks of disease are also well documented. Between 1347 and 1351 roughly a third of the population of medieval Europe was wiped out by bubonic plague, which is carried by fleas that live on rodents. In 1793, 10 percent of the population of Philadelphia succumbed to yellow fever, which is spread by mosquitoes. And in 1875 the son of a Fiji chief came down with measles after a ceremonial trip to Australia. Within four months more than 20,000 Fijians were dead from the imported disease, which spreads through the air when its victims cough or sneeze.

According to conventional wisdom in biology, people and invading microorganisms evolve together: people gradually become more resistant, and the microorganisms become less virulent. The result is either mutualism, in which the relation benefits both species, or commensalism, in which one species benefits without harming the other. Chicken pox and measles, once fatal afflictions, now exist in more benign forms. Logic would suggest, after all, that the best interests of an organism are not served if it kills its host; doing so would be like picking a fight with the person who signs your paycheck.

But recently it has become clear to epidemiologists that the reverse of that cooperative paradigm of illness can also be true: microorganisms and their hosts sometimes exhaust their energies devising increasingly powerful weaponry and defenses. For example, several variants of human immunodeficiency virus (HIV) may compete for dominance within a person's body, placing the immune system under ever-greater siege. As long as a virus has an effective mechanism for jumping from one per-

son to another, it can afford to kill its victims [see "The Deadliest Virus," by Cynthia Mills, January/February 1997].

If the competition were merely a question of size, humans would surely win: the average person is $10^{17}$ times the size of the average bacterium. But human beings, after all, constitute only one species, which must compete with 5,000 kinds of viruses and more than 300,000 species of bacteria. Moreover, in the twenty years it takes humans to produce a new generation, bacteria can reproduce a half-million times. That disparity enables pathogens to evolve ever more virulent adaptations that quickly outstrip human responses to them. The scenario is governed by what the English zoologist Richard Dawkins of the University of Oxford and a colleague have called the "Red Queen Principle." In Lewis Carroll's *Through the Looking Glass* the Red Queen tells Alice she will need to run faster and faster just to stay in the same place. Staving off illness can be equally elusive.

THE CENTERS FOR DISEASE CONTROL and Prevention (CDC) in Atlanta, Georgia, has compiled a list of the most recent emerging pathogens. They include:

• *Campylobacter,* a bacterium widely found in chickens because of the commercial practice of raising them in cramped, unhealthy conditions. It causes between two million and eight million cases of food poisoning a year in the United States and between 200 and 800 deaths.

• *Escherichia coli* 0157:H7, a dangerously mutated version of an often harmless bacterium. Hamburger meat from Jack in the Box fast-food restaurants that was contaminated with this bug led to the deaths of at least four people in 1993.

• Hantaviruses, a genus of fast-acting, lethal viruses, often carried by rodents, that kill by causing the capillaries to leak blood. A new hantavirus known as *sin nombre* (Spanish for "nameless") surfaced in 1993 in the southwestern United States, causing the sudden and mysterious deaths of thirty-two people.

• HIV, the deadly virus that causes AIDS (acquired immunodeficiency syndrome). Although it was first ob-

served in people as recently as 1981, it has spread like wildfire and is now a global scourge, affecting more than 30 million people worldwide.

• The strange new infectious agent that causes bovine spongiform encephalopathy, or mad cow disease, which recently threw the British meat industry and consumers into a panic. This bizarre agent, known as a prion, or "proteinaceous infectious particle," is also responsible for Creutzfeldt-Jakob disease, the brain-eater I mentioned earlier. A Nobel Prize was awarded last year to the biochemist Stanley B. Prusiner of the University of California, San Francisco, for his discovery of the prion.

• *Legionella pneumophila,* the bacterium that causes Legionnaires' disease. The microorganism thrives in wet environments; when it lodges in air-conditioning systems or the mist machines in supermarket produce sections, it can be expelled into the air, reaching people's lungs. In 1976 thirty-four participants at an American Legion convention in Philadelphia died—the incident that led to the discovery and naming of the disease.

• *Borrelia burgdorferi,* the bacterium that causes Lyme disease. It is carried by ticks that live on deer and white-footed mice. Left untreated, it can cause crippling, chronic problems in the nerves, joints and internal organs.

HOW IRONIC, GIVEN SUCH A ROGUES' gallery of nasty characters, that just a quarter-century ago the Egyptian demographer Abdel R. Omran could observe that in many modern industrial nations the major killers were no longer infectious diseases. Death, he noted, now came not from outside but rather from within the body, the result of gradual deterioration. Omran traced the change to the middle of the nineteenth century, when the industrial revolution took hold in the United States and parts of Europe. Thanks to better nutrition, improved public-health measures and medical advances such as mass immunization and the introduction of antibiotics, microorganisms were brought under control. As people began living longer, their aging bodies succumbed to "diseases of civilization": cancer, clogged arteries, diabetes, obesity and osteoporosis. Omran was the first to formally recognize that shift in the disease environment. He called it an "epidemiological transition."

Like other anthropologists of my generation, I learned of Omran's theory early in my career, and it soon became a basic tenet—a comforting one, too, implying as it did an end to the supremacy of microorganisms. Then, three years ago, I began working with the anthropologist Kathleen C. Barnes of Johns Hopkins University in Baltimore, Maryland, to formulate an expansion of Omran's ideas. It occurred to us that his epidemiological transition had not been a unique event. Throughout history human populations have undergone shifts in their relations with disease—shifts, we noted, that are always linked to major changes in the way people interact with the environment. Barnes and I, along with James Lin, a master's student at Johns Hopkins University School of Hygiene and Public Health, have since developed a new theory: that there have been not one but three major epidemiological transitions; that each one has been sparked by human activities; and that we are living through the third one right now.

The first epidemiological transition took place some 10,000 years ago, when people abandoned their nomadic existence and began farming. That profoundly new way of life disrupted ecosystems and created denser living conditions that led, as I will soon detail, to new diseases. The second epidemiological transition was the salutary one Omran singled out in 1971, when the war against infectious diseases seemed to have been won. And in the past two decades the emergence of illnesses such as hepatitis C, cat scratch disease (caused by the bacterium *Bartonella henselae*), Ebola and others on CDC's list has created a third epidemiological transition, a disheartening set of changes that in many ways have reversed the effects of the second transition and coincide with the shift to globalism. Burgeoning population growth and urbanization, widespread environmental degradation, including global warming and tropical deforestation, and radically improved methods of transportation have given rise to new ways of contracting and spreading disease.

We are, quite literally, making ourselves sick.

WHEN EARLY HUMAN ANCESTORS moved from African forests onto the savanna millions of years ago, a few diseases came along for the ride. Those "heirloom" species—thus designated by the Australian parasitologist J. F. A. Sprent because they had afflicted earlier primates—included head and body lice; parasitic worms such as pinworms, tapeworms and liver flukes; and possibly herpes virus and malaria.

For 99.8 percent of the five million years of human existence, hunting and gathering was the primary mode of subsistence. Our ancestors lived in small groups and relied on wild animals and plants for their survival. In their foraging rounds, early humans would occasionally have contracted new kinds of illnesses through insect bites or by butchering and eating disease-ridden animals. Such events would not have led to widespread epidemics, however, because groups of people were so sparse and widely dispersed.

---

*Global Warming could allow the mosquitoes that carry dengue fever to survive as far north as New York City.*

---

About 10,000 years ago, at the end of the last ice age, many groups began to abandon their nomadic lifestyles for a more efficient and secure way of life. The agricultural revolution first appeared in the Middle East; later, farming centers developed independently in China and Central America. Permanent villages grew up, and people turned their attention to crafts such as toolmaking and pottery. Thus when people took to cultivating wheat and barley, they planted the seeds of civilization as well.

With the new ways, however, came certain costs. As wild habitats were transformed into urban settings, the farmers who brought in the harvest with their flint-bladed sickles were assailed by grim new ailments. Among the most common was scrub typhus, which is carried by mites that live in tall grasses, and causes a potentially lethal fever. Clearing vegetation to create arable fields brought farmers frequently into mite-infested terrain.

Irrigation brought further hazards. Standing thigh-deep in watery canals, farm workers were prey to the worms that cause schistosomiasis. After living within aquatic snails during their larval stage, those worms emerge in a free-swimming form that can penetrate human skin, lodge in the intestine or urinary tract, and cause bloody urine and other serious maladies. Schistosomiasis was well known in ancient Egypt, where outlying fields were irrigated with water from the Nile River; descriptions of its symptoms and remedies are preserved in contemporary medical papyruses.

The domestication of sheep, goats and other animals cleared another pathway for microorganisms. With pigs in their yards and chickens roaming the streets, people in agricultural societies were constantly vulnerable to pathogens that could cross interspecies barriers. Many such organisms had long since reached commensalism with their animal hosts, but they were highly dangerous to humans. Milk from infected cattle could transmit tuberculosis, a slow killer that eats away at the lungs and causes its victims to cough blood and pus. Wool and skins were loaded with anthrax, which can be fatal when inhaled and, in modern times, has been developed by several nations as a potential agent of biological warfare. Blood from infected cattle, injected into people by biting insects such as the tsetse fly, spread sleeping sickness, an often-fatal disease marked by tremors and protracted lethargy.

A SECOND MAJOR EFFECT OF AGRICULture was to spur population growth and, perhaps more important, density. Cities with populations as high as 50,000 had developed in the Near East by 3000 B.C. Scavenger species such as rats, mice and sparrows, which congregate wherever large groups of people live, exposed city dwellers to bubonic plague, typhus and rabies. And now that people were crowded together, a new pathogen could quickly start an epidemic. Larger populations also enabled diseases such as measles, mumps, chicken pox and smallpox to persist in an endemic form—always present, afflicting part of the population while sparing those with acquired immunity.

Thus the birth of agriculture launched humanity on a trajectory that has again and again brought people into contact with new pathogens. Tilling soil and raising livestock led to more energy-intensive ways of extracting resources from the earth—to lumbering, coal mining, oil drilling. New resources led to increasingly complex social organization, and to new and more frequent contacts between various societies. Loggers today who venture into the rain forest disturb previously untouched creatures and give them, for the first time, the chance to attack humans. But there is nothing new about this drama; only the players have changed. Some 2,000 years ago the introduction of iron tools to sub-Saharan Africa led to a slash-and-burn style of agriculture that brought people into contact with *Anopheles gambiae*, a mosquito that transmits malaria.

Improved transportation methods also help diseases extend their reach: microorganisms cannot travel far on their own, but they are expert hitchhikers. When the Spanish invaded Mexico in the early 1500s, for instance, they brought with them diseases that quickly raged through Tenochtitlán, the stately, temple-filled capital of the Aztec Empire. Smallpox, measles and influenza wiped out millions of Central America's original inhabitants, becoming the invisible weapon in the European conquest.

IN THE PAST THREE DECADES PEOPLE AND their inventions have drilled, polluted, engineered, paved, planted and deforested at soaring rates, changing the biosphere faster than ever before. The combined effects can, without hyperbole, be called a global revolution. After all, many of them have worldwide repercussions: the widespread chemical contamination of waterways, the thin-

ning of the ozone layer, the loss of species diversity. And such global human actions have put people at risk for infectious diseases in newly complex and devastating ways. Global warming, for instance, could expose millions of people for the first time to malaria, sleeping sickness and other insect-borne illnesses; in the United States, a slight overall temperature increase would allow the mosquitoes that carry dengue fever to survive as far north as New York City.

Major changes to the landscape that have become possible in the past quarter-century have also triggered new diseases. After the construction of the Aswan Dam in 1970, for instance, Rift Valley fever infected 200,000 people in Egypt, killing 600. The disease had been known to affect livestock, but it was not a major problem in people until the vast quantities of dammed water became a breeding ground for mosquitoes. The insects bit both cattle and humans, helping the virus jump the interspecies barrier.

In the eastern United States, suburbanization, another relatively recent phenomenon, is a dominant factor in the emergence of Lyme disease—10,000 cases of which are reported annually. Thanks to modern earth-moving equipment, a soaring economy and population pressures, many Americans have built homes in formerly remote, wooded areas. Nourished by lawns and gardens and unchecked by wolves, which were exterminated by settlers long ago, the deer population has exploded, exposing people to the ticks that carry Lyme disease.

Meanwhile, widespread pollution has made the oceans a breeding ground for microorganisms. Epidemiologists have suggested that toxic algal blooms—fed by the sewage, fertilizers and other contaminants that wash into the oceans—harbor countless viruses and bacteria. Thrown together into what amounts to a dirty genetic soup, those pathogens can undergo gene-swapping and mutations, engendering newly antibiotic-resistant strains. Nautical traffic can carry ocean pathogens far and wide: a devastating outbreak of cholera hit Latin America in 1991 after a ship from Asia unloaded its contaminated ballast water into the harbor of Callao, Peru. Cholera causes diarrhea so severe its victims can

die in a few days from dehydration; in that outbreak more than 300,000 people became ill, and more than 3,000 died.

The modern world is becoming—to paraphrase the words of the microbiologist Stephen S. Morse of Columbia University—a viral superhighway. Everyone is at risk.

Our newly global society is characterized by huge increases in population, international travel and international trade—factors that enable diseases to spread much more readily than ever before from person to person and from continent to continent. By 2020 the world population will have surpassed seven billion, and half those people will be living in urban centers. Beleaguered third-world nations are already hard-pressed to provide sewers, plumbing and other infrastructure; in the future, clean water and adequate sanitation could become increasingly rare. Meanwhile, political upheavals regularly cause millions of people to flee their homelands and gather in refugee camps, which become petri dishes for germs.

More than 500 million people cross international borders each year on commercial flights. Not only does that traffic volume dramatically increase the chance a sick person will infect the inhabitants of a distant area when she reaches her destination; it also exposes the sick person's fellow passengers to the disease, because of poor air circulation on planes. Many of those passengers can, in turn, pass the disease on to others when they disembark.

THE GLOBAL ECONOMY THAT HAS arisen in the past two decades has established a myriad of connections between far-flung places. Not too long ago bananas and oranges were rare treats in northern climes. Now you can walk into your neighborhood market and find food that has been flown and trucked in from all over the world: oranges from Israel, apples from New Zealand, avocados from California. Consumers in affluent nations expect to be able to buy whatever they want whenever they want it. What people do not generally realize, however, is that this global network of food production and delivery provides countless pathways for pathogens. Raspberries from Guatemala, carrots from Peru and coconut milk from Thailand have been responsible for recent outbreaks of food poisoning in the United States. And the problem cuts both ways: contaminated radish seeds and frozen beef from the United States have ended up in Japan and South Korea.

Finally, the widespread and often indiscriminate use of antibiotics has played a key role in spurring disease. Forty million pounds of antibiotics are manufactured annually in the United States, an eightyfold increase since 1954. Dangerous microorganisms have evolved accordingly, often developing antibiotic-resistant strains. Physicians are now faced with penicillin-resistant gonorrhea, multiple-drug-resistant tuberculosis and E. coli variants such as 0157:H7. And frighteningly, some enterococcus bacteria have become resistant to all known antibiotics. Enterococcus infections are rare, but staphylococcus infections are not, and many strains of staph bacteria now respond to just one antibiotic, vancomycin. How long will it be before run-of-the-mill staph infections—in a boil, for instance, or in a surgical incision—become untreatable?

ALTHOUGH CIVILIZATION CAN EXPOSE people to new pathogens, cultural progress also has an ob-vious countervailing effect: it can provide tools—medicines, sensible city planning, educational campaigns about sexually transmitted diseases—to fight the encroachments of disease. Moreover, since biology seems to side with microorganisms anyway, people have little choice but to depend on protective cultural practices to keep pace: vaccinations, for instance, to confer immunity, combined with practices such as hand-washing by physicians between patient visits, to limit contact between people and pathogens.

All too often, though, obvious protective measures such as using only clean hypodermic needles or treating urban drinking water with chlorine are neglected, whether out of ignorance or a wrongheaded emphasis on the short-term financial costs. The worldwide disparity in wealth is also to blame: not surprisingly, the advances made during the second epidemiological transition were limited largely to the affluent of the industrial world.

Such lapses are now beginning to teach the bitter lesson that the delicate balance between humans and invasive microorganisms can tip the other way again. Overconfidence—the legacy of the second epidemiological transition—has made us especially vulnerable to emerging and reemerging diseases. Evolutionary principles can provide this useful corrective: in spite of all our medical and technological hubris, there is no quick fix. If human beings are to overcome the current crisis, it will be through sensible changes in behavior, such as increased condom use and improved sanitation, combined with a commitment to stop disturbing the ecological balance of the planet.

The Bible, in short, was not far from wrong: We do bring plagues upon ourselves—not by sinning, but by refusing to heed our own alarms, our own best judgment. The price of peace—or at least peaceful coexistence—with the microorganisms on this planet is eternal vigilance.

---

*George J. Armelagos is a professor of anthropology at Emory University in Atlanta, Georgia. He has coedited two books on the evolution of human disease:* PALEOPATHOLOGY AT THE ORIGINS OF AGRICULTURE, *which deals with prehistoric populations, and* DISEASE IN POPULATIONS IN TRANSITION, *which focuses on contemporary societies.*

# The Natural History of Art

### Beauty Is Not Just in the Eye of the Beholder. It's Embedded in Our Genes

## By Richard Conniff

NOT LONG AGO IN AFRICA, I camped in what seemed like one of the perfect places on Earth, at the edge of a stand of trees overlooking a floodplain. The stars were spangled across the sky in smoky clusters of light, and I lay in my tent listening to the distant rumble of lions and the doleful keening of jackals. In the morning, my companions and I squatted around an open fire and watched the night fade gradually into dawn on the open plain. It might have been 100,000 years ago, when our ancestors were hunter-gatherers. It might have been millions of years ago, when we were apes.

It felt like home, and the biologist I was visiting suggested that perhaps our evolution in a landscape like this had shaped much more than the way our hips articulate or our hands grasp. Maybe evolution influences what we like, he said. Maybe we like glassy, sparkling surfaces because they suggest close proximity to water. Maybe we take comfort in a certain branchy tree shape because our Pleistocene forebears roosted in such trees at night for safety from predators. Perhaps things we regard as purely cultural and artistic—like the graceful way a ballerina's ankle unbends when she is on point, in a way few men can manage—are actually products of anthropoid evolution. A woman's ankle can rotate through a much greater arc, one biologist has suggested, because our early female ancestors had to stretch from one branch to another while foraging in the trees and bushes, whereas heavier-bodied males tended to stick to flat land.

The idea that there might be a natural history of aesthetics turned out, when I

got home and began to read, to be more than idle campfire talk. Richard Coss, now a psychology professor at the University of California at Davis, largely invented the idea of evolutionary aesthetics in a paper he wrote 30 years ago as a young graduate in industrial design. Coss made the startling suggestion that we respond to art, and to our visual world, not just as aesthetes (or even Philistines) but as animals. Among other examples, he cited an abstract painting by Paul Klee, *The Snake Goddess and Her Enemy*. Coss noted that butterflies and other creatures often use false eyespots to produce alarm in predators. He suggested that Klee was eliciting an innate biological response in his viewers through similar "releasing mechanisms"—the S-shape of the snake and the use of a mask with two prominent eyes.

The idea of looking at art from the perspective of animal behavior also occurred to Gordon Orians at the University of Washington. Orians was studying how blackbirds choose where to live when he noticed that humans also select their habitat according to specific criteria, like the presence of water, large trees, open space, and distant views—criteria evoking the savanna where humans evolved. Moreover, when Orians asked test subjects to rate landscape paintings, they tended to prefer the ones that met those criteria. A John Constable landscape like *Dedham Vale* appeals to us, Orians argued, at least partly because it gives the viewer clues to finding resources and avoiding danger. Looking at it is an unconscious exercise in habitat selection: Could I live here? Is it safe to explore? Should I turn and run?

The ideas pioneered by Coss and Orians have gained increasing currency. But to many people, the animal behavior perspective on art still seems like an affront to our idea of what it means to be human. We tend to think that few things are more individual than art, and it's difficult to accept that our idiosyncratic tastes might have a common biological basis. Orians argued, for instance, that the celebrated landscape of the English country house was an unconscious attempt to recreate the environment of the African savanna. I tried this idea out recently on a British aristocrat, who replied, in a horrified tone, "No. The idea was to bring out the natural character of the English countryside." But the means her family had employed over the centuries to achieve a "natural" effect at their house included cutting down dense forests to create open vistas, introducing water holes, and otherwise turning the grounds into a savanna.

The evolutionary perspective has also been slow to take hold because research on the biology of aesthetics tends to be fuzzier than scientists (and some art historians) might like. Orians, Coss, and others quantify preferences that are expressed both verbally and by such physiological measures as pupil size and blood pressure. Then they compare these preferences across cultures (and sometimes across species) to discern whether they are a product of nature or nurture. Skepticism is the typical reaction: A curator at one prominent museum argued that art is far more likely to be influenced by various cultural developments, such as the invention of photography or the rise of Impressionism, than by evolution.

But biologists believe that ancient history—the rise and fall of different body types, survival strategies, and instincts for habitat—has a way of shaping the DNA, where it becomes a sort of ghostly puppet master. In humans, the strings tying us to our past may stretch back more than 2 million years. These strings take the form of innate propensities, things we do unthinkingly and without having to learn from our parents. As in the Klee and Constable paintings, artists often unconsciously express these same propensities.

One of the most basic inherited propensities in animals is a tendency to select a habitat where past generations have thrived. For instance, prairie deer mice live only in the grasslands of the Midwest. When scientists rear them in isolation and give them a choice between grassland and other habitats, untutored youngsters almost always choose grassland. It is in their genes, and natural selection keeps it there. For most animals, including humans, an instinct for suitable habitat—a place that offers adequate food, breeding opportunities, and shelter—is the difference between life and death. Individuals in past generations who chose badly left fewer offspring to perpetuate their foolish ways. On the other hand, individuals with an instinct for choosing good habitat tended to produce more offspring, thus spreading their instincts through the population. What has gotten programmed into our genes as a result, says Orians, is an emotional or psychological response to good habitat—and also to paintings and photos of good habitat.

Most animals appear to be biologically prepared to recognize highly specific indicators of good habitat. When yellow warblers arrive in Jackson Hole, Wyoming, each spring, the trees are still leafless and there's snow on the ground. But the warblers seem to recognize by the shape and color of the bare willow branches that this will soon become good habitat. Likewise, when scientists offer cage-reared chipping sparrows both deciduous and coniferous branches, they perch on the coniferous ones, which are a cue to their ancestral habitat.

Even if having an eye for the right habitat is encoded into the genes, individual animals can often ignore or alter these innate propensities, within limits. Peregrine falcons have evolved to nest on cliff faces. But if a falcon finds its way to New York City, which has no suitable cliffs, it doesn't suddenly act like a robin and nest in a tree in Central Park. Instead it nests high up on the next best thing to a cliff—a Fifth Avenue apartment building overlooking the park. Biologists believe people adapt in much the same way. The tenants in that building make more elaborate nests than the falcon. But evolutionary biology suggests they are also embellishing on innate propensities: Humans and falcons alike choose their roosts for the same reasons—that is, the proximity of good habitat and a safe prospect from which to view it.

It is relatively easy to demonstrate that humans have a genetically prepared negative response to nature. For example, we know rationally that handguns and frayed electrical wires pose a greater threat in the modern world than snakes or spiders. But our evolution has prepared us to fear natural threats more viscerally, and these fears stay with us even though it may be thousands of years since deadly snakes or spiders were part of our daily lives. Scientists have conducted a number of Pavlovian conditioning experiments in which subjects are repeatedly exposed to threatening images. Fear of handguns and frayed wires vanishes relatively quickly. But fear of snakes and spiders, as measured by heart rate and other autonomic nervous system activity, persists long afterward. It's in our genes.

Demonstrating that we have a biologically programmed positive response to nature is more difficult, because we don't respond so dramatically to something that's not a threat. But numerous studies since the 1970s suggest the subtle power of natural scenery to heal both body and mind. Texas A&M researcher Roger Ulrich, for instance, has shown that people who watch a calming nature video after a stressful experience have markedly lower muscle tension, pulse, and skin conductance activity after less than five minutes. This translates into significant medical benefits. Ulrich monitored patients after gallbladder sur-

gery and found that those assigned to a room looking out on trees needed far fewer painkillers than patients in rooms that faced a brick wall. Heart surgery patients in rooms with nature scenes on the wall experienced less anxiety and smoother recoveries than patients with blank walls or abstract art. Likewise, cosmonauts confined for months in outer space quickly lose interest in video programs and other diversions. They prefer to stare out the window at the untouchable Earth.

We seem to be biologically prepared to look for very specific cues about the natural world, in much the manner of chipping sparrows choosing coniferous branches. In separate surveys, Ulrich, Orians, and others have found that people respond strongly to landscapes with open, grassy vegetation, scattered stands of branchy trees, water, changes in elevation, winding trails, and brightly lit clearings, preferably partly obscured by foliage in the foreground. It's a landscape that invites exploration, promising resources and refuge at the same time. The changes in elevation—a view of distant mountains, for instance—provide a landmark to help the viewer orient himself in the scene. The winding trail and the partly obscured clearing provide mystery and entice our innate curiosity to explore. Flowers are valuable not merely for their beauty, but also because they promise fruit and honey. Orians and coauthor Judith Heerwagen note that we prefer flowers to be big and asymmetrical, traits that indicate greater nectar content. They argue that we bring flowers to hospitals because they are literally good medicine: They soothe us with the promise of better times ahead.

All this may seem like a long way from a John Constable landscape. But Orians and Heerwagen found that these habitat cues abound in landscapes by Constable and other artists. When they compared sketches Constable made on the spot with the finished paintings he produced later in his studio, they found that the artist consistently "savannafied" reality to enhance the desirable cues—stripping away foliage to expose tree branches or adding houses for refuge. Habitat cues turn up even in a portrait like Leonardo da Vinci's *Mona Lisa*. It's not just the woman who is serene; it's the setting: A winding road in the background leads through scattered trees to a brightly lit clearing, with a bridge across a river and mountains in the distance, all under a blue sky. In a subsequent study, Orians and Heerwagen applied their evolutionary perspective to 35 paintings of sunsets, by such artists as Frederick Church and Martin Johnson Heade, on the theory that sunset would have been fraught with tension for our ancestors. "When you're out walking on the African savanna," says Orians, "and the sky is getting pink, and in a half hour the lions and hyenas are going to be coming out, sunset is terrifying. We really worry at sunset about where we're going to spend the night." Orians and Heerwagen found that two thirds of the paintings included a refuge clearly accessible to the viewer—a church or a house, often with a light in the window.

Anxiety about lions is of course irrational in the context of an English or American landscape. But biologists say we are built to make snap judgments about such landscapes, without conscious thought. "Behavioral sciences were dominated until fairly recently," says Ulrich, "by theories that put emphasis on conscious, deliberate thinking as a source of feelings. But such an animal would have been highly dysfunctional: 'There's something moving. By golly it looks like a snake. Last time I saw a snake somebody got bitten. Hey, maybe I should feel a little bit afraid.' Well, no." When we see a snake, it pays to jump faster than we can say the word. It takes less than a quarter of a second for the body to register a physiological response to a threat, and somewhat longer—a second or two, according to Ulrich—to register a positive stimulus.

But wait. Unless they are deranged, don't people in a museum know they are looking at paintings on a wall, not real landscapes or real snakes? In traditional criticism, our aesthetic responses are practically defined by being unreal and having no pragmatic application. Seeing an Andy Warhol painting of a Campbell's soup can does not make us reach for a spoon, and neither should a painting of a sunset make us imagine we are out on the savanna with no place to sleep.

But biologists argue that aesthetic and real-life responses differ only in degree. "Alfred Hitchcock was great at this," says Nancy Aiken, author of *The Biological Origins of Art.* "You see a knife coming down and you don't have to see the victim; you know it hits. You might actually gasp and grab hold of the arms of the chair. The blood pressure is going up, the palms are sweating. It's this internal, visceral alerting response. We're physiologically preparing for flight from danger." It takes the conscious brain a moment to remind us there's no real danger.

So should we judge art by what makes the palms sweat, or by what soothes the troubled brow? One art historian who dismissed the idea that biology and art have anything to do with each other suggested that I look up a recent book called *Painting by Numbers: Komar and Melamid's Scientific Guide to Art.* Vitaly Komar and Alexander Melamid, Russian immigrants, commissioned polls in various countries of what people want in their paintings. To Melamid, the uniformity of the results suggested genetic imprinting: "In every country the favorite color is blue, and almost everywhere green is second. . . . Everywhere, the people want outdoor scenes, with wild animals, water, trees, and some people." The two artists then painted each country's "most wanted" image. Kenya's, for example, featured Jesus Christ rising out of a lake with Mount Kilimanjaro in the distance, a hippo grazing on the shore, a family preparing dinner with mortar and pestle, and a blue sky. The point, of course, was parody.

At times, the biological point of view seems to come perilously close to Komar and Melamid's perspective, without the satiric edge. Ulrich, for instance, writes about "the need for research to establish scientific guidelines to help interior designers select art that is reliably stress reducing and physiologically supportive. . . ." But he is talking only about art in hospitals and in other medical contexts, where he believes the sole critical standard is whether art "improves outcomes in patients, and if it doesn't, it's bad art."

The idea of any scientific guidelines for art is guaranteed to raise hackles. And listening to Ulrich, you can easily imagine the tort already festering in some medical malpractice lawyer's brain: "That Jackson Pollock painting killed my client." In truth, figuring out just what constitutes therapeutic art can be difficult. In the mid-1990s, Duke University Medical Center installed a whimsical courtyard sculptural arrangement called *The Bird Garden,* inspired by Florence Nightingale's belief that good art in hospitals can be an "actual means of recovery." It consisted of 10-foot-tall steel pieces commemorating birds that are now extinct, like the dodo and the passenger pigeon. Patients looking at the courtyard sculptures soon began to project their troubles onto the art. One piece reminded them of hands reaching up from the grave. Another piece, depicting an owl, disturbed them by seeming to stare with one glowering eye. A psychologist like Coss might have informed hospital administrators that chimpanzees will avoid looking at a toy with prominent eyes, gorillas feel threatened by the blank stare of binoculars, and "one of the most primitive avoidance responses to form exhibited by man today is gaze aversion to the unyielding stare of a stranger." The hospital has since removed the sculptures and redesigned the courtyard with inoffensive plants.

But all of this raises the question of why the rest of us, who don't happen to be in hospitals, actually seek out disturbing art. If evolution shapes what we like, why don't we stick with tranquil savannafied landscapes? Why go to a museum to see a painting by George Stubbs, who never left Europe but depicted lions sinking tooth and claw into the necks of terrified horses? What do we find so compelling about a J.M.W. Turner seascape of a storm, which seems to swirl across the canvas without horizon or anything else to give the viewer a foothold? From an evolutionary perspective, says Orians, we find such paintings fascinating because they help us prepare. We look at them for the same reason that we rubberneck at car wrecks or watch "Shark Week" on the Discovery Channel: to learn how to avoid getting into the same situation. Seeing Hitchcock's *Psycho* terrifies us—and reminds us to lock the bathroom door. Art is a message about survival. We are also built to seek thrills, preferably in a safe context. A painting in a museum allows us to experience Turner's perfect storm without strapping ourselves to a mast and risking shipwreck, as the artist did.

Some of the most intriguing ideas about the interplay between visual pleasure and peril continue to come from Coss, who has studied everything from the predator response of California ground squirrels to the design of visual stimulation for astronauts on NASA spacecraft. In his current research, Coss is learning how various primate species protect themselves from leopards, which have preyed on them (and us) for more than 3 million years. Crab-eating monkeys, for example, have a visual system that is highly sensitive to the color yellow, apparently for easier detection of leopards. Coss has also found that a patch of spotted fur no larger than a football will produce alarm even in bonnet macaque populations that have not been exposed to leopards for generations. He theorizes that leopard spots also elicit an innate predator response in humans. This may be why heads of state like Mobutu Sese Seko, the late dictator of Zaire, wear leopard-skin robes and hats.

The zigzag scaly pattern on snakes also appears to elicit an innate arousal in many animals. Coss flips through a clothing catalog to a photograph of a woman in a Gottex bathing suit. The pattern comes, he says, from a venomous Asian pit viper. It makes him wonder about the intended effect: "If you have something that catches your attention in clothing and you combine that with the body of a person who is not going to harm you, it might make you more interested. It's not going to make you fearful, because it's not a frightening context."

Churches and temples seem to use snakeskin patterns to slightly different effect, Coss suggests. The snakelike tile patterns in old mosques and cathedrals "might enhance the religious, fervent emotions," eliciting a mix of "awe and reverence." Or these patterns may simply help keep worshippers awake: "These are things that attract attention," he says, "and it doesn't wane, we don't habituate well to it, and the pattern doesn't become neutral." Our visual world is full of these biological cues, often deployed without conscious thought to their origins, and responded to in the same unthinking fashion, says Coss.

In certain public spaces, particularly stairways and corridors, Coss believes complex visual details, such as patterned wallpaper or conspicuous graphics in the carpeting, may serve a social function by deflecting the gaze of approaching strangers. In other contexts, these details may be subtly oppressive. Not long ago, for instance, I stayed in a beach rental that I came to think of as "knotty pine hell." After a while, I figured out what was making me so uncomfortable: The knots in the wood paneling were paired like unblinking eyes all around me.

The scientific evidence, says Orians, is that our visual environment profoundly influences our physical and mental health, much as a suitable habitat makes for healthier animals in the zoo.

I was thinking about all this back home, on the porch of the house my wife and I recently built on the Connecticut shore. The porch columns around me suddenly felt like tree trunks and the ceiling became the forest canopy, with the paddle fan fluttering overhead like leaves in the breeze. It dawned on me that what we had created was no more than an elaborate replica of that camp site at the edge of a forest in Africa. From my refuge, I looked out at a perfect shopping list of biological habitat cues: There was a grassy lawn, a footpath winding through a scattered stand of branchy trees, a brightly lit clearing in the distance, partly obscured by vegetation, and beyond that, a deep-blue swath of water. I closed my eyes and could feel the puppet strings of evolution tugging at my turn-of-the-millennium soul.

---

Richard Conniff responds viscerally to paintings. "There are times when I go into museums and I want to eat the pictures," he says. "It's a subliminal response that's both calming and exciting." Seascapes at a museum near Conniff's home in Old Lyme, Connecticut, inspired him to seek the source of aesthetics in human history "I've always wondered why a swirl of colors is so compelling," he says. Conniff has written about the natural world for *Outside* and *The Atlantic Monthly.* His latest book is *Every Creeping Thing: True Tales of Faintly Repulsive Wildlife.*

# Dr. Darwin

*With a nod to evolution's god, physicians are looking at illness through the lens of natural selection to find out why we get sick and what we can do about it.*

## Lori Oliwenstein

*Lori Oliwenstein, a former DISCOVER senior editor, is now a freelance journalist based in Los Angeles.*

PAUL EWALD KNEW FROM THE BEGINNING that the Ebola virus outbreak in Zaire would fizzle out. On May 26, after eight days in which only six new cases were reported, that fizzle became official. The World Health Organization announced it would no longer need to update the Ebola figures daily (though sporadic cases continued to be reported until June 20).

The virus had held Zaire's Bandundu Province in its deadly grip for weeks, infecting some 300 people and killing 80 percent of them. Most of those infected hailed from the town of Kikwit. It was all just as Ewald predicted. "When the Ebola outbreak occurred," he recalls, "I said, as I have before, these things are going to pop up, they're going to smolder, you'll have a bad outbreak of maybe 100 or 200 people in a hospital, maybe you'll have the outbreak slip into another isolated community, but then it will peter out on its own."

Ewald is no soothsayer. He's an evolutionary biologist at Amherst College in Massachusetts and perhaps the world's leading expert on how infectious diseases—and the organisms that cause them—evolve. He's also a force behind what some are touting as the next great medical revolution: the application of

*"If you look at it from an evolutionary point of view, you can sort out the 95 percent of disease organisms that aren't a major threat from the 5 percent that are."*

Darwin's theory of natural selection to the understanding of human diseases.

A Darwinian view can shed some light on how Ebola moves from human to human once it has entered the population. (Between human outbreaks, the virus resides in some as yet unknown living reservoir.) A pathogen can survive in a population, explains Ewald, only if it can easily transmit its progeny from one host to another. One way to do this is to take a long time to disable a host, giving him plenty of time to come into contact with other potential victims. Ebola, however, kills quickly, usually in less than a week. Another way is to survive for a long time outside the human body, so that the pathogen can wait for new hosts to find it. But the Ebola strains encountered thus far are destroyed almost at once by sunlight, and

even if no rays reach them, they tend to lose their infectiousness outside the human body within a day. "If you look at it from an evolutionary point of view, you can sort out the 95 percent of disease organisms that aren't a major threat from the 5 percent that are," says Ewald. "Ebola really isn't one of those 5 percent."

The earliest suggestion of a Darwinian approach to medicine came in 1980, when George Williams, an evolutionary biologist at the State University of New York at Stony Brook, read an article in which Ewald discussed using Darwinian theory to illuminate the origins of certain symptoms of infectious disease—things like fever, low iron counts, diarrhea. Ewald's approach struck a chord in Williams. Twenty-three years earlier he had written a paper proposing an evolutionary framework for senescence, or aging. "Way back in the 1950s I didn't worry about the practical aspects of senescence, the medical aspects," Williams notes. "I was pretty young then." Now, however, he sat up and took notice.

While Williams was discovering Ewald's work, Randolph Nesse was discovering Williams's. Nesse, a psychiatrist and a founder of the University of Michigan Evolution and Human Behavior Program, was exploring his own interest in the aging process, and he and Williams soon got together. "He had wanted to find a physician to work with on medical problems," says Nesse, "and I had long wanted to find an evolutionary biologist, so it was a very natural match for us." Their collaboration led to a 1991 article that most researchers say signaled the real birth of the field.

NESSE AND WILLIAMS DEfine Darwinian medicine as the hunt for evolutionary explanations of vulnerabilities to disease. It can, as Ewald noted, be a way to interpret the body's defenses, to try to figure out, say, the reasons we feel pain or get runny noses when we have a cold, and to determine what we should—or shouldn't—be doing about those defenses. For instance, Darwinian researchers like physiologist Matthew Kluger of the Lovelace Institute in Albuquerque now say that a moderate rise in body temperature is more than just a symptom of disease; it's an evolutionary adaptation the body uses to fight infection by making itself inhospitable to invading microbes. It would seem, then, that if you lower the fever, you may prolong the infection. Yet no one is ready to say whether we should toss out our aspirin bottles. "I would love to see a dozen proper studies of whether it's wise to bring fever down when someone has influenza," says Nesse. "It's never been done, and it's just astounding that it's never been done."

Diarrhea is another common symptom of disease, one that's sometimes the result of a pathogen's manipulating your body for its own good purposes, but it may also be a defense mechanism mounted by your body. Cholera bacteria, for example, once they invade the human body, induce diarrhea by producing toxins that make the intestine's cells leaky. The resultant diarrhea then both flushes competing beneficial bacteria from the gut and gives the cholera bacteria a ride into the world, so that they can find another hapless victim. In the case of cholera, then, it seems clear that stopping the diarrhea can only do good.

But the diarrhea that results from an invasion of shigella bacteria—which cause various forms of dysentery—seems to be more an intestinal defense than a bacterial offense. The infection causes the muscles surrounding the gut to contract

more frequently, apparently in an attempt to flush out the bacteria as quickly as possible. Studies done more than a decade ago showed that using drugs like Lomotil to decrease the gut's contractions and cut down the diarrheal output actually prolong infection. On the other hand, the ingredients in over-the-counter preparations like Pepto Bismol, which don't affect how frequently the gut contracts, can be used to stem the diarrheal flow without prolonging infection.

Seattle biologist Margie Profet points to menstruation as another "symptom" that may be more properly viewed as an evolutionary defense. As Profet points out, there must be a good reason for the body to engage in such costly activities as shedding the uterine lining and letting blood flow away. That reason, she claims, is to rid the uterus of any organisms that might arrive with sperm in the seminal fluid. If an egg is fertilized, infection may be worth risking. But if there is no fertilized egg, says Profet, the body defends itself by ejecting the uterine cells, which might have been infected. Similarly, Profet has theorized that morning sickness during pregnancy causes the mother to avoid foods that might contain chemicals harmful to a developing fetus. If she's right, blocking that nausea with drugs could result in higher miscarriage rates or more birth defects.

DARWINIAN MEDICINE ISN'T simply about which symptoms to treat and which to ignore. It's a way to understand microbes— which, because they evolve so much more quickly than we do, will probably always beat us unless we figure out how to harness their evolutionary power for our own benefit. It's also a way to realize how disease-causing genes that persist in the population are often selected for, not against, in the long run.

Sickle-cell anemia is a classic case of how evolution tallies costs and benefits. Some years ago, researchers discovered that people with one copy of the sickle-cell gene are better able to resist the protozoans that cause malaria than are people with no copies of the gene. People with two copies of the gene may die, but in malaria-plagued regions such as

tropical Africa, their numbers will be more than made up for by the offspring left by the disease-resistant kin.

Cystic fibrosis may also persist through such genetic logic. Animal studies indicate that individuals with just one copy of the cystic fibrosis gene may be more resistant to the effects of the cholera bacterium. As is the case with malaria and sickle-cell, cholera is much more prevalent than cystic fibrosis; since there are many more people with a single, resistance-conferring copy of the gene than with a disease-causing double dose, the gene is stably passed from generation to generation.

"With our power to do gene manipulations, there will be temptations to find genes that do things like cause aging, and get rid of them," says Nesse. "If we're sure about everything a gene does, that's fine. But an evolutionary approach cautions us not to go too fast, and to expect that every gene might well have some benefit as well as costs, and maybe some quite unrelated benefit."

---

*"I used to hunt saber-toothed tigers all the time, thousands of years ago. Now I sit in front of a computer and don't get exercise, so I've changed my body chemistry."*

---

Darwinian medicine can also help us understand the problems encountered in the New Age by a body designed for the Stone Age. As evolutionary psychologist Charles Crawford of Simon Fraser University in Burnaby, British Columbia, put it: "I used to hunt saber-toothed tigers all the time, thousands of years ago. I got lots of exercise and all that sort of stuff. Now I sit in front of a computer, and all I do is play with a mouse, and I don't get exercise. So I've changed my body biochemistry in all sorts of unknown ways, and it could affect me in all sorts of ways, and we have no idea what they are."

Radiologist Boyd Eaton of Emory University and his colleagues believe such biochemical changes are behind today's breast cancer epidemic. While it's impossible to study a Stone Ager's biochemistry, there are still groups of hunter-gathers around—such as the San of Africa—who make admirable stand-ins. A foraging life-style, notes Eaton, also means a life-style in which menstruation begins later, the first child is born earlier, there are more children altogether, they are breast-fed for years rather than months, and menopause comes somewhat earlier. Overall, he says, American women today probably experience 3.5 times more menstrual cycles than our ancestors did 10,000 years ago. During each cycle a woman's body is flooded with the hormone estrogen, and breast cancer, as research has found, is very much estrogen related. The more frequently the breasts are exposed to the hormone, the greater the chance that a tumor will take seed.

Depending on which data you choose, women today are somewhere between 10 and 100 times more likely to be stricken with breast cancer than our ancestors were. Eaton's proposed solutions are pretty radical, but he hopes people will at least entertain them; they include delaying puberty with hormones and using hormones to create pseudo-pregnancies, which offer a woman the biochemical advantages of pregnancy at an early age without requiring her to bear a child.

In general, Darwinian medicine tells us that the organs and systems that make up our bodies result not from the pursuit of perfection but from millions of years of evolutionary compromises designed to get the greatest reproductive benefit at the lowest cost. We walk upright with a spine that evolved while we scampered on four limbs; balancing on two legs leaves our hands free, but we'll probably always suffer some back pain as well.

"What's really different is that up to now people have used evolutionary theory to try to explain why things work, why they're normal," explains Nesse. "The twist—and I don't know if it's simple or profound—is to say we're try-ing to understand the abnormal, the vulnerability to disease. We're trying to understand why natural selection has not made the body better, why natural selection has left the body with vulnerabilities. For every single disease, there is an answer to that question. And for very few of them is the answer very clear yet."

One reason those answers aren't yet clear is that few physicians or medical researchers have done much serious surveying from Darwin's viewpoint. In many cases, that's because evolutionary theories are hard to test. There's no way to watch human evolution in progress—at best it works on a time scale involving hundreds of thousands of years. "Darwinian medicine is mostly a guessing game about how we think evolution worked in the past on humans, what it designed for us," say evolutionary biologist James Bull of the University of Texas at Austin. "It's almost impossible to test ideas that we evolved to respond to this or that kind of environment. You can make educated guesses, but no one's going to go out and do an experiment to show that yes, in fact humans will evolve this way under these environmental conditions."

Yet some say that these experiments can, should, and will be done. Howard Howland, a sensory physiologist at Cornell, is setting up just such an evolutionary experiment, hoping to interfere with the myopia, or nearsightedness, that afflicts a full quarter of all Americans. Myopia is thought to be the result of a delicate feedback loop that tries to keep images focused on the eye's retina. There's not much room for error: if the length of your eyeball is off by just a tenth of a millimeter, your vision will be blurry. Research has shown that when the eye perceives an image as fuzzy, it compensates by altering its length.

This loop obviously has a genetic component, notes Howland, but what drives it is the environment. During the Stone Age, when we were chasing buffalo in the field, the images we saw were usually sharp and clear. But with modern civilization came a lot of close work. When your eye focuses on something nearby, the lens has to bend, and since bending that lens is hard work, you do as little bending as you can get away with. That's why, whether you're conscious of it or not, near objects tend to be a bit blurry. "Blurry image?" says the eye. "Time to grow." And the more it grows, the fuzzier those buffalo get. Myopia seems to be a disease of industrial society.

To prevent that disease, Howland suggests going back to the Stone Age—or at least convincing people's eyes that that's where they are. If you give folks with normal vision glasses that make their eyes think they're looking at an object in the distance when they're really looking at one nearby, he says, you'll avoid the whole feedback loop in the first place. "The military academies induct young men and women with twenty-twenty vision who then go through four years of college and are trained to fly an airplane or do some difficult visual task. But because they do so much reading, they come out the other end nearsighted, no longer eligible to do what they were hired to do," Howland notes. "I think these folks would very much like not to become nearsighted in the course of their studies." He hopes to be putting glasses on them within a year.

THE NUMBING PACE OF EVOlution is a much smaller problem for researchers interested in how the bugs that plague us do their dirty work. Bacteria are present in such large numbers (one person can carry around more pathogens than there are people on the planet) and evolve so quickly (a single bacterium can reproduce a million times in one human lifetime) that experiments we couldn't imagine in humans can be carried out in microbes in mere weeks. We might even, says Ewald, be able to use evolutionary theory to tame the human immunodeficiency virus.

"HIV is mutating so quickly that surely we're going to have plenty of sources of mutants that are mild as well as severe," he notes. "So now the question is, which of the variants will win?" As in the case of Ebola, he says, it will all come down to how well the virus manages to get from one person to another.

"If there's a great potential for sexual transmission to new partners, then the viruses that reproduce quickly will spread," Ewald says. "And since they're reproducing in a cell type that's critical for the well-being of the host—the helper T cell—then that cell type will be decimated, and the host is likely to suffer from it." On the other hand, if you lower the rate of transmission—through abstinence, monogamy, condom use—then the more severe strains might well die out before they have a chance to be passed very far. "The real question," says Ewald, "is, exactly how mild can you make this virus as a result of reducing the rate at which it could be transmitted to new partners, and how long will it take for this change to occur?" There are already strains of HIV in Senegal with such low virulence, he points out, that most people infected will die of old age. "We don't have all the answers. But I think we're going to be living with this virus for a long time, and if we have to live with it, let's live with a really mild virus instead of a severe virus."

Though condoms and monogamy are not a particularly radical treatment, that they might be used not only to stave off the virus but to tame it is a radical notion—and one that some researchers find suspect. "If it becomes too virulent, it will end up cutting off its own transmission by killing its host too quickly," notes James Bull. "But the speculation is that people transmit HIV primarily within one to five months of infection, when they spike a high level of virus in the blood. So with HIV, the main period of transmission occurs a few months into the infection, and yet the virulence—the death from it—occurs years later. The major stage of transmission is decoupled from the virulence." So unless the pro-tective measures are carried out by everyone, all the time, we won't stop most instances of transmission; after all, most people don't even know they're infected when they pass the virus on.

But Ewald thinks these protective measures are worth a shot. After all, he says, pathogen taming has occurred in the past. The forms of dysentery we encounter in the United States are quite mild because our purified water supplies have cut off the main route of transmission for virulent strains of the bacteria. Not only did hygienic changes reduce the number of cases, they selected for the milder shigella organisms, those that leave their victim well enough to get out and about. Diphtheria is another case in point. When the diphtheria vaccine was invented, it targeted only the most severe form of diphtheria toxin, though for economic rather than evolutionary reasons. Over the years, however, that choice has weeded out the most virulent strains of diphtheria, selecting for the ones that

---

*"We did with diphtheria what we did with wolves. We took an organism that caused harm, and unknowingly, we domesticated it into an organism that protects us."*

---

cause few or no symptoms. Today those weaker strains act like another level of vaccine to protect us against new, virulent strains.

"You're doing to these organisms what we did to wolves," says Ewald.

"Wolves were dangerous to us, we domesticated them into dogs, and then they helped us, they warned us against the wolves that were out there ready to take our babies. And by doing that, we've essentially turned what was a harmful organism into a helpful organism. That's the same thing we did with diphtheria; we took an organism that was causing harm, and without knowing it, we domesticated it into an organism that is protecting us against harmful ones."

Putting together a new scientific discipline—and getting it recognized—is in itself an evolutionary process. Though Williams and Neese say there are hundreds of researchers working (whether they know it or not) within this newly built framework, they realize the field is still in its infancy. It may take some time before *Darwinian medicine* is a household term. Nesse tells how the editor of a prominent medical journal, when asked about the field, replied, "Darwinian medicine? I haven't heard of it, so it can't be very important."

But Darwinian medicine's critics don't deny the field's legitimacy; they point mostly to its lack of hard-and-fast answers, its lack of clear clinical guidelines. "I think this idea will eventually establish itself as a basic science for medicine, " answers Nesse. "What did people say, for instance, to the biochemists back in 1900 as they were playing out the Krebs cycle? People would say, 'So what does biochemistry really have to do with medicine? What can you cure now that you couldn't before you knew about the Krebs cycle?' And the biochemists could only say, 'Well, gee, we're not sure, but we know what we're doing is answering important scientific questions, and eventually this will be useful.' And I think exactly the same applies here."

# Scientists and Religion in America

*Science and religion are engaging in more active dialogue and debate, but a survey suggests that scientists' beliefs have changed little since the 1930s, and top scientists are more atheistic than ever before*

## by Edward J. Larson and Larry Witham

*EDWARD J. LARSON and LARRY WITHAM had the idea of redoing James H. Leuba's survey while Witham was interviewing Larson on the topic of American scientists' religious belies. Witham did the legwork for the survey; Larson, the analysis. Larson, the Richard B. Russell Professor of History and Law at the University of Georgia, won the 1998 Pulitzer Prize in history for his book* Summer for the Gods. *He attends a United Methodist church in Athens, Ga. Witham has written several fiction and nonfiction books and covers religion news for the* Washington Times. *Reared as a Lutheran, Witham is comfortable with Leuba's God.*

A stone's throw from the Potomac River in Washington, D.C., a bronze statue of Albert Einstein reposes in a garden beside the National Academy of Sciences. Could there be a more fitting individual than this mythic figure to symbolize the highest echelon of scientists in America?

Having fled to the U.S. from the secular horrors of Nazi Germany because of his religious heritage, Einstein never ceased musing about religion and once challenged quantum uncertainty by famously denying that God plays dice with the universe. Late in life, however,

he concluded, "In their struggle for the ethical good, teachers of religion must have the stature to give up the doctrine of a personal God."

Now, at the turn of the millennium, comes a movement bent on reconciling science and religion. New books hail the divine in physics, biology, even computer information theory. Last year "SCIENCE FINDS GOD" emblazoned the cover of *Newsweek,* and other leading newsmagazines picked up the theme. More conferences than ever feature dialogues between the "two ways of knowing." By one report, U.S. higher education now boasts 1,000 courses for credit on science and faith, whereas a student in the sixties would have long dug in hardscrabble to find even one. Scientists who are older and tenured, it is said, feel it is time to give witness to their once closeted or newly found faith.

The movement is far from spontaneous, however. The cover stories followed a major symposium at the University of California at Berkeley, "Science and the Spiritual Quest," underwritten by the deep pockets of the Templeton Foundation, whose founder, financier-philanthropist Sir John Templeton, is profoundly interested in reconciling religious belief with modern science. He calls it "humility theology," emphasizing the need for par-

tisans on both sides to recognize limits to their way of knowing and leave room for the other. The Templeton Foundation has also supported many of those new college courses on the topic, created cash rewards for scholarly papers, and financed countless other academic lectures and conferences—all designed to stimulate scholarly discussion of the relationship between science and religion within the framework of humility theology. Striving to keep pace, some evangelical Protestant organizations—most notably the well-funded Campus Crusade for Christ—have sponsored conferences and collegiate lectures pitching their views on the subject.

Yet in institutional science, where the brightest men and women do their work, the wheels grind slowly and exceedingly fine. For many, the result is an intellectual aversion to the supernatural. Even if science were to find God, as *Newsweek* reported in what would have been (if true) the news story of the century, would scientists recognize it?

Charles Darwin is honored as an exemplar of the scientific spirit. Patiently, Darwin doubted and tested his theory of evolution for 20 years before he published it. He fretted even longer over religion before opting for agnosticism. "I feel most deeply that the whole subject is too profound for the human intellect," he wrote late in life. "A dog might as well speculate on the mind of Newton. Let each man hope and believe what he can."

And what does the typical scientist hope and believe? An early pioneer who sought to answer that question was Bryn Mawr College psychologist James H. Leuba. In 1914 and again in 1933 Leuba surveyed American biological and physical scientists on their views regarding what he described as "the two central beliefs of the Christian religion": a God influenced by worship, and an afterlife. He maintained that without these "fundamental dogmas" Christianity could not survive. And it was appropriate to inquire about these beliefs among scientists, he asserted, because scientists "enjoy great influence in the modern world, even in matters religious."

To see if scientists' beliefs had changed since his day, in 1996 and in 1998 we again asked American scientists Leuba's two questions: Do you believe in (1) "a God in intellectual and affective communication with man . . . to whom one may pray in expectation of receiving an answer" and (2) "personal immortality." Yes, no, and don't know or agnostic were the only options offered. Responses were strictly anonymous.

Our surveys' questions generated significant criticism, as they did in Leuba's day. "Why such a narrow definition [of God]?" asked one of our respondents, writing in the survey margin. "I believe in God, but I don't believe that one can expect an answer to prayer." Another respondent added, "I consider it quite possible to be a deeply religious person while rejecting belief in a personal God or in personal immortality."

Leuba resolutely defended his questions in response to similar complaints. "I chose to define God as given above because that is the God worshipped in every branch of the Christian religion," he wrote. Because we could track changes over time only by using Leuba's precise questions, we accepted the risk that responses could understate religious belief.

The polling closely tracked Leuba's methods. First we surveyed a random sample of biological and physical scien-

> *"In their struggle for the ethical good, teachers of religion must have the stature to give up the doctrine of a personal God."—Albert Einstein*

tists (the latter included mathematicians) listed in the standard reference work *American Men and Women of Science,* just as Leuba did in 1914 with the then *American Men of Science.* Leuba's second quarry, "greater scientists," was based on a random sample of persons so designated by stars next to their listings. That distinction is no longer made in *American Men and Women of Science,* so we fell back on the much more elite membership rolls of the National Academy of Sciences (NAS), whose core biological and physical science sections we surveyed in their entirety. By survey response standards, the two questions touched a nerve then and now, with better than half those polled responding each time.

## THE 40-PERCENT SOLUTION

One number rings down through more than eight decades: 40 percent. Four in 10 of Leuba's scientists believed in God as defined in his survey. The same is true today. Somewhat more, about 50 percent, held to an afterlife in Leuba's day, but now that figure is also 40 percent.

Thus, one of Leuba's predictions, which we shall call his general theory of disbelief, failed. Progress in science, he wrote around 1914, would demand "a revision of public opinion regarding . . . the two cardinal beliefs of official Christianity." He expected religious disbelief to grow among both "American scientists and Americans in general. But scientists today no more jettison Christianity's "two cardinal beliefs" than their counterparts did in 1914. Gallup surveys suggest the same about the general population.

In the second part of Leuba's survey—his poll of the scientific elite—he

found much higher levels of disbelief and doubt. In 1914 fewer than one in three of Leuba's "greater" scientists expressed belief in God and only a slightly larger fraction in immortality. In 1933 more than 80 percent of top natural scientists rejected both cardinal beliefs of traditional Christianity.

We shall call Leuba's second theory his special theory of disbelief. The "greater" scientists were less accepting of the supernatural than were "lesser" scientists, Leuba postulated, because of their "superior knowledge, understanding, and experience." The special theory is alive and well today: "You clearly can be a scientist and have religious beliefs," University of Oxford chemist Peter Atkins told the British press when the 40-percent result was announced in 1997. "But I don't think you can be a real scientist in the deepest sense of the word, because they are such alien categories of knowledge."

The 1998 NAS members perhaps provide a more immaculate sample of the elite than Leuba's starred entries did. Congress created the National Academy of Sciences in 1863, and after naming its first members Congress empowered them and their successors to choose all later members. Its current membership of 1,800 remains the closest thing to peerage in American science.

And their responses validate Leuba's prediction of the beliefs of topflight scientists generations from his time. Disbelief among NAS members responding to our survey exceeded 90 percent. The increase may simply reflect that they are more elite than Leuba's "greater" scientists, but this interruption would also please Leuba. NAS biologists are the most skeptical, with 95 percent of our respondents evincing atheism and agnosticism. Mathematicians in the NAS are more accepting: one in every six of them expressed belief in a personal God.

## ZIGGURAT OF BELIEF

Nevertheless, what stands out is an image of American natural science that has not fundamentally changed since 1914. Measured by religious belief, professional science is like a pyramid, or a three-tiered ziggurat. At the top is acute disbelief. Scientists in the middle are significantly less believing (by more than half) than citizens in general. The wide and heavy base is more firmly sunken into religious America—evidence suggests that there is more personal religion among physicians, engineers and members of other technological occupations that involve applied science.

Unveiling this pyramid would strike many learned people as much ado about the obvious. "Today the higher the educational attainment, or the higher the scores earned on intelligence or achievement tests, the less likely are individuals to be Christians," notes intellectual historian Paul K. Conkin. He could say the same of higher income, too.

Some risk lies in sorting aside the "lesser" scientists to crown the "greater" one, but the distinction does have its value. Of course, theists can scratch their heads and ask, Were not Copernicus, Kepler and Newton also great? Were not each of them profoundly and personally religious? Why are there not more theistic Newton types in the upper echelons today? Are the deepest contemporary scientific minds drawn to atheism, or, to paraphrase Darwin, does the environment of an elite science society select for the trait of disbelief?

Legendary evolutionary biologist Ernst Mayr, an NAS member since 1954, made a study of disbelief among his Harvard University colleagues in the academy. "It turned out we were all atheists," he recalls. "I found that there were two sources." One Mayr typified as, "Oh, I became an atheist very early. I just couldn't believe all that supernatural stuff." But others told him, "I just couldn't believe that there could be a God with all this evil in the world." Mayr adds, "Most atheists combine the two. This combination makes it impossible to believe in God."

University of Washington sociologist Rodney Stark, an early researcher on the spread of secularization in a religious society, points out, "There's been 200 years of marketing that if you want to be a scientific person you've got to keep your mind free of the fetters of religion." He argues that although demographics make a difference—a professor teaching in South Dakota is likely to be more religious than an academic in Chicago—higher education on the whole winnows out the idea of God or people who hold to it. In research universities, "the religious people keep their mouths shut," Stark says. "And the irreligious people discriminate. There's a reward system to being irreligious in the upper echelons." Stark suggests that perhaps more NAS members are religious than think it politic to admit.

The NAS, like many scientific organizations, lives off the commonweal. The academy's primary work (done in conjunction with the National Research Council) is to produce on average one technical report a day to advise Congress and other lawmakers, calm unwarranted public fears about science hazards, lobby for research funds, and promote good science and public interest in the field. The NAS is mindful of its obligation to serve the public, but it can be a delicate course to maneuver. Disbelief and belief have often become a major public relations issue for science in religious America.

"I asked some people at the NAS why they don't have a section on evolution," says William B. Provine, an evolutionist and science historian at Cornell University. "Too controversial." Yet, to its credit, in 1998 the NAS issued a report proudly promoting the teaching of evolution in public school. "Whether God exists or not is a question about which science is neutral," the report cautiously begins, before launching its broadside of scientific arguments against religious objections to teaching evolution. But the irony is remarkable: a group of specialists who are nearly all nonbelievers—and who believe that science compels

*Are the deepest contemporary scientific minds drawn to atheism, or do the higher echelons of academia select for the trait of disbelief?*

such a conclusion—told the public that "science is neutral" on the God question.

Religion was an unavoidable subject at the news conference at which the report was released. Eminent panelists reiterated that most religions have no conflict with evolution and that many scientists are religious. "There are many outstanding members of this academy who are very religious people, people who believe in evolution, many of them biologists," offered NAS president Bruce Alberts. Of course, he did not claim that these "very religious" NAS members believed in a God as defined in Leuba's survey—traditional Jewish, Christian or Muslim theism, that is—but that would have been a natural interpretation of his statement by many in the general public.

## BALANCING ACT OR COWARDICE?

The NAS showed similar concern for public opinion in a 1981 policy statement it adopted as a rearguard action after two states mandated equal time for "creation science" in public school biology classes. "Religion and science are separate and mutually exclusive realms of human thought whose presentation in the same context leads to misunderstanding of both scientific theory and religious belief," it said.

These rules of the game suit many in the broad middle but are less satisfying to some scientific atheists and to many scientific religionists. British zoologist Richard Dawkins calls the NAS statement "a cowardly cop-out. I think it's an attempt to woo the sophisticated theological lobby and to get them into our camp and put the creationists into another camp. It's good politics. But it's intellectually disreputable." Antievolutionists such as Phillip E. Johnson, a Berkeley law professor and frequent speaker for the Campus Crusade for Christ, thrive on such clarity and find Dawkins the perfect foil. "My colleagues and I want to separate the real science from the materialist philosophy," Johnson countered on a PBS *Firing Line* debate.

Dawkins is well known for his uncompromising views and has likened belief in God to belief in fairies. He considers it intellectually dishonest to live with contradictions such as doing science during the week and attending church on Sunday.

Eugenie C. Scott, director of the anticreationist National Center for Science Education, is mindful of the public relations dividends at stake when combatants such as Johnson and Dawkins insist that the debate between science and religion, belief and nonbelief, evolution and creation, brooks no compromise. One of her showdowns came in the fall of 1997. On the agenda for the board of the National Association of Biology Teachers (NABT) was a vote about its 1995 "Statement on the Teaching of Evolution." The statement had become infamous in creationist circles because it said the evolution is "an unsupervised, impersonal, unpredictable and natural process"—which to some implied atheism.

Two reputable scholars, religious historian Huston Smith and philosopher Alvin Plantinga, suggested that the board drop the words "unsupervised, impersonal," to save biology teachers the grief of having to defend them. The board voted down this proposal. Then, with only hours to spare, Scott persuaded the board to reverse itself. NABT director Wayne W. Carley said the change was good, honest science. "To say that evolution is supervised is to make a theological statement."

But the vote came across in the popular press as scientists kowtowing to creationists, and thus began what Scott calls "*l'affaire* NABT." A counter group of

biologists disparaged her concern for public relations, insisting that indeed evolution *is* unsupervised and impersonal.

Such is the balancing act that materialists in science must play, living and working as they do in a traditionally Christian culture. Matt Cartmill, president of the American Association of Physical Anthropologists, weighs into the debate mostly on the side of humility in science. "Many scientists are atheists or agnostics who want to believe that the natural world they study is all there is, and being only human, they try to persuade themselves that science gives them the grounds for that belief," he wrote in *Discover* magazine last year. "It's an honorable belief, but it isn't a research finding."

Some scientists try to make it so, however. At its 1997 annual symposium in New Orleans, the Society for Neuroscience heard about the "God module," a spot in the brain that apparently produces religious feelings. The evidence came from the gold mine of brain research, the mentally damaged: patients with temporal lobe epilepsy have religious experiences in their seizures. Christian antievolutionist Johnson shot back: "You may be sure that scientific materialists will never discover a 'materialist module,' meaning a brain part that causes people to fantasize that they can explain the mind in strictly materialist terms."

At the 1998 Science and the Spiritual Quest conference in Berkeley, funded by the Templeton Foundation, more than 20 scientists, including a physics Nobel laureate, testified that science either led them to God or was not an obstacle to faith. The conference encouraged scientists to engage in public discussion of God, including (but not predominantly) Leuba's God who answers prayers.

Some pointed out that both science and faith make big presumptions, whereas

others suggested that the cosmos contains hints of a mind. Astronomer Jocelyn Bell Burnell, a devout Quaker best known for her discovery of pulsars, finds a place for both science and religion in her life. "I don't think God created the world in any physical sense," she told the gathering of 350 people. "But that's not to say there isn't a God." For her, God just *is*—a private, interior experience tells her so. She said that some people want to put God in that little nanosecond gap after the big bang, but her faith did not need God in any gap.

Late in his distinguished career, astronomer Allan Sandage stumbled on the question theists in science love to ask their agnostic colleagues: Why is there something rather than nothing? "I never found the answer in science," he confided to the Berkeley assembly. "To stop the divine discomfort, I had to do something." He simply "decided to believe," Sandage explained, adding that the belief "turned out to be correct." Sandage's conversion experience makes him a rare "bridge person," linking different camps of theists. His testimonial approach appeals to evangelicals, yet he also fits right into venues organized by liberal Christians. The same could be said of noted Princeton geologist and NAS member John Suppe, who also "got religion" after getting scientific fame, in his case arriving at faith through a search for meaning.

## INTELLIGENT DESIGN AND NOAH'S FLOOD

Quite a different wing of the debate was evident in 1996 at the Mere Creation Conference on science and God sponsored by the Campus Crusade for Christ, convened at conservative Biola University (formerly the Bible Institute of Los Angeles). An im-

---

*The story of evolution is "a rich resource for persons who are seeking a theistic presence in their lives."—Ursula Goodenough* pressive succession of orators spoke on evidence in science for a God. This wing is populated mostly by "old-earth" creationists. They admire conventional science, with its evolved cosmos and eons of time, and can accept everything about evolution except the hard parts: turning chemicals into life and fish brains into human consciousness. They hanker for a science that is God-friendly, a discipline allowing such terms as "intelligent design" and "theistic science." Behind this movement is the Leuba-defined God of early 20th-century Protestantism who answers prayers and promises an afterlife.

Further to the theological right loom the so-called scientific creationists. They seek to give the Bible's "young earth"—created rapidly a few thousand years ago as dated by the genealogies in Genesis—a good name in science. Their central research program is flood geology, which seeks evidence of a Noachian worldwide flood and uses this catastrophe to account for the earth's major geologic features. They would have been in enemy territory, so to speak, at the spiritual quest conference in Berkeley, with its vague personal gods and poetic interpretations of Genesis. A few flood geologists with secular doctorates in science attended the Biola meeting, but the old-earth camp wants to convert such people to ancient time, to work together on poking holes in orthodox neo-Darwinian evolution, which they find implicitly atheistic.

## BISHOPS AND ECOLOGY

Yet it is in evolution that some scientists find a secular religion. One such is cell biologist Ursula Goodenough, a past president of the Institute for Religion in an Age of Science [see the review of her book *The Sacred Depths of Nature;* SCIENTIFIC AMERICAN, May]. For her, there can be religion without a God or the supernatural. "I consider myself a nontheist," she told the "Epic of Evolution" conference at Chicago's Field Museum in 1997. Her religion, she explained, goes by the name "religious naturalism" (as distinct from philosophical naturalism) and puts forth the evolution story as a rich re-

source for those seeking a theistic presence in their lives.

Concern for the environment has provided common ground for nonbelieving, humanist scientists and liberal religionists. Carl Sagan broke the ice between these camps with his 1990 open letter welcoming and challenging the religious community to get on board the movement to save the planet. The next year Sagan stood beside a robed Episcopal bishop in Manhattan's Cathedral of St. John the Divine as they co-chaired the joint appeal by science and religion for the environment.

Last fall a similar alliance strolled the halls of Evolution Central, the American Museum of Natural History in New York City. One paleontologist at the museum, the noted anticreationist Niles Eldredge, says it was all to the good. But, he is quick to add, the environment may be the only thing science and religion can civilly discuss. "There's an ecological component to all concepts of God," Eldredge told the *New York Times.* For those wary of public relations debacles the friendly focus on ecology can easily obscure the troublesome God question, a welcome side effect for scientists concerned about public support for their discipline.

This rapprochement over the environment is all the more remarkable considering that among all the categories of scientists polled, NAS biologists wanted the least to do with the supernatural. "The modern biologist really thinks that if we go down to the level of DNA, we understand things," biologist Lewis Wolpert commented on our survey results. "If you are a physicist, in a world of quantum mechanics and the big bang, it is so bizarre and ludicrous that the concept of understanding almost disappears." Thus, a physicist may see gaps left for God. Similarly, mathematicians can be Platonic and perceive the beau-

tifully concocted math of the human mind as charting the order of a divine intellect.

Fred Hoyle, who coined the term "big bang" in derision, is famously quoted (speaking in support of ideas like the anthropic principle) as saying that it is staggering to see the universe so fine-tuned when there is no God to have done it. Of course, theists contend that that's the point: How else could the big bang have generated the precise conditions needed to produce carbon-based life? But to an evolutionary biologist such as NAS member John C. Avise, "Only natural selection comes close to omnipotence, but even here no intelligence, foresight, ultimate purpose or morality is involved. Natural selection is merely an amoral force, as inevitable and uncaring as gravity."

Avise simply does not see a too-orderly-for-chance world in his science. "By all objective scientific evidence, our immediate biological fates, like those of other species, are influenced profoundly by genetic gods and other natural forces," he notes in his 1998 book, *The Genetic Gods,* before quoting the words of William Provine: "Our modern understanding of evolution implies . . . that ultimate meaning in life is nonexistent."

Philosopher of science Michael Ruse has made a career of studying how biologists do their work and spin their theories. And he's all for naturalism; it is matter only, all the way down. Yet as an early member of the modern historical school of science, he cannot but see social factors influencing both disbelief among biologists and membership selection in the NAS. Do great minds tend to turn atheistic, or do such academies welcome only atheists? "It is a bit of both," Ruse says. Overtly religious members would doubtless feel tension, especially if their beliefs were theologically conservative.

---

*"A dog might as well speculate on the mind of Newton. Let each man hope and believe what he can."—Charles Darwin*

Lutheran theologian Philip Hefner is no fan of fundamentalists and sees himself as pro-science. His journal *Zygon* is dedicated to linking science and faith while avoiding the extremes of either camp. As a student of theologian Paul Tillich, Hefner is on personal terms with symbols and myths. Myths can overpower at times, he says, and science is at fault as much as religion. Sadly for America, its greatest myth about science and religion is a legal melodrama, the 1925 John Scopes "monkey trial." This myth has clung tenaciously to American intellectual life ever since, Hefner says.

"The myth is," he continues, "that scientists are courageous loners who are willing to die for the truth. Organized religion is ipso facto opposed to intellectual freedom and the freedom of truth. Organized religion is the enemy. When heave comes to shove, organized religion will kill the courageous scientist." Hefner sighs over this predominant morality play. "History is just showing that it's not true," he days. "But you'll never get that across."

So the debate goes on, largely pressed by those on the side of religion—conservative, moderate and liberal—who seek the authority of science for their views. In an earlier age, it was scientists who sought the imprimatur of the church, but now that the power and the glory have shifted to science, most modern scientists seem not to care what the church thinks of their science. They generally view religion as a relic of the past or as a private matter beyond the realm of scientific discourse. Yet thanks perhaps to Templeton's influence and the rise of postmodern relativism, many on both sides now sound willing to admit limits to their way of knowing. And at least in the U.S., where the government funds basic research and regulates its applications, some politically savvy scientists recognize the value in downplaying the negative implications for the supernatural that arise from their study of the natural.

## Further Reading

SCIENCE AND RELIGION: SOME HISTORICAL PERSPECTIVES. John Hedley Brooke, Cambridge University Press, 1991.

THE SOUL OF THE AMERICAN UNIVERSITY: FROM PROTESTANT ESTABLISHMENT TO ESTABLISHED NONBELIEF. George M. Marsden. Oxford University Press, 1994.

SUMMER FOR THE GODS: THE SCOPES TRIAL AND AMERICA'S CONTINUING DEBATE OVER SCIENCE AND RELIGION. Edward J. Larson. Basic Books, 1997.

LEADING SCIENTISTS STILL REJECT GOD. E. J. Larson and L. Witham in *Nature*, Vol. 394, page 313; July 23, 1998.

WHEN ALL THE GODS TREMBLED: DARWINISM, SCOPES, AND AMERICAN INTELLECTUALS. Paul K. Conkin. Rowman & Littlefield, 1998.

SKEPTICAL INQUIRER: SPECIAL ISSUE: SCIENCE & RELIGION, Vol. 23, No. 4; July/August 1999.

# Test Your Knowledge Form

We encourage you to photocopy and use this page as a tool to assess how the articles in **Annual Editions** expand on the information in your textbook. By reflecting on the articles you will gain enhanced text information. You can also access this useful form on a product's book support Web site at **http://www.dushkin.com/online/.**

NAME: 

DATE: 

TITLE AND NUMBER OF ARTICLE: 

BRIEFLY STATE THE MAIN IDEA OF THIS ARTICLE: 

LIST THREE IMPORTANT FACTS THAT THE AUTHOR USES TO SUPPORT THE MAIN IDEA: 

WHAT INFORMATION OR IDEAS DISCUSSED IN THIS ARTICLE ARE ALSO DISCUSSED IN YOUR TEXTBOOK OR OTHER READINGS THAT YOU HAVE DONE? LIST THE TEXTBOOK CHAPTERS AND PAGE NUMBERS: 

LIST ANY EXAMPLES OF BIAS OR FAULTY REASONING THAT YOU FOUND IN THE ARTICLE: 

LIST ANY NEW TERMS/CONCEPTS THAT WERE DISCUSSED IN THE ARTICLE, AND WRITE A SHORT DEFINITION:

ANNUAL EDITIONS revisions depend on two major opinion sources: one is our Advisory Board, listed in the front of this volume, which works with us in scanning the thousands of articles published in the public press each year; the other is you—the person actually using the book. Please help us and the users of the next edition by completing the prepaid article rating form on this page and returning it to us. Thank you for your help!

## ANNUAL EDITIONS: Physical Anthropology 01/02

### ARTICLE RATING FORM

Here is an opportunity for you to have direct input into the next revision of this volume. We would like you to rate each of the 42 articles listed below, using the following scale:

**1. Excellent: should definitely be retained**
**2. Above average: should probably be retained**
**3. Below average: should probably be deleted**
**4. Poor: should definitely be deleted**

Your ratings will play a vital part in the next revision. So please mail this prepaid form to us just as soon as you complete it. Thanks for your help!

### RATING

### ARTICLE

1. The Growth of Evolutionary Science
2. Darwin's Influence on Modern Thought
3. Curse and Blessing of the Ghetto
4. The Saltshaker's Curse
5. The Fortune Teller
6. The Five Sexes, Revisited
7. Machiavellian Monkeys
8. What Are Friends For?
9. Dian Fossey and Digit
10. The Mind of the Chimpanzee
11. Dim Forest, Bright Chimps
12. To Catch a Colobus
13. Coping With Crowding
14. Are We in Anthropodenial?
15. These Are Real Swinging Primates
16. The War Between Men and Women
17. The Myth of the Coy Female
18. A Woman's Curse?
19. What's Love Got to Do With It?
20. Apes of Wrath
21. Sunset on the Savanna

### RATING

### ARTICLE

22. Early Hominid Fossils From Africa
23. A New Human Ancestor?
24. Scavenger Hunt
25. *Erectus* Rising
26. Hard Times Among the Neanderthals
27. The Gift of Gab
28. The Dating Game
29. Who Were the Neandertals?
30. Fate of the Neandertals
31. Archaeologists Rediscover Cannibals
32. The Lost Man
33. Black, White, Other
34. Racial Odyssey
35. Culture, Not Race, Explains Human Diversity
36. The Tall and the Short of It
37. Profile of an Anthropologist: No Bone Unturned
38. Gorilla Warfare
39. The Viral Superhighway
40. The Natural History of Art
41. Dr. Darwin
42. Scientists and Religion in America

(Continued on next page)

## BUSINESS REPLY MAIL
FIRST-CLASS MAIL  PERMIT NO. 84  GUILFORD CT

POSTAGE WILL BE PAID BY ADDRESSEE

**McGraw-Hill/Dushkin**
**530 Old Whitfield Street**
**Guilford, CT 06437-9989**

---

## ABOUT YOU

Name _____   Date _____

Are you a teacher? ☐   A student? ☐

Your school's name _____

Department _____

Address _____   City _____   State ____ Zip ____

School telephone # _____

## YOUR COMMENTS ARE IMPORTANT TO US !

Please fill in the following information:
For which course did you use this book?
_____

Did you use a text with this *ANNUAL EDITION*?  ☐ yes  ☐ no
What was the title of the text?
_____

What are your general reactions to the *Annual Editions* concept?
_____

Have you read any particular articles recently that you think should be included in the next edition?
_____

Are there any articles you feel should be replaced in the next edition? Why?
_____

Are there any World Wide Web sites you feel should be included in the next edition? Please annotate.
_____

May we contact you for editorial input?  ☐ yes  ☐ no
May we quote your comments?  ☐ yes  ☐ no
_____